Routledge Revivals

Ethics & Atonement

Ethics & Atonement

W. F. Lofthouse

First published in 1906 by Methuen & Co.

This edition first published in 2018 by Routledge
2 Park Square, Milton Park, Abingdon, Oxon, OX14 4RN
and by Routledge
711 Third Avenue, New York, NY 10017

Routledge is an imprint of the Taylor & Francis Group, an informa business

© 1906 by Taylor & Francis

All rights reserved. No part of this book may be reprinted or reproduced or utilised in any form or by any electronic, mechanical, or other means, now known or hereafter invented, including photocopying and recording, or in any information storage or retrieval system, without permission in writing from the publishers.

Publisher's Note
The publisher has gone to great lengths to ensure the quality of this reprint but points out that some imperfections in the original copies may be apparent.

Disclaimer
The publisher has made every effort to trace copyright holders and welcomes correspondence from those they have been unable to contact.

ISBN 13: 978-1-138-60569-5 (hbk)
ISBN 13: 978-1-138-60571-8 (pbk)
ISBN 13: 978-0-429-46228-3 (ebk)

ETHICS AND ATONEMENT

BY

W. F. LOFTHOUSE, M.A.

WITH A FRONTISPIECE

METHUEN & CO.
36 ESSEX STREET W.C.
LONDON

First Published in 1906

CONIVGI DILECTISSIMAE
SINE CVIVS
AVCTORITATE OPE CONSILIO
HOC OPVSCVLVM
NEC CONFECTVM NEC INCEPTVM
FVISSET

PREFACE

THE attempt to add to the many books that deal with the Atonement needs some excuse. Although, however, the subject has been so widely discussed, there is one side from which it has not often been approached, the side of those who are not greatly concerned with theology, but are keenly interested in morals and in life. Yet it is from this side that most people come to the consideration of the Atonement. Hence questions are often asked which treatises on the Atonement do not appear to answer, and the Atonement itself, instead of being the illuminating centre of theology, becomes a stumbling-block in the way of any real acceptance of religion.

In the following pages I have endeavoured to maintain that the doctrine of the Atonement is not an artificial theorem or an inexplicable or unethical dogma, but that it has its roots in the foundations of all human life, and is really the highest expression of the law of all moral and social progress; and that ethics itself is of little use, as a practical science, unless completed by the Atonement.

I have to thank Professor Palmer of Harvard University, the Rev. J. S. Lidgett, M.A., Warden of the Bermondsey Settlement, and my colleague, Dr J. G. Tasker, for valuable advice in connexion with large portions of the book. To Mr Lidgett's work,

"The Spiritual Principle of the Atonement," I gladly acknowledge my great obligation. My chief debt, from the first page to the last, I owe to my wife, to whom the conception of the book in large part is due, and who has helped to shape the thought of every chapter, and the language of every paragraph.

The frontispiece is a copy of Fra Angelico's fresco of Christ on the Cross with S. Dominic, in the cloisters of the Monastery of S. Mark in Florence, from a photograph by Alinari of Florence. The Biblical quotations in the book are from the Revised Version throughout.

HANDSWORTH COLLEGE
July 1906

CONTENTS

CHAP.   PAGE

I. ETHICS IN THE BIBLE.
1. Religion in the Bible not opposed to Morality . . 1
2. Morality in the New Testament as Self-Renunciation . 8
3. Its Foundation in the Covenant . . 11
4. The Covenant both an Agreement and a Gift . . 16
5. Hence, the Importance of the Three "Theological" Virtues 19
6. Righteousness Fulfilled in Love, in the Sphere of the Family 22

II. ETHICS OUTSIDE THE BIBLE.
1. Divorce between Ethics and Religion in Ethical Writings 26
2. Non-Religious Character of Ethics in Greece and Rome 29
3. Neglect of Ethics by Christian Thinkers . . 34
4. General Course of Ethical Thought after the Reformation 39
5. The "Impasse" in Modern Ethics, and the Way Out . 45

III. DUTIES AND PERSONS.
1. Duty, Pleasure, and Self-Realisation . . . 52
2. The Isolated Individual Non-existent . . . 55
3. Duty and the Personal Bond of Union . . . 59
4. The Personal Bond in the New Testament . . 64
5. The Importance of the Personal Bond implied by Sociology and by the Intuitional and Æsthetic Views of Ethics 69
6. The Personal Bond and Casuistry . . . 75
7. The Personal Bond and the Unity of Virtue . . 80

IV. RECONCILIATION.
1. Need of Further Consideration of Personality . . 82
2. Sin as the Breaking of the Right Relation between Persons 84
3. Sin in the Bible; the Old Testament and Sacrifice . 87
4. Sin in the New Testament: Atonement or Reconciliation 90
5. Reconciliation, Forgiveness, and Punishment . . 99
6. Contrition and its Awakening 106

CONTENTS

CHAP.
V. MEDIATION.

	PAGE
1. The Influence of Mind on Mind	111
2. How can the Injured Person Influence the Mind of the Injurer?	118
3. An Example	121
4. Christ as the Mediator	125
5. The Place of Vicariousness in Christ's Mediation	133
Note on New Testament Passages relating to the Atonement	143

VI. ANGER AND FORGIVENESS.

1. The Fear of Divine Anger in Religion	148
2. Modern Revolt against the Idea of Divine Anger	151
3. The Place of Divine Anger in the Bible	154
4. The Place of Anger in Ethical Conduct	160
5. Positive and Negative Anger	163
6. Anger and "Repentance" in God	167
7. Christ and the Anger of God	171
8. Anger and Fatherhood	176

VII. SYMBOLISM AND REALITY.

1. The Shedding of Blood upon the Cross	180
2. References to the "Blood" in the New Testament	185
3. Connexion between the Death and the Resurrection of Christ in the New Testament	188
4. Sacrifice in the Bible and in Ethnic Religions	195
5. The Two-fold Attitude to Sacrifice in the Bible	198
6. The Permanent and Universal Significance of Sacrifice	202
7. The Metaphorical Character of Sacrificial Language	209
8. Sacrifice and Reconciliation Complementary	212

VIII. THE GOD-MAN.

1. Christ "One with" God and Man	216
2. Christ's own Claim to Unity with God	219
3. Its Historical Reality and its Limits	223
4. Impossibility of Rejecting the Claim	229
5. Christ's Claim to be the Son of Man	232
6. The Holy Spirit and Christ's Union with Man	235
7. The Personal Character of this Union	240

CONTENTS

CHAP.   PAGE

IX. PERSONALITY.
1. Can these Claims be Philosophically Justified? . . 244
2. Transcendental and Common-sense Views of Personality 247
3. Personality as Inclusive 251
4. "Great Personalities" 253
5. The Supreme Personality 258
6. Personality the One Medium of Divine Revelation . 261
7. Personality the One Medium of Atonement . . 264

X. ATONEMENT AND THE RACE.
1. The Worth of Good Acts apart from Faith in Christ . 266
2. Goodness of Act and Goodness of Character . . 272
3. Faith in Christ as Dependent on Human Presentation . 274
4. The Test of Goodness Primarily Moral and not Religious 277
5. Goodness and Communion with Christ . . . 280
6. The Pre-existence of Christ 284
7. The Timelessness of Christ 286
8. The Atonement as a Principle for all Time . . 289
9. Faith in the Principle of the Atonement and in its Embodiment 294
10. The Ethical Necessity of the Atonement . . 296

A FRESCO IN SAN MARCO

Oh ancient mystery of love unknown !
We, with the saint, would kneel and here adore,
Dumb in our thanks, and humble evermore
For this dear love that left us not alone.
We wandered 'mid the thorns that made His crown ;
He sought us in the wild ; with travail sore,
E'en there for us His kingly state He wore
Yet laid aside, for our dark sin to atone.

Our spirits find a home beneath His gaze,
Weary, estranged, and with much wandering blind,
Lost in the night till He had brought us thence.
Men's searching only led us to a maze,
Darker for subtleties of human mind ;
Here we but love, and know our impotence.

K. L. L.

ETHICS AND ATONEMENT

CHAPTER I

ETHICS IN THE BIBLE

I. ONE of the distinctions oftenest made at the present day is between religion and morality. There never was a time when the authority of morality was more readily acknowledged, at least in theory; there never was a time when religion was called more frequently and imperiously to stand on the defensive. We turn to the poets or philosophers for moral inspiration: we leave the Bible unread. It is seldom recognised that there is one ideal common to all the Biblical writings; that ideal is Righteousness. In Biblical language, Righteousness is, broadly speaking, right conduct in the eyes of God; hence we can speak of the Righteousness of God himself, as well as of the Righteousness of man. Righteousness is indeed ordinarily associated with the Old rather than the New Testament; but neither Amos nor Isaiah is a more passionate exponent of the nature and obligation of Righteousness than is S. Paul; there is hardly a page of S. Paul's writings but glows with some vindication, some enforcement, of its claims. And S. Paul only echoes the spirit of the teaching of Jesus.

In the discourses reported in the Gospels there is far more of the proclamation of sheer morality than is often supposed. From the Sermon on the Mount, with its detailed duties, and its emphasis on motive,

ETHICS AND ATONEMENT

right up to the last discourse on the Judgment of the World, there is one and the same insistence on the difference between right and wrong. Nor is it without reason that the early writers on Christianity dwell far oftener on what the Christian has to do than on what has been done for him by his Saviour. The Epistle of James repeats the teaching of Jesus as well as the Epistles of John; Polycarp, Barnabas, and Hermas carry us back constantly to the former; they hardly so much as suggest the latter.

In spite of this, Christian teachers have not seldom allowed themselves to speak slightingly of mere morality; and the "preaching of the law" has often been regarded as unreconcilable with the preaching of Christ. An Archbishop of Canterbury once stated that among the many sermons to which he had listened, he had not heard one on the duty of common honesty—an experience by no means unique.

On the other hand, there has grown up a positive suspicion of religion, as softening the rigidity of the moral outline. Many a man has turned his back on religion—and this not only in Roman Catholic countries — who would resent with heat any imputation of moral laxity. We are all agreed that the State must enforce and teach morality; but also that it must be very careful how it touches religion. The most influential preachers and advocates of morality have often been men who cut themselves off from Christianity as generally accepted, like T. H. Green, or from religion altogether, like J. S. Mill.[1] In ancient

---

[1] A short time ago a striking example of our modern attitude was issued in the form of a "non-religious syllabus" of ethical teaching in connexion with a provincial board school. An elaborate list of duties was therein formulated, closing with instruction as to " man's place in the world, and

ETHICS IN THE BIBLE

Greece, Socrates and Aristotle were not irreligious; but to them, as to the majority of men in their time, religion was a matter primarily for the priests; what concerned the thinker and the practical man, they would have said, was that very different thing, right conduct.

But it is against this separation that the Bible is in reality one long protest. The Jews were unlike the heathen nations, as it has been well remarked, just because "there was nothing of that wide separation between religion and morality which among other nations was the road to all impurity"; to the Jew, the inspiration to right conduct was found simply in the will and approbation of Jehovah. No one can read the Old Testament without seeing that the Jew traced back to Jehovah all his law; but the law included not only the ritual directions for feasts and sacrifices, but also the more personal rules to be carried out in the dealings between man and God and between man and man, from the Ten Commandments onwards. From Nathan standing before David, or Isaiah in the midst of the corrupt civilisation of the later Jewish monarchy, to Malachi rebuking the community repatriated in Judæa, the denunciations of the prophets are levelled, not at neglect of the Levitical laws, but at the defiance, in ever-changing forms, of the Moral Law. "Cease to do evil, learn to do well." This is their constant refrain. Idols themselves are an abomination because of the degrading associations of their worship; to do evil is to be faithless to Jehovah, the jealous God. And even where the offence seems to be purely against the

the value of noble rules of life," with the note that "it is not designed that this scheme shall in any way interfere with the ordinary Bible readings and explanations."

ordinances of ritual, the personal and ethical element is the root of the disobedience; the real sin is the sin against the moral will of the Divine Lawgiver. The ritual is only an index of the moral. If Nadab is punished for offering strange fire, it is for the pride which overshot Jehovah's command. If Nehemiah protests against the breaking of the Sabbath, the real cause of his anger is the heartless treachery which would make gain out of the cause of his city's danger.

In the New Testament the connexion is even closer. All that part of the Jewish Law which might seem to imply "religion without morality," and which indeed had divorced the two in the unscrupulous hands of the Pharisees, was definitely put on one side. Christ, who came to fulfil the law, did so by lifting it back to its old place as the will of God, and proclaiming it the ruler of the ethical relations of man to man. Significantly enough, Christ has often been taken to be the champion of morality against religion, as well as of religion against morality. Every one who has studied social problems, and, in so doing, has come to the conclusion that the improvement of society must go hand in hand with the moral reform of the individual, has been compelled to recognise Christ as an ally or a leader. Mazzini, who believed as strongly as Gambetta that "le clèricalisme c'est l'ennemi," and Mill, who was one of the keenest opponents of religion as it is commonly understood, were alike in their admiration of "the morally perfect being, Christ."

It is this double attitude of Christ which is the keynote of the teaching of the Bible. The Bible defends, now religion, and now morality, without the least suspicion of inconsistency in so doing. The passages which most distinctly emphasize morality

ETHICS IN THE BIBLE 5

are also the most distinctly religious. This is true even of the ceremonial books of the law. " If anyone sin and commit a trespass against the Lord and deal falsely with his neighbour in a matter of deposit or of bargain or of robbery, . . . he shall restore the thing which he took, and he shall bring his guilt offering unto the Lord, and the priest shall make atonement for him before the Lord, and he shall be forgiven." [1]

Many such passages could be quoted to show that duties to man are also looked upon as duties to God ; the codes of the Old Testament are in this respect very different from the recently discovered and more " business-like " code of Hammurabi. But the union of the two aspects of life is naturally much more prominent in the prophetical writings, as when Isaiah, declaiming against the rich who " join house to house and lay field to field till there is no room," and " rise up early in the morning that they may follow strong drink," and " draw sin as it were with a cart rope," proceeds " therefore is the anger of the Lord kindled against his people " ; or when Zechariah, expounding God's thought to do well to Israel, adds, " these are the things that ye shall do,—speak ye every man the truth with his neighbour . . . let none of you imagine evil in your hearts against his neighbour, for all these are the things that I hate, saith the Lord." [2]

The spirit of the New Testament teaching on this union of conduct and religion is less easy to represent

---

[1] Lev. 6^{2-7}. Compare Ex. $23^{22\ 33}$, where the duty of separation from the Canaanites is inculcated in a precaution against being made to sin against God by them ; also Lev. 25^{17}, "ye shall not wrong one another, but thou shalt fear the Lord thy God," and the juxtaposition of partly ritual and purely moral provisions in Dt. 22 $^{1-9}$.

[2] Is. $5^{8\ 11\ 18\ 25}$; Zech. 8^{14-18}. Compare the famous passages in Mic. 6^{8} ; Hos. 6^{6} ; and Jer. 7^{5-8}.

6 ETHICS AND ATONEMENT

by individual passages. The fact referred to above, that Christ is claimed as an ally by every social and ethical reformer, is perhaps the best proof for the place of ethics in his own utterances. A few outstanding sayings may be quoted: " Every idle word that men shall speak, they shall give account thereof in the day of judgment, for by thy words thou shalt be justified, and by thy words thou shalt be condemned."[1] " If thou wouldest enter into life, keep the commandments."[2] Our familiarity with such words has blinded us to their immense significance. The parable of the sheep and the goats, where, as Seeley says, all virtues are gathered up into the one virtue of benevolence, gives us its real lesson in the assertion that the ultimate decision of a man's fate will depend on the place of common self-denying kindness in his life. The fourth gospel might at first sight seem to lay stress on the purely religious side of the Christian life. But even here, love itself is unmeaning if it does not imply the practical beneficence of "love to the brethren." The teaching of the epistles is not less clear. An antithesis has often been insisted on between S. James and S. Paul in this respect. It is apparent on the first reading of the Epistle of S. James (perhaps the oldest book in the New Testament) that the interest is primarily ethical and practical. "The hire of the labourers who have reaped your fields, which is of you kept back by fraud, crieth ; and the cries of them which have reaped are entered into the ears of the Lord of Sabaoth."[3]

---

[1] Mt. 12$^{36\ 37}$.   [2] Mt. 19^{17}.
[3] Ch. 5^4. Compare Amos 5$^{12\text{-}14}$. Add to this the well-known description of " pure religion and undefiled " in James 1^{27}. See the striking parallels in Mt. 25^{43} and Mic. 6^8, also James 2^{17}, admirably expounded by Tolstoi ; "one of the chief distinctions between true faith and its

On the other hand, it is pointed out that with S. Paul the condition of salvation is faith; but the faith that saves is emphatically the faith that works, and that without works is dead. This is made abundantly plain in the ethical sections of every one of the longer epistles. Only one to whom conduct and belief were in thought inseparable could have written, while introducing a detailed list of duties, "be not conformed to this world; but be ye transformed by the renewing of your mind; that ye may prove what is that good and acceptable and perfect will of God"; or, "for this ye know of a surety, that no whoremonger or unclean person, nor covetous man, who is an idolater, hath an inheritance in the kingdom of Christ and of God"; and immediately afterwards, "ye were sometimes darkness; but now are ye light in the Lord; walk as children of light."[1] This can only mean that duties to men are service to God. Whenever law is mentioned in the New Testament, even in the Epistle to the Hebrews, the merely ritual side is entirely neglected, vulnerable as it was; it is the moral side which is attacked for its imperfection, and then reaffirmed and exalted in him who came to fulfil it.

But far more convincing than any array of texts is the consideration of the general attitude of Old Testament and New Testament alike to God and the law of God. The belief in God never receives any philosophical or metaphysical justification. It is rooted, not in the intellect but in the conscience. What

corruption is that when it is corrupted, man demands of God that in return for his sacrifices and prayers, God should fulfil his desires—should become the servant of a man; whereas according to true faith, man feels that God demands of him, a man, the fulfilment of His will, —demands that man should serve Him."

[1] Rom. 12^2; Eph. $5^{5\,8}$.

8 ETHICS AND ATONEMENT

differentiates Jehovah from other gods is his righteousness; and the demand for righteous dealing in his people, and the appeal to his own righteous dealing with them, are sufficient credentials for his messengers. For a speculative religion the Semites had no genius; and the refusal to accept the allegiance of ritual observances, which occupied the field of religion for other Semites, was pressed home on the Hebrews by prophet and even by priest, as the supreme vindication of Him who claimed to be above all gods. In the New Testament, the credential of the gospel is the single assertion, "this one thing I know, that whereas I was blind, now I see"; and this seeing, for Nicodemus as for the woman of Samaria, means beholding and obeying a Saviour from sin, the Christ who came to restore men from systems (whether Jewish or pagan) which neglected ethics but respected observances, to a system whose only sacrifice was that of a broken and a contrite heart.

II. We may take it, then, that right conduct is the beginning and end of Biblical religion; the beginning, because God comes to man first of all with a law; the end, because it was to fulfil the law that Christ himself was sent into the world. But what is the standard of this right conduct? Is it the same in the Old Testament and in the New? Does it not seem as if in actual fact Christ supplemented rather than fulfilled and reaffirmed the law as laid down in the Old Testament? Job, ch. 31, may be taken as a picture of the Hebrew conception of the moral ideal; and we cannot overlook its large and inclusive majesty. It embraced the mutual relations of mankind in their widest application; it affirmed the universal worth of justice, truthfulness, and sincerity, though it had little to say of bravery or self-sacrifice; it made much of personal purity and self-control, and exalted patriotism from being the discharge of a duty to one's fellow-citizens, into the rendering of an honour to the national God. Nor can we withhold our admiration when we find the Hebrew ideal extolling the man who could stand proud and unreproved in the gate, saying nothing of the mortification of the saint, though commending the position of the man who has no riches either to abuse or to enjoy; passing over love, as a general attitude to mankind, in the attention it pays to a large-hearted hospitality, especially to the needy and the stranger within the gate. We are conscious of moving within a narrower world when we turn to the moral ideal of the Sermon on the Mount and the Epistle of S. James.

This is true. Passing from the attractive picture of the Hebrew, clothed in his varied robes of righteousness, to the John-the-Baptist-like figure, clothed in skins, and wandering, as it were, with no abiding city here, in deserts and mountains and caves, we seem to enter a moral atmosphere at once cramping and austere. Christianity has raised to a pre-eminence which many have called vicious the virtues of humility, long-suffering, self-abnegation; bidding its followers to "bear the reproach of Christ," as its phrase is; actually to count as gain the hatred of that world which "lieth in the evil one"; to despise, forsooth, all that makes for right conduct in the forum or on the battle-field;—"a religion for women and slaves"! In a word, Christianity, it is urged, preaches self-denudation, not self-realisation. Unlike the Hebrew, the Christian must empty himself, we are reminded, of one recognised and admired virtue after another, till there is no form or comeliness that men may desire ; only the bare frame—of love.

All this is apparent when we turn to the short lists of virtues permitted to the Christian ; these lists, indeed, are few as well as short, since so much of the ethical teaching of the New Testament is devoted to cautions against the wrong-doings of paganism. The "fruits of the Spirit" include long-suffering, kindness, meekness, self-control, and goodness or beneficence ; they do not include patriotism, justifiable self-assertion, and "reasonable self-love." The man whom Christ pronounces blest is the man who would gain nothing but contempt or amused toleration from a pitying world—poor in spirit (poor-spirited, as his neighbours would immediately call him), merciful, eager only for that unprofitable thing, goodness, and welcoming every scorn and rebuff, like "a lamb led to the slaughter." The would-be follower of Christ must sell all that he has, must hate his own parents and family, and even his own life—"else he cannot be my disciple"; he must crucify the flesh with the affections and lusts thereof. It was the Son of thunder who considered that hatred shut the heart to the light of God as effectually as murder ; it was the Pharisee of the Pharisees, the fiery and passionate Saul, who warned against all bitterness and wrath and clamour, who gloried in tribulation, and counted all on which the Jew most prided himself as refuse, and was willing to regard himself and be regarded by others as the filth and offscouring of the world.

The same ideal of self-renunciation, of stooping to gain what seems at best a problematical conquest, of non-resistance to evil, of willingness to endure suffering and wrong, is to be met with in the rest of the New

Testament. The disciple who, to avoid the contumely of an unpopular connexion, said of his master, " I never knew him," is found urging that " when you do well and suffer for it, ye shall take it patiently," adding poignantly " for hereunto were ye called, because Christ also suffered for you " ; or in other words, recalling the Beatitudes, " if ye shall suffer for righteousness' sake, blessed are ye " ; or again, " inasmuch as ye are partakers of Christ's sufferings, rejoice." [1] The whole duty of man, according to New Testament ethics, might be summed up in the significant words of S. James, "the wisdom from above is first pure, then peaceable, gentle, easy to be entreated, full of mercy and good fruits, without partiality and without hypocrisy." [2] And this was precisely the aspect of Christian conduct that impressed the heathen. Beneath the caricatures of Celsus and Lucian, we can distinguish the zeal for hospitality,—that strange hospitality which had excited the world's hostility to "the friend of publicans and sinners,"—the suspicion of wealth or influence, the meekness which gave the other cheek also and did not resist evil.

III. The world has not erred in regarding this ideal of conduct as distinctively Christian ; alien alike to the Old Testament and to paganism. Where then shall we look for its source?

In the environment of early Christianity, some have replied. The circumstances of the church in its beginning made such an ideal inevitable. The Old Testament was inseparable from the religion of a nation, and of a nation which had constantly to assert itself and its God before the Gentiles. Self-repression there would have meant annihilation. All the morality

[1] 1 Pet. $2^{20\ 21}\ 3^{14}\ 4^{13}$. [2] James 3^{17}.

12   ETHICS AND ATONEMENT

of the Old Testament, it is said, sprang from this ruling idea or grew side by side with it; and when the nation, after the crisis of the exile, became a church, this national morality surrendered its prominence to the ritual and apocalyptic teaching of the later prophets. The religion of the New Testament, on the other hand, is from the very beginning, the religion of a church. But it was no established church; its members were sent out as sheep among wolves; not as soldiers in a victorious army, like the warriors of Joshua or David, but as the upholders of what seemed a lost cause. For them, propagandism by the sword was out of the question; Christ was no Mohammed; nor were his apostles capable of sustaining the rôle of Caliph; theirs was rather, of necessity, the "way" of the Buddhist, whose hope of overcoming the world lay not in affirmation, but in renunciation and abstraction.

Further, the virtue of humble endurance has seemed, to exponents of this view, the only virtue possible for the majority of the earliest converts. "Not many mighty, not many noble," were called. Christ himself had startled his hearers by emphasizing the dangers of wealth and resources; he laid it down as an axiom that it was better to be poor than rich; he even despised the favours of the rich, and his attitude of pity to the rich man has been a riddle to the world ever since. For such men as he chose, only two courses were possible, self-renunciation and endurance, or attempt at revolution. The latter would have meant ruin. That endurance as a policy is superior to resistance, has been urged with all his vigour and acumen in our time by Tolstoi. Tolstoi attributes the continuance of Christianity to the rule of the survival of the fittest, owing to its adaptation to the principle of non-resistance. In the following sentences he has given us a modern paraphrase of the equally clear-cut teaching of our Lord. " The chief difference on this point between the teaching of Jesus and of the world is this,—the latter considers labour a special merit in a man, giving him a claim on others, and enabling him to assert his right to a larger sustenance in proportion to the amount of his labour; the former considers it a necessary condition of life, and food an inevitable consequence. . . . However bad the master be, he will feed his labourer as he will his horse; will feed him so that he may work as long as possible,—that is, he will contribute towards the attainment of the greatest good for the man." " A Christian's certainty of provision for his needs will be as great among the heathen as among Christians. He labours for others, consequently, he is necessary to them, and will be cared for. A dog that is useful is fed and taken care of; who, then, would not take care of a man needed by all?"[1]

Whether this is exactly our Lord's meaning or not, Tolstoi would be the last man to claim originality in advancing the view. What he did claim was that he was re-asserting a truth too clear and concise to be tolerated by the centuries which had buried it. The strength of the early Christians was, though in another sense than Isaiah's, " to sit still." Passive resistance and passive endurance approximate. Christianity was the leaven, not the lump to be leavened. The leaven works in secret; its secrecy is its security. To choose the alternative which meant revolution would have destroyed the church in the first two centuries of its existence.

[1] " Work while you have the Light."

14 ETHICS AND ATONEMENT

But can this view of Christianity, as founded on non-resistance, be upheld ? Let us turn to the great figures of these early years, when its first outlines had not become dimmed. In their natures, as in their creed, is a distinctly combative element. How did they reconcile it with this alleged non-resistance? There is much in what they wrote and said and did that implies a habit of most strenuous resistance. Even in the epistles of his old age, S. John is a "son of thunder" still; S. Paul's personal keynote was boldness, the boldness of a good soldier of Jesus Christ; and how strange the paradox conveyed by that warlike simile! The Apocalypse is a simple proclamation of war to the knife with society; the humble note of non-resistance is finally drowned in the clanging warfare of Michael and his angels. Even Jesus, who was not to strive or cry, or to cause his voice to be heard in the streets, could fling the crowd of hucksters out of the temple; and the thunder of the reiterated "Woe!" with which he defied those who were travestying the religion of his Father, still rolls in magnificent scorn. No one can read his burning words to the ruling classes in Jerusalem without feeling that the sin which he denounced was a personal matter to him, and that the honour of his Father which he was defending was the honour of the jealous God, who bade His servants do much beside sitting still and enduring. If non-resistance is the foundation of the religion of the New Testament, not only has Christianity, as Tolstoi complained, been one long unfaithfulness, but the New Testament itself is unintelligible; and the attitude of the men who did most to shape the tradition of Christian life and thought becomes an insoluble enigma.

ETHICS IN THE BIBLE

But the New Testament cannot be so interpreted. No true lover of S. Paul or S. John or of Christ could continue to misunderstand them thus. The foundation of Christian ethics is the New Commandment, love; love to one another. But what does this love mean? Does it really imply what is foreign to the Old Testament? We cannot understand it apart from a deeper principle, which is not a precept but a fact; the love of the Father to Christ, and of Christ to the disciples. "As the Father hath loved me, so have I loved you; continue ye in my love." And it is significant that at the moment when Christ made his disciples feel that he was at last speaking clearly to them, he emphasized this "new commandment" as he had never done before; and that he chose this as the moment in which to make use of an expression which is as rare in the New Testament as it is common in the Old, the Covenant. "This is the New Covenant in my blood." Hence, at the very centre of the new, the Church of Christ, we have the link with the old, with Israel, the Covenant people. This expression demands a short consideration.

There can be, indeed, no doubt that the conception of the Covenant is the fundamental conception of the Old Testament, within which that of righteousness itself is contained. True, in spite of its early appearance in Genesis, the Covenant may not have been the earliest religious idea consciously held in the mind of Israel. But it is none the less inseparable from every part of the Old Testament; it meets us in the Law, in the Prophets, and in the Writings; and in each case just when the spirituality and intensity of the revelation, if we may so speak, reaches its highest level. God's dealings with the Patriarchs are represented in Deuter-

16 ETHICS AND ATONEMENT

onomy as being a Covenant.[1] It was a Covenant which God formed with Moses and the Israelites at Sinai.[2] The so-called Priests' code may be said to be built up on the idea of the Covenant. In the earlier Prophets the Covenant is but seldom mentioned, though the Covenant idea must be admitted to underlie all that is said of Jehovah's special and indestructible relation to His people.[3] But Jeremiah and Ezekiel base this indestructibility on the fact of the Covenant,[4] and both look forward to a new Covenant,—new, because unlike the old one, it will be kept.[5] This conception is developed more fully in the second part of Isaiah,[6] and where prophecy reaches its culmination in the picture of the Servant, the Servant himself becomes the Covenant of the people.[7] In the Psalms righteousness is almost synonymous with keeping the Covenant, wickedness with breaking it; the Covenant is naturally spoken of side by side with the Law, though while God gives the Law, He Himself must keep the Covenant.[8]

IV. At first sight, there seems something unnatural in this view of God, as at once a lawgiver and a bargain-maker. But the Covenant is no mere bargain; it is a Covenant of love, made because Love saw that without it, man could not be saved from himself, or from the disobedience to Law which meant death. In fact, the whole spirit of the Old Testament is enshrined in Augustine's prayer, "Give what thou commandest, com-

---

[1] 4^{31} 7^{12} $6^{10\ 18}$, etc. [2] Ex. 24; Dt. 4^{13} 9^9, etc.
[3] Hos. 2^3 12^9; Am. 3^2; Is. $28^{15\ 18}$ 33^8. [4] Jer. $11^{34\ 35}$ 31^{31} 7^{22}; Ezek. $16^{8\ 59}$.
[5] Jer. 31^{38}; Ezek. 36^{24}; Jer. $33^{14\text{-}16}$; Ezek. $37^{21\text{-}28}$.
[6] 55^3 56^6 61^8. [7] 42^6 49^6.
[8] Pss. 25^{10} 44^{17} 74^{20} 78^{10}. Compare Neh. 1^5 and Dan. 9^4, "God, which keepeth covenant and mercy with those that love him and keep his commandments"; also Ezra 10^{34}.

ETHICS IN THE BIBLE 17

mand what thou wilt."[1] The Law and the Covenant went together because the Covenant was to ensure the power of keeping the Law to him to whom it was given. Man struck no bargain with God, nor God with man; instead, man was admitted to certain rights with God, by God's free grace; he became, not a subject of the Law, but a partner, as it were, with the Lawgiver. He is an accused man at the bar of the judge; but he is also the assessor on the judge's bench; bound to implore forgiveness when he has broken his part of the Covenant; but able to plead with God that God should not Himself prove unfaithful.

Can this conception of the Covenant, then, be found in the New Testament? There is certainly a very striking parallel where we might least have expected it, in the writings of John. John emphasizes repeatedly the connexion between keeping the commandments of Christ and experiencing the love of God.[2] But this is more than a parallel; for it is based on a similar but deeper relation between God and man. Of himself, man has no more right before God in the New Testament than he has in the Old. God is as supreme as if he were an oriental despot. But the gospel is one long proclamation that man may be admitted to certain rights before God: that he should be no longer a prisoner at the bar, but one who knows no condemnation, who is at peace with God, who is—and here the Old Testament is finally transcended—a son. In the earliest teaching of the gospel the apostles were con-

[1] " Da quod jubes, jube quod vis."
[2] 1 Jn. 2^5, 4^{12}; *cf.* Jn. 14^{23} and 1 Jn. 5^3, "this is the love of God, that we keep his commandments"; *cf.* Dt. 4^1, "hearken unto the statutes and unto the judgments which I teach you, to do them, that ye may live and go in and possess the land which the Lord God of your fathers giveth you." *Cf.* also 6^{24} and 8^1.

B

18   ETHICS AND ATONEMENT

tented with taking the Old Testament conception of the Covenant and announcing that the new Covenant had now been brought about.[1] But in the first place the content of the conception is in the later writings transformed, inasmuch as the rights were found to be far more than those even of a favoured subject: and all legal phraseology becomes but a cold medium for so warm and glowing a reality. And in the second place, men are clothed with these new covenant rights not directly by God but through a third person, a mediator, the Son of God, who extends to them his own privileges, connoting a son's relationship with his father. It can hardly be necessary to quote passages to show that in the New Testament men are made sons, and made sons through Christ; but whether we take S. John's cardinal expression of the gospel, "Beloved, now are we the sons of God,"[2] or S. Paul's, "God sent forth his son . . . that he might redeem them which were under the law, that we might receive the adoption of sons," it is equally certain that this new relationship is founded in God's free grace, as much as was the Covenant in the Old Testament; and that the keeping of the commandments is not its cause, but its effect. We receive the spirit of adoption, of son-making.[3] Christ himself says little about the formal aspects of the new relationship; he simply claims for himself a unique closeness to God; but his favourite names for God are My Father, The Father, Your Father—never Our Father; he bids his followers love their enemies, that they may become sons of their Father who is in heaven; he has for ever connected the thought of the repenting sinner with that of

---

[1] See Acts 3^{25}, "Ye are the children of the prophets and of the covenant which God made with our Fathers." *Cf.* 2^{16}.

[2] I Jn. 3^2.   [3] Gal. 4^3; Rom. 8^{15}.

the returning son, and in his last prayer of consecration he claimed for his disciples the possession, through himself, of all that he had with God,—joy, sanctification, oneness; the general sharing of what was his own.[1]

V. It is when we view the gospel in this light that we see why the three theological virtues, faith, hope, and love, must needs take precedence of the four "cardinal" virtues, bravery, self-control, justice, and wisdom,—or of any others. If the acceptance of the gospel means entering into a new relation with God through Christ, then obviously the first necessity is faith, the heart-whole acceptance of that position and of the mediator who brings us there. This may sound far enough from the traditional definitions of faith. Faith indeed in the New Testament is used in varying senses. In the Synoptics, it is the unquestioning faith which laughs at difficulties or impossibilities, and takes Christ confidently at his word, either for the healing of leprosy or the removing of mountains. In the Epistle to the Hebrews, faith is not so much personal confidence in Christ, or allegiance to him, as that general confidence in the unseen which becomes the foundation of every other virtue; a psychological faculty, a "principle making for heroism."[2] With S. Paul, faith takes primarily a legal or forensic aspect; in faith, man sets his hand and seal to the Covenant, and thereby is pronounced just; stands before God in the very position of the sinless Christ. But it is not forensic only; it becomes a principle whereby the righteousness imputed to him works itself out in his life, even as God himself, by the power which raised Christ from the dead, works in him, to will and to work of his good pleasure. To S. John, faith, as belief in Christ's divine person, em-

[1] Mt. 5^{45}; Lk. 15; Jn. $17^{14\ 19\ 20\ 24}$.   [2] Bruce, in "Hasting's Dict. Bib." ii. 334.

20 ETHICS AND ATONEMENT

braces every gift and every grace. S. John brushes aside, as comparatively unimportant, any individual or passive results of faith; faith is that immediate reception of Christ's own account of himself which means life. But there is no real conflict between these four leading presentations of faith, any more than there is conflict between the teaching of S. Paul and S. James on the same subject. The object of faith in each is ultimately Christ. Christ is the captain and completer of faith. Salvation is not from faith; it is from Christ. It is by faith, because by faith, by self-commitment to Christ alone can we experience his saving power, whereby sin is forgiven, alienation is brought to an end and our adoption into God's family is accomplished. "Without faith it is impossible to please Him." For the ethics as for the very acceptance of Christianity, faith comes first, as inevitably as hope, the projection of faith upon the future, comes second.

"Thou shalt love thy neighbour as thyself." "Love one another." These are central words on the lips of Christ, and necessarily so, if our account of the new Covenant is correct. Man stands in a certain relation to God, through Christ. That relation is not of subject to King but son to Father. The reason why love is emphasized in the New Testament, is that it is no longer in opposition to a nature "red in tooth and claw" that man has to preserve his allegiance to God; he is brought into the security of a family circle. "To Jesus, the spirit of the kingdom was no other than the filial spirit, and the reign of God is simply God's rule over His family."[1] This will explain why in the New Testament there is a measure of reserve in the call for love, but none in the call for faith. Faith is the mark

[1] Clarke, "Outlines of Theology," p. 277.

of the true filial attitude, of which hope is the abiding mark,—hope for yet fuller communion with the Father. If the society which Christ came to found is ethical through and through, as we cannot too often remember, it is a society, a kingdom, presided over by a Father. There the disciple, the subject, finds that to love his father and to love his brethren are one and the same thing. There love identifies itself with law, and law again with life; and S. Paul travels from height to height till he reaches the very mount of transfiguration where they who think no evil, who bear all things and believe all things, see God face to face.

The foundation then of the Christian virtues is the Christian attitude of man to God, and it is this fact which explains the large place assigned, as we have already noticed, to the characteristics of humility, sincerity and non-resistance to evil. It also explains the note of strenuous resistance therein. The New Testament gives no list of unconnected virtues like Aristotle's. Bravery, prudence and patriotism may be fine things: but the garment of Christianity is the seamless robe of pure simplicity and not the embroidered vestment of a Jewish high priest, nor the pallium of a Roman consul. Now to this attitude of faith which "works by love," there are three great foes: the spirit of the Pharisee who thanks his God that he is different from his brethren: the Judas-kiss which simulates that holiest bond of brotherhood and desecrates it: and the defiance of the family tie which, instead of simply neglecting the brotherly love that bears all things, and the love of enemies that claims them for friends, rejects the idea of brotherhood with scorn, and turns friends to enemies. It is the Christian attitude of man to God, thus understood, which necessitates the rooted aversion and contempt with which the world is regarded. How can the friendship of the world be other than refuse and filth? How can the principles of worldly prudence, repaying injuries, resisting evil, refusing forgiveness, be other than criminal folly, when even to think of them is to harbour disloyalty and treachery to God and to God's order? It is hate alone which is hated: scorn alone which is despised. Pride, insincerity, treachery: these are the ever-deepening circles which lead to the ice of some Dantesque abyss, the three vices against which the most terrible of the New Testament woes are hurled. Meekness, sincerity, endurance are the successive steps to the very rose of heaven, the dwelling of God the Father, who so loved the world that He gave to it, through His son, the great secret of sonship and brotherhood.

VI. Righteousness, it was said, is the mark of the Old Testament and New Testament alike, and we have seen that there is really no reason to doubt or alter that statement. God's covenant love is at the foundation of both. Yet there is a difference between the righteousness of the Old Testament and that of the New. The emphasis is changed. It is laid in the New, not so much on the things to be done, as on the way in which they are done, or on the man who does them. Christian ethics is not a certain view of right conduct between man and man: it is rather the principle of right conduct of one Christian to another, or to those who are meant to become Christians. The progress involved in Christian ethics is not "from status to contract," but from contract to status. The Covenant itself rests on status rather than contract.

And S. Paul never wearies of urging that Christians "are not under the law but under Grace." Now S. Paul,

ETHICS IN THE BIBLE

equally with Christ himself, repudiates the idea of doing away with either law or the law. Christ said with perfect definiteness, " I am come not to destroy the law but to fulfil it." Still, Christianity does recognise a difference. The law, as fulfilled or to be fulfilled, by the Christian, and in Christ, is no longer a code: it is transformed to a privilege whereby those who love him shall keep his commandments as proof of their love, take his yoke upon them and so find rest to their souls. Even to the Jew, law is not simply a matter of codes: it is " Torah," instruction, intended, as Psalm 119 abundantly shows, to point out the way of blessedness. The Jew had the " Torah " of Jehovah; the Christian had the " nomos " of Christ. But to the Jew " Torah " came first; by the " Torah " was Jehovah approached: to the Christian, Christ came before the law as well as after it, and in rapt contemplation of Christ the law faded out of sight altogether.

Is the law, then, to be regarded, by Christian ethics, as antiquated? On the contrary, " So act as men that are to be judged by a law of liberty." The life of the Christian exemplifies the paradox of a service, a slavery, which is perfect freedom. To this paradox all obedience, as it grows perfect, invariably tends. A law that is " heteronomous," imposed from the outside, can never be perfectly obeyed. As soon as obedience is perfect, from the heart, the law ceases to be heteronomous and becomes self-imposed: the obeyer of the law becomes his own dictator, and is, as such, a free man. His law is a law of liberty. Freedom means not deliverance from law, which would be anarchy, but voluntary acceptance of law, self-identification with law. Hence, Christ makes his followers free, not by releasing them from restrictions, but by making them members of his

24 ETHICS AND ATONEMENT

own body, joint heirs with himself, making his own attitude to the law, which is the same as his Father's, their attitude also. This conception of freedom is not, as is sometimes supposed, confined to S. Paul among New Testament writers, though it is S. Paul who most carefully elaborates it. The mere fact that S. James also glories in the idea makes it difficult to believe that Christianity is here a debtor to Stoicism. True, the Stoic prided himself on his freedom: but on freedom itself, and also on the way to it, there is between Stoicism and Christianity fundamental disagreement. The Stoic's freedom consists in aloofness from all the entanglements of a busy and passionate world, an $\dot{a}\pi\acute{a}\delta\epsilon\iota a$: the Stoic is above law because he condescends to acknowledge no law which can command him. He gains his lofty pinnacle through unremitting practice, constant cultivation of habit: if the entanglement is too clinging, he has the desperate remedy of suicide. The Christian is not without law: he glories in being under the law, but under the law to Christ. Freedom, to the Christian, does not consist in being unbound, but in being bound completely. A man may seize my hand with his and bind it fast,—that is slavery. Another may seize my will with his and hold it fast, so that with his mine moves inevitably and with perfect contentment,—that is freedom.

Now, in what system of human relationship is this attitude of the subjects of law to the law itself and to the lawgiver carried out? To a certain extent in any free state where the body politic legislates for itself, or where the acts of the legislative body are freely and heartily accepted by the whole nation. Yet this at best is an approximation. In practice, a minority will always exist to find fault with the majority; and some laws will receive at best but a forced and unwilling obedience. But in the system for which we are in search nothing that is enforced can be tolerated: perfect love must cast out fear and unwillingness alike. Not in the civic or political realm, but only in the ideal family relationship can we reach our object. It is there alone that we have in its completeness the relation, not of contract, but of status, where law itself is forgotten by the side of the unity of the personal will existing between the parents and the children. And this is precisely the conclusion to which, as we have said, we are led by every page of the New Testament. The family indeed is the end, as it is the beginning, of human society. The relations of father and son have been from everlasting and shall be to everlasting. Here in our human life nothing nobler is known than the devotion, affection, sacrifice and unity of the perfectly welded family; and Christ's clearest descriptions of the relations of men to God and to their fellows which he came to found, imply and rest upon the perfect understanding, based on obedience and love, that lives between the Father and the Son. Nowhere in the New Testament is there a completer expression of the ideal of the "new creation" to which all the other books bear their witness, than in Christ's "high priestly," or more correctly, filial and brotherly prayer, consecrating the whole family to God—"that they may all be one: even as thou, Father, art in me and I in thee; that they also may be one in us . . . that the world may believe that thou didst send me."

CHAPTER II

ETHICS OUTSIDE THE BIBLE

I. ALL this may be conceded as true of the Biblical view of conduct; but most people will feel that the Biblical view of conduct is very different from that of ordinary ethics. Ethics, as that branch of philosophy which deals with right or proper conduct, has to take into consideration everything about conduct except the one thing which to the Bible is central, namely, God. Now by this we do not necessarily intend anything disrespectful to ethics; ethical investigation, in its universal appeal, is perfectly justified if it can "do without that hypothesis." And there is this further reason for the neglect of God. In the preceding chapter we have been constantly referring to the Hebrews; ethics as a whole points back rather to the Greeks; it derives its inspiration rather from the Athenian academy than the lake of Galilee; and to Greek thought, as distinct from Greek religion, God was at best a shadowy being, about whom it was as well not to speak with too much confidence or detail.

This attitude has characterised ethics throughout its history. No writer on ethics, even in the last century, was distinctively Christian. Martineau came nearest to being so; but the tone of the "Types of Ethical Theory" is different from that of the "Study of Religion"; piety is there; but it is held in leash.

ETHICS OUTSIDE THE BIBLE

Martineau's elaborate defence of the doctrine of responsibility is pervaded by the loftiest moral enthusiasm; but its author, save for his striking literary allusions, might never have heard of the Bible. T. H. Green took up his parable against Hedonism with Hebraic vehemence; his contention for the transcendental against the material reminds the reader of Elijah's contention for Jehovah against Baal; but his Eternal Consciousness is no more God, than is the Hegelian trinity of Being, Essence, and the Absolute identical with the Trinity of Christian theology.

Sidgwick, Herbert Spencer, and J. S. Mill have even less to do with Christian or theistic belief; their concern is right conduct; but they mean conduct only as it affects the happiness of the individual or the continued existence of the race. Going back to the previous century, we may seem to find a difference of tone in the Anglican divines, Paley and Butler. Paley urged that men must needs practise morality, in their natural wish to be happy; because if they did not do so, God would take care that they were unhappy, at least on the other side of the grave. But such a God, existing to ensure reward or punishment after death, has no more to do with Christian ethics than have any of the "sanctions" of Paley's follower, Bentham. Bentham, indeed, would have as little of God as he would of the idea of Duty; and he held that men were forced to that kind of conduct which is called right, by the various pains or pleasures caused by our own bodies, by state regulations, by social opinion around us, or by the fears or hopes which religious people may entertain and teach regarding the future.

28 ETHICS AND ATONEMENT

Butler's is a greater name. Butler shrank from any view of God which would make Him a mere master of a celestial steelyard, to redress the uneven balances of earth; Butler's special contribution to ethics was the stress which he laid upon conscience; yet in Butler's presentation, conscience was little more than an instinct of morality, considered quite apart from any connexion with a Divine implanter; and the real guide of human conduct, as he asserted, was that reasonable self-love, to which any divine action was happily accommodated, and with which conscience itself could never clash. How different the teaching of the New Testament; there, conscience is not rigidly marked off from other conceptions, such as the new law in the heart, the wisdom coming from above, or even the witness of the Spirit; but there is nothing in the New Testament about "reasonable self-love." Butler's view, though valuable enough, confirms our assertion, that writers on ethics have consistently neglected distinctive Christian teaching.

Butler points back to Hobbes; Hobbes was the author, intentional or unintentional, of a thoroughgoing attack on morality in general. He no more than Bentham believed in any such thing as intrinsic Right; what we call right, said Hobbes, is simply that which is enforced by law; and law is simply the creation of a social convention or contract, without which our natural master-desire for power would fling us at each other's throats all day long. Hobbes took up the question, answered by him in this ingenious fashion, just where it had been dropped when Christianity had gradually closed the schools of the Greek and Roman philosophers, more than a thousand years before. Before Hobbes, ethics had not been actually neglected by Christian writers; but it followed, with a few necessary changes, the lines already laid down by Plato and Aristotle.

II. It is indeed impossible to understand ethical problems, or even to form a correct judgment as to what is valuable or the reverse, in ethical writings, without going back to the Greeks. Justin, who suffered martyrdom in the reign of Marcus Aurelius (166 A.D.), spoke of Socrates and Plato as if they had received almost as definite an inspiration as the Hebrew prophets;[1] and certainly if they lack the mysterious and well-nigh unearthly majesty of Amos and Isaiah and Ezekiel, there is a clear and penetrating sunlight, as if from Mediterranean skies, in their pages. We find there a knowledge of the affairs of life, as distinct from its underlying principles, not to be gained from the lightning flashes and deep thunderclouds of the seers of Israel and Judah. "There is nothing new under the sun"; and the reader of Greek philosophy is startled again and again to find how much of his modern thought has been anticipated more than 2000 years ago; some questions, keenly enough debated then, have hardly had their turn with us as yet. At the same time, he experiences all the fascination that dwells in the freshness of the early world; the Greeks, as the Egyptians told them, were always children; and to the end, when Greece was preparing to hand on the torch of thought to the quickly wearied hands of Rome, her thinkers preserved something of the naïveté and directness of children; we may well wonder whether they are not for this reason nearer to the Kingdom of Heaven than their successors who, sixteen centuries later, put on one side that Gospel of

[1] Apol. ii. ch. 10.

the Kingdom for which Greek ears had listened in vain.

The Greeks, too, had all the child's practicalness. They had not felt "the heavy and the weary weight of all this unintelligible world" as we moderns have learnt to feel it; ethics was somewhat of a light-hearted business to them, as it cannot be to us; and they could devote themselves to it with what Stevenson whimsically called "the superior earnestness that properly belongs to play." Theirs was the matter-of-fact object, to discover how to live well, and reach true well-being and happiness. Socrates led the way; all through his life, he had to face the Sophists, the professors of the art of success, as a greater than he had to face the Pharisees, the professors of the art of the religious life. But Socrates was himself also a professor of the art of success. If we can only know, he used to assert, the real nature of virtue, we cannot possibly do anything but embrace her; while vice, "to be hated, needs but to be seen." A man's true business is to find out what is the useful, the beautiful, and the good. Now in these statements there are implied two very serious questions. First, granted that we may really come to know what is the true nature of virtue, how may we bridge over the gulf that still remains, and act virtuously? "To will is present with me"—and that is a stage beyond knowing—"but how to perform that which is good, I find not." And secondly, is it the fact that the good and the useful—to say nothing of the beautiful—always coincide? On the contrary, the difficulty with most of us is to reconcile the alarming divergence of the good from the useful, and still more from the pleasant. Within the limits of these two questions has lain the field of ethics ever since;—how to make practice answer theory, and how to make advantage or pleasure answer right and duty.

It was some little time, however, before these questions shaped themselves explicitly in men's minds. Socrates simply stated what would be the result when the answers were found, and then went on to consider the real meanings, or the definitions, of the several virtues. The greatest of his followers, Plato and Aristotle, left him far behind in their grasp of the facts which ethics has to take into account; but like him, they believed in and sought after a knowledge which would inevitably translate itself into conduct, and a good which would at once approve itself as the goal of all desire and the crown of all usefulness. Thus they are at once practical and speculative. As a result, they have given us sketches of complete moral life, which are as different from the ideals of the early Christian monks or of the later English philosophers or divines, as one of the Elgin marbles is from an early Italian S. Sebastian or a Dutch Burgomaster by Rembrandt. Plato's search for the true essence of goodness led him to the conception of a form or "idea" of goodness, imperceptible to any of the senses, and only to be known by a mind kindred to it, after a prolonged and most careful training;—a "soul of goodness," which is the source of all goodness in the things or people that are called good in our lower and material world. And he has left us a noble and astonishing picture of a man, the eye of whose soul has been turned—"converted," to use his own word—to this spiritual goodness, as from shadows to the sun, with every faculty of his mind called out in eager appreciation of that hidden treasure. Burning with a glowing passion for the great and supreme Idea, like the passion of the lover for his beloved, he walks through

32 ETHICS AND ATONEMENT

the toilsome world of the practical life, solves its problems, endures its scorns, and in all literalness, labours as seeing the invisible.

Aristotle, who wrote his Ethics to explain the true nature of Well-being or Blessedness—the word he used means as much the one as the other—found it in a well-rounded and mature life, where every power should have full employment, according to the standard of virtue and judged by the rules of right reason.[1] This rather portentous definition is elucidated when we learn that to Aristotle, virtue consists in allowing each faculty, in all matters connected with pleasures and pains, to go exactly to the right limit of exercise, in knowing how far to give the rein to natural desires, to love of honour or to high spirit, or even to playfulness and jesting; and in being able by long practice and training, to restrain each faculty at that point. Virtue, or excellence, to Aristotle consists in intelligent and habitual self-control.

It is here that he takes occasion to describe to us the character who appears most to excite his admiration;[2] the "high-souled" man, who knows that he is worthy of great things, and claims them; who will be dependent on none, beholden to none; who loves to give rather than to receive; who will not deign to recount his own exploits, but requires that others should remember them; who preserves a leisurely and courteous demeanour in all circumstances; never at a loss; never in a hurry; always master of himself, of his position, and of other people; a kind of Olympian among men, preserving the readiness of the Christian to serve and to impart, but only by robbing it of its brotherly sympathy and love, and then clothing it in the stiff aristo-

[1] Nic. Eth. ii. 6. [2] *Ib.* iv. 3.

cratic garb of conscious superiority and worth. We should indeed be unjust to Aristotle if we thought his last words on ethics were the description of a prig, insufferable because so well schooled and capable. His discussions of justice, freewill, friendship and wisdom gain rather than lose in pregnancy from the limitations of their time; but his ideal of character undoubtedly tends to the coldly correct, the faultlessly sublime; there is no distracting conflict of the good and the useful in such a life; but then there is no moral conflict at all; still less is there any sympathy with one whose ambition it was to be a fool for Christ's sake. We are never greatly roused by one who boasts of being "constant as the Northern star"; and Aristotle's paragon, in attaining his proud stability, loses our sympathy and forfeits his own connexion with the actual conditions of life. Plato has inspired the mystic in each subsequent age; Aristotle has been the model of the formal and systematic theologian. Plato finds his echo in Jacob Behmen; Aristotle in Thomas Aquinas.

Duty, and Pleasure; each has been regarded as consistent with the other so far; but no longer. With the schools of the Cynics and the Cyrenaics, contemporaries of Aristotle himself, came the division. The Cynic catchword was Duty and not Pleasure; that of the Cyrenaics, the Pleasure of the moment; and the antithesis was handed on to the far more influential sects of the Stoics and the Epicureans. The latter were not mere devotees of the senses; nor indeed, were all the Cyrenaics, as readers of Pater's "Marius the Epicurean" will remember. But the false step had been taken when pleasure and gratification, however exalted and refined, had been distinguished from duty and its responsibilities. Life to the Epicurean seemed

c

best to be fulfilled when the first thought was for freedom from the unpleasant or the irksome. He aimed at an ideal of tranquil, dispassionate ease. The same even dispassionateness was the aim of the Stoic also; but it was to be reached along a very different path; the world denied, desires trampled under foot; virtue enthroned; Zeus himself taken into partnership with the sage; Duty obeyed as supreme lord. The sage is to practise all the virtues, to keep his own soul free from all disturbance and every whisper of lust, calmly following life according to nature and in harmony with himself. He alone is free; he is at once priest, prophet and king;[1] and he is fully at liberty to put an end to his existence, either in order to serve his friends, or to escape dishonour or even simply pain to himself.

III. Such was the highest type of pagan thought when Christianity started out on her career of conquest; and such too, was the noblest combatant in the long struggle which lasted on for her through the remaining years of the classical period. That struggle has continued, with an existence independent of the newer doctrines of Christianity, ever since. The spirit of the combatants may have changed; they may have understood their own battle-cries differently; but the battle-cries have been the same. On the one side, to use our modern names, Hedonism or Utilitarianism, the cult of satisfaction and advantage; and on the other, Intuitionism, the obedience to direct commands speaking within the soul. But into the arena of the conflict, Christianity never really stepped. The mind of Christianity has had little patience even for questions so great as these. Like Jesus in the gospel story, Christianity seems to

[1] A striking description is given in Stobæus, Ecl. ii. 16.

ETHICS OUTSIDE THE BIBLE 35

have asked, half contemptuously, of the warring sects, "who made me a judge and a ruler over you?" Her relations with ethics were confined, in the age immediately following the Apostles, to the simple enforcement of obvious points of morality; and then, before there was time to see the need of digging beneath these to their foundations, great problems of theology on the one hand and of Church organisation on the other arose to demand instant and absorbing consideration. The nature of Christ, the means of salvation, the slavery or freedom of the human will, —all these had to be decided before there could be leisure to settle what a man's duties were, or whether he had any duties, properly speaking, at all. And before the decisions could be made, the barbarians had swept in on the old civilisation, and reduced all, for a time, to chaos.

Yet it must not be supposed that the practice of ethics had been neglected. Even the dark ages, when Goth and Vandal were doing their worst, were the ages, not of vices only, but also of saints. The Church, indeed, had become saturated with commercialism, and winked at high-handed sins, or even excused them, with an appalling callousness. Lecky's picture of Christianity in Europe before Charlemagne, dismal as it is, cannot be called exaggerated.[1] Yet there was a change, and the human mind had become possessed of ideas unknown before the birth of Christ. Human life had gained a new sacredness; there might be murders and massacres on a frightful scale; but gladiatorial shows, the exposure of infants, and suicide, were no longer thought to have "no harm" in them. Women attained a position denied to them, both in

[1] Lecky's "History of European Morality," vol. ii. ch. iv.

Greece and Rome, for centuries. Slavery died, though it died hard. Humility was admired even when it was not practised; asceticism—by no means a bad thing in an age when every passion leaped forth unchecked in its worst forms—captivated the minds of thousands; reverence, liberality, and the forgiveness of injuries took on a definiteness unknown to Seneca and Marcus Aurelius. The Church, as a corporation at once secular and religious, fostered a new spirit of personal independence, an independence from all external "worldly" control, as complete as was the obedience which she claimed for herself in all matters of faith.

All this, however, was far enough from a merely ethical advance. It was the direct though perhaps unconscious result of the religious belief of the time. Any independent thought, between the sixth and the tenth centuries, would have been impossible. If human life was more sacred, the reason was that the death of the body was not the end; to send a living person to the grave was to drive him before the judgment seat. Women were treated with a new respect, because women shared with men the blessings of redemption. Almsgiving was practised as it never was in the heathen world, because it was a distinct means of benefiting one's own soul. The schoolmen were too close students of Plato and Aristotle to neglect altogether the separate treatment of ethics; but they wedged it in between masses of theology; and they were for the most part content with re-arrangements of the conclusions of their Greek philosophical masters, or the Bible, or both. The great contests of the Scholastic age lay far away from the field of ethics. The importance of reason as

ETHICS OUTSIDE THE BIBLE 37

compared with faith; the relation of the understanding to the will; the antithesis of nominalism and realism; these were the intellectual objects of interest; and Christian duties might have been forgotten altogether by the regular authorities of the Church, had it not been necessary to lay down rules for the practice of penance and the guidance of father-confessors. Only by the impulse that led Luther and Calvin to the discovery of St Paul was the moral image of Christ restored as the example of the Christian; then at last ethics was proclaimed as of the very essence of Christianity.

Yet even at the Reformation, interest was soon diverted into other channels. Luther himself called the Epistle of James, that magnificent manual of Christian Ethics, an epistle of straw, since he failed to find therein a statement of the doctrine of justification by faith. He could accuse Romanism of fostering immorality, as the Romanists accused him of teaching antinomianism; but to both parties, the question "what must I do to be saved?" quite obscured the other, "what must I do when I am saved?" The Calvinists, and especially our own Puritans and Covenanters, were the Stoics of the Reformation; their devotion to Duty was clothed with a sternness which made it irresistible; but to Duty itself, as distinct from the will of the Lord, they never consciously gave a thought. Since the Reformation, ethics has continued to hold a subordinate place in religious discussion. Those who debated most keenly the freedom of the will had yet no doubt about man's responsibility for keeping the ten commandments and the new commandments of the Gospel. The later conflicts with Deism and Unitarianism never extended to ethical subjects, and the various elements in German Reformed circles, Evangelicalism, Pantheism, Rationalism, took the prosaic matter of conduct for granted.

It is not strange, then, that theology has left systematic ethics for the most part untouched. Christianity, indeed, has given vigorous and uniform support to morality; but that is a very different thing. The assertion borne out by the facts is that theology, the precise consideration of the objects of the Christian consciousness, has done little or nothing for the scientific examination of our ideas of conduct. Science consists in the quest for definitions; ethics, as a science, consists in the quest for definitions on all subjects connected with conduct considered as right and wrong. Theology has laboured to give us precise notions of what we mean by God, sin, grace, salvation, and the like; though—such have been its limitations—of so obvious an idea as Personality, whether applied to God or man, it has till quite recently deigned to take very little notice. On the exact meaning of Justice, Gratitude, Benevolence, and even Purity, it has preserved silence. Still less has theology attempted to give a definite ruling on the relation between our intuitions and the considerations of our interest or of general utility, although this relation has the clearest bearing both on theology and on religion as a whole. In common with nearly all religions, Christianity has given a prominent place to rewards and punishments, future and present; but as to the influence which ought to be exerted by such hopes and fears on right conduct, there has been the widest difference among Christian teachers and writers.

Further, scientific Christian thought has paid little attention to psychology. Its incursions into psychological territory have been chiefly for the purpose of deciding whether the nature of man is tri-partite or bi-partite. But without psychology, there can be no clear appreciation of the problems of morality. Even to think of the good, in the most general way, suggests the question What is it that is good? the act by itself, or the will? the intention, the desire or the motive? How are we to distinguish these from one another? Does susceptibility to temptation lessen or increase goodness of character? Should we endeavour to form good habits, or is it the case, as has been affirmed, that "to form habits is to fail in the moral life"? Is the moral value of an act diminished by the pleasure with which it may be performed, or the advantage which may follow? How far are our moral judgments and convictions liable to be modified or warped by wish or by any sudden impulse? These questions have long been recognised as besetting the morality of "common-sense"; a wrong answer to them—and every one has to give some sort of answer—may easily involve a serious deflection from right conduct; and it is not surprising if the common-sense even of Christians, left without the guidance of precise Christian thought on these problems, has at times failed and brought discredit on the worthy name by which it is called.

IV. Theology has left ethics, for better or for worse, to go its own way. What has been the result for ethics? Ethics, as we have seen, has equally neglected theology. Ancient ethics, whose course we hurriedly traced up to Christian times, has had its successors, but outside the Church. If we turn again to Hobbes we shall observe that he took up the debate where the Stoics and Epicureans had left it, and in his masculine way gave a new philosophic basis to Epicureanism;

not the old refined Epicureanism of the garden, aiming at the tranquil meditative life, and the casting out of all fear; but the fundamental egoism which lay beneath such a refinement of self-interest—"I must do the best for myself," unhindered by any *a priori* considerations of duty whatever. Duty, Hobbes discovered, was no innate idea in the human breast, but an invention of Society. The primary aim of all human beings, he held, is power; and if we recognise certain tempting things as not to be done, and never dream of trying to indulge every desire for power, it is not because of any heaven-descended law, but for the sake of our own general convenience. The original selfishness of human nature, he pointed out, is evident enough from the police measures of civilisation; if no restrictions were placed on our conduct, our condition would be as odious as that of the savage. To make life pleasant or even tolerable, our aboriginal and lawless thirst for power has been put under the control of an arbitrary tyrant,—king or state,—who has been constituted to keep other people's hands off us, and ours off them.

Hobbes thus took his stand on psychology and on a somewhat imaginative view of history. His opponents fought his extraordinary but highly ingenious contention on his own ground. Their success was complete, in driving Hobbes off the field; but only partial, inasmuch as room was still left for others. The replies, indeed, were various; but they all maintained in one form or other, that the laws of morality are independent of any humanly constituted authority, whether tyrant or legislator; they were "eternal and immutable," as Cudworth said. The Christian Platonists found the law of Right to be seated in

ETHICS OUTSIDE THE BIBLE 41

man's reason; Shaftesbury in a kind of æsthetic sense, by virtue of which a cultivated "taste," as it were, would lead us to select goodness and reject vice; Butler, more powerfully, in the unique faculty of conscience. On the other hand, Hartley derived our veneration for the Good from the fact of its association, through our natural feelings of sympathy with one another, with the Pleasant. The Utilitarians, from Paley and Bentham to J. S. Mill, likewise held that the natural object of man was that conduct which would bring the greatest amount or intensity of happiness, and that it was idle to think of virtue, save as a means to this supreme end. This view was modified by distinguishing between the individual and the general happiness; but as soon as it was necessary to exhort the individual to labour for the happiness, not of himself, but of society,—which might be a very different thing—the old difficulty about Duty reappeared. Duty is a term which the Utilitarians suspected. They do indeed leave us with a feeling that we "ought" to aim at others' happiness: but for this "ought" there is no foundation save in so far as "we ought" means "it is to our advantage."

It will not have escaped the reader that these theories contain a good deal of ambiguity. What is meant by "natural"? Is the word used in the sense that it is "natural" for a clock to indicate the correct time, or that it is "natural" for the clock to deviate from the correct time? What is man's "nature," and how is it related to the Universe, and to the central principle of the Universe, God? It is here that ethics, if debarred from theology, will yet persist in falling back on metaphysics. Only a few years after the appearance of Hobbes' great work, the "Leviathan," Spinoza produced his system of "Geometrical Ethics," by which he deduced all the laws of morality from the construction of the Universe; man, he asserted, is a "mode" of the infinite substance, which is God; his will is necessarily determined by something else, and so cannot be free; sin can have no real existence, as the only real thing is God; and to know and love God is alike the truest virtue and the highest felicity of the soul.

The greatest name, however, in modern ethics is that of the German philosopher, Kant. Kant was well acquainted with the metaphysics of Spinoza and of those who followed him; he saw that metaphysics was often only a broken reed to the moralist, and he therefore returned to psychology; but his psychology was of a far deeper kind than that of the English school. To him, the fundamental fact of human nature, on its practical side, was the definite and, to use his own word, "categorical" imperative of duty;—Do this, apart from any thought of consequences whatsoever. Since this imperative exists, and is binding on every man by the very terms of his manhood, it must be capable of being obeyed; that is, man must be free— free to obey it; and indeed, only in obeying it can man be free at all; disobedience means enslavement to some tyranny or desire, imposed by something outside our true being. And thirdly, since man cannot be regarded as an isolated existence, but is a member of a race, the imperative must be the same in all men, and it must include humanity in its compass; "Act so that the rule of your own conduct could be the rule for all your fellow-men." You can, he says, because you ought; and you ought, not because you have been so trained or accustomed or advised, or because any

ETHICS OUTSIDE THE BIBLE

preference, however laudable, would so suggest, but because you are a rational being. Here we seem to rise above the antithesis between duty and pleasure to that between duty and the very negation of humanity. But in practice, the old problem of conduct is left untouched; duty faces pleasure still; the only difference is that instead of either defying the allurements of pleasure or trying to turn pleasure into an ally, Kant warns us against the perils of experiencing it, not only in wrong-doing, but even in the act of obedience to duty itself.

Hegel, Kant's great successor in German thought, went further, and with an unequalled breadth of grasp, bade us at last rise above the ceaseless contradiction to a self-realisation that should be at once our highest duty and our deepest joy. True progress is the identifying of my own particular and "subjective" will with the universal and "objective" will; and progress, in which my own small self merges into the universal self, or the "Absolute," must be the highest satisfaction. Here is no longer a question of war to the knife between duty and pleasure; the universe of rational beings is an organism—a great building, as St Paul might have called it; to the growth of that building all that exists must contribute; thus, in a new sense, "whatever is, is right," since it forwards the general good, the reconciling of all opposites in a single magnificent synthesis; "all partake the joy of one," and each part finds its own realisation, its own true and perfect being, in accepting and obeying the law of the whole. Hegel thus did consciously what Plato and Aristotle, two thousand years before, had done unconsciously; the legacy both of the Greeks and the German is a morality not of conflict but of reconciliation.

44 ETHICS AND ATONEMENT

Hegel's powerful influence, at least in his own country, soon waned, though for metaphysical and scientific rather than ethical reasons. In his zeal to reach the Absolute, he could not brook the delay of patient scientific investigation. In England, the last half of the nineteenth century, after two hundred years of patient investigation of psychological laws, went far to shift the ground from psychology to biology. The history of the human race ceased to be considered as the advance of one generation on the achievements of another, brick placed on brick in the great edifice of civilisation; it was viewed rather as the development from within of one great living creature,—the same, though changing from age to age. Every generation inherited, not the labours, but the very disposition and character of its predecessors; every generation, plunged into the struggle for existence, inevitably used, yet slowly modified, the powers with which it had been endowed. The struggle itself meant a constant weeding out of the less capable; only those survived who had certain qualities, or had them in a certain measure; by virtue of their possession of these qualities—which of course varied in different periods and environments —the actual survivors were held the fittest to survive; though, by a strange piece of circular reasoning, the only possible test of this fitness to survive was actual survival. The effect of this view on ethics was to change the meaning of the word Good; the good could only be that which made an individual fit, *i.e.*, able to survive. Hence, strictly speaking, we could only know whether an individual deserved to be called good by knowing whether he continued to exist and to propagate his kind.

Now it is certainly possible, on this standpoint of

biological ethics, to speak in a very exalted strain of moral exhortation ; and when that which survives is not the individual but the race, a great deal can be said by way of urging the individual to self-effacement and self-sacrifice to gain the glorious end of racial victory in the struggle. As a matter of fact, many of the supporters of this school have not been slow to avail themselves of the language of the New Testament. But biology none the less leaves us as badly off as psychology; if in its ethics it uses the word "ought," it leaves that word with no foundation. Why must I turn away from what happens to be agreeable simply because I am told that posterity may have a fuller existence thereby? The advice to live for existence is only too easily translated into "let us eat and drink, lest we die to-day instead of to-morrow"; and as life apart from happiness or pleasure will appeal to very few, we find ourselves after all where we were before; the arena is the same as that in which Stoics and Epicureans were fighting when St Paul arrived in Athens.

V. "What a barren result! Better leave ethics alone, if she can do no more for us than this." But this is not to assert the barrenness of ethical study. On the contrary, the history of ethics has been a history of progress ; psychology, metaphysics, biology, have been successively introduced ; and the conceptions of duty and right, happiness and pleasure, have been successively enlarged and modified. Some cruder ideas have been definitely put on one side. We shall not go back to Hobbes or Shaftesbury ; nor to Butler. We cannot say "the way does not lie here" without being nearer to the assertion "the way lies there." It is the business of ethics, as Martineau says, "to strip from the current judgments their accidental, impulsive and unreflecting character; . . . to interpret, to vindicate and systematize the moral sentiments, constitutes the business of this department of thought."[1] Doubtless, if ethics can reinstate us critically where we stood intuitively, it will have done good service. But it has done more than this. It has analysed the common man's sentiments by turning on them the light of one scientific study after another. Butler, Kant and Hegel have closed doors through which the speculation of the past has often wandered to no purpose; they have opened doors through which their successors have already advanced, and we may hope will advance still more. But that advance so far has been spiral; higher up, and with a wider outlook, rather than further on. As regards practical ethics, it would seem that Lancelot Gobbo spoke nearly the last word; "Budge, says the fiend; budge not, says my conscience. Conscience, say I, you counsel well; fiend, say I, you counsel well . . . and on my conscience, my conscience is but a kind of hard conscience; the fiend gives the more friendly counsel." Few would give to the opponent of conscience so outspoken a name as that which Gobbo used; few would state the two alternatives so baldly; there is oftener a conflict of duties (real or imagined), or of interests, to complicate the issue; but the issue is fundamentally the same, and even here, if ethics can help us to see, and understand, both the "fiend" and "conscience" more clearly, it may help us also to give the verdict to the right claimant.

We readily admit that between the combatants in one army and those in the other, there is little difference in actual conduct. Neither side has a monopoly of the

[1] "Types of Ethical Theory," vol. i., Introd.

virtues or of the advantages of life. The student of Herbert Spencer may be, and doubtless is, as excellent a father and as worthy a citizen, as the devoted adherent of Martineau. Knowledge of the philosophic sect to which a man belongs "cometh not with observation." If there were any standard by which we might compare the positive services rendered by individuals to mankind, we might find that J. S. Mill surpassed both Butler and Kant. But we cannot set these results of individual lives to the credit of their respective schools. If, diverging on questions of principle, they have approximated to a common ideal of conduct, we shall suspect that some other influence has been at work, more powerful than their theories. A good man will do good, whatever his views on the true basis of conduct, and a bad man will do evil. If, then, each type of ethical theory can point to noble lives among its supporters, and must confess to ignoble ones, the natural conclusion would seem to be that the types themselves do not matter; and the man in the street may well be forgiven if he professes no concern in theories of ethics, and fails to sympathise with those who do.

But it still remains true that "as a man thinketh in his heart, so is he." To cease from the effort to find the true theory, means to lay oneself open to the theory that first presents itself, and this will generally prove to be "all I can be sure of is my own happiness; so I will make for this directly or indirectly"—a type which has been repudiated alike by Bentham and by T. H. Green. It may be true that the majority of men have very little opportunity or power for abstract thought on this subject; but they are led by those who have. Neither Hume nor Schleiermacher, Rousseau nor Huxley may have been widely understood in their time; but the influence they have exerted, even over those who have hardly heard their names, has been considerable. If it comes to be agreed among the leaders of thought that ethical principles can safely be neglected, the popular mind will not be slow to make this very neglect the foundation for new principles of its own. It has never been easy to move the mass of men to sustained effort by appealing to their sense of duty, or even to their "natural" desire for the greatest good of the greatest number. Let it be supposed that neither the veneration for right, nor the endeavour after the widest good, will seriously alter a man's attitude to himself or his fellow-men, and the field will be left open to the untutored and random verdicts of "common-sense"; verdicts which, however creditable in individual cases to our common humanity, are only fit to be the beginning of rational enquiry, and are most unfit to be the end of a life's experience.

Here then lies our danger at the present time. Ever since the days of Aristotle, with every advance in thought, the issues remain practically unchanged. Palamon and Arcite may summon their allies, one after another, into the lists; but the real combatants are Palamon and Arcite still. And while the theoretical battle has raged on, the spectators who have been waiting to give in their allegiance to the victor, and even perhaps the combatants on the field themselves, are beginning to wonder whether they are not fighting for a shadow. Once let them believe this, and the conflict will come to an end, not with victory, but with a dishonourable peace. In the general discredit of ethics, should that ever come about, and with the chamber swept and garnished of ethical theories, we shall be the prey of the delusive temptations, too powerful in every age, which tell us that desires are meant to be gratified, and bid us gather our rosebuds while we may. It was this danger which moved Socrates to take up his parable against the Sophists, and argue—till most people were weary of the sound of his voice—that moral distinctions really did exist; and we may have to seek a new Socrates to do the same for us. Happily, the instincts of duty and of self-repression are as native in us, and as free from perilous connexion with theory, as the instincts of gratification. But duty is commonly sent to play the heroic part of Leonidas at Thermopylæ. It holds the pass, though wearied and outnumbered, for a time: but sooner or later it is taken in the rear; the insidious voice is heard—"I must; but why must I? Why cannot I please myself?" To that all-important question, ethics must give an answer. To decide what that answer shall be, is the task of the future.

To sum up. Ethics, as distinct from Christian ethics—that is to say, the ethical systems which have been able to do without "the hypothesis of God," or have regarded him merely as the dispenser of rewards and punishments on a more than human scale,—have made steadfast advance in the analysis of the leading and mutually opposing ideas which they received from Socrates and his two great followers. However they have varied or combined or disguised these two ideas, they have not, save in one instance, carried us beyond them; nor, as it seems, is there a likelihood that they will be able to do so. Had the different investigators kept these ideas together, and endeavoured, as Plato and Aristotle had endeavoured, to find a place for both in the perfect life —had they even kept to the thought of self-control, and then asked what is the "self" that controls or is controlled—they might have accomplished a great deal which, as things are, has proved beyond their power. And yet suggestions for such a course were not far to seek. Wordsworth has sung of a time

> "When love is an unerring light,
> And joy its own security";

and he has touched on a truth hidden even to Kant in the lines that follow :—

> " Stern lawgiver ! yet thou dost wear
> The Godhead's most benignant grace ;
> Nor know we anything so fair
> As is the smile upon thy face."

Browning characteristically goes further, and rises in thought to

> "The ultimate angels' law,
> Indulging every instinct of the soul,
> There where law, life, joy, impulse are one thing."

It has more than once been pointed out that in the very parables of Christ the appeal is not to duty apart from happiness, nor to happiness apart from duty ; the great object is that which is best for the soul ; and this best cannot be tied down within the narrow categories of pleasure or pain, when it means receiving in this life a thousand-fold more than has been given up,—" with persecutions." There is a profound truth in the lines of the German poet,

> "Nicht Schmerz ist Unglück, Glück nicht immer Freude ;
> Wer sein Geschick erfüllt, dem lächeln beide."[1]

Perhaps this experience is better known to plain earnest men and women than to philosophers. It is at

---

[1] Haym's "Humboldt." "Pain is not unhappiness, Happiness not always joy ; he who fulfils his destiny, wins smiles from both."

all events very different from the philosophic assertion that to gain a desired end, the means that reason prescribes must be welcomed, even when in themselves painful. Is there not a state of mind in which the claims of the pleasant and the unpleasant are superseded as completely as the sensations of pain and of its absence are superseded for the soldier in the heat of battle, or as the considerations of danger and of safety for the dam defending her whelps? If so, we are on the way to a reconciliation of the long strife. It is along this path that our discussion will now attempt to proceed.

CHAPTER III

DUTIES AND PERSONS

1. THE last chapter closed with the unreconciled opposition between duty and advantage. Each, by itself, would seem to make a triumphant appeal to common-sense: every one is familiar with the stern mandates of duty, whether he is in the habit of obeying them or not; every one is equally familiar with the maxim that "honesty is the best policy"; and believes with the Utilitarians that it pays to be good, and even, within limits, that what pays must be good. On the other hand, at a nearer view, the strength of these two principles lies rather in their mutual antagonism; each would be hopelessly weak were it not for the weakness of the other. Each has lived on, indeed, not so much for its own sake as to afford a refuge from the difficulties of the other. If Utilitarianism is to be a system at all, it necessarily comes to lay down definite rules and affirm a definite end. Unless it is to be a merely natural science, describing what people are observed to do and choose, and therefore not ethics at all, it must assert the imperative which it sets out by denying. Why ought I to seek my happiness (or other people's) in the way my Lord the Utilitarian is pleased to direct? why ought I to seek other people's happiness at all, or even my own? Every science is either descriptive or normative. It must either state antecedents and consequents, or

DUTIES AND PERSONS 53

lay down regulations. Science knows but two sentences, the conditional and the imperative. Utilitarianism has never been content simply with the conditional, it has refused to say nothing more than "if A happens B will follow," as if it were one of the natural sciences; but it can only indulge in the imperative by denying itself. Once tell me what pleasure I ought to choose, and, with an *ipse dixit* as flagrant as that of the dogmatic moralist, you lay on me an obligation which is distinct from pleasure and alien to it.

From such inconsistency we are driven back to the Intuitionist and his law of duty. All intuitionist views approach to the typical view of Kant. Duty is the immediate deliverance of our consciousness. " I must act as a rational being because I am a rational being." But the arguments urged against this view seem as convincing as those urged against its opponent. They fall mainly under two heads; in the first place, Kant's statement may be true as to his own experience, but we cannot help questioning whether it is true as regards the experience of others. Some people do not hear the dictates of conscience as clearly as others: some hardly hear them at all. Very few hear them in Kant's form. That men are rational beings, and that they must act in a manner appropriate to rational beings, may doubtless be evident to the philosopher and to other people when they are under philosophical instruction; but it is as far from the average man's consciousness as are the laws of higher mathematics. The voice of duty speaks in particulars long before it speaks in generals. "Do this" and "do that" come long before the abstract "do your duty," and if there are immediate deliverances of the human mind as distinct from philosophical deductions from conduct, they look to the needs of the immediate present instead of to some timeless sphere of reality.

There is a second objection, which arises from the abstractness of Kant's formula. The formula does not provide any specific "do this" or "do that" at all. We are not all of us really as God, "knowing good and evil." We need direction. But Kant's theory endows all mankind with an invariable standard of morality which would, in effect, rob humanity of its title by attempting to abolish its chief limitation. No two men coincide altogether in their views of right, and to place before every one of us the simple command "do your duty," is to set mankind at variance with itself and to leave every man doing that which is right in his own eyes. "Formal self-consistency cannot result in material precepts or prohibitions"; it makes them impossible. Kant saw this; but as soon as he tried to deduce material precepts, *e.g.* respect for property, from his categorical imperative, he became artificial and unnatural, as unnatural as when his moral purism compelled him to regard even love and affection as hindrances to duty. A lawgiver who should be content with saying "you must obey the law," without telling us the provisions to be obeyed, would do us little service; nor is it enough to tell us this; for we must take into account the persons who are to obey the law, or with whom the law is to be obeyed. We have called this law of duty formal, but in reality it is rather the raw material which must be run into moulds of many different shapes before it can minister to the needs of man, varied and changing as they are. What would Kant say to the child whose parents could not convince him of the inherent necessity of truth-telling, and who could only be persuaded to "truth it" (to use a child's words), as a dignified concession on his part to the demands of a conventional society which persisted in making things uncomfortable for those who asserted their moral independence? Doubtless there is in most people a "formal" consciousness of duty,—certain things must be done,—as there is in most people a sense of utility,—certain things will pay. But neither can be exalted into a principle capable of explaining all the facts of the case. If we attempt to regard them as more than auxiliaries, we find in them nothing but contradictions.

We are thus left at an impasse. The path to a full understanding of moral life does not lie through either of these gateways. There remains a third gate, of which we had a hint in the last chapter—the gate which bears the legend "Self-Realization." Let us see where this path leads. What is meant by Self-Realization? Self-realization starts with anything but self. It may be true that primitive man was what we should call a selfish creature. It may also be true that civilized man has instincts as brutal and as savage. Nevertheless every man, savage or civilized, is bound to his neighbour by ties not of his making or choosing, which neither he nor we can neglect. In the true realization of this interdependence between his neighbour and himself lies the essence of true self-realization.

II. There is no such thing as an isolated individual. Such an individual, as Aristotle remarked, would be either an animal or a god. A ray of sunlight may contain all the colours of the rainbow; but if we are to perceive the separate colours, the ray must be split up artificially. Every man, woman, or child whom we meet is something more ; son, father, wife, or sister. Every human being represents a graduated scale of human relationships. He is a member of a family, a tribe, a community. It is not to the Crusoes, the Selkirks, the Thoreaus of this world that we must look for the typical man. It is rather to the savage, building his mud hut as much for wife and child as for himself, or to Walt Whitman, embracing all the world with his cheery "allons, camarados!" The supreme fear, to the marooned sailor, is solitude. The pangs of hunger and the torture of thirst would lose half their terror if he shared them with a fellow castaway : when borne in isolation, these sufferings are eclipsed by the naked misery of isolation itself. The punishment of Cain, the first man to violate this law of true interdependence, was to be driven forth a wanderer on the face of the earth; and it was heavier than he could bear. Man is by nature a πολιτικὸν ζῷον. In his most rudimentary stage, even before the rise of the family, man is a member of a tribe. As such, he is by no means his own master. Neither duty nor advantage can appeal to him. He must move in the trammels of the tribal life—he can in fact conceive of himself as doing nothing else. He must obey the tribal customs or rules, and share in the tribal plenty or penury. An injury to the tribe is an injury to him, an injury to him is an injury to the tribe. Only in the tribe can he be said to live at all. This tribal enclosure of the freedom of man is constantly suggested in the Old Testament. Amalek, Edom, and many another tribe are condemned and punished for crimes committed by individuals even in the distant past. Israel is made to flee before Ai because of one man's disobedience. On the other hand, the cities of the plain

DUTIES AND PERSONS

might have been saved had ten righteous men been found therein.

Within the larger unity of the tribe springs up the smaller unity of the family. Just as anthropology has made it certain that the tribe comes first, so in his ideal republic, Plato has subordinated the family, or even made it disappear before the dominant personality of the πόλις. Still, logically, as Aristotle felt, the order is—first the family, then the tribe.

> " Man is made of social earth,
> Child and Brother from his birth."

In all civilized communities the individual realizes that he is a member of a family long before he realizes he is a member of a state. He is as little bound to the family as to the tribe by the simple ties of duty or of interest. The real tie is more elementary. Unless the husband or child is to be gibbeted as unnatural (that severest condemnation !), both the griefs and the joys of the family are his ; his griefs and joys are theirs. It is only in a family that the man really lives. The family is his wider self or personality. The paralyzing effect of the effort to stifle the love born of the family bond is vividly pictured in Charles Reade's noble story, " The Cloister and the Hearth," where Gerard, from a distorted view of the moral greatness required of him, sought to attain it by hiding himself from his wife and child and mortifying his body in the wilderness. It was not simply to herself that Margaret won him back, but to life ; and life, thus re-born in the family, led him at once to participation in the interest of the community. To come back to this life was also to come back to nursing the sick in his plague-stricken parish. Readers of George Eliot's " Romola "

58   ETHICS AND ATONEMENT

will remember the moral ruin which overtook Tito, the man who knew of no ties save those which he had broken. Similar stories are familiar enough in the sordid records of the modern police court.

The law of the family, moreover, is a much more intimate and binding thing than the law of the tribe. The family needs no policeman, because it has other sanctions far more powerful and searching; and, just as perfect freedom is the offspring of perfect law, so a man's truest self has a more untrammelled freedom for realization in the family than in the undifferentiated unity of the tribe. But these are not the only organisms in which the individual finds his truest self. The completeness of the family bond leads a man, as it led Gerard, into wider interests. In the Florence of the thirteenth century, no man was eligible for public office unless he had first incorporated himself with the Gild of his special trade or profession. That constituted his only credential. To have been nurtured in the family is to have the best credential for still higher development in whatever direction. Further (to continue the simile), no one would regard his incorporation in the Gild as an end in itself; it was a means of reaching a wider citizenship. Thus, the identification of the individual in the wider "self" of the family is naturally reproduced in many other sets of relationships, political, social, or religious. What may sometimes be looked on as a hobby, at other times as unselfish devotion to a cause or a party, is simply the passing from narrower to wider interests and sympathies. We gravitate to each other; we live and move in other people; the recluse is an abortion. The strength of the monastic system itself lay not in its enforced seclusion, but in the absolute interdependence which it entailed on every member of the brotherhood. The great penalty of any disease is that it cuts off one of the main avenues to the wider self. The ancient city state, the feudal system, the medieval church and the medieval chivalry, the monastic orders, the numberless communities and brotherhoods of the middle ages, equally with the trades unions, the clubs, the religious denominations and even the co-operative societies of modern times, are witnesses to the instinct for aggregation and organization in human nature;—witnesses, as the Christian would add, to the principle which finds its highest expression in the union of all believers in Christ. It is a false view of history which regards the basis of all this common life and endeavour as utilitarian or even entirely voluntary. Every society which has failed to recognise this principle—not the principle merely of mutual self-sacrifice at a crisis, but of constant sharing in interest and aim,—all partaking the joy, or grief, of one—is doomed to disintegration into powerless units. At the moment when Arthur's knights set forth on separate quests, the glory of the Round Table had departed.[1]

III. As Herbert Spencer has shown us, all development, in the social as in the physical world, means progressive organization and interrelation. We repel a slight on our church or our club as vigorously as one on ourselves. The fine heritage of the "impossible loyalty," bestowed on one by the public school or the university,

---

[1] Shakespeare has given forcible expression to the connexion between the severing of natural ties and political or social decay;—"Love cools, friendship falls off; brothers divide; in cities, mutinies; in countries, discord; in palaces, treason; and the bond cracked between son and father; . . . we have seen the best of our time."—"King Lear," Act I. sc. ii.

is gained by another through a trades association, or by the link of a common profession or occupation, predilection or sport. Even the social life to which chance circumstances may lead, will prove the soil for the plant which flowered alike in the knightly orders of the middle ages and the patriotism of the ancient republics. What is wanted is the badge of a corporate aim, the symbol of the life of the one in the many.

This aim may be selfish, and the life narrow. The city to which the patriot devotes his life may be following a mean and sordid policy; the society into which a man merges himself may be no better than that of professional burglars; or it may be a society like that of the Jesuits, with its curious mixture of truth and falsehood, nobility and intrigue, but aiming always at its own aggrandisement and that of its church. Still, in the meaner as in the higher forms of co-operation, the principle is the same. Even selfishness becomes less despicable, though possibly more dangerous, when it is not for myself but for my party. Themistocles, the Athenian general, intriguing for his city, is very different from Themistocles, the disgraced exile, intriguing for his own safety. Self-realization in a wider community, founded as it is in human nature, is itself the foundation of goodness.

These considerations have often been urged to support the ethical theory connected with the name of Hegel. Hegel, as a recent exponent (Professor R. Mackintosh) has pointed out, cared little himself for this dying to live, this losing oneself to find oneself in a larger life; but his followers, in Germany, and still more in England, have often spoken as if the ethical development of the individual lay through a succession of wider selves; as if family and society, the nation and humanity, led the human unit to the Absolute Self or God. That is not asserted here. Doubtless there is a personality that may belong to a family or a tribe, a church or a nation; but a man's value would be lost if he merely sank his own personality in this greater one. To a certain degree, indeed, it is true that every crowd or accidental combination of individuals makes up a collective self. We can even speak of the character of a mob. But to call such a fleeting and evanescent product of a day's incident by the name of person, is purely metaphorical, and metaphors, strictly interpreted, are untrue. The crowd could not exist, save because of the separate personalities composing it; nor could the society or the family. Personality implies permanence of character. Hence, we do God no injustice by placing him within the confines of personality; to place him outside these, in fact, is to become a pantheist. But, in the great collective of Humanity, where is the definiteness that can merit such an attribute? A family is not conscious of itself as an ultimate existence in the same sense that every one of its members is self-conscious; it can be split up;—it is continually being split up, in fact; and can be understood only from its component parts. What can be asserted apart from all fear of metaphor, is that "no man liveth to himself"; that every human being links himself, in his aims, his fears, and even in his desire for self-preservation, to his fellows.

This law, we contend, is a law of nature: descriptive and not merely normative: and it is more fundamental than either the law of self-interest or the law of duty. The greater part of life, for most of us, is taken up with actions that are neither selfish nor unselfish. The mother does not seek to save her child because it is her duty, nor because it is to her advantage. Husband and wife seek for no external reward, obey no external command, in the mutual sacrifices of their daily intercourse. And what is obvious in these closest relationships can be traced to a less remarkable degree in all others. The categorical Imperative, in spite of Kant, is not fundamental; no more are the dictates of Egoism. The Ten Commandments, on which the Old Testament moral order is based, themselves arise out of the inevitable kinship in tribal and social life which they regulate. So, on a careful consideration, does the Sermon on the Mount. All laws are the solidifications of customs; customs are but the expressions of the life of the individual in his relation to other individuals. Neither Egoism nor Altruism, neither the "I ought" nor the "I should like" cover the "I must" of the lover, the husband, the mother, the friend, or the fellow-citizen. Self-preservation comes first; but self-preservation includes the preservation of others united with myself by this primary instinct of devotion to the common life. The true basis of ethics, therefore, is neither self-interest nor duty; it is what the Greeks would call κοινωνία, that instinct for fellowship which separates man from the beasts that perish, and without which man speedily degenerates into a lower organism.

Actual experience enforces this conclusion. We may speak of duties, but we are far more conscious of persons. All duties have reference to persons, and it is the existence of persons which makes duties possible. An abstract conception of duty without regard to persons for whom it is performed, like that of Wordsworth's famous "Ode to Duty," may be beautiful and even inspiring, but it is as imperfect as are harmonies conceived in the brain of the musician and allowed to remain there unwritten and unperformed. If I act honestly, it is for the sake of my customer or even of my rival; not for the sake of an abstract law of conduct, — even less because "honesty is the best policy." However true that axiom may be, my action, if based upon it, becomes not so much honest as sagacious. If I refuse a bribe, I may do so in deference to my own self-respect, or for the respect I bear to my party or my employer. In either case, I am thinking about persons more than about the duties I may owe to them. To take another example; bravery on the battlefield may be either devotion to the honour of your regiment, consideration for the safety of others, or fear of your own disgrace—perhaps a mixture of all three. In any case, a bravery that possessed none of these elements, and was merely impersonal, if it were possible at all, would bend like a reed at the first breath of danger. Every appeal to courage has ended with the personal note—remember your country, your king, your wife, your home. Nelson might signal "England expects every man to do his duty"; but duty meant loyalty, patriotism, personal devotion. Sidney Carton was actuated by no philosophy of self-sacrifice, but by pure admiration for the heroism he saw in his fellow-prisoners and as pure a desire to save the life of Evrémonde. Plato defined bravery as "loyalty to principle in the face of danger"; but in the case of bravery, as of other virtues, he took care, in his ideal republic, to lay what he thought would be an unassailable foundation of mutual confidence and love. If we consider the self-regarding virtues, the very name proves the point we are urging. Self-respect, self-control, imply a struggle for a self not yet fully matured, and for what is none the less a person because it is identical with the agent. Kant came very near this in one of his three statements of the Categorical Imperative,—"Act as if every man were a member of the kingdom of ends," an end of action in himself. Kant only restates the Golden Rule, "Thou shalt love thy neighbour as thyself." In this form of the precept, as in the other, "Do unto others as ye would that they should do unto you," duty is hardly suggested as a principle of conduct; it is the personal bond of union which is enforced.

IV. This disappearance of duty as such is even more noticeable when we turn to that great manual of Ethics, the New Testament. The Bible does, as a matter of fact, recognise motives both of self-interest and of duty, the former more particularly in appeals to the Israelites to obey the Mosaic law, "that their days may be long in the land": the latter in the moral exhortations of the prophets, "Cease to do evil, learn to do well." But in the Old Testament, these two appeals fade away before another: and in the New Testament, it is not too much to say that all duties are stated in terms of the personal. S. Paul, for instance, gives no list of purely abstract duties; his insistence on the personal gives his ethical directions a curiously simple flavour. Alone among the New Testament writers he devotes a special section of his letters to matters of practice and conduct, and in these he applies the general teaching of the earlier sections to actual members of particular churches, once even mentioning two of those members by name. It is not however the rule alone, but the rule as wrought out in the lives of persons, that interests him; how husbands should comport themselves to their wives, children to their parents, slaves to their masters, friends

DUTIES AND PERSONS 65

to friends. Nothing can be more distinct from the point of view of the ordinary moralist, from Aristotle downwards, than Paul's treatment of his subject. We are accustomed to consider the moral agent, while he develops his character and practises his virtues, as thrown out against a background of ill-defined aids or hindrances; as shadows thrown on the screen of an imaginary or contentless background. The "great-souled man" of Aristotle, the moral connoisseur of Shaftesbury, or the common-sense servant of conscience described by Reid and Stewart, are almost as abstract, and we may almost say as unreal, as the "economic man" of the Manchester School. But the men and women of whom and for whom S. Paul writes, live, breathe, and struggle, "creatures not too bright or good for human nature's daily food," tried by jealousy, stirred by misunderstandings, torn by doubts, shaken by hypocrisy, harassed by pride; they had to wring their morality from the common ingredients of daily intercourse, where men and women must work back from the experimental to the theoretical. They must have the love that vaunteth not itself, is not puffed up, doth not behave itself unseemly. They must be warned against thinking of themselves more highly than they ought to think; they must be of the same mind one toward another. Even a glaring case of immorality is treated, not as a violation of any law of duty or of conscience, but as an act of disloyalty to what ought to be the closest of human ties. Ritual observances and church collections alike are made dependent on the right attitude to "the brethren." Paul's greatest ethical utterance is reached in the famous chapter on love, and love can only exist within human relationships. The individual is no

E

more. He has become the member of an ethical community, a spiritual family.

With all this, the Biblical references to conscience are in entire harmony. There is no definite teaching on the subject of conscience in the Bible; and the word itself is exceedingly rare. This may account for the atmosphere of mystery which has enveloped the subject in later writings, Christian as well as non-christian. Otherwise we can hardly conceive the appearance, in the same communion, of views so dissimilar as those of Butler and Paley; the one placing conscience now by the side of, and now in control of man's reasonable self-love, the other condemning it at best to be the servant of his hopes and fears.[1] True, in the Old Testament there is ample recognition both of repentance and remorse; the stories of Cain, of Balaam and of David, would be unintelligible apart from the consciousness of a wrong done and a law violated. Some of the most touching and penetrating passages in the Psalms are those which tell of God's nearness to the broken heart. "If I regard iniquity in my heart the Lord will not hear me," and "Thy word have I laid up in my heart that I might not sin against thee." But in every case where law is mentioned as dwelling in the heart, it is the law of God. The law to the Hebrew is of no importance save on account of the lawgiver. "Take for example, the cry of the Psalmist, 'Against thee, thee only, have I sinned,' and the cry of Wordsworth in the 'Ode to Duty,' 'Oh! let my weakness have an end!' . . . If the substance of the two cries is the same, if they refer to two similar conditions, wherein do they differ? The point of view is different, that is

[1] See ch. ii. pp. 27, 28.

DUTIES AND PERSONS 67

all. While each expresses the essential union of the finite or imperfect being with the infinite or perfect one, yet in the religious case the stand is taken at the point of view of the perfect one, while the moral man looks at it from the opposite end, the point of view of the imperfect one."[1] The moral man starts from his own attitude to the law, the religious man from God's attitude to him.

In the New Testament there are abundant references to law; and the bulk of these, when not actually referring to the provisions of the Mosaic code, occur in two letters of S. Paul, to the Galatians and to the Romans. While S. Paul was engaged in the controversy against the Jewish legalists, in connexion with these two churches, his voice rang out like a trumpet, whether he was speaking of the law written in the heart or of the law of Christ. But there is a gradual diminuendo in that trumpet blast as the controversy itself gradually died away. Outside these two letters, indeed, he hardly uses the word. Even within them, he never refers to an impersonal moral law,[2] and in later years he felt himself at liberty to use a less austere presentation of the same conception, not modifying the stringency of the command, but bringing it into more intimate relation with the person of Christ. His desire is "that ye may be filled continually with the knowledge of his will in all wisdom and spiritual understanding." Christ himself spoke much about light, as illuminating the mind and the heart, but that light can only be authentic when it

[1] G. H. Palmer, "Field of Ethics."
[2] In Rom. 2^{12} 5^{13}, etc., "law" stands for a system given by God to the Gentiles, though not so distinct and detailed as that which he gave to the Jews. Of law outside any relation to God, Paul had no conception.

comes from him who was the light of the world.
There is a whole world of difference between the
pagan's ethical conception, high as it was, "nocte
dieque suum gestare in pectore testem" ("night and
day to carry your own recording angel within your
breast"), and the religious confidence of the man who
has learned to find the centre of his moral life in God ;
"when he giveth quietness, who then can condemn?"

"I am the light of the world"; "no man cometh
unto the Father but by me"; "come unto me; take
my yoke upon you and learn of me." These sentences
lead us to the very heart of Christ's moral teaching.
Much of that teaching was a development, and what
appeared to be a reconstruction, of the Mosaic law.
But what most impressed his hearers was that he
spoke not as an exponent or a commentator of the
law, but as the lawgiver explaining his own code.
"He spoke with authority and not as the scribes"; "I
say unto you"—in other words, the important part of
the command was, that he gave it. The other part
of his teaching is yet more intimately connected with
himself. Most leaders have taken pains to leave
behind them a trustworthy policy; and they have
sought to give that policy a foundation independent
of the attitude of their followers to themselves. With
Jesus Christ, policy and leader were inextricably
joined. The policy could only be carried out by
those who were rooted and built in him. Apart from
himself there was no policy. Christ was no teacher
of a system. He *was* the system; "the way, the
truth, the life." Individual duties, individual moral
instincts pale before the splendour of that living bond
which was to bind the disciples with him and with
each other; "apart from me ye can do nothing." His

DUTIES AND PERSONS

last words to them were one long charge to love one another as he had loved them. We are often reminded that Christ taught little about the church; but to base conduct on this personal attachment was, in itself, to found a church. Christ's conception of ethics finds its logical fulfilment in the words, "ye are the body of Christ and separately members thereof"; "and whether one member suffereth all the members suffer with it, or one member is honoured, all the members rejoice with it."

V. This further consideration of New Testament ethics has carried us rather beyond our present point. We have been arguing that right conduct rests on a basis, not of interest nor of duty, but of personal attachment,—a growing into others, as we may call it. The New Testament, as we have seen, hurries beyond this into the thought of attachment to one special person. Its position is that "Christ himself is the Christian law."[1] But this principle, even if it transcends our own contention, does not violate it, but gives it, *à fortiori*, valuable support. Similar support is lent by other systems which might seem at first sight to have little connection with our own. It lies beyond our present limits to discuss the contentions of other schools in any detail, but a few observations may serve to indicate our general meaning.

Herbert Spencer has rendered an abiding service to ethics in attempting to replace empirical reasoning, utilitarian or intuitionist, by going back to the first beginnings of ethical life in the race, in order to "establish morality on a scientific basis." All ethical precepts, he argued, rose out of the primary necessity of preserving the life, not of the individual only, but of

[1] "Ecce Homo," ch. x.

the tribe or social organism to which the individual belonged. For that organism the individual had constantly to sacrifice himself; and thus egoism became the teacher of altruism, both alike leading to "actions conducive to the maximum quantity of life." But all sociology teaches that in primitive times, at least, there was no such social contract as is here implied. We shall either make Hobbes' mistake, or else be compelled to recognise that men did not say to one another, "I will help to defend you if you will help to defend me." Macaulay's famous lines in "Horatius" are true, not simply of Rome, but of the earlier stages of all societies which have "survived."

> "Then none was for a party
> Then all were for the state;
> Then the great man helped the poor,
> And the poor man loved the great : . . .
> The Romans were like brothers
> In the brave days of old."

Again, many Utilitarians have had much to say about sympathy and its pleasures. Mill has clearly stated their position in the following passage:—"It is this (namely, a natural basis of sentiment for utilitarian morality), which, when once the general happiness is recognised as the ethical standard, will constitute the strength of utilitarian morality. This firm foundation is that of the social feelings of mankind, the desire to be in unity with our fellow-creatures, which is already a powerful principle in human nature. . . . Society between human beings, except in the relation between master and slave, is manifestly impossible on any other footing than that the interests of all are to be consulted. Society between equals can only exist on the understanding that the interests of all are to be regarded

DUTIES AND PERSONS 71

equally."[1] Sidgwick, who refers to this classical passage of Mill, speaks of a possible sympathetic development, when the average man will never "feel prompted to sacrifice the general good to his own," and disclaims any wish "to depreciate the value of sympathy as a source of happiness, even to human beings as at present constituted. . . . Certainly in a Utilitarian's mind sympathy tends to become a prominent element of all instinctive moral feelings that refer to social conduct: as in his view the rational basis of moral impulse must ultimately lie in some pleasure won or pain saved for others; so that he never has to sacrifice himself to an impersonal law, but always for some being or beings with whom he has at least some degree of fellow feeling."[2] This is undoubtedly true, but what is the origin of this fellow feeling? Surely it is something which requires explanation. How do I come to welcome the good news which the morning's post brings to my neighbour, while possibly it brings as bad news to myself? Does the Utilitarian mean that this sympathy ought to exist, or that it does exist as a matter of fact? If he means that it ought to exist, he is telling us that we ought to find our happiness in each other and not simply in ourselves. If he means that it does exist, he is simply advocating the view that, to a greater or less extent, we are members one of another, rejoicing with those that rejoice and weeping with those that weep. In either case we must claim him as an ally of our own contention, that there is something in human nature beside the self-interest of the individual.

Perhaps the strongest proof that duties imply persons

[1] "Utilitarianism," ch. iii.
[2] "Methods of Ethics," bk. iv. ch. vi.

could be found in the writings of the professed champions of duty themselves. We have already referred to Kant's statement of his rule, " act as if every one around you were an end in himself." And T. H. Green, in his development of the Kantian ethics, shows that the idea of the good as it presented itself to Kant, implies a distinctive social interest on our part which must be taken to be a primary fact. If we are to treat others as ends, we must be conscious, not simply of ourselves, but of others, as persons; in other words, we must love them as ourselves, if not to the same extent, yet in the same manner. There is nothing good,—this Kant has made plain,—save the good will. This good will can only be for the common good: and when Green shows how this common good develops, extending its area, gradually but steadily—so that the objects of the good will are no longer confined within a man's own city walls, but are found outside the limits of city or of race—he is telling us of the extension, not of a duty, but of a deeper moral feeling still. Like John Wesley, every good man is gradually led to the point where he must say " the world is my parish." When he does so, his conception of duty may very possibly have remained the same; what will have developed is the strength and extension of the bond which unites him to the persons sharing his ethical world. The very exposition of "duty for duty's sake" becomes the statement of the law of self-realization.

In a well-known passage, Aristotle says that the brave man is influenced, not by fear of disgrace nor by love of honour, but by the moral beauty of the brave act.[1] This principle of the $καλόν$, the beautiful, with its power of exciting spontaneous admiration, occupied a

[1] Nic. Eth. iii. 7.

DUTIES AND PERSONS 73

large place in Greek thought, and in later times it has been again exalted to one of the main incentives to right conduct by Shaftesbury, and, in a slightly different form, by Hutcheson and Adam Smith. And there can be no doubt that such admiration exists, in all save the utterly degraded, not only as a passive emotion, but as an active stimulus. We admire noble conduct in others; and we wish to be admired ourselves, if not for what is truly admirable, at least for some counterfeit or imitation. Henry the Fifth exclaiming,

> " If it be a sin to covet honour,
> I am the most offending soul alive,"

and Sir Willoughby Patterne playing the refined and beneficent country squire before his dependents and guests, are by no means ambitious in the selfish sense of the word; they acknowledge the glamour of the ideal at which they aim. A similar aim, though of far nobler kind, was his who was said to have endured the cross, despising shame, for the joy that was set before him,—a joy which was surely subjective rather than objective, because it depended solely on the ideal attained. This aim is as real as is love of self-interest or as the desire for fame. Its reward, however, is not external but internal; not in the applause or the payments of an admiring world, nor even in the doing of the act itself, but in the having done it.

But here two questions arise; what kind of actions reach this æsthetic standard, and by whom is the standard set? The standard is undoubtedly set by the community or by those individuals whom the agent selects as his judges. He aims at the standard, not because it is a standard, but because it has the approval of certain persons. He is thinking, not of it, but of them. The words of the epitaph of the Spartans who fell at Thermopylæ would show this: "Oh stranger, tell the Lacedæmonians that here obedient to their words we lie." We might even quote the half-ironical words of Persius, "Your knowing a thing is no good unless your neighbour knows that you know it.

As to the first question it might be said that the actions which reach this standard are all actions which we can call good. This only raises the further question, "what are good actions"? As a matter of fact the actions which excite approbation or respect, and secure their accomplishment by their own moral beauty, often in the face of great difficulty, are not often instances of stoical adherence to duty. There must be a dash of self-forgetfulness, of loyalty, of passion, before we find ourselves forced to recognise them as fine or noble or heroic. Curtius, leaping into the chasm in the Roman forum; Kent, braving alike the dangers of nature and of the state to be near his old master, the self-impoverished Lear; Wilberforce, devoting his magnificent energies and prospects to a cause which seemed certain to bring him nothing but failure and contempt; all these inspire us with admiration, because the only reward possible to them is the consciousness of serving the common good. On the other hand, Æneas, surrendering the friendship of Dido, with all its allurements and advantages, to fulfil the behests of his own destiny, arouses no enthusiasm. Both missionary and tradesman make sacrifices; both may be men of honourable and stainless conduct; but the issues of their self-sacrifice are widely different. It is the man who lays down his life for his friends, not the man who identifies his life and his livelihood, whom we admire. The instinct of admiration for moral beauty is real;

DUTIES AND PERSONS

but it is no statue, however exquisitely carved, with which we fall in love. Clogged as we may be by indolence, dragged backwards by selfishness, wrapped in the mists of ignorance of ourselves and suspicion of others, we feel an impulse for something that we can share with others alike in a thousand "nameless unremembered acts of kindness and of love," and in the supreme crises of a life of conscious endeavour after the lofty fulfilment of duty; it is this which carries us on to the end of human life, the one thing for which we desire all that is desired.

VI. We now face a problem with which every system of ethics has to reckon. Granted that we have our general principle, how shall we apply it to the details? I must find the end of my being in the common good; very well; but how shall I know how much of my interest I must postpone to that of my friend, or how much of the truth I ought to tell to my servant? It must be admitted that from pure ethics to applied ethics there is always a great and even momentous chasm to overleap, whatever be the principle we choose to adopt. If we prefer to take our stand with the Intuitionists, and to say—"I must just do what is right, and rely on my conscience to tell me," the chasm still yawns before us. For instance, let us consider what all would admit to be a virtue and a duty, benevolence. I ought to do good to other people, to my friend and my servant, as well as to my wife and family. But questions immediately arise; am I to do for them what they happen to wish for, or what I know, or think, to be the best thing for them? Am I to aim at their happiness, or at their perfection? What right have I to decide what they ought to have or to want? Again, benevolence is commonly opposed in thought to justice; benevolence goes beyond justice. But if I go beyond justice with one, shall I not be in danger of falling behind justice with another? If I choose to help my friend, I shall be unable to do what I might otherwise have gladly done in carrying out my benevolent impulses to my servant. If I give away half-a-crown to the first case of need I meet, I may have nothing for the next. Further, if I enjoy doing the kindness, as I shall do when it is done from an impulse of benevolent affection, am I not thereby leaving the sphere of strict virtue? "Love all men"; but the self-sacrifice that springs from love is not self-sacrifice at all in the ordinary sense; and hence sterner moralists have bidden us to eliminate affection from our mind altogether, which is to transform benevolence to a bare and very uncompromising justice. Again, justice and truthfulness will be universally recognised by Intuitionists as virtues, right in themselves. But what is justice—to give to every man his due, to our enemies as to our friends? Must we give what we think is his due, or what he claims as such,—what the law tells him is his, or what we think ought to be his? Plato could ask these questions, and we have hardly got beyond his answers. And must we always tell the truth, and to everyone? Are all the points to be stated to a madman or to an invalid? Are we to tell the whole truth to every question of an unduly inquisitive child? How shall we even decide when the inquisitiveness is "undue"? Can we ever allow, in a law-court or elsewhere, the *suppressio veri* or the *suggestio falsi*? And so we might go on.

"No," the Utilitarian would reply; "you are simply delivering yourselves into our hands. Casuistry is the rock on which Intuitionism and the 'duty philosophy'

DUTIES AND PERSONS 77

founder. There is no rescue save by the maxim of the general happiness." That is to say, in deciding between the conflicting claims of my generosity or my truthfulness, I must be guided by considerations of the general happiness, and of any two courses, if one will yield, as far as I can tell, thirty-fold, and the other sixty-fold, I "must" choose the latter, even if my own private happiness should form part of the thirty-fold, and be absent in the latter case altogether. And it will not be my own satisfaction only that "must" be thrown overboard. If truthfulness itself should happen to give the thirty-fold but not the sixty-fold returns, then apparently, truthfulness must go also. Against the Utilitarian we have argued sufficiently already. We have only to remark here that in the matter of application he is no better off than the Intuitionist. For in the first place, this calculation of results is bound to be both lengthy and precarious. Take a case suggested by Sidgwick, the bequest of property. How far may a man neglect his children for his collateral relatives? Or, if he has no children, will the general happiness be more surely attained if he leaves his money to poor relations, or to the waifs and strays of the London streets? If the balance falls for the waifs and strays, most people, though not for utilitarian reasons, will "feel" that there is something wrong, even if they acknowledge the perfect adjustment of the utilitarian scales. And in any case, the desire for general happiness, by itself, is no thread to guide the way through the labyrinth. Even supposing that it were, no one but a recluse could stop to work out the necessary sums. We may nourish the best intentions of setting our sails to the trade winds of calculation and circumstance, but we shall be hurried out of our course by the wayward gusts of selfishness or even of passion, or the bewildering cross-currents of complete unselfishness or of partiality. Nor can the trade winds themselves be relied upon; and to have nothing to do with preferences, sympathies, and emotions, as the colder Utilitarian demands, is to turn our backs on the compass. When Regulus was standing with his weeping family, his imploring countrymen and the urgent need of his country on the one side, and the horrors of the Carthaginian torturer and his own faithfulness to his word on the other, would his decision and the decision of posterity have been the decision of Utilitarian morality?

Casuistry would seem, then, to threaten the Utilitarian as dangerously as the Intuitionist, and we might fear that nothing but the ingenuity of a Jesuit father-confessor would suffice to unravel the innumerable problems of right and wrong as they arise in the ever-varying circumstances and combinations of daily life. But for most of us, Protestants as well as Catholics, this difficulty, like so many others, is, to a certain extent at least, "solved by walking." As a matter of fact, there is one person who cares for none of these things, and is troubled by no inelastic theory, either of duty or of interest, but who is equipped with a rule which is only complete when it is applied—the man who cares for the common good. After all, "love is an unerring light." The surest way to know how to treat a person is to be interested in him; nor is a good mother—nor a good Sunday-school teacher—ever bewildered by the conflicting claims of two children, nor by the more loudly conflicting claims of love and duty—the two are for her synonymous. Psychology has as yet given no account of the phenomenon, and those who

DUTIES AND PERSONS

are habitually guided by it have not been able to explain it; but "he that loveth his brother abideth in the light; there is none occasion of stumbling in him"; it is through hatred of his brother that a man "walketh in the darkness and knoweth not whither he goeth, because the darkness hath blinded his eyes."[1]

This is not to affirm that first thoughts are always best, or that every wandering impulse of a good heart may prove a safe guide. But, as Sir Philip Sydney said, "the philosopher, setting down with thorny argument the bare rule, is so hard of utterance and so mistily to be conceived, that one that hath no other guide but him shall wade in him till he be old before he shall find sufficient cause to be honest." It is by a wise love, and not by calculation, that the father will know when not to spare the rod lest he spoil the child; it is a wise love that will teach him how he must "scourge every son whom he receiveth." The surgeon as he guides his knife thinks nothing of his fee, or of the personal gratification of his patient; he is aiming at the ends of his art and at the good of mankind; and we, whether we cut or unravel the knots of life, are the best surgeons when we think least of result or of gratification. Every well-ordered family is an illustration of this truth; not intuition, but a healthy instinct, leads us to do right to those nearest to our heart.

"For there the more each one '*our* good' can cry,
So much the more can each claim as his own."[2]

And the more we extend the family attitude, and, in sober literalness, regard other people as our brothers and sisters, the more steadily does the light burn; we need neither to cut the knot nor to unravel

[1] 1 John 2⁹ ¹⁰. [2] Dante, *Purg.* xv. 55-57.

it; we give a firm pull at the strands, and they come asunder.

And this, we may add, has always been the teaching of Christianity: "If any man willeth to do his will, he shall know of the teaching"; and those who aim at the common good find that they have no trouble about the details. Augustine stated, in bold paradox, "Love God, and do what you please," whatever might be the conflicting claims of generosity or truthfulness, of family affection or patriotism. The religious man will say that the Holy Spirit leads him into all truth, and we, taking our stand on the ground of ethics, can assert that to treat everyone as an end in himself is to reach the solution that shirks no issue, but renders casuistry unnecessary.

VII. One final consideration. It is an old question, Are the virtues one or many? On our showing, there is no real difficulty in the discussion; there is but one virtue, the right attitude—the "family" attitude, as we have represented it—to those who surround us; loyalty to the true relations in which we stand to other people. Almost without exception, other systems outside the Bible have ignored the fact that virtue has its origin among persons. What is bravery save loyalty in the face of danger, not to principles but to persons, my comrades and those who depend on me? What is temperance but my loyalty to them, and to myself as one of them, in the face of temptation to bodily excess? Even the most self-regarding of the virtues stand on the same plane; for my self-respect is rooted, not simply in my attitude to myself, but to the society of which I am a member, and which I respect even more than I respect myself. Virtue, in fine, is an attitude, and consists not in doing, but in being; the

DUTIES AND PERSONS 81

"virtues" are the different expressions of that attitude. And this has been the character of all virtue grown on Christian soil. The Stoic ideal has been banished by the teaching of S. Paul and of his Master, as completely as the Epicurean. Christian teaching may have emphasised different qualities at different times: humility, control of the passions, especially in the relations between the sexes, or humanity and philanthropy; but the Christian character has in all ages been recognised as resting on a turning of the soul, as Plato called it,[1] a conversion, to a new view of God, of man, and of oneself. Whether we take great churchmen like Hildebrand or Anselm, great soldiers like Bayard or S. Louis, or that treasure-house of all medieval thought and sentiment, Dante, or the scholars and philanthropists of the Renaissance and the Reformation and of later years, Pico de la Mirandola or Ulrich von Hutten, Wesley, or John Howard or Mazzini, we see that it is no thought of individual excellence or virtue that has moved them, but rather the strong reaching-out of sympathy and heart to the persons around them and the great Person above them—"the love that moves the sun and the other stars."

[1] περιστροφὴ ψυχῆς, Plato, *Republic*, vii. 521.

CHAPTER IV

RECONCILIATION

I. WE may now pause for a moment and look back over the ground which we have traversed. We began with observing the wide difference commonly supposed to exist between morality and religion. That difference, we found, does exist, but not in the fashion commonly imagined. Religion, and especially the Christian religion, certainly takes account of morality, but in a manner of its own. Righteousness is a matter of right conduct between persons, and is only possible when those persons are in a right relation to each other. To please God, Christianity teaches, we must have found our way into God's family, and consequently must be able to look upon God as our Father, and upon other people as our brothers and sisters, actual or potential. This can only be done when we have first been enabled to take up the right relation to a third person, "the Son," as he is often spoken of in the New Testament, or Christ himself. The teaching of ordinary ethics, on the other hand, knows nothing of these personal readjustments. It is rather concerned with the vain attempt to decide the dispute between our sense of duty and our natural desire for pleasure or advantage; and it ends, either in laying down a general law or formula which we must apply to individual instances ourselves, or in turning itself into a system of psychology. Thus the difference between the two would be, not the difference between the moral and the non-moral, but the difference between what has a basis in personal experience, and what has not.

But further consideration showed us that ethics itself implies far more than the moral action of the isolated individual. "No man liveth to himself." It is by not recognising this that the majority of ethical systems have failed to hit the mark. Quite apart from the express teaching of Christianity, a thorough survey of the conditions demanded by any system of ethics shows that all duties, and all satisfactions of wrongs done, imply persons, and that conduct, either to be right or to be in any real sense advantageous, necessitates the right relation between persons. In this way, ethics may be said to bear its testimony to religion, or at any rate to religion as it appears in Christianity. True, ethics as such has nothing to say about God; but it points to the conception of humanity as one great family; the only account it can give of duties that is of any value, is that they are the natural actions of one member of a family to another,—actions which are based on a community of interests, in which the joy and pain of all are shared by each. Such a family may surely be said to imply a father; and we might thus say, to adapt Aristotle's description of metaphysics, that Christianity is ethics "with its head on."[1] To both Christianity and ethics, righteousness is based on the same type of conduct, has the same value, and springs inevitably from the same kind of personal relations. To both, acts refer us back to an attitude, doing rests upon being, and all the "virtues" are but separate manifestations of one principle of Virtue.

[1] Eth. Nic. vi. 7.

Here then we might feel inclined to stop. We cannot expect to put the head upon ethics without the aid of theology, or at least of metaphysics. And indeed, without allowing a place to metaphysics, we cannot do justice to ethics. This is plain from the stress that we have had to lay on personality. What is the meaning of "You" and "I"; of your relation to me and mine to you? These questions are metaphysical; they lie outside the sphere of ethics proper, though not outside the sphere of Christianity; but any system of ethics which ventures to neglect them will break down. As a matter of fact, it will generally be found that "you cannot make the slightest concession to metaphysics without ending in a theology."[1] These questions we shall endeavour to take up later on. At present, however, we might claim to have settled the opposing contentions of ethics and religion. But to have done this is not to have reached the end of our discussion, but only the beginning of a new chapter. With the statement of these right relations and the conduct that properly belongs to them, ethics abruptly leaves us, with no word as to how those relations may be formed or, if broken, restored; while religion pushes forward into realms unknown to the purely ethical investigator, realms where at first sight morality seems to be left behind altogether.

II. One of the great complaints often urged against Christianity is that it deals with the visionary and the impracticable. It is too good for the rough-and-tumble of every day life. The business man, we are assured, must of course be fairly honest, but we cannot expect him to practise the absurd magnanimity of the New Testament, to feed and even to love his enemy, and to

[1] Martineau, Preface to "Study of Religion."

reject all sound business policy by lending and hoping for nothing in return. A complaint, however, may fairly be made on the other side; if Christianity is impracticable, is not ethics more impracticable still? This can hardly be denied. Ethics, in fact, is built up on a condition of society which cannot at present be found. That personal relation to one another which is the necessary condition for all right conduct—what if that is non-existent? Take away this foundation-stone, and the whole edifice trembles. To tell us that there is nothing good except the good will, and that we must aim at the common advantage for the pure love of it, is very interesting, and if the good will were more potent within us, it might be very profitable. "That mankind is a community," as Butler asserts, "and that we all stand in a relation to each other, that there is a public end and interest of society which each particular is obliged to promote, is the sum of morals." But if it is the sum of morals, it is not the sum of what we need for living the moral life. Conscience, as Butler tells us again, if it had "power as it had manifest authority, would absolutely govern the world."[1] True; but the very point on which we wish for information is, how can it gain this power? The real obstacle to human progress is not ignorance as to what we ought to do or to be, but the moral estrangement between man and man; and the really visionary and unpractical proceeding is to tell us what follows from the right relations, when those relations are broken to start with. How am I to act as a brother to my neighbour, when his hand is against mine, and mine, for purposes of self-protection, has to be against his? " Thou shalt love thy neighbour as thyself."

[1] "Sermons on Human Nature," Ed. Bohn, p. 406.

I admit that I ought to, but hatred has already taken up all the room, and love cannot get in ; nor can I, by my own unaided power, make a place for it. There are many things by which I feel justifiably alienated from my neighbour. Just as it takes two to make a quarrel, so it takes two to constitute the "right relation"; however anxious I may be to do my part to my neighbour, I can do nothing unless he is ready to do his. I have not only to change my own attitude ; I have to change his, or wait till he changes it for himself. Again, it may be "natural" for me to seek the common good ; but I am continually conscious of a whole army, or rather a mob, of conflicting and self-regarding impulses which seem to me just as "natural," and often a great deal stronger. Often, too, the leaders of this mob are certain blind passions ; and these, though quite distinct from anything that I can call definitely selfish or unselfish, demand a gratification which, fiercely sought at the moment, turns out to be contrary to the real advantage both of others and of myself as well.

These signs of what theology has defined as "original sin" are not the only influences that sunder me from others. If all are my brothers, how am I to overstep the barriers raised by differences of race, nationality, and creed ? I cannot feel to a black man as I can and do to a white. The dirt of a Kaffir kraal, or even of an East End tenement, is enough, for physical reasons alone, to impede me in discharging my moral obligations to beings who are abhorrent to me, or indeed in perceiving that I owe them any obligations at all. The lynch law whose application to a white man is unthinkable, may appear perfectly just when set in motion against a negro. Divergences of temperament rise

RECONCILIATION

between me and my neighbour, making even the ordinary civilities of life seem hard. One Christian may feel to Shylock an antipathy just as unreasoning as another (to use Shylock's own illustration) may feel to "the harmless necessary cat." What is there in the counsels of ethics which will enable me to overcome this, and place me where there is neither Jew nor Greek, bond nor free? I ought to seek the common good; I willingly labour for my own family; I find no difficulty in giving up time for the business of my club or my friends or my church; but when it is a matter of denying myself or taking up a new attitude to those who have laid me under no "obligation"—the very word is significant—the promptings to brotherliness lose their force and are forgotten.

Thus the charge of impracticability hurled at religion rebounds with startling force against any preacher of pure morality who ventures to employ it. And perhaps this is the reason why the study of ethics with so many people has fallen into disrepute. The attempt to disregard the maxims of ethics would be as foolish as the conduct of an engineer who should attempt to construct an engine without a diagram; but the diagram is not the engine, nor even its motive power; and however complete the mechanic's knowledge of the right running of his engine, that knowledge will be of little use unless he has the tools and the skill to repair a broken crank or an injured valve. Ethics, as we have been considering it, furnishes an admirable manual for criticism, but cannot be looked upon as a technical handbook; where is the philosophy that shall be—as Cicero said in his eulogy of Brutus— a "lex non ita disputandi, sed ita vivendi," a rule, not of theoretical discussion, but of active life?

III. The Bible, unlike ethics, does not stop here; it

does not stop even with describing our relation both to one another as members of the family, and also to God as its head. It starts off, so to speak, on a new tack; and having emphasised, as we have already seen, the value of right conduct, now proceeds to emphasise the value of suffering. Not a word is said to diminish the importance of what we have already laid down; morality lives on every page of the Bible; but by its side lives something else. The ordinary manual of ethics neither occupies itself with the cost of morality, nor dwells on the necessary effort to maintain it. But the Bible, besides the fulness of its "do this" and "be this," has very much to say about paying the price. It provides, that is to say, not only for doing right, but for repairing wrong. In the Old Testament the books of the law contain many directions for moral conduct, both for the individual and for society,—the earlier sections of the law, indeed, more than the later ones. But the earlier as well as the later laws have their piacular provisions. If wrong has been done, the penalty has to be paid, to God as well as to man. True, all the sacrifices were not intended to be the means of propitiation for wrongdoing; many were simply the expressions of worship, or of the community of life between the worshipper and his God; many others were the visible embodiments of gratitude; but there were others that partook strictly of the nature of a penalty; a recompence had to be given for property or rights misappropriated; and a life had to be offered for the sin committed—the pure, unblemished victim killed by the wrongdoer, or for him, to "atone for" his sin.[1] The inner significance of this act is often left without emphasis and perhaps was often

[1] See especially Lev. 5-7, 16. It will be noted that trespass offerings are provided for ritual as well as moral uncleanness.

RECONCILIATION

absent from the mind of the worshipper. But the heifer or the lamb, itself unblemished, and therefore regarded as unsoiled by sin, was offered instead of the soiled life of the worshipper, and on his behalf. In other words, when the relation between God and man was broken, it was restored as soon as the sinner in repentance presented, not himself, but a being which was at all events without conscious sin, and with which he identified himself before the altar. As was the victim, so, by this presentation, was the offerer in the sight of God.

Many of the most familiar passages in the Psalms, as in the Prophets, read at first blush almost like protests against this sacrificial view of the law; but the protest is only against the preservation of the husk and the loss of the kernel. In sacrifices there can be no great proportion between the enormity of the offence and the penalty ordained for it; and it was dangerously easy for the worshipper to shelter himself behind the protection of a ritual act from the necessity of a moral change. But the most striking feature of the Psalms is the very feeling that gave the sacrificial system all its value, the sorrow for sin, for the broken relation, coupled with the welcoming of affliction which could be felt as a means of restoring the sinner to God. " Before I was afflicted I went astray." " It is good for me that I have been afflicted, that I might learn thy statutes." The clearest expressions of the renewing power of sorrow occur in the 51st Psalm. " Thou delightest not in sacrifices, else would I give them; thou hast no pleasure in burnt offering. The sacrifices of God are a broken spirit. A broken and a contrite heart, O God, thou wilt not despise." The true remedy for wrong doing has been found when the Psalmist has become able to say, " I will declare mine iniquity, I will be sorry for my sin," or to pray, "O Lord, have mercy upon me, heal my soul; for I have sinned against thee."

Much of the history of Israel reads like the aimless and sorry twisting of a tangled web; but to the men who brooded over it, it was not simply a story of suffering, but of renewal through suffering to the righteousness which had been lost. The disasters of the exile, as well as those which preceded it, were simply means for reconstruction of the old pure national life out of "the remnant that escaped." As such the exile itself was understood by the most powerful of the prophets. The national calamities were not the result of Assyrian or Babylonian violence and greed. They were ordained by the hand of Jehovah, and the great prophet of the exile has given expression, in the classical passage describing the chastisement of the Servant of the Lord, to the redemptive power of suffering. One of the most human stories in the Old Testament is the account of David's repentance for the sin of numbering the people. He almost courted the pressure of God's hand on himself and on those whom he ruled, because he realised, at least in part, the enormity of his own sin and the depth of his love for God. We cannot deny to the old warrior the delicacy of conscience that revealed to him God's utter purity of abhorrence at that sin. He would not allow the dutiful liberality of Ornan to rob him of the privilege of paying the full price, "the uttermost farthing."

IV. But in this respect, as in many others, the Old Testament is simply the adumbration of the New. The New Testament is unique among religious books, both by its insistence on morals, by its view of the basis of morality, and also by the stress laid on suffering

RECONCILIATION

and its value. Other systems have grappled with the question of suffering; but they have at best left it as they found it—a problem, an obstacle, a stumbling-block. The New Testament, in a plane of teaching which is sometimes distinct from that of ethics, and sometimes inseparable from it, views all suffering in the light of what is, in its view, the supreme act of suffering; and regards suffering as a means to the right action which is impossible otherwise,—the constant "bearing about in the body the dying of Jesus, that the life also of Jesus may be manifested in our body."[1] And since right action, as we have seen, is a matter of restored personal relations, the New Testament everywhere carries suffering into the transfiguring light of reconciliation.

In other words, the whole system of life as understood by the New Testament writers, with a unanimity which is striking even if it is not complete, centres round the life and death and resurrection of Christ. The four gospels view these three historical facts from somewhat different standpoints, whose mutual independence only emphasizes their common loyalty to Christ; and the epistles add their testimony with equal distinctness, yet with as clear a perception of the three central points of interest. To them the problem of suffering and of evil, whether hinted at or boldly stated in the Old Testament, culminates both as difficulty and as solution in the person of Christ. The life of Christ, ending in a violent death and crowned by the resurrection from the dead, was viewed under the three main aspects of filial obedience, sacrifice and reconciliation. That is to say, when the first Christian writers thought of Christ,—and indeed to judge from their writings they

[1] 2 Cor. 4^{10}.

thought of little else—they thought of him now as the son who knew and did and loved his father's will, whose passion was to be about his father's business, who even by suffering learnt obedience ; now as the fulfilment of the Old Testament sacrificial types, the priest, or the victim, in the one great sacrificial act which rendered all others superflous ; and now as the mediator between God and man, the reconciler between those whose sins he bore and Him into whose presence no sin could come.

At times it has seemed to theologians as if these three aspects were really three separate and individual characters successively assumed by Christ, instead of three stages in our recognition of the working out of the one ruling idea embodied in the reconciler's life ; consequently there has always been a tendency for some one of the three aspects to obscure the other two. We have forgotten the reconciler in the sacrifice, or the sacrifice in the obedient son. The insight which governed the compilation of the New Testament, balancing its different elements of biography, history, treatise, and apocalypse, was similar to the insight of the individual writers in perceiving the necessity for the emphasis to be laid on each of the offices that are therein involved. It is true that these writers do not always mention all three offices in the same breath. Often they speak as if one alone were present in their thoughts ; but they can each be shown to have felt and appreciated all three, and to have seen that obedience implies sacrifice, and sacrifice reconciliation. To them the part is equal to the whole.

It is not indeed their business to remove apparent contradictions. Of such, it has been urged, the New Testament contains many ; and often its various references to Christ seem to involve considerable incon-

RECONCILIATION

sistencies, as will be obvious from the following fairly representative passages: "The son of man came ... to minister, and to give his life a ransom for many."[1] "Thou wast slain, and hast redeemed us to God by thy blood."[2] "As by one man's disobedience many were made sinners, so by the obedience of one shall many be made righteous."[3] Or, "The first man Adam was made a living soul, the last Adam was made a quickening (life-giving) spirit;"[4] which we may set side by side with the fuller passage, where separate functions seem to be assigned to the death and the life of Christ, "If when we were enemies we were reconciled to God by the death of his son, much more, being reconciled, we shall be saved by his life."[5] Or again, contrast the words, "The high priest of our profession, Christ Jesus,"[6] with "Christ, our passover, is sacrificed for us,"[7] and with "Christ was once offered to bear the sins of many."[8] Again, "It is expedient for you that I go away; for if I go not away the comforter will not come to you, but if I depart I will send him unto you,"[9] may be placed by the side of "Verily, verily, I say unto you, he that believeth on me hath everlasting life,"[10] and also, "Jesus said unto them, I am the bread of life. He that cometh to me shall never hunger, he that believeth on me shall never thirst."[11] In relation to these last two passages, a fresh aspect is presented in the words, "Whom God hath set forth as a propitiation through faith in his blood."[12] Further, contrast, "Christ hath redeemed us from the curse of the law, being made a curse for us,"[13] with, "being made per-

---

[1] Matt. 20^{28}. [2] Rev. 5^9. [3] Rom. 5^{19}. [4] 1 Cor. 15^{45}.
[5] Rom. 5^{10}. [6] Heb. 3^1. [7] 1 Cor. 5^7. [8] Heb. 10^{14}.
[9] Jno. 16^7. [10] Jno. 6^{47}. [11] Jno. 6^{35}. [12] Rom. 3^{25}.
[13] Gal. 3^{13}.

94 ETHICS AND ATONEMENT

fect, he became the author of eternal salvation unto all them that obey him."[1] To which we may add, finally, Christ's own words, " I came down from heaven not to do mine own will, but the will of him that sent me,"[2] coupled with S. Peter's comment, "who his own self bare our sins in his own body on the tree, that we being dead to sins might live unto righteousness."[3]

Thus we are saved by Christ's death, Christ's obedience, Christ's life. Christ is at once the high priest and the victim. He insists on the absolute necessity of simple faith in himself, while at the same time he is not simply the object of our faith but also the propitiation for our sins ; again, to secure the full blessing for us he must retire in favour of another. He is at once made a curse or made sin, and made perfect or fully consecrated as priest ; and, finally, the object of his coming is represented as solely to do God's will, and also to reconcile to God those who had been aliens by his death. But these inconsistencies, as we shall try to show later on, do not affect the real unity of the writers' thoughts of Christ : they testify to the depth of the apostolic consciousness of the results of Christ's life ; and it would be hard in any case to suppose that the writers leap from one view to another without consideration of what would be involved in the gap they were leaving.

Further, it is urged that this line of teaching lies outside morality ; and this extra-moral teaching, we are often told, originated only with the men to whom the life of Christ was a datum, and not with Christ himself. Christ, it is said, sided with the moralist, and was content with repeating the warning of the prophets, though with a sweetness and variety all his

[1] Heb. 5^9. [2] Jn. 6^{38}. [3] I Pet. 2^{24}.

RECONCILIATION

own, "Cease to do evil, learn to do well." He did not care, it is argued, to enlarge on his own obedience to God. He did not proclaim himself either priest or unblemished lamb led to the slaughter, nor did he think it necessary that any third person, or even himself, should stand as mediator between the returning prodigal and the Heavenly Father. Now it is quite true that Christ did not go about proclaiming himself the Son of God or the Mediator, nor did he himself expound any "plan of salvation;"[1] yet the unprejudiced reader of the gospels, even taking into account the Synoptics alone, will wonder at nothing more than at the star-like aloofness, majestic, free, of this solitary figure. How did he make his unique authority felt by all men, Pharisee and common man alike, without any personal insistence upon it, while all through his brief life, "his heart the lowliest duties on herself did lay"? Even in the fourth gospel, supposed as it is to be coloured by the theologising of a later age, Christ is never represented as saying: "I am the Priest: I am the King: I am the atoning sacrifice;" but, "I am the way:" "I am the good shepherd:" "I am the light of the world:" "I am the bread of life." He never said explicitly, "I am the Son of God;" he only wrapped this claim in the quiet, though none the less startling statement, "I and my Father are one;" or "No man cometh unto the Father but by me." Even in S. Matthew, besides the direct words, "The Son of Man is come to lay down his life for many," we have the equally direct claim to uniqueness in, "No man knoweth the Son, save the

---

[1] *Cf.* G. B. Stevens, "The Christian Doctrine of Salvation." "The ransom passage is a figure of speech occurring only once. It is not claimed that the idea which is deduced from it appears elsewhere in the Synoptics," p. 117.

96 ETHICS AND ATONEMENT

Father, and no man knoweth the Father save the Son, and he to whomsoever the Son willeth to reveal him."[1] And when at last he came to speak plainly of his approaching death and resurrection to his disciples, he did not indeed enlarge upon the theological significance of these events. He spoke of them as of what was going to befall their dearly loved friend and teacher; but the manner of his speaking of them showed that he regarded them, and wished his disciples to regard them, as the culmination of the mission of one whose meat and drink it was "to do the will of him that sent him," and to be ever "about his Father's business"—of one who, at his coming, was announced as, "Jesus, who should save his people from their sins."

All this is enough to show that Christ was not merely a prophet born out of the prophetic age. In spite of all that he said of the necessity and charm of goodness, he also said much that neither Buddha, Mohammed, nor Confucius dared to say. Doubtless there is more theology in the early Christian writings than in the words that we can attribute to Christ himself. But whence came this theology? If Christ only said, "I am the teacher; hear my words," how did they come to represent him as saying, "I am the redeemer; be saved through my death"? Whence this elaborate teaching common to the various writers of the New Testament? There was no council of Nicea among the apostles, held to formulate even a single Christian doctrine. The only intellect among them capable of elaborating such a system as that which is expounded or implied by them all was S. Paul's, and S. Paul was the last man to whom the other apostles would turn for information concerning the master whom they had

[1] Matt. 11^{27}.

loved, and for the explanation of the inner meaning of the life which he had lived before them. Had their view of that significance been quite simple, concerned with obedience alone, or with sacrifice alone, its diffusion through the early church, on the supposition that it had no basis in the actual teaching of Jesus, would have been less difficult to understand. But the view actually held, as we have seen, is highly complex. Each of the writers gives some importance to every separate element in Christ's life. The only exception is the high priesthood of Christ, of which the Epistle to the Hebrews makes much and the other writings leave unmentioned. The only writing in which there appears to be no direct teaching that implies the atonement is the Epistle of S. James, and even S. James speaks of the law of liberty, and reminds his readers that God brought them forth by the word of truth. To him also Christ is no mere teacher. He is the Lord to whom S. James renders " bond-service " as completely as he renders it to God Himself; and the whole epistle implies the reconciliation between man and God brought about by the death of Christ.

Now the very complexity of the view thus held demands an explanation. If the apostles did not get it from one another, or from Christ, where did they find it? Did they all light independently upon the same combination of functions,—obedience, reconciliation, and sacrifice,—by accident? If there had been no basis for all this in the teaching of Christ, the gospels as we have them would have been impossible. If history really denies such a view to Christ, they would either have conformed to historical accuracy and omitted all reference to the atonement, or they would have been written from the theological standpoint of a later age and have

98 ETHICS AND ATONEMENT

made the atonement as prominent as it is in the epistles. The place the atonement actually occupies in the gospels—in the fourth as well as in the other three, where it is seen like an object under the surface of clear water—is unintelligible, unless Christ really spoke on the subject himself. The position of the atonement in the epistles, whatever be the view of inspiration accepted by the reader, can only be explained by one supposition; the various writers, meditating independently, though in the same circle of thought, on the events of Galilee, Calvary, and Olivet, interpreted those events by the teaching they had received, as they found that teaching, in its turn, developed and explained by the events themselves;—or as they themselves preferred to say, the spirit of Christ, not yet given to them while they were listening to their master's words,[1] made plain to them the meaning of both words and life. Our purpose however does not lead us into the details of criticism. It is enough for us to recognize, by the side of the universal importance of morality in the New Testament, and inseparable from the words of Christ himself, the insistence on something besides mere conduct, and the picture of an obedience and a suffering which become the means of reconciliation and of restoration.

The New Testament writers thus refuse to be content with "you must do this" or even "you must be this." To be content with the first, they hint,[2] would be a cruel mockery; to be content with the second would be still more cruel. They insist on proceeding to a third assertion, "your sins are forgiven, you are made a new creature, through the death of Christ, by faith in his blood." Herein lies the opposition between ethics and religion. Ethics complains that religion brings in an extraneous

[1] Jn. 7^{39}. [2] Rom. 7^{24}.

RECONCILIATION 99

and superfluous dogmatism. Religion accuses ethics of stopping short before any solid vantage ground is gained. And herein lies the problem of Christian ethics, which is to show why, from the "do this" and still more the "be this" of ordinary ethics, we must go on to the "new creature in Christ Jesus."

V. After all, it is not strange that reconciliation, in some form or other, should figure so largely in the Bible; for in the Bible, as we have seen, all right conduct is a personal matter and stands in personal relations. The Old Testament indeed may be called the book of severed relations, the New Testament the book of the knitting up of severed bonds. The two together rest on estrangement and restoration, disobedience and forgiveness. Wounded love returning good for evil, the "seeking" and "saving" of the lost is, to use Delitzsch's phrase, the "Ariadne thread" that runs through the whole volume from Genesis to Revelation. Nor, again, is it strange that ethics should, for the most part, have omitted all thought of reconciliation, remaining content with the definitions and sanctions of duties. But when from duties we are driven back upon persons, when we recognize that wrong is really an outrage upon persons, making a breach which must be healed before right can be done once more, reconciliation can no longer be left out of account. Unless the system of ethics is to be a castle in the air, a mere summary of ideals, wrongdoing and the broken relations between man and man must be facts for its consideration. Before we can do more than gaze upon the sweet fields beyond the flood, we must find some way of crossing the Jordan which separates us from the possession of the rightly ordered and harmonious life. How is this crossing to be effected?

If we are right so far, all wrong acts imply wrong attitudes. You cannot indeed regard any act as isolated. The man who lies has forgotten that he owes the duty of truthfulness to the man to whom he lies. The mother who ill-treats her child has violated or repudiated the great debt of mother-love laid on her at the child's birth. The employee who cheats his employer forgets that honesty is the only ground on which they can both stand with safety, and that his insecure foothold on that ground implies insecurity to his employer also. Every act of wrong-doing takes its character from the position both of injurer and injured. The injurer does wrong, not absolutely, but to the particular person injured. He violates the demands of their relation to one another. Now this violation demands satisfaction. It is a crime which, as we should say, must be atoned for. It cannot simply be regarded as non-existent. To take the short and easy method of saying, "do right and sin no more," would be to commit a further wrong, for which satisfaction would be as needful as for the offence which had just been so easily dismissed. Does the employer, the poorer by £500 through the dishonesty of his cashier, summon the defaulter to his room and simply tell him "never to do it again"? The man who accepted such a superficial view of his own dishonesty would be almost as foolish as the employer who suggested it. The first offence may be overlooked; but what security is there within the culprit that it will not occur again? There must be, at least in his own conscience, the heavy underscoring of the act, which will make him disown the fault and in some degree place him where he was before. This underscoring is owed to him by his employer, as part of the sacred duty, owed by all men to each other, not to make it easy for an offence to be repeated.

It is the same with the lie told by a man to his friend. The friendship cannot be the same after the lie as before it. The wrong, unatoned for, would live on to interfere with all the confidence and openness without which friendship is but a name. Until this need of satisfaction has been recognized by injured and injurer alike, the restoration of real friendship is impossible. Every man has in him something of the instinct of the discharged bankrupt who, though legally free from all claims of his creditors, cannot rest till out of the proceeds of a new and more successful business he has paid to each twenty shillings in the pound. The difficulty is that in the moral life the new business cannot be begun until this full payment has been made. Who is to give the wrong-doer the means with which to make this payment? A youth has committed a shameful act of cowardice.[1] Cowardice may be foreign to his real nature; he may have bitterly repented of the act, and loathed himself, from the very moment that the act was committed. But how shall he find the only relief that can be real, and render the act undone? However unblemished may be his reputation for courage among those who have never known the one black passage in his life, however he may try to "atone for" that dark hour by years of patient and unfaltering bravery, the act is still done, and even when it is unsuspected by others, it weighs on his conscience with a load not to be shaken off. Things can never be the same between him and the human race to which at a crucial moment he has been unfaithful.

It is one of the paradoxes of human nature that when

[1] As in Conrad's striking story, "Lord Jim."

102 ETHICS AND ATONEMENT

a man once realises the wrong he has done, he will welcome and even long for the chance of making some reparation that shall place him where he was before he had yielded to the temptation. It is this instinct which lies at the root of the great systems both of sacrifice and penance. No agony can be greater than that of the wrong-doer who finds that all reparation, all restitution, is unavailing; who cannot, by any sacrifice, induce the world to cry quits with him. Not only the extremity of human wickedness, but the extremity of human misery was reached when Judas, making the one attempt at atonement left him, flung the thirty pieces of silver upon the Temple pavement before the priests, and found even that despairing attempt brutally foiled. There is profound truth in Bunyan's story, characteristically retold in Browning's "Ned Bratts," of the old scoundrel who, coming to see his life of robbery and theft in its true light, and doubting his own moral capacity for rectitude, came before the judge and begged to be hanged out of hand.

"To pay the debt" is the idea underlying all punishment. He who sins must smart for it. When a wrong has been done, the injured man, or society acting for him, exacts a certain amount of suffering as an equivalent. Most punishment is no doubt deterrent as well as retaliatory; intended, that is, to prevent future crime as well as to "make up for" the past. But all punishment, to be recognized as in any sense just, must hold some proportion to the crime; "an eye for an eye, and a tooth for a tooth"; and the infliction of fines, from the carefully graduated Saxon system of the "Were-Gild" to the procedure of the modern police-court, implies,

RECONCILIATION

in the frankest manner, this conception of a debt to be discharged.[1]

But there is really no equivalence, or at least equipollence, between suffering and crime. Would it not seem an insult, when a man's firstborn son has been killed, to offer to the parent of the murdered lad a sum of money? At how many pounds sterling shall we estimate a lie to a friend, or treachery to our country? By how large a cheque shall we restore, not only the money which we have stolen from one who trusted us, but also the right, of which our sin had robbed him, to look upon us as capable of trustworthiness and honesty? What can be more pitiable, or more inevitable, than the impotent distress of the bankrupt or the thief, who, after paying the penalty of his wrong-doing appointed by the law, finds that he is not one whit safer in himself, or one step nearer to restored relations of confidence or credit with his fellow-men? The equilibrium which wrong disturbs is a personal one, and the restoration must be personal also. Such a transaction as this it is obviously impossible to state in terms of monetary payment; and it is as impossible to state it in terms of infliction of pain. To do this would necessitate a quantitative comparison between pain and injury,—so much injury equal to so much pain; but both pain and injury defy any such computation. The same pain differs in quality with the nervous systems on which it is inflicted; one man's agony would merely be another man's discomfort; and to the same man the pain itself may vary in intensity at different times. Further,

---

[1] *Cf.* Dante, "Purgatory," x. 139, where the sufferers through pride rejoice in their pain, as the means of unliving their past, and exclaim with passionate regret, "I can no more."

apart from all this, who would venture to construct a fixed scale of moral delinquencies to set by the side of the sliding scale of man's moral attainments? In the view both of the injurer and the injured, the same offence may at different times or in different circumstances be felt as anything between a trifling misdemeanour and an almost irreparable sin. A sensitive mind will regard the utterance of a few disloyal words as an enduring and ineffaceable stain upon his conscience demanding years of reparation. With the busy and well-seasoned politician, a biting attack on a foe may weigh no more than a gnat's sting. The guilt of every wrong act must be estimated with reference to the amount of the excuse or the temptation; but it will also depend on the position of the one offended, a parent or a benefactor, a life-long friend or a casual acquaintance.

Here it will perhaps be urged that what is properly punishable is not the wrong act but the wrong motive. A highly reprehensible motive may result in what seems a peccadillo, while under other circumstances it might have resulted in an outrageous crime. From the point of abstract justice all wrong motives are equally reprehensible. If I am resolved to defy the law of right, it does not matter whether a pin, a five-pound note, or my friend's reputation is stolen. The first act as well as the last would deserve condign punishment, or rather would involve a guilt which no punishment could atone for. But as a matter of fact, in human nature, good and bad motives are so perplexingly intertwined that only supreme justice can disentangle them; and where motives are as various as the persons who employ them, where shall we find that nicely graduated scale of pain which could be pronounced efficient, because exactly corresponding with the motives it is to punish?

Punishment, then, is an inadequate means of restoration, for two reasons. First, because of the impossibility of assigning an adequate quantity of retribution to any given wrong, or of employing the simple method of a pound of flesh; and secondly, because the existence and significance of wrong act and wrong motive alike is wholly independent of the pain and loss which punishment implies. There remains therefore forgiveness as a yet untried bridge over the gulf. But what does forgiveness mean? To some people it means no more than the processes we have already considered; that is, it means one of two things, either punishing the offence and then regarding it as done with, or else not punishing at all and regarding the offence as uncommitted. But neither of these processes is necessarily forgiveness: the judge may pass the sentence of punishment and the Home Secretary may send the order for the reprieve, yet can we say that either of these in any sense constitutes forgiveness? Both the remission and the infliction of punishment may be consistent with forgiveness: they may also be consistent with the gravest injustice. True forgiveness must pass beyond the offence to the offender, and must take into account the moral motive and attitude which begot the offence. Sin lies not in the single act but in the general attitude. Therefore forgiveness ought primarily to take into consideration the attitude and not the act. And forgiveness, like duty, is a matter of relations between persons, and persons in a special position in regard to one another. It takes two to quarrel, and we must also admit that it takes two to make up a quarrel. You cannot forgive, any more than you can punish, a block of stone or a piece of wood. You may whip your dog for disobedience and then pat him in token of restored favour: but what is forgiveness to you, to him can hardly be more than animal satisfaction at a well-known token of affection; real contrition there cannot be. And without contrition in the object of your forgiveness, forgiveness sinks to the level of indulgence.

VI. Contrition, not punishment or its absence, is the condition of forgiveness. A mother has concentrated all the interest and vigour of her life on her only son; so much so, that all his joy is her joy and—such is the mystery of love in the human heart—his pain is also hers. Grown to manhood, the son, embittered at some great disappointment, leaves home and plunges into evil courses. Wearied with the husks that the swine did eat, he returns to find her wonderful love still undiminished; but can she forgive him? The purer her nature, the more she will resent and loathe the sin that drove him from her. Only when the wanderer, by not only suffering from the consequences of that sin but repudiating the motive that underlay the sin itself, has become acquainted with contrition, can she allow her love to express itself in forgiveness. Hermione can indeed receive back the husband whose suspicion had done her the foulest wrong, but only when he has learned to say,

"Whilst I remember
Her and her virtues, I cannot forget
My blemishes in them, and so still think of
The wrong I did myself: which was so much,
That heirless it hath made my kingdom; and
Destroyed the sweet'st companion that e'er man
Bred his hopes out of."[1]

[1] "Winter's Tale," Act V. sc. i.

RECONCILIATION

To take another instance. The crime of Peter was only less despicable than that of Judas. His was the base desertion of a friend in need, a friend whom he had sworn to support even to the death. Could such an act as this be "washed in Lethe and forgotten"? It could, because after meeting his Lord's look, he "went out and wept bitterly." In that moment Christ knew that Peter renounced the meanness and cowardice that had prompted the sin; and he showed it when he asked the tender question, "Lovest thou me?" and when he commanded him to undertake a new work of grave responsibility, as if he had never made the great refusal; while Peter himself was able to answer with all the confidence of the child restored to the old footing of unbroken personal relations, "Thou knowest all things. Thou knowest that I love thee."

Forgiveness, therefore, is dependent on contrition. What, then, of the unrepentant? Here we are confronted by a new problem. One of the chief characteristics of sin is to harden the sinner: how is the uncontrite sinner to be forgiven? Must the pitying, merciful man hold himself sternly aloof from the friend who has wronged him until the wrong-doer comes to him with the words, "I repent"? How if he never comes? Must the mother shut out the disobedient child from her tender heart until the little one comes shyly whispering, "I am sorry"? Every true heart would repudiate such an acquiescence in alienation. Real love, instead of wistfully mourning over the breach, seeks at once to repair it. Its difficulty is not how to forgive but how to render forgivable; how to work upon the wrong-doer so that he may utter the words, "I am sorry," and be set where he was. How is the injured to reconcile the injurer to himself? How can he mediate between himself and the sinner?

He can only do it in one way; by suffering the shame which the wrong-doer ought to feel. The suffering that leads to repentance is not the suffering that is consequent on punishment, or on those awkward consequences of sin that are sooner or later inevitable—even a Judas may feel these; but on the uncontrollable repulsion towards the sin that has made the breach. The wrong-doer may be far from feeling this. It may be the last thing that, after his sin, he is capable of feeling. Punishment may only drive him the further away from such restorative sorrow. But this is precisely the grief that may be felt by the injured person. He must feel it, if there is to be any chance of reconciliation. Here is the great work of the reconciler. It is the injured who must go to seek the injurer, who must place himself at the prodigal's side, bearing with him the consequences which the prodigal can feel and also those deeper sorrows which as yet he cannot feel. It is when the child sees how his disobedience has made his mother grieve that its true meaning flashes in upon his own spirit, and he too grieves, not over the result, but over the sin. It is when the young man sees his self-indulgence bringing a blush of shame to his father's cheek that he realises within himself his father's hatred of his sin. For there is something contagious alike in sin and in the shame for sin. A traitor in the ranks may soil a whole company by his own treacherous designs; a dishonest clerk may infect a whole office. And shame, too, is not leaden-footed: it flies from one mind to another, and many a man has not felt his own shame until he saw it seated on the honourable brows of his comrades. Cæsar could turn the mutinous sentiments of his veterans into self-reproach, by addressing them with the scornful expression, "Quirites," "civilians." Here, too, we learn from practice rather than from precept; we kindle our emotions at the flame of the emotions of others. If I wish to inspire others with "the scorn of scorn, the hate of hate," I must myself first of all despise rightly and hate nobly; and all else that I can do to rouse those feelings will be from first to last subordinate to the presence of right passions in my own breast. If, then, I would bring another to suffer for his sin, so that he may repent, I must first suffer myself. Any man who would win the title of saviour, must know how to bear the sins of others.

Most minds have felt the pathos of the story of the girl who leaves her father and her village home to plunge into the excitement of life in a great city; she sends no word of her surroundings, but her father, month after month, and year after year, sets the door of the cottage open each night, with the quiet words, "some day she will return." She returns at last, broken down in body and mind, the piteous wreck of her former self,—brought back by the love which in her saddest degradation she had never forgotten, as it had never failed her,—to find the forgiveness which she had first despised and then despaired of, in her father's strong embrace. The father's love had conquered; yet, touching as is the picture of the old man calmly waiting year after year, it was not his to put forth that greatest love, that went forth to seek and to save the lost. His daughter had not sunk to the depths if she could be brought back by what to her was only a memory. Such memories have often served only to repel. The supreme love will not rely on a memory, however tender; it has other weapons. To follow the unfaithful friend or the wandering child into the abyss; to bear the ill-will of others, the odium of the sin, as if oneself the malefactor; to suffer the gibes and the contemptuous hatred even of the wrong-doer, until the old affection, wounded and half dead from the blow of the unforgotten injury, begins to reawake from its stupor,—this is the steep but royal path of complete reconciliation. This is to turn a sinner from the error of his ways, and cover a multitude of sins. This, further, is true mediation; because in acting thus the reconciler comes between the sinner and his sin, or rather between the sinner and the moral authority which he has defied and turned into his foe, and replaces him in that sacred bond of personal relationship which he had outraged by his disobedience.

We can now see why a treatise on ethics that is to have any practical value cannot stop where most writers on ethics lay down their pens. Prevention is doubtless better than cure; but in the presence of disease it is useless to be satisfied with reciting maxims of health. To "ascertain necessary relations" and to "deduce from necessary principles what conduct must be beneficial and what conduct must be detrimental"[1] in a perfect state of society, may be the end of Absolute Ethics; the end of a system of ethics that is to help society to perfection, must be Reconciliation.

[1] Herbert Spencer, "Data of Ethics."

CHAPTER V

MEDIATION

I. THE problem of suffering is one of those ever-recurring riddles whose answer, hidden from the wise and prudent, is often revealed unto babes. Why suffering, indeed, should ever be allowed in God's fair world, no human ingenuity has been able to explain. But the fact remains that when suffering takes the form which we were considering in the last chapter, suffering and salvation become synonymous. No face is more beautiful than the face that has been marked by the lines of grief; grief born of no personal weakness or self-indulgence or sin, or of its sad fruit, remorse; but the grief that accompanies the entering in to the sin of others; and such an entering in, to the sensitive soul, must be more bitter than the knowledge of self-committed sin. This grief has no admixture of selfishness, and it is selfishness which is the sting of purely human grief; freed from selfishness, grief grows akin to the "divine compassion," which links man most closely to God. Such suffering presents no difficulty to the mind. It is not a curse, but a blessing. In every age, human nature would have been infinitely the poorer had no tears been shed for the frequent sinning and the unmanly repentances of those whose own hearts had never known the pangs of honest self-condemnation.

Further, suffering of this kind is the most potent

means by which man influences man. It is not of course the most conspicuous; but the grass on the hill-sides grows green because of a thousand hidden streams which only rise to the surface on the slopes far below. Obedience, at least outwardly, may be forced by some "commanding personalities," who have never learnt to "weep with those that weep," nor to "rejoice with those that rejoice." But all those who have exercised an empire over the inner loyalty and devotion of men have wielded a sceptre wreathed with starry tears of compassion; and the two figures which have enchained the abiding admiration and love of centuries are those of the Buddha and of Jesus of Nazareth—the one flinging aside all human bliss to court the knowledge of pain, in order that the path of escape therefrom might be made known to his fellow-men; and the other bearing our sins in his own body on the tree.

All this will be familiar to the experience of serious people; but it rests on a principle which has perhaps been insufficiently considered. Man does not generally realise that his most valuable asset is himself, and that his greatest powers are those resident in his own mind and will,—in what we call his personality. We have often had to use the term humanity; and if humanity is anything more than a collective term for an indefinite number of individuals existing at this or any other time, it is because humanity is really an organism, of which each part has a distinct and definite function to discharge towards the rest. With a weapon borrowed from the outside world, a stick or a stone, I can affect the outside world, or any part of it, a man or a tree. There is a weapon not borrowed from the outside world, but given me at my birth, my will, by which I

MEDIATION

cannot affect a tree or a rock, but by which I can move another living person. It may indeed be replied, "Yes, but this is not confined to humanity: by your will you can influence an animal also." Yet I have only to think of the limitations of the power of the human will over the animals to feel that I have here another proof that the will is properly a link, and the only link, between man and man.

This power of the will, which in some of its manifestations approaches the weird and the uncanny, is only becoming tardily recognised by Science. It has received in some quarters the descriptive name of Personal, or even Animal Magnetism; and although there may be no scientific basis for such nomenclature, the fact is indisputable that the mental attitude of one person may always influence that of another. This may certainly be claimed by psychology as a scientific law, though not at present capable of accurate measurement. It is a matter of common and trivial observation that you can often make a person turn round by looking even at the back of his head. The terror of a few may throw a whole crowd into a panic; the confidence of the leader of a forlorn hope may turn his dispirited company into a band of heroes. As the proverb reminds us, one black sheep will infect a flock; and, happily for us, the reverse is also true, and true oftener in the mental than in the physical world. What we sometimes speak of as the "atmosphere" of a person is only another illustration of the same fact; education, for instance, is beginning to realise this; and though the mind of the teacher may contain much that is beyond the conscious attainment of the child, it is precisely this larger knowledge by which the child's mind is most vitally influenced. As we have seen in another connexion, it is what we are that affects people far more deeply than anything that we can do.[1]

But we need not stop here. It is only of late that the word Suggestion has come to be used, at least by psychologists, in a technical sense. Under the influence of hypnotism, a sane and healthy person will respond like an automaton, to suggested impulses entirely foreign to him in his normal state; and even when the hypnotic trance is passed, the commands laid upon him in his sleep will be obeyed when he is fully awake. This suggestion appears to "work" as efficaciously over the body as over the mind; and however strange and bizarre its phenomena, it is only the scientific application to abnormal conditions of a principle active in the commonest intercourse of life. We are always suggesting to other people. The greatest personalities are those which are capable of inspiring faith—believe, and "all things are possible to him that believeth."[2] And this faith is two-fold; I believe in the man who inspires me; and his inspiration makes me believe in myself;—believe, for example, that I can accomplish the task that seemed impossible, or bear the pain at which I trembled.

If I am thus made to believe, I can make others believe also. What I feel, you will feel, if I feel it strongly enough; especially if I consciously "will" you to feel it. The exceptions to this law are, we may at once admit, multitudinous—more numerous, it might be urged, than the instances of its fulfilment. But this is only to say that we do not yet fully understand the conditions. There is also a law which most religious people accept, that prayers are answered.

---

[1] *Cf.* Emerson's well-known sentence, "What you are speaks so loud that I cannot hear what you say." [2] Mark 9^{23}.

MEDIATION 115

Now, as every one knows, many prayers go unanswered. This, however, is not made a count against the law itself, but against the attitude of the individual petitioner. Prayer, if it is to be answered, is to be offered "in the name of Christ"; and who shall say that when the request is unanswered, the condition has none the less been adequately fulfilled?

In what circumstances this wireless telegraphy between mind and mind can act, or how one mind needs to be attuned to another, as it were, in order to receive its messages or its commands, is doubtless as yet beyond our knowledge; in that vast "region beyond," the terms of the psychologists do but serve as boundaries defining the extent of the unknown; but that messages and commands are so conveyed, is a fact which every student of life has verified by experience. Was it not this mysterious power of self-communication which made the stern straight figure of General Nicholson, silent and pre-occupied as he often appeared, a tower of strength to those dispirited regiments before Delhi to whom he had nothing to bring except himself? History, indeed, abounds in such examples; as when Nelson, reaching the fleet that was to conquer at Trafalgar, instantly made every man under his command conscious of Nelson's courage throbbing in his own breast; or when Napoleon, escaping from Elba, without a single gun, without a single private, threw the legitimist France into transports of passionate imperialism. In the American civil war, it is said that no appeal to patriotism, no hope of victory nor fear of defeat, could rouse, in the civilian recruits of the South, the burning zeal and the indomitable patience born of the rough soldiers' song, "That's Stonewall Jackson's way."

116 ETHICS AND ATONEMENT

Nor is the secret of the power of the popular orator or preacher to be traced to any other source. "He spake with authority and not as the scribes" was said of one who, above all other men, scorned the dogmas of the schools, and communicated, not his ideas, but himself. He was himself "the truth." And in the classical example of oratorical achievement, when Mark Antony roused the Roman citizens to feverish enthusiasm for the tyrant they had just condemned, he used no argument, but simply, as with the magic touch of a wizard's rod, transferred his own sentiments to their minds. John Wesley's influence over rough mobs was hardly less magical; and a similar influence has often been observed at outbreaks of religious excitement, in which it is the personal attraction of the preacher, more than his arguments, more even than his appeal, that "breaks down" his audience. Herein lies the great hope of every reformer; enthusiasm will always serve as wings to carry him into hearts into which the mere dead weight of his convictions and his reasoning could never force an entrance. Many a pupil knows that the greatest debt he owes his teacher is not for the spoken lesson, but for the impulses and ideals which not even the teacher could ever have put into words. Readers of the "Ring and the Book," that most subtle example of Browning's psychological analysis, will remember the strange effect of Pompilia's character both on Caponsacchi and on Guido, inspiring in the one case immeasurable awe and reverence, and in the other, unspeakable hate; not that the innocent girl ever dreamt of influencing anyone; but, as the poet is careful to show, an authority streamed from her, greater than her own, and born of the divine which dwelt within her.

So much for the phenomena; the exact scientific description we may leave to psychology; it is the psychologists who have to decide how much therein is physical and how much psychical, and how much, perhaps, spiritual. For us, the important point is that personality exerts a real influence, an influence exerted by nothing else known to us. I cannot be what I am without affecting others to a greater or less degree. The only question is, what makes that degree greater or less? What do we mean by calling some personalities strong and others weak? Why do some persons affect me more than others? And why do other people feel the force of personal influence differently from myself? The answer is not so hard as it seems; strength of personality, as Illingworth has pointed out, is proportionate to the number of points of contact between the active personality and the passive. A man may have a strong effect on me, who has no effect at all on my neighbour. A strong personality, in the absolute sense, has points of contact that enable him to affect and "invade" the majority of men he meets. Personality, in fact, is not exclusive but inclusive. We are persons, that is to say, not by our power of self-isolation, but by our power of transcending that isolation and linking ourselves to others, and others to ourselves. The doctrine of the familiar lines,

> " Each in his separate sphere of joy or pain
> Our hermit-spirits live and move alone,"

is for most of us unfortunately too true; but the more we possess of the great gift of personality, so much the more are we able to escape from the solitude of our hermit-cells, austere or self-indulgent, and join in a life which relates us to other lives, with common joys, common aims, and common experiences. Caliban was not a person; Prospero was; and even Trinculo, to the non-personal Caliban, was a kind of god.

This power of affecting others, then, to a greater or less degree, is a matter of experience; and its main condition is affinity. In each part of my mental being, will, intellect, and emotion, I must be able to "get at" the mental being of others. Of the three, the readiest vehicle for this invading power is emotion. The electric current will fuse where the hammer would break or crush; the strongest will becomes doubly strong when suffused with rich and eager feeling. All the great leaders, of nations as well as of religions, have been men of strong passions; Pitt as much as Gladstone, Calvin as much as Luther, Mohammed as much as Paul. The greater the whole personality, the deeper the emotions the stronger is the influence, the "invasion," the self-communication.

II. Let us now return to our previous conclusion, that personal reconciliation involves the suffering of the wronged. We have already seen that in reconciliation between two persons, something more than reconciliation is necessary. Reconciliation is the healing of a wrong attitude to an individual; but I cannot place myself in a wrong attitude or a wrong relation to an individual, without placing myself in an equally wrong relation to the humanity of which that individual is a part; and if I would set myself right with the individual, I must set myself right with humanity; I must acknowledge my sin, not only against the command that forbids me to tell a lie or act unkindly to Thomas or John, but against the command that forbids me to do so to men in general. But, if our argument in chapter iii. was right, we cannot stop even here. We think of something more than Thomas or John; but that something more is not humanity; it is a Person standing behind or manifested through humanity. It is not formal duty, but personal will, which stands over us in the moment of our repentance. "Against Thee, Thee only, have I sinned, and done this evil in Thy sight."[1] This is the instinctive conviction of all religion and even of all morality; though he has outraged Bathsheba and murdered Uriah, it is before God alone that David trembles. Otherwise, the conception of a moral God could hardly have arisen. Unless God were interested in my conduct to my neighbour, religion could be nothing more than ritual. What could suggest this interest taken by God in my conduct to men, except the conviction that my conduct to men is part of my conduct to God? It may of course be urged that mankind has been under a "strong delusion," and that this conviction, if it exists, does not prove that there is any such thing as God at all. We can at this point only reply that if, as we are forced to believe, every system of ethics implies the existence of God, reconciliation implies reconciliation to God. It may be that we can form no clear idea of this God, whether as "Jehovah, Jove, or Lord"; we may be unable to rest in the conception of either Mohammedan, Platonist, or Christian; but the fact remains that behind our duties to persons there is our duty to a Person, dim or even invisible, from the notion of whom we cannot shake ourselves free.

The question of reconciliation thus becomes far more difficult than at first sight appeared. Reconciliation, to be complete, cannot be effected without the

[1] Ps. 51^4.

120 ETHICS AND ATONEMENT

aid of mediation, even though the person of the mediator be contained in the injured party himself. The true type of reconciliation is reconciliation by mediation; and when it is with God that we need a reconciliation, the further difficulty arises; by what mediation can we approach the unapproachable, or gain access to an offended Majesty, from whose very presence we are interdicted by the limits of our existence? Or, since reconciliation must, at least in most cases, start from the side of the wronged, how is God to approach us? This is the problem that has always confronted Deism of every shade. And Deism, unable to find a solution, becomes a more hopeless creed than Atheism itself. For if my sins are sins against God, and with God no true reconciliation is possible, it would be better for me if there were no God at all. The Christian claims that he has the solution; he asserts that there is not only a chasm to be bridged—which every one must admit—but that it has been bridged, and that the bridge remains, that it may be crossed yesterday, to-day, and for ever, by the divine feet.

How then has the abyss been spanned? Let us again try the method of analogy. For any reconciliation, A, the injured, and B, the injurer, must touch one another. Circumstances, even in human affairs, may render impossible a direct *rapprochement* between the two. This difficulty is often prominent when the need for reconciliation is specially felt by outsiders. In a great labour dispute, or in strained diplomatic relations between two countries, many others will suffer besides the parties immediately concerned; and the obvious expedient has always been that some third party, if possible a *persona grata* with both the disputants, should use his good offices as mediator, or should come

MEDIATION

forward, as one who comprehends the wrong inflicted by B upon A, the possible provocation felt by B, and the extent of the resulting estrangement in the minds of both; and thus be able to represent A to B, and B to A. Even if one of the parties should be anxious to find a way of reconciliation, the conciliator may still be necessary; and where Elisha remains in his house, and Naaman is going away in a rage, Naaman's servants, by showing their master the other side of the case, and saying to him what Elisha himself might have said,—by "representing" Elisha to him, when he would not have been likely to listen to Elisha in person,—can bring the quarrel to an end.

But these instances only take us along a small part of the way that we have to traverse. Most well-disposed persons have earned something of the blessing of the peacemaker, and have spent some time, as George Herbert's "Country Parson" spent his spare hours on Sundays, in "reconciling neighbours that are at variance," and have induced each to see the other's position by taking each position themselves in turn. But we are not now dealing with a simple quarrel, where both parties have an equal right to feel offence; we have to consider the case in which one party has done the wrong and the other has suffered it; and where the injured, wishing to recall the injurer to himself, is yet separated by a gulf which he cannot cross.

III. We may be forgiven if we use a more lengthy illustration to serve our purpose. Let us imagine a father who is anxious to set up his son in business, and with that object makes over to him a part of his estates situated in a foreign country, and sends him abroad to supervise them. But the son proves no faithful steward of his father's trusts, and news comes home of the estates badly managed, and of money squandered and wasted. The father is compelled to read therein the evidences, not only of ignorance and thoughtlessness, but of wilful ingratitude and dishonesty: his messages of expostulation and reproof, he gathers, are left unread, or only further incite to disobedience and profligacy; until he learns at last that his son is a penniless outcast and as good as dead to him. What can he do? He would gladly take the first steamer and hasten to his boy's rescue. But that is impossible. He has public and private engagements which will not at the time admit of so long an absence; nor could a person in his position conduct a search for his son through the bazaars and alleys of a foreign city with any hope of success; for there his very dignity would alienate his son's associates and his son himself. His personal grief is intense; his commercial interests have suffered greatly, and even the good name of his family is becoming soiled and tarnished. His very love makes him the more angry. His anger makes him the more eager to "commend" his love to his son, and bring him back to penitence, obedience, and honour. But he himself is helpless; his son will not come to him; he cannot "get at" his son. Letters do no good; nor could he dream even of sending out a confidential clerk on such a mission, either for his son's sake, or for his own. He has but one resource, and one which he almost shrinks from contemplating, so great is the personal sacrifice which it involves. His elder son, who is a partner with him, is brought into the closest relations with him daily, and between the two there exists a confidence which makes the ruin of the younger son only the more bitter. It is the elder son who must go. If he cannot

MEDIATION

restore the erring lad, no one can. But though the elder son must go, it will not be as the honoured representative of a well-known name; in such a guise, he would be as helpless in the search as his father; to excite suspicion would be fatal; he must be prepared to appear as one of the ordinary inhabitants of his brother's far-off hiding-place.

The elder son, eager as his father, starts out on his mission, and soon finds the prodigal, whose very notoriety prevents a lengthened concealment. But this is merely the beginning of his task. To go up to him and say, " Come home with me," would simply drive him further off. There are mountains of suspicion to be crossed, and passionate tempests of wilful sin to be allayed. The path to win his brother demands the most skilful tact, the most unwearying patience; and his strongest appeals must be lived rather than voiced. Thus to lay siege to his brother's heart, he must enter his brother's surroundings; surroundings which will fill his pure soul with a daily and increasing horror and indignation, mingled with an overwhelming and abiding sorrow. But such a task is his father's bidding, and his own deliberate choice. This, however, is not all: to enter his brother's surroundings means to enter the shadow of his brother's shame. More deeply than the degradation of the filthy purlieus in which he lives, must he feel the touch of the blackness of his brother's soul; the constant contact with a sin, in one so near akin to him, which is entirely foreign to his own nature and his own experience. And with this shame there rises in his heart a deep displeasure and wrath at such iniquity in the son of his father—a son who is no longer a son, but whom he has to win back to sonship. The prodigal's deadened mind has almost forgotten that sin must arouse anger—such pure resentment as will from time to time break forth from his brother; he is surprised still more as he realises, in spite of himself, that this terrible sternness is joined with a tender and self-abnegating affection that softens him while he shrinks from it.

Thus the elder son proves himself the true mediator. All the wrath and all the love that have burned in the father's breast, animate his own, and are revealed before the astonished eyes of the prodigal; and, on the other side, all the shame which the prodigal should have felt, and which, if felt, would have begotten in him the healing force of penitence, he beholds in his brother's conduct, and hears in his brother's words. The elder son represents, and even, by the power of sympathy, in his own mind identifies himself with, the prodigal to his father; while at the same time he represents the father to the erring son. But his brother is not only startled; he is frightened, and frightened into antagonism. Fear of a holiness that he cannot comprehend; rage at the skill that has discovered and invaded his retreat; hatred, all the greater—paradox as it sounds—because of his brother's love, a love throbbing with sinless anger; all these hurry him into resistance to the appeal whose strength he feels, but will not acknowledge. But at last love accomplishes its perfect work; for this work, in the elder brother, does not consist simply in loving, but in laying down all that makes life valuable, and tasting the very bitterness of death, to attain his father's desire and his own—to redeem the prodigal. It would take a stronger than the poor weak-willed lad to resist such untiring force, or to close the heart for ever to the violence of such self-forgetful pity.

Slowly, then, hostility gives way to shame—the shame

MEDIATION

that is poured into his heart from his brother's. And now we begin to observe the working of that strange law of personality which we have just been considering. His brother's strong emotion communicates itself to him. What his brother felt, he now comes to feel for himself; the filial obedience he has observed in his brother, he now comes at length to desire; and shame begets in him, what it could not have begotten in his brother's unsullied heart, penitence and contrition. He has reached the point where reconciliation is actual. But the enormity of his sin now confronts him; how can he dare to return to the father whose love, recognised at last, he has outraged and trampled upon? The abyss seems to him wider than before; how can he ever make atonement? But the elder brother calms his fears. "You cannot make atonement," he says; "but your father asks for none; atonement, reconciliation, is already accomplished; I am the sign of his forgiveness; your contrition shows that you now hate the sin as he hates it himself, and as his true son must hate it. Return with me; and as he receives me, he will receive you." "I see it now," replies the younger man; "I could not face my father alone; but I can stand before him, if I can stand at your side; if he looks at you when he looks at me, I can bear his glance; and with you close to me at home, I can be a real son to him." To live that life will be hard enough; it will involve many a struggle; but success is sure.

Thus the second difficulty is conquered; the son has been brought to desire reconciliation; he has been brought to see that reconciliation is possible; he is reconciled, through his brother's sufferings, obedience, and love.

IV. The significance of this parable will be manifest.

ETHICS AND ATONEMENT

It is evident that when we wish to represent the dealings of God with man, any human analogy must at best fall far short of the truth; our eyes can follow the road that leads to the full knowledge of God, but before we see the end of the road, it has passed over the horizon. Yet there is much in our parable which corresponds to reconciliation, as we find it in the New Testament. The parable hinges on mediation, the mediation of the elder son. Now in the actual language of the New Testament, there is comparatively little about mediation. S. Paul only employs the term in two passages, in one of which he is not speaking directly of Christ; and even in the Epistle to the Hebrews, the mediator of the new or better Covenant is but three times referred to.[1] By Christ himself the word is never used. The conception, however, is found everywhere—in the Gospels, as in the rest of the New Testament. Everywhere, Christ is felt to stand midway between God and man, to bring together those persons who would otherwise have been for ever apart.[2] He called himself habitually the Son of Man; he allowed himself to be recognised and saluted as the Son of God. His mission was to be the reconciler; he came to reconcile both Jew and Greek to God through his cross; Christians are reconciled to God through the death of His Son; through Christ, God reconciles all things unto Himself; and Christ has made peace through the blood of His cross. He is the Door, the Way; no one comes unto the Father except by him.[3] Even God's love to the world

---

[1] Gal. $3^{19\ 20}$; 1 Tim. 2^5; Heb. 8^6 9^{15} 12^{24}.

[2] "Only the personal can heal the personal, and God must become man that man may come again to God."—Schelling, quoted in Fairbairn's "Christ in Modern Theology."

Eph. $2^{6\ 16}$; Rom. 5^{10}; Col. $1^{20\ 21}$; Jn. 10^9 14^6.

MEDIATION

can only issue in His sending Christ into it; only by their faith in Christ can men receive God's gift of eternal life, and of this very gift, Christ claims the power of bestowal.[1] In Christ's last prayer, as we have it recorded in Jn. 17, he speaks of himself throughout as the channel of God's best gifts; "I manifested thy name unto the men whom thou gavest me out of the world"; "the glory which thou hast given unto me, I have given unto them"; "that they may be one, even as we are one"; "these things I speak in the world, that they may have my joy fulfilled in themselves." Finally, this conception appears, not only in a theologian like S. Paul or S. John; but in the earliest preaching of the disciples at Jerusalem; to them also Christ is the sole means of restoring the relations between men and God which sin had broken; "Neither is there any name under heaven, that is given unto men, whereby we must be saved."[2]

But we can go further. To recognise fully the complete relation of Christ to God and to man, we must leave behind individual passages; we must consider what used to be spoken of in evangelical theology as the "plan of salvation"—that definite and harmonious conception of man's redemption which binds the different books of the New Testament into one volume. We start here from the point which we had previously reached, the need of reconciliation between man and God; to this need, ethical consideration had of itself led us; and as we saw, the Bible is explicit enough thereon. Unaided, man cannot get back to God, either by the sacrifices of the Jewish ritual, or by that moral life which S. Paul calls the wisdom of the Greeks; and God's magnificence,

[1] Jn. 3^{16} 10^{28}.   [2] Acts 4^{12}.

though it must needs yearn over man, cannot, by the mere force of its sinlessness, restore man to his due allegiance; all the glowing descriptions of God's moral sublimity in the prophets only leave "the high and holy place," in which He dwells, unapproachable. That holy place is not yet the new Jerusalem, wherein are enrolled the spirits of just men made perfect; it is still the mount that burned with fire, surrounded with blackness and darkness and tempest and all the terrors of Sinai. John the Baptist, the last and greatest of the prophets, could preach repentance, but he could not inculcate it; he was doomed to decrease before the light of a Sun that was to rise "with healing in its wings." In one way alone could the deadlock be solved.

And it was solved. There came one who taught in a manner which surprised every one, not because he had a new message, but because he taught "with authority," as if he were God himself. More than this, he lived as no man had ever lived before; without sin; the meekest of men, yet making the most astounding claims, not only to purity ("which of you convicteth me of sin?" he could triumphantly ask), but to divine knowledge and divine functions; a power more than man's he actually and habitually exercised, both over the body, and—far more wonderful—over the soul. He lived, in fact, as if he were God, and the people around him felt it. But he lived as man also; that is, as man would live if he were sinless. And because he was sinless, the consequences of sin were to him a far more terrible burden than they would have been to any man or woman who had sinned. In the midst of human iniquity, conscious of every human temptation, beholding every hideous consequence of sin in the disease and

MEDIATION 129

misery around him, indignant at the wide-spread ruin of ignorance and death, "he was found in fashion as a man, and became obedient unto death." Nor was this death the ordinary end of existence that must befall every man soon or late. It was the direct outcome and completion of his life. His sinlessness could not but provoke the bitterest hatred from the sinfulness round him; that hatred pursued him relentlessly and condemned him to the foulest of deaths; a death which he could have escaped with ease, had he been less faithful to his mission of representing each of the two parties,—had he consented to be less completely God or less completely man. His death, indeed, was deliberately faced and sought. But he did not seek death as the suicide seeks it. The suicide rushes to death as a means of breaking loose from life and finding a welcome oblivion. To Christ, death was the final act of his obedience, the completion of his reconciling and redeeming purpose. The two noblest heroines of Greek tragedy, Antigone, laying down her life for the laws of abstract Justice, and Alcestis, laying down hers to redeem her own husband from the power of death, chant, as their death-song, the glories and bliss of life; Christ himself, in Gethsemane, shrinks from the cup that he is to drink; but he girds himself to meet the last dread companion of human nature, with all the added terrors which it had for him, in order to consummate his Father's will,—to "redeem those who through fear of death were all their lifetime subject to bondage." It was in this way that he paid the full penalty of the sin he loathed and came to destroy, experiencing at length upon the cross all its accumulated suffering, as if he himself had been the sinner. On the cross were felt the consequences of the utmost human sin. The two thieves at the side of Christ suffered, but justly, and for their own misdoings; but he had done nothing amiss; he was bearing the sins of the world.

What was the effect on mankind? How did this suffering reconcile the injurer to the injured? Through the power of self-communication, possessed by all to whom we can attribute personality, and therefore pre-eminently by Christ. In the life and in the death of Christ, man saw God's hatred to sin, God's love to himself; and he saw his own ideal attitude, hatred to sin, obedience to God. Hence, at first, came the instinct of repulsion to one who made him hate what he had chosen. Then, as the example, the sufferings, the very spirit of Christ worked upon him, as he saw sin in its true and proper ugliness and horror, repulsion gave way to penitence. To look on the sufferer whom he has pierced, is to long to get back to God, and, with a new alarm, to feel the impossibility of doing so.[1] But his fears are calmed. He no sooner recognises that no

[1] Compare the statement of the Atonement recently made by Sir Oliver Lodge :—" The perception of something in the Universe which not only makes for righteousness, but which loves and sympathises in the process; and yet is no mere indiscriminate charity, weakly relieving a man from the consequences of his blunders or stealthily undermining his powers of self-help, but a true benevolence, which healthily and strongly and if need be sternly convinces him that the path of duty is the path of joy, that sacrifice and not selfishness is the road to the heights of existence, that it is far better to suffer wrong than to do wrong;—such a perception inevitably raises man far above 'the yelp of the beast'; 'saves' him, saves him truly, from æons of degradation, and enables him to 'stand on the heights of his life with the glimpse of a height that is higher.' Selfishness long continued must lead to isolation and so to a sort of practical extinction: it is like a disintegrating or repulsive force in the material cosmos, while unselfishness is like a cohesive and constructive force." "Suggestions towards the Re-interpretation of Christian Doctrine;" *Hibbert Journal*, vol. i. No. 7.

MEDIATION

reparation of his own can cover the extent of his sins, than he learns that to attempt to cover them is needless. Christ is no separate person acting for him; Christ is identified with him. He has been entered by Christ's hatred of sin; he can now share Christ's filial relation to God, and even, by virtue thereof, Christ's ease in the presence of God. He has passed over the abyss; he feels a new filial obedience, poured into him by the all-righteous Christ; he is the very righteousness of God in Christ, as Christ was made sin for him.[1] He is a new creature in Christ. Christ is the new self, the new person, within him. His faith in Christ, the confident flinging of himself upon Christ till he abides "in Christ" is what, in all literalness, saves him. Many a struggle there will be in the future; many a bitter memory of the past; many a bitter experience of its results in the present; but he will know that success is sure, and that defeat is at once changed to victory.

The correspondence of all this with our parable will be clear. The gulf between the injurer and the injured; the desire of the injured father to remove it; the mission of the reconciler who comes from him, and is in fullest sympathy with him; the reconciler's sufferings, borne in order to represent the father to his prodigal son, and to bring the son back to his father; the son's hatred and suspicion, gradually changed to loving repentance and an intense desire for the restoration of the old filial and natural life; the fulfilment of this desire through the emissary of the love that wrought his penitence; and the new-found obedience inspired in him by his restorer. In one point, however, the correspondence stops short. There was and could be nothing in the parable about the reconciler's death.

[1] 2 Cor. 5^{21}.

In the actual "plan of salvation," the death of Christ is not the end, but the beginning; it reveals God's love; it also reveals man's sin, as the life of Christ by itself could not do; and it is in fact regarded as imparting to man the new life and the new obedience or righteousness. As a matter of fact, the presence of the death of Christ in the evangelical account makes clear what in the parable was necessarily vague and unconvincing. Christ's death was the completion and crown of his obedience; it was the consummation of his sufferings; and it was the utmost consequence of the sin that he was bearing. It was indeed the inevitable expression and result of the nature of the sin for which he was making atonement, that the Sinless One should die. Thus was it made clear to mankind that sin was "exceeding sinful," and that it contained within itself the seeds of dissolution, which, unchecked, brought forth death. Thus, in the death of Christ, man not only felt, but saw, his own punishment; the sword hanging over his own head, had fallen on him who knew no sin. In the doom laid on Christ, he saw at once his own guilt, and his own means of escape.

The death of Christ was the means by which the life of Christ became available as the new life, the source of the new obedience, in man. The law of personal influence with which our chapter began, however real, is at best vague and obscure; the personality of one man can flow in some unknown way, and to some unknown extent, into that of another. But after Christ's death came his resurrection; and that outward event had its spiritual counterpart in the experience of every believer. The power of Christ's death showed itself as the power of an endless life. From the moment of Christ's resurrection from death, he was felt, in the clearest and most definite manner, not simply to have imparted an influence, but to be living his life in the lives of those who "believed on him," that is, who accepted him as their means of crossing the abyss, and of regaining their sonship to God. So profound is the believer's participation in the sufferings of Christ, that he cannot stop even at the point of Christ's death. He feels—he cannot help feeling—that he dies with Christ, realising that the corn of wheat must fall into the ground and die; only so can it share in the resurrection to new life. But as Christ spoiled death of its dominion, the Christian knows also that having died with Christ, the dominion of death over him is broken; he has entered the risen life along with his Saviour. In the company of Christ, he gains all that the Father has to give.

V. We have so far made no reference to what is known as Vicariousness. This has been an intentional omission. It will, we hope, be conceded that our account of Reconciliation, or Atonement, is in harmony with ethics; it is, in fact, as we have observed, just what is demanded by ethical considerations. But is it in harmony with Theology—with the true interpretation, that is, of the language of the New Testament? We must first ask what is meant by the vicariousness of Christ's sufferings. We mean that he suffered instead of us. When we call his sufferings representative, we mean that he suffered on our behalf. The difference sounds unimportant; but between the two phrases lies a whole theological gulf. To say, bluntly, that Christ suffered instead of us is inconsistent with the view taken in this chapter; it is also inconsistent, rightly understood, with the view steadfastly maintained throughout the New Testament.[1] It implies, first, that God, being angry with man for his sin, must demand a penalty; secondly, that the due penalty, if it were paid by man, would appease the wrath of God; thirdly, that the penalty demanded by God is beyond the reach of man's payment; fourthly, that Christ, seeing this, in pity to man stepped in and substituted himself, thus appeasing God and leaving man nothing else to do, save to take advantage of the arrangement.

Now, what does this mean? That God is less hostile to sin than to the doer of the sin. Sin has been committed; very well, it must be punished; the punishment is the important thing. If Christ is to bear anything instead of us, it can only be the brunt of the pain to be inflicted. It may be urged that this view is found in the well-known expression of our Lord Himself, "to give his life a ransom for," that is, instead of, "many." Now Christ's death is certainly spoken of in some passages as a ransom; but these passages are too few to allow us to think that this term expresses a habitual attitude of thought in Christ towards his sacrifice. Nor can we press the figure far; since directly we attempt to do so, and ask, "To whom was this ransom paid?"—surely not an unnatural question —we find that there is no answer; it could not have been paid to God, since there was no wish in the ransomer to induce God to give man up to some one else; nor could it have been given to the devil—a

---

[1] Compare W. B. Pope, "Compendium of Christian Theology," vol. ii. pp. 269-271; especially the words "the doctrine (of the New Testament) is not that a penalty has been endured by Christ instead of his people . . . it is rather that a sacrificial offering has been presented by him instead of the race;" that is to say, that there is a vicarious goodness, but not vicarious suffering.

gross idea that few besides Gregory of Nyssa could have dared to entertain; nor even to man's own self, since to ransom man from himself for himself is too subtle a conception even for scholastic theology. But if the Sacrifice is to be spoken of as a ransom at all, the wonder is, not that the phrase "instead of" occurs —it was hardly avoidable—but that it only occurs once.[1]

Still, this thought of Christ as our Substitute is natural enough when God is regarded as an autocrat, whether as a Byzantine Emperor, or as a Feudal monarch of Western Europe. To such a monarch, *lèse majesté* will be the one thing which he cannot endure, and the vindication of his own honour will be of far more importance to him, than the attitude of the offender, either in rebellion or in repentance. Majesty so outraged could only be satisfied by the rebel himself, or by a substitute; and it was easy for theologians to see such a substitute in Christ. The highest form of this substitutionary theory is set forth by Anselm; sin has, so to speak, cast a slur upon God; to atone for this, something more than obedience, which has been man's duty from the first, is required; man himself cannot render this something more; yet it must be rendered, and by man; hence the sinless Christ, God-man, by rendering what could never have been required from him, both satisfies God, and gains as the extra reward he is entitled to claim, the deliverance of man.

[1] δοῦναι τὴν ψυχὴν αὐτοῦ λύτρον ἀντὶ πολλῶν (Mt. 20²⁸ = Mark 10⁴). The compound ἀντίλυτρον also occurs once (1 Tim. 2⁶), but its substitutionary force is neutralised by the ὑπέρ ("on behalf of") which immediately follows. The customary word is ὑπέρ, which is used in this connexion in nearly every book of the New Testament.

It would ill become us to depreciate Anselm's work; the philosophical acuteness and religious reverence of his view drove many an idle and fantastic speculation from the field, and ushered in a new era of thought upon the whole subject. On the other hand, the royalty of the "father which is in heaven" is not one which is greatly concerned with its personal honour, and it thinks far more of the sinlessness of its subjects. To offer to God a substitute, is to misunderstand the depth of His anger toward sin, and the eagerness of His jealous desire for the sinner's return.

But it is possible to show that each of the four assertions of the substitutionary view is at variance with Biblical teaching. In the first place, we may indeed say that God is angry with man because of his sin; but if we are to describe the attitude of God with care, we must say that God is primarily angry with sin for the sake of man. Even the story of the Fall makes this clear; else, why should God, proclaiming an unconquerable enmity to the serpent, retain so burdensome a charge as the redemption of man, instead of casting him off altogether? Throughout the Old Testament, punishment, at least as regards God's "chosen people," is almost always restorative or "medicinal," not an end in itself. God does not desire to make men suffer, however rebellious they have been. What he desires is to have them back, although to bring them back, he must make them suffer. God's anger against man is gone, as soon as man returns; he then hears the promise "I will heal their backslidings, I will love them freely." The penalty is not demanded because God is angry with man, but because by means of penalty alone can man be made to realise that God is angry with sin. In the New

MEDIATION 137

Testament punishment fades out of sight before sin, forgiveness, justification.

The second assertion was that the due penalty, if it could be paid by man, would appease the wrath of God. Without this, the whole theory would fall to pieces; but there is nothing in the Bible about man's appeasing the wrath of God.[1] All that man is bidden to do is to repent and "convert," or return, in both Dispensations alike. The word "Propitiation" occurs three times in the New Testament;[2] but both S. Paul and S. John describe that propitiation as set forth by God; that is to say, it is not man that propitiates God, but, paradox as it may sound, God that propitiates Himself.

To assert, in the third place, that the penalty demanded by God is beyond the reach of man's payment, is correct simply because for sin there can be no payment, only renunciation. Otherwise, we should be in danger of falling back into the atmosphere of Romanism, which changed penitence to penance, and inspired the soothing belief that when the price had by some means or other been paid, the sin did not matter, and might even be continued on similar terms.

The fourth statement is embodied in Miss Gilbert's familiar lines:—

> " He knew how wicked men had been,
> He knew that God must punish sin;
> So out of pity Jesus said
> He'd bear the punishment instead."

[1] The ritual words, *Kipper* and *Kopher*, may have their roots in some pagan idea about appeasing the deity—covering or smearing his face, so to speak—but it is safe to say that this significance is forgotten in the ritual books of the Mosaic Law, where the " covering " is that of the sinner or the sin itself, by the priest or by God (see Driver's " Deuteronomy," p. 425). In the Prophets, the pagan significance is expressly repudiated.

[2] 1 Jn. 2^2, and 4^{10}, ἱλασμὸς, and Rom. 3^{25}, ἱλαστήριον.

But if we cannot get rid of sin by bearing the punishment, no more can Christ himself, by bearing the punishment for us; if the terms of such a transaction could be carried out at all, it would make no difference whether they were carried out by the principal or by a surety. And even if Christ's sufferings could be flung as a shield between ourselves and the punishment we deserved, we should still be left sinners as much as before. Christ might have performed penance for us; he could not have redeemed us. If redemption means the endurance of a certain amount of suffering in the place of someone else, redemption is impossible, and the words of the Psalmist are true, "None can by any means redeem his brother, nor give to God a ransom for him." The only effectual ransom, even in the Old Testament, is through prayer and penitence. The Old Testament attitude, indeed, is well summed up in the following passage in Job :—

"If there be with him (a man who is being chastened with pain) an angel, . . .

To shew unto man what is right for him,

Then he is gracious unto him, and saith,

Deliver him from going down into the pit, I have found a ransom. . . .

He prayeth unto God, and he is favourable unto him ;

So that he seeth his face with joy ;

And he restoreth unto man his righteousness.

He singeth before men, and saith,

I have sinned, and perverted that which was right,

And it profited me not ;

He hath redeemed my soul from going down into the pit."

MEDIATION

And what is true of the Old Testament is true of the New. It cannot be too strongly affirmed that there is only one doctrine of sin and redemption in the Bible. " The law was given by Moses; grace and truth came by Jesus Christ ; " yet Jesus Christ solemnly warned his hearers that every man would be judged according to his works. In both the Testaments the wages of sin is death, the gift of God is eternal life.

But we have another and severer count against this theory of substitution. It must lead us, if fully thought out, to eliminate the mercy of God, and to distinguish between the attitude of the Father, who demands the penalty from us, and that of the Son, who steps in to pay our debt. If such an interposition has taken place, we have but to appeal to God's justice, apart from any yearning love for the sinner; we are in the position of a man who has received a cheque from a friend and expects it to be honoured when he presents it at the bank. We may feel gratitude to Christ for thus interfering; but the favour of Christ renders needless any favour from God. Such a distinction between the Father and the Son is its own refutation.

There is indeed a substitution and an interposition ; but it is not this. Christ did bear something for us; but it was not the punishment ; it was the sin.

> " The burden, for me to sustain
> Too great, on thee, my Lord, was laid ;
> To heal me, thou hast borne my pain ;
> To bless me, thou a curse wast made."

The burden of sin, too great for the prodigal to bear, or even to realise, was laid on the mediator ; there was laid on him, that is to say, the iniquity of the sinner, who, though he had committed the sins, was both too weak and too unstable, ever to bear them himself. By his voluntary self-identification with the sinner's degradation, the mediator may even be said to have been made a curse on the sinner's behalf, so that he might extend blessing to him who had merited nothing but his father's curse. "He was wounded for our transgressions, he was bruised for our iniquities; the chastisement of our peace was upon him; and with his stripes we were healed"; "The chastisement of our peace" is the discipline which led to our peace—though, had it been exerted simply upon us, it could have led to nothing save more rebellion. It led to our righteousness also; "by his knowledge shall my righteous servant make many righteous."[1] God's abiding claim for righteousness from us has still to be met. The difference is, that now, through our Redeemer, we are able to meet it.

Christ, then, was not our Substitute, in the popular sense of that term, as bearing the pain instead of us. As we have seen, it is far nearer the truth to call him our representative. But in what sense can he be called by this name? Not simply that he is identified with us, so that his act is our act; not simply that we send him as our ambassador to God; nor again that God sends him as his ambassador to us. Rather, he is *the* Representative, the Mediator, from each side to the other; he comes down from God to us; he suffers for us; he brings God close to us; and we

---

[1] *Cf.* G. A. Smith's "Isaiah," vol. ii. pp. 353 ff.; Delitzsch's Isaiah, vol. ii. pp. 293, 309 (Engl. Ed., 1894). "The vicariousness which this passage represents is not the vicariousness of literal substitution and legal transfer, but the vicariousness of real experience, in which the faithful and righteous bear on their heart the woes and burdens entailed by the careless and the sinful."—G. B. Stevens, "The Christian Doctrine of Salvation," p. 122.

through him are brought close to God, and live his life before God.[1]

But the question may now be asked, If Christ did not bear our sufferings instead of us, have we still to bear them ourselves? When, by his knowledge, the Servant made us righteous, did he fail to set us free from pain? Suffering he has certainly left possible to us; but this is not because of his failure, but because of his success. He came to call sinners to repentance. But repentance is no flowery path to contentment; it is a long and arduous passage from wrong to right. The sting of suffering, as of death, is sin; and it is this which has been removed for us, by Christ. For the true exposition of repentance, we might turn to Dante, the Poet of Repentance. Medieval Catholic as he is, he will have no bargaining with God; he sees clearly enough that God looks forward and not back, or that he looks back only because of the inevitable influence of the past on the future. Sin, even when it has been pardoned, entails suffering; life, even after justification, involves growth; and though in the picturesque setting of his poem, he places the process beyond the grave, his "Purgatorio" is simply a long comment on S. Paul's command, "work out your own salvation with fear and trembling." The dwellers in Dante's Purgatory are men and women who have experienced the assurance of forgiveness; they are "saved"; they walk in the light; their victory is assured; but though their joy is supreme, their sufferings are even greater than before, inasmuch as they now realise the perfection of the righteousness which their sin has offended. Oderisi, cramped and bowed to the ground

---

[1] These two meanings of substitution are well brought out in T. H. Green, Lecture on "Justification by Faith." Works, vol. iii. p. 194.

beneath his burden on the terrace of Pride, and Guido Guinicelli, disappearing within the flame-wreath on the terrace of Unchastity, can praise God as joyfully as the saints in the Rose of Heaven, though their body be enduring anguish; and Buonconte, preserved from falling into hell by "one little tear" of repentance in the hour of his mortal weakness, is content to wait for unspecified years outside the actual gate of Purgatory, because he knows that hell's angel has been finally robbed of his prey.

Other considerations remain; but they must be left over for subsequent chapters. Why God is angry with sin; how and why He punishes it; how the Christian feels himself forgiven through the death of Christ, and how Christ is made one with the human race, and at the same time is divine—of all these questions we have but touched the fringe. But the answers to them must depend on Christ's position as Mediator; this we have tried to study; and our study has at least convinced us that the accusations of immorality, levelled so often against the Atonement, can only hit, not the doctrine itself, but a misconception that obscures the real truth which they attempt to damage. There is no baseness, and no legal fiction in the Atonement; all the noblest instincts of mankind, all the unselfish struggling to raise a fallen brother, all the intense determination to overcome evil with good, all the passionate yearning for righteousness, all the deep loathing of impurity, and the indignant enmity against death, selfishness, and dissolution, are "writ large" in the mediating work of Christ.

MEDIATION

NOTE TO CHAPTER V.

It is impossible to prove any theory of the Atonement by quoting texts. Passages can be adduced with equal cogency to support the most diverse views of this great theological fact, and to destroy them. Again, there is no passage in the New Testament which contains a careful elaboration of the doctrine. Even the *locus classicus* in Rom. iii. cannot for a moment claim to be exhaustive. As we pointed out in chapter iv., the single yet complex view of the central figure of the Atonement is presented in ways as diverse as are the characters of the individual writers. Exactly the same is true of the Atonement itself. The Mediator is successively represented as the Shepherd who lays down his life for the sheep, the ransom, the advocate, the propitiation, the sacrificial lamb, and the priest who makes the Atonement for the sins of the people. We are redeemed by his blood, his death, and even his obedience. The representation is surprisingly many-sided, yet each of these many sides is referred to as a matter of familiar thought that needs no enlargement, by nearly every one of the sacred writers. Somehow or other an elaborate conception of the Atonement had very early taken shape and spread through the various circles of Christian thought and preaching. We must explain and amplify "scripture by scripture" in order that we may collect the scattered fragments of the picture into one whole. This will inevitably entail the treatment of passages apart from their context; but the dangers of this proceeding are minimized by the fact that many of the so-called Atonement passages stand curiously clear of their surroundings; it is therefore all the easier to fit them into the larger context of the general plan of the New Testament teaching on this subject.

In this note an attempt is made to show how each of the elements in our interpretation is borne out by the actual words of the New Testament. Some of the more familiar passages have been already referred to in the text. Others which may seem to militate with our view will be dealt with in subsequent chapters. We subjoin at the end of our citations a more detailed reference to Romans 3^{21-26}.

1. *The Gulf between God and Man caused by Sin.*

"God hath shut up all unto disobedience."—Rom. 11^{32}.

"The scripture hath shut up all things under sin."—Gal. 3^{22}.

"You, when ye were dead through your trespasses and sins

144 ETHICS AND ATONEMENT

... and were by nature children of wrath even as the rest."—Eph. 2^{1-3}.

2. *God's Desire to bridge the Gulf.*

"God so loved the world that he sent his only begotten son."—Jn. 3^{16}.

"Herein is love, not that we loved God, but that he loved us and sent his son to be the propitiation for our sins."—1 Jn. 4^{10}.

"He that spared not his own son, but delivered him up for us all, how shall he not also, with him, freely give us all things?"—Rom. 8^{32}.

3. *Christ's willingness to act as Reconciler.*

"The son of man is not come to be ministered unto, but to minister, and to give his life a ransom for many."—Matt. 22^{28}.

"My meat is to do the will of him that sent me, and to accomplish his will."—Jn. 4^{34}.

"I and the Father are one."—Jn. 10^{30}.

"Even as thou gavest him authority over all flesh; that whatsoever thou hast given him, to them he should give eternal life."—Jn. 17^2.

4. *Christ represents God in Humanity.*

"One Mediator between God and men, himself man, Christ Jesus, who gave himself a ransom for all."—1 Tim. $2^{5\ 6}$.

"God sent forth his son, born of a woman, born under the law."—Gal. 4^4.

"He that hath seen me hath seen the Father."—Jn. 14^8.

5. *Christ feels as Man feels.*

"We have not an High Priest that cannot be touched with the feeling of our infirmities, but one that hath been in all points tempted like as we are, yet without sin."—Heb. 4^{15}.

"The Son of man hath not where to lay his head."—Matt. 8^{20}.

"Jesus, therefore, being wearied with his journey, sat thus by the way."—Jn. 4^6.

"Jesus wept."—Jn. 11^{35}.

"When Jesus had thus said, he was troubled in the spirit, and testified and said, 'Verily, verily, I say unto you, that one of you shall betray me.'"—Jn. 13^{21}.

(Compare the whole narrative of Gethsemane.)

6. *Christ feels as Man should feel towards Sin.*

"When he had looked round about on them with anger, being grieved with the hardening of their hearts."—Mark 3^5.

MEDIATION

"He beheld the city and wept over it."—Luke 19⁴¹.
"Through the obedience of the one shall the many be made righteous."—Rom. 5¹⁹.
"God, sending his own son in the likeness of sinful flesh, and as an offering for sin, condemned sin in the flesh."—Rom. 8³.

7. *Christ bears our sin.*

"Who his own self bare our sins in his body on the tree."— 1 Pet. 2²⁴.
"Christ also, having been once offered to bear the sins of men."—Heb. 9²⁸.

Under this heading we might refer to the passages which speak of Christ as the Lamb, the victim, which, in the Old Testament language, bears the sin of the offerer :—

"Behold the Lamb of God which taketh away the sin of the world."—Jn. 1²⁹.
"I saw in the midst of the throne . . . a lamb standing as though it had been slain. . . . Worthy is the lamb that hath been slain to receive the power."—Rev. 5⁶ ¹².

And, with a slightly different reference,

"Our passover also hath been sacrificed, even Christ."— 1 Cor. 5⁷.

8. *Christ dies for us.*

"The good shepherd giveth his life for the sheep."—Jn. 10¹¹.
"Greater love hath no man than this, that a man lay down his life for his friends."—Jn. 15¹³.
"While we were yet weak, Christ in due season died for the ungodly."—Rom. 5⁶.
"Who gave himself for our sins."—Gal. 1⁴.
"That by the grace of God he should taste death for every man."—Heb. 2⁹.

It is noticeable that in all these passages "for" is ὑπέρ, "on behalf of."

9. *We die through him.*

"I have been crucified with Christ."—Gal. 2²⁰.
"Our old man was crucified with him, that the body of sin might be done away."—Rom. 6⁶, *cp.* 5¹¹.
"We thus judge that one died for all, therefore all died."— 2 Cor. 5¹⁴.
"Ye died and your life is hid with Christ in God."—Col. 3³.

146 ETHICS AND ATONEMENT

10. *Reconciliation, Forgiveness, Cleansing, through Christ.*

" For if, while we were enemies, we were reconciled to God by the death of his son, much more, being reconciled, shall we be saved by his life."

"Jesus Christ, through whom we have now received the reconciliation."—Rom. $5^{10\ 11}$.

Other reconciliation passages have already been quoted in the text.—*Cp.* Eph. $2^{14\ 15}$. "He is our peace . . . having abolished in his flesh the enmity."

"God was in Christ reconciling the world unto himself."— 2 Cor. 5^{19}.

"Through his name every one that believeth on him shall receive remission of sins."—Acts 10^{43}.

"In whom we have our redemption through his blood, the forgiveness of our trespasses."—Eph. 1^7.

"Thou wast slain and didst purchase unto God men of every tribe and tongue."—Rev. 5^9.

"How much more shall the blood of Christ . . . cleanse your conscience from dead works to serve the living God?"—Heb. 9^{14}.

"That he might sanctify the people through his own blood."— Heb. 13^{12}.

"The blood of Jesus his son cleanseth us from all sin."—1 Jn. 1^7.

For this special reference to the blood of Christ see pp. 185 ff.

11. *New life in Christ.*

"Even so reckon ye yourselves dead unto sin, but alive unto God in Christ Jesus."—Rom. 6^{11}.

"If ye then be risen with Christ."—Col. 3^1.

"Of him are ye in Christ Jesus, who was made unto us wisdom from God and righteousness and sanctification and redemption." —1 Cor. 1^{30}.

"Wherefore if any man is in Christ he is a new creature."— 2 Cor. 5^{17}.

"Of his fulness we all received."—Jn. 1^{16}.

Cp. "As many as received him to them gave he the right to become the children of God."—*v.* 12.

"Unto him that loveth us and loosed us from our sins by his blood; and he made us to be a kingdom, to be priests unto his God and Father."—Rev. $1^{5\ 6}$.

In the passage in Rom. 3, the following points are emphasised :

MEDIATION

1. The aim of God is, to manifest His own righteousness and to bring about righteousness in man.—*vv.* 21 and 26.
2. All alike have sinned.—*v.* 23.
3. The gulf is crossed from the side of God through Christ.—*vv.* 24 and 25.
4. The salvation of man is through faith in Christ.—*v.* 25.
5. And through faith man is justified.—*v.* 26.

It will be noticed that in this passage nothing is said of the sufferings of Christ, much less of his bearing any penalty. He is set forth as a propitiation to show God's righteousness.—*v.* 25. Does "justification" mean making righteous or counting as righteous? If our interpretation is correct this long standing dispute will be at an end. As we have seen, it is by faith in Christ that the sinner receives, flowing into his own life, the life of Christ. He is thus able, through Christ, to take up Christ's attitude before God, and to live a life of obedience to God, to stand before God in the attitude of Christ. Because of the first he becomes righteous, because of the second he is counted righteous. By one and the same act of faith he enters into the new filial relation, through Christ; and manifests the new filial obedience, in Christ.

It was stated on p. 90 that the conception of the suffering Messiah binds together the Old and New Testaments. The remedial suffering, which in this passage S. Paul does not emphasize, has already been set forth once for all in Messianic prophecy in the 53rd chapter of Isaiah. So completely did the prophet grasp the extent of this timeless act, that every writer in the New Testament felt it needless to enlarge thereon : it was enough to quote his words. If there is a silken thread of Redemption running through the Bible, its colour surely gleams forth scarlet in this transcendent description of him by whose stripes we are healed.

But Christ is something more even than Atonement : he is Life (John 2^{25}). He made Atonement for us because to do so was the fullest expression of himself : he could not have avoided the cross : he could not save himself. We may therefore fitly close our list of passages by quoting the two great statements, not uttered with direct reference to the Atonement, but as the Laws of Life :—

"Except a grain of wheat fall into the earth and die, it abideth by itself alone : but if it die it beareth much fruit."—John 12^{24}.

"He that loveth his life loseth it : and he that hateth his life in this world shall keep it unto life eternal."—*v.* 25.

CHAPTER VI

ANGER AND FORGIVENESS

I. HITHERTO the argument has led us forward, step by step. We have seen that the ordinary systems of ethics leave us with a demand for a reconciliation. And we have seen how precisely the reconciliation which is demanded is supplied by the New Testament presentation of the Atonement. In the New Testament we have the complete type, the ἰδέα, as Plato would put it, of all imperfect human reconciliations, of all the means, that is to say, whereby broken human relations are restored. But we have not yet exhausted all the aspects of this typical reconciliation. We have still to deal with the wrath of God. For this we may seem hardly to have left a place. Yet it is there, as we shall see, and it is overlooked in neither the Old Testament nor the New. In most treatises on the Atonement it occupies an important place, in some the most important place. The Atonement implies propitiation. A person who is propitiated is presumed to be angry. When he is propitiated he forgives, and forgiveness, again, implies the putting away of wrath.

This is to approach the subject from the standpoint of the person offended. On the other side, in the mind of the sinner, the very sense of sin rouses fear, either of the law he has transgressed, or of the person who represents that law. The consciousness that I have deserved punishment makes me tremble at the thought there is some one to punish me. I tremble the more when I

ANGER AND FORGIVENESS 149

reflect that that some one is not man but God. From Lucretius to Herbert Spencer the root of religion itself has been sought in fear; not simply fear of powers greater than man's, but of those powers as offended and avenging. *Primus in orbe deos fecit timor.* The modern evolutionist, when he asserts, with a far wider knowledge of paganism than Lucretius possessed, that religion is born from the fear of ghosts or departed ancestors, is able to point out that all religions have their aspect of terror. And every missionary will agree that, to the heathen at least, there has been given the spirit of fear, shown by a thousand cruelties willingly practised and patiently endured. The dark mysteries of the Arician Grove, the hideous tortures and self-mutilations of Indian devotees and African wizards, the human sacrifices practised at some period in every land from Britain to the Polynesian isles, and offered in the forests of Greece even while Paul was preaching at Athens, suggest the anger of gods unknown, and therefore feared the more.[1] With human sacrifice the Old Testament has made us familiar. The interesting and remarkable passage in 2 Kings 3 relates that the king of Moab, in desperate straits from the attack of the king of Israel and his allies, as a last resort, sacrificed his eldest son, and that when this became known to the allies, including Jehoshaphat, king of Judah, they refused to fight any longer against an enemy who had taken such potent means to change the anger of his god into favour. The fear and consternation roused in times of danger, have always reflected themselves in contemporary religion,

---

[1] The prolonged initiation ceremonies of the Australian aborigines and many other primitive tribes prove that the infliction of pain is not always the result of fear. See Spencer and Gillen, "Native Tribes of Central Australia," p. 329, and G. S. Hall's "Adolescence," vol. ii., p. 232.

150   ETHICS AND ATONEMENT

for races who live hard lives always have hard gods; and the religion of Israel itself, as the prophetic writings make abundantly clear, lost its brightness in an unnatural gloom when the national horizon became overcast and stormy.

Nor has Christianity been altogether free from these influences. It will not be denied that the dominant note of early Christianity, as of every great revival that has followed it, is one of joy and exultation, a note strikingly echoed in the early inscriptions of the catacombs. But the great formative periods of Christian theology have been times of strain and stress and even of paralysing terror. Augustine, elaborating the doctrine of grace while Alaric was sweeping over Europe; Anselm, writing his "Cur Deus Homo" amidst the fierce struggle of the papacy with emperors and kings for the right of investitures; Aquinas, composing his "Summa Theologiæ" when the quarrels of pope and emperor divided Christendom into two hostile camps and when the words of Bernard of Clairvaux seemed to be truer than when they were written, "Hora novissima, tempora pessima sunt, vigilemus"; Luther, whose doctrine of justification by faith was proclaimed in the years that saw the mad outbreak of the Peasants' War, and elaborated during the ghastly desolation of the thirty years' struggle,—have stamped all subsequent theology, as no others have done, with their vigorous creative personalities, but have also darkened it with the gloom which surrounded their days and nights of thought. Their views of God and their presentment of salvation were alike tinged with not a little austerity born of their environment as well as of their own character, and we shall not be surprised if their minds were thus led to dwell on those darker

ANGER AND FORGIVENESS

passages of the Bible which dealt with judgment, anger, and retribution.

II. But this is just the point at which ethics would seem to come into collision with religion once more. In ordinary ethics anger is a thing to be regarded with suspicion. Anger is never predicated of the good man save in certain extenuating circumstances. To attribute it to God is almost to deify immorality. To Greek philosophical thought anger in the deity was abhorrent. To Plato anger in its noblest form was at best an ally of that part in man which was akin to the divine. Aristotle allowed his deity no passion, least of all anger. In Buddhism, that curious amalgam of ethics, religion, and agnosticism, anger, in common with all desire, is expressly forbidden, and is indeed the direct opposite of the gentle lowliness which has made Buddha the idol of half Asia. In the ethics of the self-assertive West, we should have thought anger would have occupied a more prominent or at least a more definite place. As a matter of fact this is not so; and indeed, except in writers so outspoken as Hobbes and Mandeville, ethics has generally refrained from recognizing the existence of man's elemental passions and impulses.

Three influences have aided this result. The tendency of all utilitarianism to regard man as a machine, moved by hopes and fears, incentives and deterrents, leaves no scope for anger. You cannot be angry with an engine or a brute. In the next place the type of character which we call Machiavellian,—whose representatives, perhaps, have been more prominent than numerous,—finds anger equally illogical, though for a different reason. Bacon, our English Machiavelli, admits that "to seek to extinguish anger utterly is but a bravery of the stoics," yet asks, "why should I be angry with a

152 ETHICS AND ATONEMENT

man for loving himself better than me? And if any man should do wrong merely out of ill-nature, why yet it is but like the thorn or briar which prick and scratch because they can do no other." A nobler element of opposition to anger has arisen from that spirit of gentleness which has voiced itself in Europe, as in Asia, in varying tones for the last twenty centuries. The gentleness of Buddha has been rivalled in the writings of Seneca and Epictetus, and the influence of Christianity, leaving these far behind, has created a wide-spread enthusiasm for humanitarianism even where its more specific teachings have been overlooked. Many an opponent of revealed religion has exalted sympathy and altruism to a degree which would make us think that anger had almost been eradicated from human nature.

Against all this there has been but a single important protest; it came from the "modern Aristotle," Bishop Butler. Butler believed in the necessity of resentment; though for his sermon on the subject he chose as his text, significantly enough, the words, "Love your enemies"; nor has he a word to say in favour of the anger whose object is the person who has done the wrong. The value of his discussion is rather psychological than moral, and consists in the emphasis he lays on anger as that which is naturally aroused against vice. "Every man naturally feels indignation upon seeing instances of villainy and baseness, and therefore cannot commit the same without being self-condemned." He goes on pertinently to add, in his somewhat awkward way, "we should learn to be cautious lest we charge God foolishly by ascribing that to him, or the nature he has given us, which is owing wholly to our own abuse of it."

ANGER AND FORGIVENESS 153

S. Paul himself bade his followers "be angry and sin not," but he also gave them the caution against "letting the sun go down upon their wrath." No book has exalted forgiveness as the New Testament has dared to exalt it. The teacher who bade forgive until "seventy times seven," who commanded his disciples not to resist evil, went further and expressly identified the sin of anger with that of murder. He himself, as it was remarked of him, was content to endure also the gainsaying of sinners; while the same qualities that he looked for in man and showed in himself he found even in God. "Be ye merciful as your heavenly Father also is merciful, for he is kind to the unthankful and the evil." The mercifulness of God, indeed, is emphasised throughout the whole Bible, in words which for familiarity, as for beauty, have never been surpassed. The Psalmists, the Prophets, and the Apostles vie with one another in exalting the love and the grace of him whose "loving-kindness is in the heavens," and who "daily beareth our burdens";[1] of whom they could say, "In all their afflictions he was afflicted . . . in his love and in his pity he redeemed them";[2] "I will heal their backslidings, I will love them freely";[3] "God commendeth his own love toward us";[4] "I am persuaded that neither . . . height nor depth nor any other creature shall be able to separate us from the love of God";[5] and more significant still, "God is love."[6]

Can it then be surprising that wrath should seem irreconcilable with such a presentation of God, or that

---

[1] Ps. 36^5 68^{19}.   [2] Is. 63^3.
[3] Hos. 14^4, where the words immediately follow "for mine anger is turned away from them."
[4] Rom. 5^8.   [5] Rom. $8^{38\ 39}$.   [6] 1 Jn. 4^{16}.

154 ETHICS AND ATONEMENT

a theologian should confidently write, "The notion of the affection of wrath in God has no religious worth for Christians, but is an unfixed and formless *Theologumenon*."[1] The familiar couplet of the quaker poet:

> "Nothing can be good in him
> Which evil is in me,"

aptly expresses our modern feeling that anger, evil in us, is incompatible with the idea of God. We can hardly tolerate, in these days, the reading of those "imprecatory psalms" where God is represented as blasting his enemies, or even where he is implored to do so; still less can we conceive that God should be angry with the human race as a whole. What we have learnt from the Bible about God's love makes us shrink from that which we read in the Bible about God's wrath; the New Testament has educated us to discount what has often been presented to us, by its foes, as New Testament theology; the very fortress to be attacked has been the armoury to provide weapons for its assailants.

III. But if wrath is really so foreign to the nature of God as revealed in the Bible, we must in fairness ask, how it came and still comes to be attributed to him. Does Theology persist in calmly denying the most sacred convictions of Ethics? Or, to ask a question which must necessarily come first, What really is the place of wrath in the Bible? The great characters of the Old Testament undoubtedly exhibit wrath, and even, on occasion, ferocity; but we can no more conclude from this that the Bible commends such feelings than we can conclude that the Bible commends falsehood or lust. On the other hand, instances of forbearance and

---

[1] Ritschl, "The Christian Doctrine of Justification and Reconciliation."

ANGER AND FORGIVENESS 155

forgiveness in their histories are just as prominent, and, considering the state of society at the time, far more remarkable. In the prophets, again, are strong and unsparing denunciations, all the more perplexing because spoken expressly on behalf of God. S. Paul might be almost echoing the tone of the prophets when he said "Behold the goodness and severity of God." "Therefore is the anger of the Lord kindled against his people; . . . for all this his anger is not turned away, but his hand is stretched out still." "Wherefore my fury and mine anger was poured forth, and was kindled in the cities of Judah."[1]

It is noticeable that this wrath of God is said to burn as fiercely against Israel as against the surrounding nations of heathenism; against the very people, that is, towards whom the tenderest care is manifested; "he will rejoice over thee with joy; he will rest in his love; he will joy over thee with singing."[2] "I will be as the dew unto Israel."[3] The prophetic attitude, indeed, in denunciation, is that of Amos; "You only have I known of all the families of the earth; therefore will I visit upon you all your iniquities";[4] a passage which is echoed with striking fidelity by the Psalmist; "Also unto thee, O Lord, belongeth mercy; for thou renderest to every man according to his work."[5] Here, the narrow and nationalist view is transcended, but the principle that God's love and God's wrath must go together, is the same. What could be more relentless than the following—"He cast upon them (the Egyptians) the fierceness of his anger . . . he made a path for his anger";[6] or the terrible passage in which Ezekiel, trembling at

[1] Is. 5^{25}; Jer. 44^6.   [2] Zeph. 3^{17}.   [3] Hos. 14^5.
[4] *Cf.* Dt. 28^{63}; Am. 3^2.   [5] Ps. 62^{12}.   [6] Ps. $78^{49\ 50}$.

156   ETHICS AND ATONEMENT

the thought that Jehovah will destroy all the residue of Israel, receives the reply, " Mine eye shall not spare, neither will I have pity, but I will bring their way upon their head."[1]

All these, it may be urged, and the numerous kindred passages, are not worthy of serious attention; they are simply projections of the writer's personal feelings of indignation and resentment into what he conceives to be the mind of God; and they are to be classed with the "barbaric" commands to "go and smite Amalek and . . . slay both man and woman, infant and suckling, ox and sheep, camel and ass"[2] and to "destroy all the places wherein the nations which ye shall possess served their gods; . . . and ye shall destroy their name out of that place,"[3] or the statements that "Jehovah will have his foes in derision."[4] But what shall we say of the actual words of Christ? If not "barbaric," they are even more severe. "Woe unto thee, Chorazin; woe unto thee, Bethsaida . . . it shall be more tolerable for the land of Sodom in the day of judgment than for thee."[5] "Whoso shall cause one of these little ones that believe in me to stumble, it is profitable for him that a great millstone should be hanged about his neck, and that he should be sunk in the depths of the sea"; "so shall also my Heavenly Father do unto you (be wroth and deliver to the tormentors), if ye forgive not every one his brother from your hearts"; "Then shall (the king) say . . . Depart from me, ye cursed, into the eternal fire, which is prepared for the devil and his angels."[6] Could anything be more significant than the reiterated woes hurled by Christ against the

[1] Ezek. $9^{8\ 10}$. [2] 1 Sam. 15^3. [3] Dt. $12^{2\ 3}$.
[4] Ps. 2^4 59^8. [5] Mt. 11^{24}. [6] Mt. $18^{6\ 35}$ 25^{41}.

ANGER AND FORGIVENESS 157

Pharisees and the lawyers, which are reproduced by S. Luke as well as by S. Matthew, or the narrative of the cleansing of the Temple with the peremptory scourge of small cords at the outset of his ministry, which we owe to S. John? Not even the most frightful passages of the Apocalypse, with all its images of torment borrowed from Old Testament poetry, can eclipse the uncompromising sternness of the gentle prophet of Nazareth.

The same impression, it must be confessed, is gathered from the judgments of God narrated or foretold in the Bible, the fall of Sodom, of Tyre, of Babylon; and the great disasters of history have inevitably appealed to readers of the Bible as God's vengeance wrought upon a deliberately sinful world. The destruction of Jerusalem, the ravages of Attila, "the scourge of God," or the terrors of the earthquake at Lisbon, seemed to contemporaries to show a persistence of anger as bitter as any of the dark foreshadowings of the prophets of Judah.

But, it will be urged, is not all this—including even the words of Christ himself—tinged with what we call anthropomorphism? Have we not been guilty of the old folly of supposing that God is "altogether such an one as ourselves"? And what right have we, because we are angry with opponents or evil-doers, to imagine that God is angry also? The reply is simple. If we cannot credit God with our wrath, neither can we credit him with our gentleness and humanity. To the majority of mankind, even at the present day, whether on the burning plains of India, in the malarial jungles of Africa, or among the volcanoes of the Southern seas, to speak of the love of God would seem far more of a self-projection of the human into the divine, than to speak of his wrath. If we are to gather the divine character from nature, there is as much evidence for wrath as for mercy. But if we are to gather it from the Bible, we shall find little evidence for a God who either only hates or only loves. In God, as our quotations above have hinted, hate and love are corollaries of one another, and cannot exist apart; God is represented as one who, to borrow the words used of a medieval disciple of the prophets, loves well because he hates,—"hates the evil that hated loving."

This may sound a paradox; and the whole presentation of God's anger in the Bible, we must admit, would be paradoxical, were it not for the attitude of Christ. But here, as in every other point, if we have seen Christ, we have seen the Father. Apart from Christ, the God who poured out such bitter wrath even against his own chosen people, might well seem irreconcilable with the God who is slow to anger and of great kindness, who hath not dealt with us after our sins, nor rewarded us after our iniquities. Further, Christ's own conduct might easily be thought hopelessly inconsistent, even soft hearted, to the Pharisees, who after having been reproached most bitterly for their accounted virtues, saw him refuse to condemn a woman taken in gross sin. Christ's anger was real; but it was the hate of hate and the scorn of scorn; it was no capricious outburst of petulance or wounded pride; he could heal the ear of Malchus; he could pray for the rough soldiers as they jeered at his suffering upon the cross; but for hypocrisy, callousness and pride he had no mercy. It was not the single act, however sinful, that roused the slumbering fire of his wrath; it was the attitude of self-sufficiency recognizing the need of no saviour and therefore finding no salvation. It was the plant poisoned from the root that he would cast into the fire. The act

ANGER AND FORGIVENESS 159

could be pruned, as it were, and cut away from the vine, by the hand of the skilful and tender husbandman. It is when the savour is lost that the salt can only be cast forth to be trodden underfoot of men. And yet, greatest paradox of all in this man of paradoxes, he came to seek and to save that which was lost.

Now let us look at the question in another way. It does not need a Dante to show us that these Christ-abhorred sins are also just the sins towards which no self-respecting man could show mercy. Wisdom is justified of her children. This is true also of the Old Testament. What are the objects of God's hatred? Fraud and deceit, high-handed violence, ingratitude, perversion of justice, and all the nameless abominations of heathendom;—"let none of you imagine evil in your heart against his neighbour, and love no false oath, for all these are things that I hate, saith the Lord."[1] Is that a hatred which can be put down to "anthropomorphism" or the national ferocity of the Jews?

For other nations it might be true to say, "Sua cuique deus fit dira cupido" (each turns his own fierce desire into a god). Those who would accuse Israel of making this mistake must remember that it was a prophet of Israel who likened the love of God to the boundless tenderness of a husband winning back to himself a "wife of whoredom"; and it was another who prophesied that Israel should be a third with Egypt and Assyria. There is no more striking attribute of God in the Old Testament than his "jealousy." To the character of God, as we conceive it, nothing could seem more alien. Of all the vices of human nature none is more contemptible than jealousy. But this jealousy of God is of a different

[1] Zech. 8^{17}.

fibre. There is a great difference between jealousy for a person and jealousy against him. Human jealousy often takes the latter shape, God's always the former. It is the consuming zeal for his people's devotion and obedience and his impatience at its being withheld which the term always expresses;—the zeal that would take fire at any obstacle placed between that love and its object, that would flame forth to consume the heathen who enticed away Israel from their allegiance, as well as to scorch the Israelite who after the false imaginations of his own heart hankered after these heathen abominations. Jealousy can be a very noble passion; it was entirely noble when it made Christ recall to those who saw him the words, "the zeal of thine house hath eaten me up."

Such is the Biblical presentation of anger. It springs from love and works for love. It may be said to illustrate the axiom of Bacon that "great bodies move violently to their place, calmly in their place." It rises when the true course of love is impeded, when the right relations are broken. It is a *vis medicatrix* which from the beginning makes for the removal of the obstacle, and, in the act of removing it, expires.

IV. But now let us turn back to ethics. Will ethics dare to assert that all anger is unconditionally wrong? Would it be a crime to be angry with Iago or with Fagin? Would not the crime consist in abstaining from anger? For Wilberforce, agitated to the roots of his being by the wrongs inflicted upon a race who had no claim upon him save the claim of humanity; for Gladstone, goaded to passionate invective by the contemplation of the sufferings of tortured Bulgaria; or for the quiet American woman, friend of Whittier and of Emerson, who flung away her literary reputation in stern wrath at the wrongs of "that class of American citizen commonly called Negro,"[1] can we have anything but complete sympathy and unstinted applause? The character of anger is decided by its object. This much we have made plain. If I am asked, "Doest thou well to be angry?" I can only answer the question as I answer the two others, "Why am I angry?" and "With what am I angry?" To be angry simply because I have been injured, to wreak my vengeance like a spoiled child on the person or thing that has thwarted me,—there is no morality in that. But anger may be the highest form of altruism. When the mind is irradiated with the flame of anger against tyranny or meanness, high-handed violence or slavish cunning, anger is then simply virtue in operation. In the first case, when my anger follows the wrong that I have suffered, real or fancied, it is the child of weakness; in the second, when it follows a wrong suffered by one whom I love, it is the child of strength.

The fact is that the more one truly loves a person, the more one hates his weakness or his sin. An employer will think but lightly of a misdemeanour that will bring fierce displeasure to a father's heart. Tolstoi has admirably illustrated this in his story of the resurrection of a dead soul. The very love that made Nehludoff join the Russian convicts in their awful journey to Siberia, that he might rescue the ruined Maslova, only made his loathing of her sin the more poignant. The mother who discovers the seeds of vice in her child, is seized with a whirl of anger and disgust against the mortal enemy that is threatening the moral life of her loved one. Her

[1] See the "Letters of Maria L. Child."

very mother-love only intensifies her loathing, and sharpens her determination to rescue him, at whatever cost of his own suffering or of hers, from what is death to him, and therefore worse than death to her. It is in this sense that we often affirm "God loves the sinner but hates the sin."

This distinction, however, is not always easy to maintain. The wrong-doer may be overtaken in a fault, and then quickly try to repent and return to the place where he was before; or he may hold to it, and continue to identify himself, as it were, with it. There is no such thing as sin in the abstract. If I fall, and having fallen, try to rise, I repudiate the carelessness that made me stumble; that carelessness ceases to exist. But if, having done the wrong, I refuse to turn from it, the wrong is not only past but present; the sin is not only something that I have done, but something that is in me. He who says, "Evil, be thou my good," identifies evil, not only with his good, but with himself. Thus, to hate the sin becomes necessarily to hate the sinner. Your friend, temporarily in need of money, betrays a secret you have committed to him. You despise the fault, while you long to receive the culprit back into the old friendship. But if your friend proceeds to brazen it out, and refuses to utter a word of penitence or of regret, your dislike of the treachery becomes inevitably dislike of the traitor.[1] A son, as in our illustration in the last chapter, leaves his father's home, disobeys his father's bidding, and comes near to breaking his father's heart. How is he regarded? With love? Yes, but with a stern pity also, which will

---

[1] Compare the way in which Percy Dacier's regard for Diana Warwick changed to contempt on his discovery that she had sold to a newspaper the state secret with which he had entrusted her. See George Meredith's "Diana of the Crossways."

be felt by him (if he can feel at all), and by his father also, as anger. What is it that has broken the filial bond and ruined the father's hopes ? The lad's sin. But if the lad holds to that sin, persists in it, refuses to be separated from it, acknowledges it defiantly as his own act and deed, it is he who is responsible, and it is on him—contradictory as this may seem—that his father's anger must fall.

This is not to assert that there need be any irritation in the father's mind; irritation is swallowed up in the far nobler emotion of righteous indignation. Such indignation would be strong within him even against a stranger who erred so; it is doubly strong when the object is his own son. In the case of any wrong, and especially in the case of such a wrong, where the son has cut himself off from sonship—has robbed his father of a son—we must take sides against the wrongdoer. For there is something that the father cares for more than for the lad; namely, the relation that binds the lad to him; nor will he sacrifice the value of that permanent relation for the sake of a transient peace. "My country, right or wrong," is no motto for the true patriot.

"I could not love thee, dear, so much,
Loved I not honour more";

this is the true philosophy of the strong man's love, which recognises that the closest personal attachment is worth little, unless ennobled by the principles of honour, truth, and loyalty underlying it. If these are gone, the old love can only clothe itself in anger until they are restored.

V. Is it, then, enough that love should merely clothe itself in anger? Love cannot be passive only; it must also be active. Anger, too, must be active as well as passive; negative, and also positive. The father, suffering from the estrangement which his son has caused, cannot force from himself the usual tokens of affection; the impulse to accord them will still be there, no doubt; but it takes two to love, as it takes two to quarrel. You cannot caress when the caress will be repulsed; the words of affection that will not be listened to cannot even be uttered; signs of tenderness cannot be cast before those who will trample them under foot. This negative anger, the withholding of what once was a joy both to give and to receive, may at times be unnoticed and unfelt by its object; at other times it may cause the keenest and most salutary grief. But there is a positive anger which the culprit must be made to feel. No advance in the science of education can obscure the wisdom of the old proverb, " Spare the rod and spoil the child."

Punishment is undoubtedly one of the most difficult and expensive modes of education. But it cannot and ought not to be dispensed with, for two reasons. In the first place, sin wherever it is found, must be attacked; the vigorous moral indignation against sin of which Butler spoke, is a necessity for every healthy mind. Where the sinner has identified himself with his sin, he must be made to see what he has done, and to pay the price. That he should do so, is inevitable sooner or later. But in addition to the internal demoralisation and disintegration consequent on sin, there must also be the outward infliction of penalty on the sin which encroaches on my neighbour's rights or destroys the true relations between man and man; " no man sinneth to himself." In the second place, punishment will often, as we say, bring a man to his senses; and he who inflicts the punishment will have to repre-

ANGER AND FORGIVENESS

sent to the culprit his own best self. Crime and penalty cannot be balanced quantitatively against one another; but the amount of pain to be inflicted will often be determined by the gravity of the warning necessary to deter others from committing the same crime, and the amount of suffering necessary to right the warped vision of the criminal. Thus the primitive conviction that the sinner deserves punishment is of abiding worth; but it is only the good man, seeing sin in its right light, who can use the words of the truism despised of children, " it hurts me more than it hurts you," and who feels his very love for the sinner goading him to inflict the punishment.

This is another paradox among the many created by this strange anomaly of punishment born of affection. Cowper once said, " I could never understand why, if my mother loved me more than other boys, she punished me when she did not punish them."[1] He did not understand, and few children could understand, that his mother's anger was not against him simply, but against him as in a false position, in a false relation to her for which his disobedience to her was responsible. We say of a person who is acting strangely that he is not himself; and common expressions often have in them more metaphysics than we think. The lunatic or the idiot, we all feel, is certainly " not himself"; he has become to us a different person; so different, in fact, that he will turn against those round whom his affections used to cluster in happier days; and we ourselves must adopt a quite new attitude to him. It

---

[1] Compare for a Greek parallel to this the charming description of the conversation of Socrates with the boy Lysis, who explains that he would be punished if he attempted to do what his parents' servants are paid for doing.—Plato, " Lysis," 208-9.

would be right neither to him nor to other people to behave to him as if he were his normal self. So with sin. We are accustomed to look upon sin as what is natural; but is this so? Is not sin as much a contravention of what is natural and healthy as lunacy itself? To use our old phrase, it destroys the right relations between man and man, as completely as does the lunatic's mental aberration. If my friend's mind gives way, I can respect him for what he was, and for what I feel that he still is in reality; I cannot respect the imbecile; I can only pity him and try by patience or firmness, or both, to heal him. And if my friend gives way in a sadder fashion, if he yields to drink or falls into immorality or flings away his old veracity, I can love him for what he was to me, for what I believe he will be again, for what I would fain think he really is, even at present; so, too, I can determine, like David in Browning's well-known poem,

"To interpose at the difficult minute, snatch Saul the mistake,
 Saul the failure, the ruin he seems now,—and bid him awake";

but I cannot love the drunkard or the liar; I must loathe the drunkenness, and I must loathe the man who accepts such a degrading yoke. Sin is a kind of lunacy; but it is a guilty lunacy. I must bring the man back to his old proper self; I must "whip the offending Adam out of him," as some savage tribes are said to scourge malignant influences even out of those who represent their gods.[1] Where the offence is a moral one, the scourging must be more than merely therapeutic; I cannot but act in sorrow; and must also act in anger.

This distinction, however unfamiliar to most minds,

[1] Frazer, "The Golden Bough," iii. pp. 127, 128.

is real; and by holding to it, we can separate anger from vengeance or from any taint of personal resentment. My love for the sinner drives me to anger; but it makes me long to rescue him from the false self with which I am angry. The mind intent on vengeance has no wish for the personal regeneration of the sinner; with his own satisfaction, his interest in the whole affair may be said to end. But the man who is wounded by his friend's sin, wishing to punish that he may free the wrongdoer from the baleful thraldom, counts the days to restoration, and watches as eagerly for the signs of returning sanity, as a nurse by her patient's bedside.

Thus it is that when the injured person is anxious to forgive, forgiveness does not depend on him at all; it depends wholly on the injurer. We might almost say that the injurer accomplishes his own forgiveness, by making it possible for the injured to forgive him. When the evil self has departed from him; when he has disowned the estranging sin, the untruthfulness or the licentiousness, and is sitting clothed and in his right mind, the anger that flamed up against sin and sinner alike is at an end. It has done its work; it has burnt away the impurity; and its object has ceased to be.

VI. We may now apply this to the consideration of the divine anger, as we have observed it to exist in the Bible. If we have eliminated resentment from the highest type of human anger, shall we leave it in the divine? If human wrath is consistent with yearning watchfulness to receive the returning sinner, shall we deny this attribute to the wrath of God? On the contrary, it is just this attribute which the Bible emphasises. There are, it is true, expressions which imply derision or vindictiveness in the Most High; but these taken by themselves are inconsistent with the general attitude of the Bible; they are also far fewer than the frequent reference made to them would suggest. In spite of a sentence like "Vengeance is mine, I will repay, saith the Lord," which does not really assert vindictiveness in God, but forbids it to man—God's wrath is the wrath of one who is just and merciful; "whose anger is so slow to rise, so ready to abate." What differentiated Jehovah from heathen gods in the minds of the prophets was that he was not vindictive or capricious, but just; not that he could show no anger, but that his anger was never inflicted undeservedly, nor prolonged beyond repentance. What differentiated God from the objects of pagan superstition in the mind of the apostles, was not the fact that God was simply love, but that children of wrath might find peace with God through Jesus Christ. Sin in the Bible is pre-eminently unnatural. It is nowhere regarded as a sad necessity; wherever it is encountered, it is protested against and opposed. God's anger is anger against man in a position where he has no business to be. When that position is deserted, God's anger does not indeed turn to love, but simply drops out of love.

But does not this make God subject to change? How can God be at one time angry, and at another time angry no longer? Are we not laying ourselves open again to the attack of Ritschl, and confusing subjective changes in our own thought of God with objective changes in God's thought of us? "All reflections about God's wrath and mercy, his patience and forbearance, his severity and pity, rest on the religious comparison of our individual situation with God in the form of time."[1] It is easy to point out that what Ritschl is here implying in God is not

[1] Ritschl, "The Christian Doctrine of Justification and Reconciliation."

ANGER AND FORGIVENESS 169

stability but lifelessness; the unchangingness not of a consistent person, but of an immovable rock.[1] But it is more to our purpose to urge that the change is not in God but in man. We may indeed read of God changing his mind, so to speak,—"repenting him," either of the evil or of the good; God is made to say "it repenteth me that I have made them" (both man and beast)[2]; Moses can cry to God "repent of this evil against thy people" after they have made the golden calf; "and the Lord repented of the evil which he said that he would do unto the people."[3] When Jerusalem was to be destroyed for David's sin in numbering the people, "the Lord beheld, and it repented him of the evil, and he said to the destroying angel, it is enough."[4] We find the same thought in the prophets; "The Lord repented concerning this (the locust plague); it shall not be, saith the Lord";[5] "The Lord is slow to anger . . . plenteous in mercy and repenteth him of the evil."[6] But this conception is sometimes brought strangely near to its very opposite; God tells Samuel "it repenteth me that I have set up Saul to be king"; and almost immediately as afterwards Samuel announces to Saul that "the strength of Israel will not lie nor repent."[7] The Psalmist prays "Let it repent thee concerning thy servants"; though a later Psalm, in a very different context, can assert that "the Lord hath sworn and will not repent."[8] Referring to the reign of Hezekiah, Jeremiah says "Did he not . . . entreat the favour of the Lord? and the Lord repented him of the evil which he had pro-

---

[1] Garvie, "Ritschlian Theology," p. 307.
[2] Gen. 6⁷.
[3] Ex. 22¹² ¹⁴.
[4] 1 Chr. 21¹⁵.
[5] Am. 7³.
[6] Joel 2¹³.
[7] 1 Sam. 15¹¹ ²⁹.
[8] Ps. 90¹³ 110⁴.

170 ETHICS AND ATONEMENT

nounced against him"; and yet, looking forward to the future, he can say with equal confidence "the whole land shall be a desolation . . . I have purposed it and I have not repented."[1]

Thus, as far as individual passages go, there seems as much authority for the one view as the other; but a closer study will convince us, that in this respect, as in the case of so many other apprehensions of God, the thought of the Biblical writers rises instinctively from the lower view to the higher; if they begin by thinking that there is change with God as there is with men, good and bad alike, they go on to see that God's ways are not as man's ways; that God's law is one, and that it is the changes in man which demand varying applications of that law. The very phrase "the righteousness of God"—that fixed law of good which is inseparable from God himself—means that God holds consistently to one moral course; that his conduct can be counted on beforehand. A very simple illustration will serve to make this plain. We speak familiarly of the rising and setting sun. Once we really thought that the sun did rise and set. Now we know that it is the earth's position, relative to the sun, which changes, and brings us either into darkness or into sunlight. We are as the earth to God's sun. Once it was easy to imagine that that sun might rise upon us in love or set in anger. A fuller revelation teaches us that when our heart is turned away from God, then there is darkness; when we can echo the words of the Psalmist, "Lo, I come to do thy will, O my God," then we move into the light.

"God is love"; but to certain things, God is for ever hate. There are desert stretches which must always

[1] Jer. 26^{19} 4^{28}.

ANGER AND FORGIVENESS 171

lie in the outer darkness of God's blasting and withering displeasure; yet just as everlasting are the green pastures lit by God's unchanging goodness and mercy. It is man's affair in which of these permanent divisions of the moral world he chooses to dwell. If he chooses the deserts, he will inevitably plunge himself in darkness and feel the blasting desolation of his dwelling-place; if he "repent him," and turn to the light, he will luxuriate in its fruitful warmth, and find rest unto his soul.

But some men find this pathway to the light long and grey, darkened by the shadows which the darkness has left on their own soul. They are in the light; but the light can only be gradually assimilated. Like Plato's cave-dwellers, they are dazzled, and almost wish themselves back in the dark; or they think themselves in the dark still; they carry the burden on their back, though they have long since left the city of Destruction. But here also the change, though real and objective, is not in God. It is felt while traversing the road that leads to God. With the Father of lights, there "is no variableness nor shadow cast by turning." The true ethical attitude to anger, so far from being opposed by the Bible, is expounded in its completeness in the Bible alone.

VII. One question must here be met. In what sense can Christ be said to have come under the wrath of God? The thought of the meek and sinless Jesus bending under the accumulated weight of the wrath of his offended Father—the wrath which should have fallen upon us—is a familiar one in popular theology. But is it one which mature consideration allows us to confirm? Ethics certainly will have nothing to do with it. How can it be right to be angry with the

172 ETHICS AND ATONEMENT

innocent instead of with the guilty, or even with the innocent as well as with the guilty? How can it be anything but monstrous that the wrath of God should fall upon his sinless son, who came to do the will of Him that sent him, and in whom he pronounced himself well-pleased? Now, that either anger or punishment should fall from God on Christ, instead of on us, we have seen to be contrary alike to ethics and to the Bible.[1] But if Christ bears with man the full penalties of man's sin, that he may reinstate man in God's favour, must he not feel the dread force of that wrath from which he would save his brethren?

Christ found man estranged from God; the object of God's love; yet, placed where he was, of necessity the object of God's wrath. Into the darkness of that separation from God Christ had to enter. His work is often spoken of as if its object were to change the mind of God; but there is nothing of this necessarily implied in the content of the word at-one-ment, or reconciliation; nor can it be found in anything that Christ said of himself. He came to save man, not by altering God, but by altering man. He altered man by entering man's world. Into man's actual feelings of hatred, wrath, suspicion, pride, hypocrisy, the shameless offspring of alienation and of broken relations, he was forbidden to enter, because of the barrier set round him by his divine infinity; into the sense of alienation itself, with all its attendant loneliness and horror, he did actually penetrate. "My God, my God, why hast thou forsaken me?"—what does this mean but that he made his way to the heart of the dreadful solitude of the sinner, and drank with him the cup of bitterness to the very dregs? More than this; for Christ that cup was

[1] See pp. 133.

ANGER AND FORGIVENESS

far more bitter than it could ever be for man. For him who had lain from everlasting in the bosom of the Father, to feel himself forsaken involved a desolation unthinkable by the sinner who had always been under God's ban. Plunged by his self-identification with man into man's mortal agony, he could not but prove how truly the soul of agony is separation from God. He alone who has known the height of love can understand the depth of hate. Only the son of God's love could know the extent of his Father's wrath; only by tasting the bitterness of their cup could he reveal to men what made it bitter, "that mercy they might find, and live."

"Then God was really angry with Christ?" No; the difficulties in the way of this view are as great as they appeared a few pages back. That Christ felt the negative signs of God's anger—that he felt himself forsaken, deserted, lying under the same cloud of wrath as was resting upon mankind,—we must admit; that God was positively angry with him, or regarded him for a moment as touched by the least sin, we must as unhesitatingly deny.[1] That the one should happen without the other is perfectly possible. In his complete sympathy, he could experience the misery of those who had turned from God; but he had never turned from God himself; and no blow from the divine hand had ever fallen upon him. If God was angry with him, when did that anger commence? Not surely till after the last of the divine voices which proclaimed him the well-beloved son. Then at some interval between the Transfiguration and the Cross? Before the raising of Lazarus? Before the majestic words were spoken to Pilate? Before the prayer for the forgiveness of

[1] Compare T. H. Green, Works, vol. iii. pp. 198-9.

those who knew not what they were doing? Any consciousness of God's anger, if it ever existed, had not arisen then Again when did God's anger come to an end? With the actual moment of Christ's death? Surely it had ended before he could cry, "It is finished," or "Into thy hands I commend my spirit." The only moment when that anger could have rested upon him was the moment when the quotation from the 22nd Psalm was wrung from his lips;—the very moment when his obedience and his sacrifice were complete; when he was actually tasting death for every man, and accomplishing that "decease" about which he had held converse with Moses and Elijah on the mount of Transfiguration, and for which he had come into the world; when he had fully learnt obedience by the things that he suffered, and when God's good pleasure in him had reached its consummation. The only time when God could have been angry was just the time when He could least of all have felt anger.

There are other considerations which make it impossible to accept the thought of God's positive anger with Christ. First of all, we never have the slightest hint that Christ contemplated enduring the anger of his Father. His attitude to God is unchanged throughout his life, from the moment when he reminded his parents that he must be about his Father's business, or in his Father's house; it is an attitude of confidence, assurance and peace. "No man knoweth the Father save the Son . . . no man knoweth the Son save the Father." His last prayer, just before entering Gethsemane, was certainly not the prayer of one approaching a superior who could in any circumstances be angry with him. In order that the Son might in the next few hours carry out his work to the full, the Father might

ANGER AND FORGIVENESS 175

for one dread instant hide his face; but be angry, never. God's favour is never spoken of, before the supreme moment, as liable to be lost; it is never spoken of afterwards as resumed. True, an impressive reticence is maintained by the evangelists, the writers of the history of the atoning life, as to Christ's inner relations with his Father in making the great sacrifice; but on the other hand, they watched his stern demeanour when he set his face to go up to Jerusalem; they saw his indignation at the grave of Lazarus; they marked the unusual agitation that shook his spirit at his last meal with them; they could follow him to the agony in the garden, and see him pain-racked and alone upon the cross; yet never once did they connect these vast emotions with God's wrath actively poured out upon His Son.

Again, had the wrath of God formed an integral part of the sufferings of Christ, we might have expected mention, and frequent mention, of it in the rest of the New Testament, and especially in the epistles of S. Paul. Of such mention there is no trace. It is the unbroken unity of Christ with God, moral and spiritual, that S. Paul, like S. John, never tires of exalting. It may be answered that S. Paul asserts this doctrine twice, in the words which tell us that Christ became a curse for us, and that God made him to be sin on our behalf.[1] What these words would seem at first sight to imply is that Christ had really sinned and come short of the glory of God, falling into the curse; this is impossible. The only other meaning is that of our own contention, that Christ entered the darkness of God's wrath, by identifying himself with the sinners he came to save. To suppose the words to hint that God cursed as a

[1] Gal. 3^{13}; 2 Cor. 5^{21}.

176 ETHICS AND ATONEMENT

sinner His Son who knew no sin, is to foist upon them an otherwise unknown doctrine, which they would never spontaneously suggest.

Lastly, the theologian who holds that God could be wroth with Christ would seem unfaithful to the doctrine of the Trinity. How could the first and second Persons in the Godhead be in any sense at cross purposes? It is not indeed easy, on any showing, to reconcile the doctrine of the Trinity with the "dealings" of the Father and the Son with one another; but in our own account we have at least maintained the unity of purpose if we have not said much about the more mysterious unity of Person. To imagine that the Father could fling the Son from him, or treat him as he would treat offending and unrepentant humanity, would make the difficulty insuperable.[1]

VIII. One possible objection remains. It may be urged that we have pressed the analogy of Fatherhood to its utmost limit, and even gone beyond it. We must reply that every analogy has its limitations, this analogy as much as the rest. Doubtless, God is more than can be expressed by calling Him the Father, either of believers, or of Christ himself. But some analogy we must have, before we can express the relation between God and man at all. Those who would warn us against too great reliance on Fatherhood, often call us, not to an exposition free from all analogy—an impossible dream on this side of the grave, where we see at best through a glass darkly—but to a lower analogy instead of a higher, that of a king or a judge. And moreover we have the precedent of Christ's own

---

[1] The emphasis laid on the unbroken unity of the Father and the Son throughout the whole of the Atonement is one of the most striking parts of Dale's treatment of the Atonement. See especially Lecture ix.

ANGER AND FORGIVENESS 177

language; did he press the analogy of Fatherhood too closely? As a matter of fact, he never speaks of God as King; the Kingdom of God or of Heaven is always the Kingdom of the Father; and this is the more remarkable since the Jewish ideas had centred round a theocracy, or royalty of God, and not on a paternal government. Strangely enough, it is for himself, and not for the Father, that he claims royalty. "When the Son of Man shall come in his glory . . . then shall he sit on the throne of his glory . . . then shall the King say unto them, etc."[1] Again, Christ hardly refers to God as judge; but frequently and impressively to his own judicial functions. In the parable above quoted, it is the Son of Man who judges; and in the fourth gospel we meet with Christ's claim that all judgment has been committed by the Father into his own hands. It is the Holy Spirit, he who carries on Christ's work in the world, that is to convince the world of judgment. We read in the New Testament, as in the Old, of God as the world's future judge; but when S. Paul looks forward to the judgment, he expects to stand "before the judgment-seat of Christ."[2]

Is it not significant that in the last supreme approach of Christ to God on earth,—the one prayer of which the full substance is given to us,—the address is throughout, and essentially, from Son to Father? And when he taught his followers to begin the "Lord's Prayer" with the same address, "Our Father," would he have introduced into that daily petition for ever recurring needs, a relation which was merely parabolic? If the word

---
[1] Mt. $25^{31\ 34\ 40}$.
[2] 2 Cor. 5^{10}. In a parallel passage (Rom. 14^{10}) S. Paul writes, "We shall all stand before the judgment seat of God . . . each one of us will give an account about himself to God." But the thought of the whole passage is none the less that of the Lordship of Christ, won by his death and life.

Father, used on such high authority, is to fail us, what are we to think of the general value of the designation? In one respect, God can never be the Father of men; He is not the author of their physical being in the sense of human parentage; but this does not detract from the completeness of His Fatherhood; in the relation of true fatherhood, the physical bond is at most only one element; to lay stress upon it often reduces paternity to a caricature; it is the moral and spiritual affinity which is the essential. Least of all can we suggest that such a physical bond constituted the Fatherhood of God to Christ. God is the "Father, from whom every fatherhood in heaven and on earth is named";[1] and His Fatherhood is also unique, not because it is metaphorical, but because it is mediated; mediated through Christ, the Son, to us, who thereby become joint-heirs with him, and are made actually, what before we were potentially, sons of God.

The question is not whether we can best compare God to a judge, a king or a father; but whether our relation to God is best expressed by that of criminals to a judge, subjects to a king, or children to a parent. That the last is the truth, the argument of this chapter has convinced us. The rule of a father ought to be, and is ideally, far sterner than that of a judge or of a monarch; the demands of a father are greater, and the anger of a father is far more terrible, because he loves more.[2] When we assert that God was not angry with Christ, we do not and dare not assert that He was not angry with us; when we assert that He did not punish Christ instead of us, we do not assert that He does not punish sin and sinners; on the contrary, He punishes

[1] Eph. 3^{15}.
[2] Compare Lidgett, "Spiritual Principle of the Atonement," pp. 229, 230.

ANGER AND FORGIVENESS 179

because He is love. To call God the Father of Christ, and, through Christ, of men,—this is not to destroy the majesty of the moral law, but to place it on its true basis and establish it there. Complete reconciliation must involve love, wrath, mediation, and restoration through the mediator. These elements form the very substance of the At-one-ment, the Reconciliation, of Christ.

CHAPTER VII

SYMBOLISM AND REALITY

1. IN Savonarola's convent at Florence, the visitor traversing the bare corridors leading to Savonarola's own cell, sees in almost every cell into which he looks, some presentment of the closing scenes of our Lord's life. The agony in the garden, the Entombment, and the Resurrection, have all been depicted in fresco on one or other of the cell walls—their only decoration—either by Fra Angelico, himself no mean theologian, or by his disciples; but the scene most often repeated is the Crucifixion. With the Medieval painter, as with the apostles, the first thing to be thought of in the gospels was Christ upon the cross; the Saviour who went about doing good was to him a less potent figure than the Saviour who died on Calvary. Not only before the eyes of the individual monk at his devotions in his own cell, but facing the entrance to the convent where no casual visitor could fail to see it, is pictured this sublime figure. You feel at once that the painter-monk leaps directly to the centre of his theology. He is not interested in the properties of the scene; he is distracted by no such accessories, however awe-inspiring, as delighted Tintoretto or Rubens; you see but the one figure, bathed in light, thrown out across a dark background; calm and serene, the agony transcended, without a trace of it left behind, and the consummating words "it is finished"

already uttered. Save for the delicate trickling of streams of blood, the idea of a death of pain is never suggested. The head bends forward, as if in blessing, not death; and if the closed eyes could open, they would rest on another figure, kneeling at the foot of the cross. And here the painter would have you see how symbolic is his treatment; for that figure is neither the Virgin nor the Magdalene nor S. John, but the founder of his own monastic order, S. Dominic. The saint looks upward in an ecstasy, his arms thrown around the cross, almost touching the Saviour's feet. Between his hands flows the blood; but the painter has carefully refrained from allowing the fingers to touch the blood, or suggesting thereby that there could be anything efficacious in actual contact with the stream.

It is always so with this early master of the Renaissance; nowhere does he insist on the hideous pain that accompanied the death on the cross. This, indeed, appears the only aspect of the crucifixion which seemed to interest so many, both of his contemporaries and of his successors; to them, the main fact is that he suffered; to Angelico, that he died. They would rouse the spectator's horror and even repulsion, only to be conquered by the sternest self-repression; he would call forth a contemplative devotion which needs no conquest at all, but has its root in joy. There is no melancholy about Angelico's crucifixion; the eye rests with delight on the well-shapen limbs—the limbs, like the life, impoverished but not imperfect; every line and curve of the picture tells of peace after strife; the complete acquiescence that hallows the consummation of a sacrifice. It was left for later painters to turn the world's central tragedy into a subject for a dissecting room study or an anatomical demonstration. It was for them to expatiate on the grosser side of sacrifice, which measured its efficacy by the anguish involved and the rivers of blood shed, as if they had actually lost all thought of sacrifice in the brutal interest of the slaughter-house. But in Angelico you feel a loving delicacy that would shield from vulgar curiosity the bodily pangs our Lord endured, leaving only the triumphant symbol of the sting of death destroyed, and death itself swallowed up in victory.

In our consideration of the Atonement hitherto, we have never yet, as it were, stood beside the cross with the soldiers, or knelt beneath it with S. Dominic. And it may seem to some readers surprising that we have been able to travel for so long towards the central thought of Atonement without doing this. Now, no one can deny that in the New Testament, the blessings of reconciliation with God are specially connected with the death of Christ, and even explicitly with his blood. That death is regarded, not simply as a means of reconciliation, but as a sacrifice; and in a sacrifice, as we are generally led to understand, the essential element is the shedding of the blood, in order to propitiate an offended deity. No one could accuse popular hymnology of neglecting this element in the work of Christ; there, as in so much of the traditional theological teaching of Catholicism and Protestantism alike, the "blood" receives due emphasis.

> "What can wash away my sin?
> Nothing but the blood of Jesus;"

or, in lines which remind us strangely of Angelico,

> "Believe, believe the record true,
>   Ye are all bought with Jesus' blood;
> Pardon for all flows from his side,

SYMBOLISM AND REALITY 183

> My Lord, my love is crucified.
> Then let us sit beneath his cross,
> And gladly catch the healing stream;"[1]

or, less tastefully, if with equally devotional feeling, the familiar lines of Cowper,

> "There is a fountain filled with blood,
> Drawn from Immanuel's veins,
> And sinners plunged beneath that flood
> Lose all their guilty stains."

This view is cherished with extraordinary constancy by the Roman Catholic mind. No one who enters a Roman Catholic church and sees the exaggerated effigies of the Saviour on the cross or the representations of the bleeding heart and the agonised face, or who looks at the gruesome objects for the use of the faithful exhibited in shop windows, can help feeling that Romanist devotion is dedicated to the apotheosis of pain, and that either the evangelists, as we have understood them, have overlooked the value of some most important accessories, or the Romanist estimation of the value of those accessories has gone grievously astray. But there is much to bear this out in both Roman and Anglican devotional literature. "If we picture these ... so that every point in the Human Form should be a sort of focus of suffering, each pierced to the utmost, Brain, Eyes, Ears, Tongue, Teeth, Arms, Hands, Feet, Nails, Back, Breast, Heart ... we have not begun the Suffering of that Divine Form."[2] The following extract from a popular religious magazine may be added, as significant of the thought of a section of the church very different from Pusey's. "Should you take a little camel's hair brush and dip it into red ink and pass it lightly over every text in the Bible

---

[1] C. Wesley. Compare Polycarp's expression, ὁ ἐρώς μου ἐσταύρωται.
[2] E. B. Pusey: Address to Companions of the Love of Jesus.

which refers to the "blood" either in the Old or the New Testament, . . . you would be amazed to find how red your Bible would look, from Genesis to Revelation. Then, should you take a sharp knife and cut out of your Bible all those crimson passages . . . you would be amazed to find what a ragged and fragmentary Bible you had left."

Yet it is not too much to say that language such as this would have been strange and even revolting to the writers of the New Testament; and to us, if we had not been accustomed to it by devotional phrases familiar to us in our earliest years, it would have been as strange as to them. What connexion, indeed, it is often asked, can there be between bloodshed and our sin? In what sense, save a purely metaphorical one, can I be made clean by being washed with blood? Even to the sanguinary rites of savages, this conception is foreign; with the Jews, though their temple might run with blood, no one washed in it. When Jesus spoke about giving his blood to drink to his disciples, they found it a hard saying. To Jews, the idea would have been abhorrent, and quite alien from the practice of their own sacrifices; though to many savage tribes the literal "drinking of blood," as a religious ceremony, is familiar enough. What is it that prevents the teaching about washing in the blood, or drinking it, from being "hard" to us, except those destroyers of thought, custom and tradition? Righteousness by the shedding of blood, would, in the realm of ethics, seem either an unreality, or, if not that, a short method to goodness as suspicious as that of indulgences and more fatally easy than that of acts of penance: little better, in either case, than superstitious reliance on charms or relics. And to any religion that can be called spiritual, such a con-

SYMBOLISM AND REALITY 185

ception would appear equally remote. How can the God who is Spirit, and who must be worshipped in spirit and in truth, be affected by the shedding of any blood, whether of bulls and goats or of Jesus of Nazareth himself?

II. But here, as so often, a distinction must be drawn between the popular theology which professes to be based on the Bible, and the language of the Bible itself. Interpretations of the Bible that seem alien to ethics, will generally be seen to have been discredited by the Bible long before ethics has found fault with them. Jesus never speaks of his own blood as having any mystical virtue, for atoning or sanctifying, save in two instances; to those who gathered round him after his feeding of the 5000 he said that only by eating his flesh and drinking his blood was it possible to receive real life; "my flesh is food indeed, and my blood is drink indeed";[1] with which we may compare his words to the woman of Samaria, about the water which he gave and after drinking which there could be no more thirst,—the living water. And when he was eating with his disciples for the last time, with the thought of his approaching death heavy upon him, though even then hardly understood by them, he said to them, in words which have become an integral part of the universal Christian ceremonial, "This is my blood of the new covenant; drink ye all of this in remembrance of me."[2] In the early preaching of Christianity, as recorded in the Acts of the Apostles, there is no mention of the blood of Christ, save in one phrase of S. Paul's, "the

[1] Jn. 6^{55}.
[2] Mt. 26^{28}; Mk. 14^{24}; also in Lk. 22^{20}, where however the expression is varied; "this cup is the new covenant in my blood, that which is poured out for you"; and the same words are found in S. Paul's account of the supper, 1 Cor. 11^{25}.

186 ETHICS AND ATONEMENT

Church of God, which he (i.e. God) purchased with his own blood."[1] And when we turn to the letters of S. Paul, the great father of systematic theology, we find that while he is constantly referring to the death of Christ, as a fact not of past history but of abiding significance, he only refers five times in all his writings to the blood, as being an essential part of the Atonement wrought by that death. The very importance of these references makes us wonder that there are not more of them. They occur in the central epistle to the Romans, and in the companion epistles, Ephesians and Colossians. "Whom (i.e. Christ) God set forth to be a propitiation, through faith, by his blood"; "Much more then, being now justified by his blood, shall we be saved from the wrath of God through him"; "In whom we have our redemption through his blood"; "But now in Christ Jesus ye that once were far off are made nigh in the blood of Christ"; and "having made peace through the blood of his cross." In addition to this, besides quoting our Saviour's own words in the institution of the Eucharist, he asks "the cup of blessing which we bless, is it not a communion of the blood of Christ?"[2] We need here to notice in passing that the expressions "in Christ" and "in the blood of Christ" seem almost interchangeable, though in the epistles the former has an immensely wider application; we may specially notice the second quotation from Romans and the two from Ephesians; all that is said to be done through or by the blood of Christ is elsewhere by S. Paul said to be done simply through or in Christ. In the first epistle of S. Peter, the

---

[1] Ac. 20^{28}. The easier reading "Christ" for "God" in this passage is rejected by the oldest manuscripts and the best scholars alike.

[2] Rom. 3^{25} 5^9; Eph. 1^7 2^{13}; Col. 1^{20}; 1 Cor. 10^{16}.

SYMBOLISM AND REALITY 187

thought occurs twice; "Unto obedience and sprinkling of the blood of Christ"; and "ye were redeemed with precious blood, even the blood of Christ."[1] S. John uses the phrase "the blood of Jesus Christ cleanseth us from all sin"; but besides this we have no further reference to it,—though in a mind so mystical as his we might justly have expected it,—save in the oft-debated words, "this is he that came by water and by blood."[2] In Revelations, which is filled with symbolism, where Christ is represented as the lamb slain from the foundation of the world, and where the powers both of heaven and hell are depicted, as in Daniel, in images borrowed from the animal creation, the saints are loosed from their sins by his blood by Christ; Christ has "purchased them to God by his blood"; "they have washed their robes and made them white in the blood of the Lamb"; and they overcame the accuser of the brethren (Satan) "because of the blood of the Lamb and because of the word of their testimony."[3]

Elsewhere in that book the word is used with no mystical or religious sense whatever. Perhaps the most striking instance of reticence is in the epistle to the Hebrews, where the sacrificial bloodshed of the old covenant is constantly referred to, but where the blood of Christ, so obviously contrasted therewith in the argument of the book, is explicitly mentioned only five times. After referring to the way in which the blood of goats and bulls and the ashes of an heifer could sanctify unto the cleanness of the flesh, he asks "how much more shall the blood of Christ . . . cleanse your conscience from dead works to serve the living God?" He refers to "the blood of sprinkling, that speaketh better things than that of Abel"; Jesus, he says,

[1] 1 Pet. 1^2 1^{19}.   [2] 1 Jn. 1^7 5^6.   [3] Rev. 1^5 5^9 7^{14} 12^{11}.

"that he might sanctify the people through his own blood, suffered without the gate," as the bodies of the animals taken for sin-offering were burned "without the camp." We have the strange expression that God "brought again from the dead the great shepherd of the sheep with the blood of the eternal covenant," where the blood is connected with the resurrection of Christ rather than with his death. And lastly, Christians have "boldness to enter into the holy place by the blood of Jesus."[1]

It cannot but be acknowledged that these few passages are a very slender foundation for a non-ethical belief in the "efficacy of the blood," such as that with which devotional writers have made us familiar, still less for the repulsive pictures of torture and agony gloated over by the school of Pusey or the Roman Catholic manuals of devotion. Horrible and nauseating as were the accompaniments of crucifixion, they are veiled with an impenetrable reserve, even by the apostle who learnt to glory in the scandal of the cross. It would have been as easy for S. Peter or S. John, eye-witnesses of that terrible event, to grow sentimental over it, as for us; they might have attributed some magical potency of healing to the blood which they had watched trickling from his wounds; but this would have been to misunderstand the miracles and to degrade the divinity of Christ; to forget both his aversion to the spectacular and his insistence on the value of the spiritual. In the New Testament, there is the intensest realisation of suffering; but there is no sentiment.

III. Now, if we seem to discount the importance of the blood, do we not also take from the importance

[1] Heb. 9^{14} 12^{24} 13^{12} 13^{20} 10^{19}.

of the death of Christ? If his blood is mentioned but seldom, his death is dwelt upon in every page of the New Testament. The apostles never wearied of contemplating that death, if contemplation it could be called, which never rested upon a single detail of the tragedy; from it they derived, with a striking unanimity, all the blessings of their experience; they gathered their garland of rejoicing from the heart of that act of shame; and the Roman citizen gloried that his Lord died the death which his city gave to a common slave. Surely if this is so, it might appear idle to warn against the devotion that rejoices in the outpouring of the blood or loves to gaze upon the pallid and strengthless limbs, bruised by the scourge and mangled by the nails, when the Saviour of the world lay dead. But it must be remembered that when we think of death, we think of something quite different from what is suggested to the Christian by the words "the death of Christ." In spite of all the consolations of religion and the elevation of death into a "passing away" or a "going home," death is still for us the end of life and life's activities; and even if our thoughts attempt to follow the dead into that dim region whither they have gone, yet our hope for "some strong bond that is to be" is inevitably obscured by the "yearning for the friendship fled." To the Christian, however, the death of Christ was but the beginning, as S. Luke finely put it, of what he did and taught; the new religion was born at the moment of the discovery that Christ's death was not the end, but the commencement, of the kingdom which he preached. How did Christ himself habitually think and speak of his death? Was it not always with a strange triumph, and with a vision of the resurrection which was to follow? He never foretold his death to the disciples, without foretelling the resurrection in the same breath, and the one was as difficult for them to understand as the other. If the Messiah was to lay down his life, he left them in no doubt that he had power to take it again. True, he was to leave his friends; but that was for their good; "it is expedient for you that I go away"; only so could the Comforter come to carry on his work; and only so could he himself promise to leave them no more. Some end his human life demanded; and that end came when his youth gave hopes of many years to come. But his death, so premature from a human point of view, merely gave him to them again in a new and more intimate way. They might speak of the death of Christ, but of a dead Christ never.

This is very noticeable in the preaching and writing of the disciples themselves. The burden of the speeches in the Acts is "You put Jesus to death; God raised him up again." S. John, while he reminds his readers that the blood of Christ cleanses from sin, and that Christ is set forth as himself a propitiation by God, never once refers to his death, outside the actual narrative of the Passion, but speaks of him simply as the source and giver of life. There is one apparent exception which proves our assertion; "I lay down my life," Jesus says, "for the sheep." This is, however, but the sign of love, of that love which is, like life itself, the very opposite of death.[1] S. Peter refers to Christ's death in several passages, but never without immediately proceeding to the resurrection which crowned it. S. James, "the brother of the Lord," is unique in the New Testament as making explicit mention neither of the death nor the resurrection.

[1] Jn. $10^{15\ 17}$; $3^{14\ 15\ 16}$.

SYMBOLISM AND REALITY 191

The letters of S. Paul, on the other hand, are filled with references both to the death and to the resurrection of Christ. On the latter subject he speaks with all the assurance of the earlier apostles; he too has seen the Lord; it has pleased God to reveal His son in him. The appearance on the road to Damascus was to him more immediately authoritative and epoch-making than were the appearances during the forty days to the twelve. In the opening sentences of his earliest epistle, he reminds the Thessalonians that they had turned unto God from idols, " to wait for his son from heaven, whom he raised from the dead."[1] In a discussion of purely moral considerations, he suddenly interjects "the body is for the Lord, and the Lord for the body; and God both raised the Lord, and will raise us up through his power."[2] This thought often recurs; the proof of our power to live the new life is the power displayed in the resurrection of Christ. "If the spirit of him that raised up Jesus from the dead dwelleth in you, he that raised up Jesus Christ from the dead shall also make alive your mortal bodies."[3] S. Paul never forgets that the resurrection would have been impossible without the death; but the value of the death is that it made possible the resurrection. Often he seems unable to mention the former without passing on with grateful haste to the latter; and the shame of the cross is to him a delightful foil to the glory of the empty tomb. " It is God that justifieth; who is he that shall condemn? It is Christ Jesus that died, yea rather, that was raised from the dead, who is at the right hand of God, who also maketh intercession for us ";[4] or he will wedge a hurried mention of the death between two references to the resurrection; "for our sake . . . who

[1] 1 Thess. 1^{10}. [2] 1 Cor. 6^{14}. [3] Rom. 8^{11}. [4] Rom. 8^{34}.

192 ETHICS AND ATONEMENT

believe on him that raised up Jesus our Lord from the dead, who was delivered up for our trespasses, and was raised for our justification." The weakness of the cross stands in perpetual contrast to the power of his present life; "he was crucified through weakness, but he liveth through the power of God." Even where S. Paul is exhorting his friends to lowliness and humility, bidding each count other better than himself, and is enforcing the precept by the powerful example of the humiliation of Christ, he cannot stop there; "He humbled himself, becoming obedient unto death, yea, the death of the cross; wherefore also God highly exalted him, and gave unto him the name that is above every name." [1]

This is not of course to assert that S. Paul can never speak of the death without going on to its immediate consequence; but it is very striking that whenever he goes no further than the death of Christ, he either brings it forward as an example of patient suffering or of the malice of his enemies; or else he implies in the context its consummation in life. "Ye also," he tells the Thessalonians, "suffered the same things of your own countrymen, even as they did of the Jews; who both killed the Lord Jesus and the prophets, and drove out us." "Walk in love, even as Christ also loved you, and gave himself up for us." Had the rulers of this world known the hidden wisdom, "they would not have crucified the Lord of glory." [2] When he writes "our Lord Jesus Christ, who died for us," and goes on "that, whether we wake or sleep, we should live together with him," he shows at once that he is by no means thinking of the death as if it were an isolated fact.

[1] Rom. $4^{24\,25}$; 2 Cor. 13^4; Phil. $2^{8\,9}$.
[2] 1 Thess. $2^{14\,15}$; Eph. 5^2; 1 Cor. 2^8.

SYMBOLISM AND REALITY

The same thing may be said of the two passages in the Epistle to the Galatians: "Far be it from me to glory save in the cross of our Lord Jesus Christ"; why should he glory therein, if the cross had not been transfigured? This he shows by adding "through which" (or, whom) the world hath been crucified unto me, and I unto the world"; "I have been crucified with Christ; yet I live; and yet no longer I, but Christ liveth in me." He describes the spirit of his preaching plainly enough; "I determined not to know anything among you save Jesus Christ, and him crucified"; but we must interpret this by his other and longer account of his preaching given in the same epistle; "I delivered unto you first of all that which I also received, how that Christ died for our sins according to the scriptures; and that he was buried; and that he hath been raised from the dead on the third day, according to the scriptures.[1]

To preach Christ as crucified was obviously, for S. Paul, the same thing as to preach him as risen. But there are places wherein Christ is referred to as a sacrifice. These might indeed seem to preclude our view; the efficacy of the sacrificial victim does not consist in its coming to life again, but in its dying. To the sacrificial aspect of Christ's death we must refer later. S. Paul seldom makes any definite allusion to such an aspect; he is generally supposed to be doing so however in the words "God, sending his son in the likeness of sinful flesh, and as an offering for sin, condemned sin in the flesh,"[2] where the word "offering" has been inserted to render the Greek prepositional phrase περὶ ἁμαρτίας, a phrase which has constantly in the Septuagint the substantival significance of "sin-offering."

[1] 1 Thess. 5^{10}; Gal. 6^{14} 2^{20}; 1 Cor. 2^2 15$^{3\,4}$.   [2] Rom. 8^3.

194 ETHICS AND ATONEMENT

But even here, S. Paul proceeds " that the ordinance of the law might be fulfilled in us, who walk not after the flesh but after the spirit," *i.e*, who are " in Christ," who possess the new life of the Spirit given by the living Christ. In Ephesians [1] we read " Christ gave himself up for us, an offering and a sacrifice to God." The other important passage is " our passover also hath been sacrificed, even Christ." [2] In this place alone is Christ definitely spoken of as a Paschal sacrifice ; and in this sacrifice, whatever may be the case with sacrifices for sin, the object is not the death of the victim, but the shedding of its blood, and this not to cleanse the worshipper, but to protect him ; it is sprinkled, not on him, but on the doorposts of his house ; and in this section of his letter to the Corinthians, the thought in the apostle's mind is not the Atonement of Christ ; but the fact that Christians have, though in a spiritual sense, a share in the passover celebration, and must therefore be free from the old leaven of bodily uncleanness.

It has been necessary to refer at this length to the writings of S. Paul, because it is upon his writings that the interpretation of the place of the death of Christ in the New Testament must be based. As Westcott says, and as we have already noticed, " the simple idea of the death of Christ, as separated from his life, falls wholly into the background in the writings of S. John ; it is only in the words of Caiaphas that the virtue of Christ's death is directly mentioned " ; and the expressions used by S. Peter, though reminding us of S. Paul's language, need that language, at once fuller and more theological, to make them clear. On the other hand, it may be urged that the gospels, themselves an important witness to the earliest Christian thought, besides emphasising

[1] Eph. 5^2.   [2] 1 Cor. 5^7.

Christ's own predictions of his death, relate the events of the crucifixion with a remarkable fulness and agreement. We have pointed out above that every prediction of the death is joined to a prediction of the resurrection. The fulness of the narrative of the crucifixion is indeed remarkable, and a matter of reverent thankfulness to every Christian; but the narrative is equally remarkable for what it omits. Everything that could point to the fulfilment of prophecy, while Christ actually hung upon the cross or endured the sufferings and humiliation which preceded; everything that could show how fully in his last hours he preserved his confidence in God and his compassion for men; everything that proved him to be, in the very article of death, triumphant over death, each evangelist is eager to relate. What they hide from us is every thought of Christ's death as the end of his existence, all cheap detail of his tortures, all mention of the horrors of death that encompassed him. The impression left by the passion narratives, when read apart from the sentimental amplifications of later ages, is that of the words of Christ in the Apocalypse, "I am the living one; and I was dead, and behold, I am alive for evermore."

IV. The significance of Christ's death, then, is not that it was merely a shedding of blood, and not by any means that it was in itself the whole act of Redemption; but that it was for him, as for us, the gate of life. But we should miss the full inwardness of that dread event, unless its sacrificial character were borne in mind as well. We have noticed that this event is not often spoken of as a sacrifice; but to Jews, whether from Galilee or from Tarsus, the thought of sacrifice—a victim slain for sin—was a constant companion; and the perpetual repetition of the phrase "on our behalf" or "on behalf of sin," is enough to show that the idea was ever in their minds, even if for some reason the word but seldom rested upon their lips. The epistle to the Hebrews fixes upon the thought which is thus taken for granted or latent in the rest of the New Testament, elaborates it, and shows it to be, for every believer in the new dispensation, the fulfilment of the old. Sacrifice, indeed, like the Covenant, is one of the links that bind the two dispensations together; and the two links are really one and the same. The Covenant was originated and continued by Sacrifice; and Sacrifice for the Jews had no meaning save within the Covenant relations between Jehovah and Israel. The Messiah was the Covenant-gift; he was set forth, according to the Isaianic prophecy, as a covenant for the people;[1] if he died for his people, or for their sins, how could that death be anything, in their eyes, save first and foremost a sacrifice?

But this seems to bring us back face to face with our old difficulty; ethics can take no cognisance of sacrifice, as the step to moral improvement. We hear again the old protest of ethics against religion; "if religion calls us to sacrifices, religion is primarily a matter for the priests; and what concerns us is not sacrifice or ritual, but right conduct." Now, however loud, and however wise, this protest of ethics may be, we cannot but observe that in all religions, and in all beliefs hardly to be honoured with the name of religion, the law of sacrifice seems to be indigenous. In the cults and the mythology of Greece and Rome, of Teutonic antiquity and of India, and behind them in the early dawn of the Aryan races as philology allows us to peer into it,

[1] *Vid. supr.* pp. 11 *ff.*

SYMBOLISM AND REALITY 197

sacrifice is at the centre of religion. The greater non-Aryan religions of China and ancient Egypt are like that of India in containing in their sacred books elaborate directions as to sacrifice; in the Semitic world, from Babylon to Arabia, and from Arabia to Phœnicia and her distant colonies, sacrifice entered into every relation of life; and the sacrifices of the Mosaic codes are simply the sacrifices of Semitic heathenism circumcised, as it were, into purity and spirituality of devotion. When we descend to the paganism of the lower and less developed races, instead of passing outside the realm of sacrifice, we find that it is as steadfastly believed in and practised as in more civilised religions. The primitive instinct of man seems to demand it; the increasing experience of man does not outgrow it. In the jungles of Africa, beneath the palms of the South Sea islands, in the Australian bush, or amid the snows of Greenland, sacrifice, in some form or other, is the recognised sequel of good and ill fortune alike, or else the appointed means of communion to bind living worshippers and their canonized ancestors. Is the god kind? he must be thanked by sacrifice; is he angry? he must be propitiated by sacrifice; is some disaster impending? by sacrifice it must be averted. Sacrifice, in the sense of ceremonial offering or slaughter, may even exist without any definite idea of a god at all. In no aspect do the most diverse religions show more variety of cult and more harmony of underlying idea, than in their sacrificial ritual. There are but three great exceptions; Buddhism, which was originally not a religion at all, but a system of philosophical atheism, rejecting the ideas of sacrifice and propitiation altogether, and holding that every act, good and bad, must work out its consequences to the bitter end;—only in later ages has Buddhism found a place both for sacrifices and gods in its hospitable bosom; Mohammedanism, which rejected sacrifices in its fierce revolt against the religious cults of heathens, Jews, and Christians alike; and modern Judaism, cut off now from sacrifices and from holy place, but only waiting for the restoration of its national life to restore the ritual for which the nation exists.

V. The Old Testament contains at first sight two totally opposite attitudes towards sacrifice; the attitude of careful and scrupulous reverence to sacrifice, as the only means of any valid approach to God; and the attitude of eager and contemptuous protest against any such mechanical mediation between the offender and the one offended. In the elaborateness of its ritual directions as to the kind of victim or offering, the manner of heaving, waving or sprinkling, the conditions of ceremonial purity and acceptance, the sacrificial portion of the Old Testament reminds us of the sacred books of paganism, and of the customs of paganism never written in books, but handed down by tradition from generation to generation. It reminds us of paganism, too, in the absence of reasons, moral or spiritual, both for its commands and for its prohibitions. Why should those creatures be "clean," *i.e.* permitted for food, which chew the cud and part the hoof, but these interdicted which fail to do either the one or the other? Why should all winged creeping things that go upon all fours be an abomination, excepting the locust and the bald locust, the cricket and the grasshopper? Some reason there undoubtedly is; but it is not stated nor apparently regarded as important. Why was it necessary, to take a very different part of the law, that on the day of Atonement, the priest should put incense upon the fire before the Lord, that the cloud of incense might "cover the mercy seat, that was upon the testimony, that he die not"? And why was he to be careful to burn the fat of the sin offering upon the altar? To these questions, too, no answer was given; nor was an answer felt to be needed. In fact, wherever religion becomes connected with external ceremonialism, custom in itself comes to be reverenced as much as the observance which custom prescribes. A spectator of the "performance" of the Roman Mass can hardly help feeling that the elaborate gesticulations and scarcely audible mutterings gain all their veneration, not from any intelligent appreciation of their meaning, but from their prescription by that depository of custom, the Church. "It hath been said by them of old time"; that was enough; but whether what was said can be justified by the criticism or the conscience of later times, was felt to be beside the mark, and of no moment. Enough that everything was done as the Law, the Torah, ordained.

On the other hand, completely to exclude the questioning spirit has always, unfortunately for most ceremonial religions, proved impossible. The enquiring minds that have persisted in asking, "Why do we do this or that?" must bear the responsibility for the growth of mythology. Beautiful or ingenious as myths may be, whether they come to us from Greece, from the "Celtic twilight," or from Hottentots or Bushmen, they show manifest signs of being originated by the customs they are intended to explain, rather than of being themselves the originators. Critics of the Old Testament have succeeded in discovering very few traces of such mythologising there. Only two sets of reasons are given for any of the multitudinous precepts of the sacrificial law;

reasons connected with the grand deliverance from Egypt; or reasons connected with the principle, always stated as axiomatic, that "the blood is the life." But even these great clues to the significance of the observances would seem to be far from leading us to the real origin of the cultus; the similarity of the Hebrew sacrifices to those of other Semitic peoples suggests that with the Hebrews themselves also, the customs existed long before some startling event or some deep conviction gave them a higher meaning and more awful sacredness.

However this may be, no moral significance is felt by the prophets to attach to the sacrifices of their time. Their attitude to sacrifices is one of frank opposition. It may be said that this opposition is really directed against profane or corrupt sacrifices, the importations of heathenism into the pure religion of Israel. "Bring no more vain oblations; incense is an abomination unto me."[1] This may be so; yet the striking point is that no such contrast is ever suggested, and that no true sacrifices are enjoined to replace the false; no sacrifices, that is, except acts of moral and spiritual obedience. "To obey is better than sacrifice, and to hearken than the fat of rams." "The sacrifices of God are a broken spirit; a broken and a contrite heart, O God, thou wilt not despise." "I desire mercy and not sacrifice." "Is not this the fast that I have chosen? to loose the bonds of wickedness, to undo the bands of the yoke, to let the oppressed go free?" "Yea, though ye offer me your burnt offerings, I will not accept them . . . but let judgment roll down as waters, and righteousness as a mighty stream."[2] This is the contrast that is universal in the prophets. It is the contrast

[1] Is. 1^{13}. [2] 1 Sam. 15^{22}; Ps. 51^{17}; Hos. 6^6; Is. 58^6; Am. $5^{22\ 24}$.

SYMBOLISM AND REALITY

that is developed by S. Paul into the contrast between faith and works.

In turning to the writers of the New Testament, our first impression is that their attitude is simply that of the prophets in the Old. The sacrifices of Judaism have no place in the dispensation of grace. The only sacrifice that is of value in the eyes of God is the Christian himself, his body and his spirit, and his offerings of prayer, of thanksgiving, and of obedience. The words "I beseech you therefore, brethren, by the mercies of God, that ye present your bodies a living sacrifice unto God" are echoed in every epistle. But this is not quite true. In the writings of S. Paul and in the Epistle to the Hebrews the Mosaic sacrifices are not treated as valueless absolutely, but as antiquated. Just as the law was the attendant or "usher" (παιδαγωγός) to bring us to Christ, so the sacrifices were shadows of good things to come, types which needed their fulfilment, sign-posts, so to speak, pointing to the goal of the whole journey, which was Christ. The sacrificial terms, as we have seen, are rarely used of the death of Christ; the sacrificial atmosphere is constantly thrown around it. The references to the shedding and the sprinkling of the blood, the slaying of the spotless victim for our sin, and the manner in which Christ himself connected his death, and his body and blood, with the new Covenant, made it impossible for the sacrificial aspect to be mistaken.

But the very fact that this aspect is hinted rather than stated openly is significant. For when the life and duties of the Christian are spoken of the case is different. The sacrificial terms at once begin to occur. The very name which S. Paul loves to give to his converts, "saints" or "holy ones," suggests the Levitical

202 ETHICS AND ATONEMENT

ceremonial at once. "Holiness" in the Law is the technical term for the condition of cleanliness, ritual and physical rather than moral, without which the priest cannot approach the altar; and "holy," when applied in the Old Testament to men, and not to God or to angels, connotes predominantly that state of ceremonial purity and freedom from defilement of any sort in which alone a worshipper can find access to God.[1] When the Christian is told to "present his members" to God as instruments of righteousness, to present his body as a living sacrifice, or to be a member of "a holy priesthood to offer up spiritual sacrifices,"[2] it is to the Law and not the Prophets that his mind is being turned. Why should the technical terms of the altar be so often used of the believer, so seldom of Christ? There can be only one answer. Where there was no danger of ceremonialism, in dealing with the daily life and conduct of the believer, the familiar language of the temple ritual could be readily and lovingly used; where there was a likelihood that the spiritual inwardness of the great redemptive act on Calvary might be forgotten, that language is used with the utmost caution. In this way, the instinct of the early Christian writers accomplished what literary art could scarcely have hoped for; the central point of their gospel is connected with the chief observance of Judaism and of all other religions, and yet raised high above it. Christ died as a sacrifice, yet a sacrifice as different from all other sacrifices as the object is from the shadow, or the reality from the type.

VI. Having come so far, we can hardly avoid a more

[1] See Lev. 17-26, and Ezek. 44.
[2] Rom. 6^{13} 12^1; 1 Pet. 2^5. Compare Rom. 1^9; Phil. 3^3; Rom. 13^6; Phil. 2^{30}, where the words for service are definitely sacrificial.

formidable question : Is there anything in this conception of sacrifice that is of permanent and abiding value for us? Granted that the conception was useful and even invaluable to believers who had been nursed in Judaism, and equally invaluable to converts whose only thought of religion had centred round pagan altars, and to whom the death of their saviour would have to be either a sacrifice or an inexplicable mystery, has it therefore any use for us, to whom the idea of sacrifice is foreign and perplexing? It may be replied that the very persistence of sacrificial terms in our religious language witnesses to their permanent value and necessity. The religious thought of all ages seems to have demanded them. But we can go further than this. For the universal system of sacrifice there must be some underlying principle. If mythology cannot furnish us with a clue to this principle, what can?

To all early religions one great thought is common, that the well-being of the community can only be maintained by personal surrender on the part of one or more of its members. That surrender may take one of many forms; the death, real or pretended, of the king, or of a priest, or of some substitute for either, specially chosen from the tribe, or taken captive in war, or fixed upon by chance; or by the destruction or special preservation of some material object, the last corn-sheaf brought from the field at harvest, for example, or the so-called "May bough," which is then treated with a veneration properly due to the divine. Beneath all the varieties of savage practice, is the belief that life can only be preserved and danger averted, by death.[1]

[1] See Frazer's "Golden Bough," W. Robertson Smith's "Religion of the Semites," Jevon's "Introduction to the History of Religion," chs. v., xi., xii., Crawley's "Tree of Life," ch. iii.

Why by death? Because death, or a representation of death, more or less dramatic, is the only way by which the life of the victim can be preserved, *i.e.* made available for the whole of the community. It is far too early as yet to dogmatise about the dim beginnings of savage practice and belief; to attempt to penetrate them is to find a mass of superstitions, guesses and half-understood truths twisted into a very jungle of illusion. The action of the law of association of ideas is enough to lead the untutored mind into a maze of fallacies ; if a chief, after breaking off a piece of an old anchor, should happen to die suddenly, his followers may begin to pay reverence to the anchor; if an English sportsman dies among the Indian tribe with whom he has lived, the tribesmen have been known solemnly to offer cheroots and brandy at his tomb ; and many a strange custom appears to be derived from the simple but mysterious theory of the virtues of "the hair of the dog that bit you."

Amidst all this dense undergrowth, however, there stand out two or three wide-spread beliefs, common to every race, found in every part of the globe, derivable from no one source, attributable to no one cause, as old as man, and as mysterious ; totemism, as it is now called, or the conviction that men are akin to different species of animals or plants; taboo, or unreasoning dread of dangerous powers supposed to be inherent in certain articles, and from them transmissible to others ; and the belief that strength and vigour and life itself reside in the blood, and can be communicated, through contact with the blood, from one living creature to another. Of the two former, traces have been pointed out, not only in the familiar religions of Greece and Rome, but in the Old Testament itself. The lists of forbidden animals

SYMBOLISM AND REALITY

may have reference to the totem-gods of other Semitic tribes, eaten sacrificially with heathen rites, and therefore to be loathed and abominated in Israel; the laws of ceremonial cleanliness may be but an elevation and a hallowing of the taboos of primitive savagery. The blood as the vehicle of the life lies at the root of the whole sacrificial system. The great difference is that in paganism sin is the last thing to be thought of; in the religion of Israel, it is the first and most important circumstance which influences the Covenant-God in relation to His people.

The real thought underlying Old Testament sacrifice is this. The worshipper feels his own guilt and sin, and knows that he cannot, as he is, appear acceptably before God. He therefore takes an animal, pure and unblemished, and representing the moral spotlessness which he himself has lost. His object is not to substitute the animal for himself, but to present the animal's spotlessness as his own. He confesses his sin; and he lays his hand upon the victim's head, to identify himself therewith; to repudiate that from which he would fain escape. But this is not enough; with the sacrificial knife of the priest, the victim's life must be actually set free. The blood is shed and caught; it is sprinkled upon the worshipper; that is to say, he receives the purity of the victim; and it is sprinkled upon the altar; that is to say, the pure life, now belonging to the worshipper, is offered to God, and accepted.

The mystic import of the blood is seen most clearly in the ritual of the Day of Atonement. On that day, two goats were employed, one being identified with the actual sins of the people, and the other with their desired righteousness; the first was driven into the wilderness; in the case of the other, its blood, like the

206 ETHICS AND ATONEMENT

blood of the bullock specially appropriated for the cleansing of the sins of the officiating priest, was solemnly sprinkled on the mercy seat in the most holy place, in the final act of dedication to God.

If such was the spirit of sacrifice, it is easy to understand the New Testament attitude to the sacrifices of the Old. To our minds there is something strange and even a little grotesque in the adoption of animal spotlessness by a human being as his own. But we must remember that to early man, as well as to vast numbers of the human race at present, the unity of all life is much more important than the distinction between animal and human life. In course of years, as we have seen, the Jewish mind was torn in two, approaching God by the only appointed way of animal sacrifices, and yet unable to see how such sacrifices could have any moral validity. The transference of animal cleanliness to a human being by sprinkling its blood on him was, after all, only a legal fiction. So was the offering of a human life by sprinkling on an altar an animal's blood. But with the death of Christ before his eyes, the Jew no longer needed to think of sacrifice as a riddle. Here was a man, sinless and undefiled and approved by many signs, and most of all by the crowning sign of the resurrection, to be more than man —the very Son of God. His blood had been shed; and by no legal fiction, but by the witness of experience, it was felt to be the source of new strength, purity, and life to every believer. The guilty shrinking from God was gone; it was replaced by a delighted consciousness of his grace.

Christ, then, is represented in the New Testament as the fulfilment of all sacrifice; he has made unnecessary any future sacrifices save that of the humble and

SYMBOLISM AND REALITY

reverent spirit. What they could not do, but only suggest, he has done, and done once for all. What was this? They suggested that purity might be transferred to one who was impure; that another's sinlessness might become mine. In Christ this was felt to be accomplished. The sacrifices therefore were fulfilled just in so far as they meant that the worshipper was enabled by them to receive the stainlessness of the victim. The sacrifices were not always so understood; indeed, they were most often understood otherwise. But in any other sense than this they had no relation to Christ. A sacrifice might be merely an act of thanksgiving, a return for mercies vouchsafed, or the present which an inferior naturally brings when appearing before a superior; or they might be an attempt to curry favour with God by offering to him something of special value to its possessor. There is obviously nothing corresponding to this in the sacrifice upon Calvary. A sacrifice might even be an attempt to strike a bargain with God, much as a Greek would sacrifice to his god before going into battle, or as a modern Italian will offer candles to the Madonna before starting on some perilous undertaking of his own,—a long journey, or even a piece of brigandage. But there was no bargaining in what was the supreme exhibition of God's free grace. Or again, a sacrifice might be offered, especially in times of plague, war, or disaster, to appease the supposed anger of the deity. "If I give up something that I love—torture myself with knives and lancets—kill my own firstborn son upon your altar—surely you will think that I have paid for the sin that has brought this trouble on me, and will stay your avenging hand."[1]

[1] Compare Micah 6⁷.

Agonised cries like these have been uttered under stress of calamity in every land, and to gods of every name; but their spirit is the spirit of the worship of Baal and not of Jehovah. What is there in the Gospels to correspond to this, or even remotely to suggest it?

Any attempted parallel between these lower forms of sacrifice and the sacrifice of Christ is precluded by a single consideration; in the former, it is the worshipper who offers the sacrifice to gain some advantage for himself; in the latter, it is not the worshipper who offers the sacrifice at all, but God. To talk of God bargaining with himself or propitiating himself for the worshipper's benefit, seems impossible. To think of God as arranging a way by which a sinful man might come before him and be accepted, is the only manner in which we can think of a God to whom belong both justice and mercy. Under the Old Covenant, the sacrifice had of course to be offered by the worshipper; but the fact that the worshipper offered it was the least important part of the proceeding; the objects of sacrifice were specially prescribed by the law, and, for a pastoral people, easily obtainable; nor was their efficacy ever enhanced by rarity or costliness. It was simply their life which the worshipper gave in place of, and as, his own. Under the New the sacrifice is offered on our behalf, that we may give, not something else, but ourselves.

Another consequence of our consideration of sacrifice now emerges into view. Sacrifices were not confined to Israel; they are found wherever man is found. And the idea of sacrifice, as the shedding of the blood, which is the life, for the benefit of the worshipper, is not Israel's peculiar possession; it is

SYMBOLISM AND REALITY 209

universal. If therefore Christ fulfilled the types of the Jewish law, he fulfilled the types of pagan custom. In this sense as well as in the more familiar one, he was not the son of the Jews only; he was the son of man. Degraded, thoughtless, and profane as the Israelitish sacrifices at times became, they still bore witness to the great sacrifice which God was to set forth in the fulness of time for the redemption of man and his restoration to the life of God himself; and however dark, repulsive, or apparently meaningless might be the sacrificial rites of Kaffir or Negro, Aztec or Hindu, they show that the isles also were waiting for his law. The obscure rites are adumbrations of the central truth of all experience; both the distorted wisdom of barbarian ages, the sayings of certain of the sages and poets of heathen civilization, have led men to conceive of the possibility of receiving the life of God into the soul of man. In the great sacrifice of the human race, there is neither Jew nor Greek, barbarian nor Scythian, bond nor free.

VII. Here, however, it may be necessary to face another objection, namely, that this sacrificial interpretation of Christ's death might be perfectly satisfactory and convincing to the Jews, accustomed to regard sacrifices as being a necessity to any religion; and also to the heathens to whom the gospel might be preached; but can it have the same significance for us? To modern Christians, the sights and sounds accompanying sacrifice, would be wholly foreign and repugnant. Would the idea ever have occurred to us, apart from the Jewish sacrifices, that without shedding of blood, there can be no remission of sins? We do not at present naturally think in terms of the altar, and it is unreasonable to expect us to do so; nor can we conceive of a spiritual effect, like conversion, following a material cause, like the shedding of blood. At best, such language is metaphorical; the metaphor does not indeed mislead, as the Levitical ritual misled, being for that reason condemned by the prophets and antiquated by Christianity; but it may none the less be misunderstood, or not understood at all. The contention of the Epistle to the Hebrews, it might be argued, is as much out of date as is the ceremonial environment of its first readers, and the doctrine of the Atonement, to be intelligible to us, must not be stated in terms of sacrifice at all.

The reply is not really difficult. The sacrificial language of the New Testament is certainly metaphorical. Now, every metaphor is literally false. To say that "the ship ploughs the sea," or "the dawn gilds the mountains," if taken literally, is both false and unmeaning. Metaphor must be expanded into simile; "as the plough cleaves the soil, so the ship cuts through the sea." So, the statement that "without shedding of blood there is no remission," if it is to be literally true, must be expanded in like manner; " just as the Jew or pagan felt that without the shedding of the pure victim's blood, his uncleanness could not be removed, so, without receiving the life of Christ, our unrighteousness cannot be remitted." We must admit that this language may be misleading; indeed, the aim of our whole argument has been to preclude the possibility of its misinterpretation; almost from the beginning, people have talked of the blood or of the cross of Christ, without comprehending their real import; but how else shall we express the truth? The highest ideas can only be embodied in forceful metaphors or clumsy periphrases. Even the Fatherhood of God may be set down as metaphorical; but

SYMBOLISM AND REALITY 211

once let us understand the simile, and there need be no fear from the metaphor. And what is theology for, save to teach us to expand metaphors into similes? There is no need to forget that in the Epistle to the Hebrews, the words are quoted with evident approval and without modification, "Sacrifices and whole burnt offerings . . . thou wouldest not . . . then hath he said, Lo, I am come to do thy will."[1]

Understood in this way, can we venture to call the language of the New Testament antiquated? The writer of the same epistle speaks almost immediately afterwards of those who would "enter into the holy place by the blood of Jesus"; what does he mean save that when we have received the life, the spirit, of Jesus, the pure Son of God, we can approach the very presence of God? When S. Paul reminds the Colossians that they "who were once far off have been made nigh by the blood of Christ,"[2] he is telling them that the life of Christ, communicated to them, has brought to an end the old separation born of ignorance and sin. Apart from this interpretation, the words which instituted the Eucharist, "this is my body, this is my blood," may give rise to the grossest materialism of transubstantiation; with it, they convey the clearest promise of the experience that can say "no longer I live, but Christ liveth in me."

We reach the full symbolical significance of the sacrifice when we notice, lastly, that there is another transference; the transference of the worshipper's guilt to the sacrifice. This is a striking part both of the ritual in the Old Testament, and of its interpretation in the New. "The Lord laid on him the iniquity of us

[1] Heb. 10⁸.   [2] Col. 2¹³.

all." It was not enough to receive the new goodness; the sin had to be confessed and repudiated. On the Day of Atonement, this repudiation was symbolised by the driving away of one of the goats into the wilderness, bearing the sins of the people. But in ordinary cases, where there was but one animal, it was easy to regard the blood as cleansing or washing away from the worshipper the sin which he had by confession transferred to it, while at the same time it bestowed on him its supposed purity. How Christ was thus "made a curse for us" we have already discussed. When we recognise the fact, we understand that the sacrifices do not enable us to understand Christ, but that Christ enables us to understand the sacrifices.

VIII. Sacrifice, then, is a moral transaction for moral ends. It is the repudiation of sin. It is the transference, to an impure life, of purity and goodness. Pain, and even death—as death is in our thought, namely, the cessation of bodily life—are inevitable accessories; but they are not insisted upon; the main point is that as the victim is accepted by God, so is the worshipper who offers it, and thus, by faith, we can claim and receive its purity. There is nothing here inconsistent with ethics. Ethics demands goodness; it cannot tell us how it is or is not to be obtained. But in taking up this attitude, do we not seem to be relinquishing the argument of the preceding chapters? There, we obtained the goodness we could not of ourselves exhibit, through being reconciled by a mediator; here, by the sacrifice of a victim. Can Christ be at one and the same time, both reconciler and sacrifice? He can. The points of view from which he is regarded now as the one and now as the other, are different; the spirit and meaning of both functions are identical. We may call the two functions, for clearness' sake, the moral and the ceremonial; when we speak of Christ as the reconciler, we are speaking in terms of morals; when we call him the sacrifice, in terms of traditional observance. And it must be remembered that when we have been speaking of sacrifice, we have been using the word in its technical sense as an offering made to God, and not in its more modern and familiar sense as the surrender of anything we may hold dear, either for ourselves or for a friend. To apply the word in this latter sense to the work of Christ is to refer rather to the moral than to the ceremonial aspect of his life. It is the victim who is made the sacrifice; it is the reconciler who, as we say, makes the sacrifice. But whether we speak of Christ as making the sacrifice, or as being the sacrifice, we mean that he so placed himself in relation both to God and to man, that he was able to communicate his spirit, his obedience, his life, to man, and thus to make man as acceptable to God as he was himself.

> "Accepted in the Well-beloved,
> And clothed in righteousness divine,
> I see the bar to heaven removed;
> And all thy merits, Lord, are mine.
> . . . .
> And lo, I plead the atoning blood,
> And in thy right I claim thy heaven."

The two aspects are mutually complementary. Christ has combined them in his simple and touching declaration, "Greater love hath no man than this, that a man lay down his life for his friends." Did he lay down his life for his friends as a sacrifice or as a reconciler? As sacrifice, he laid down his life, that it might be appropriated by others; as reconciler he gave up for his "friends" all that he held most precious, to bring them back to God. His death, as we saw when considering reconciliation, was the consummation of his life, of his obedience to God, and his loving sympathy to the wanderer; but it was also, as we saw when considering sacrifice, the means by which that life could be transmitted to and shared by those for whom it was lived. But let us be careful to understand the term "death" in its complete sense. No one who knows anything of the history of Christendom can overlook the value of the spectacle of the cross, as an appeal to the purest sympathy and the highest emotion. Agony bravely borne, injustice victoriously accepted, together with the whole contrast between the moral grandeur of the sufferer and the physical repulsiveness and disgrace of his surroundings, infallibly conduce to an ennobling pity and an adoring allegiance. The sudden rush of feeling which made the centurion acknowledge in the crucified Galilean a righteous man or even the Son of God, and which drew from Clovis, hearing for the first time the story of the cross, the eager cry "If I had been there with my Franks, that would never have happened," has surely been repeated in the experience of many of the readers of this book. But the power of the cross does not rest on a sublime spectacle, however affecting; nor does the efficacy of the death of Christ spring from the single moment when he "gave up his spirit." His whole life was one long death, his death was the complete expression of his life. The sacrificial act was real; but it was performed not simply during the few hours on the cross, but through all the years that stretched between Bethlehem and Calvary.

The mere emotion of admiration will fade and disappear. Other magnificent sacrifices have been and will be forgotten. The sacrifice and the reconciliation of Christ point severally to the two great companion truths of metaphysics, that life and character are transferable; and that only by the surrender of one's life can that life be gained, either by oneself or by another. Here, if ever, we pass out of the region of metaphor, into that of definite law. "To as many as received him, to them gave he authority to become the sons of God"; received him, that is to say, not by acclaiming him as the Messiah or even as the Son of God; but, to use his own words, by eating his flesh and drinking his blood; by taking the bread which he gave, his flesh, for the life of the world; by receiving his life as their life. "That life which I now live in the flesh, I live in faith, the faith which is in the Son of God, who loved me and gave himself up for me";—gave himself up in that life-long death to sin, lived before the eyes of an unsympathetic and hostile world, in virtue of which the believer also died to sin and rose to righteousness; that death in which he laid down his life, that not only he, but all who came to God by him, might take it again.

CHAPTER VIII

THE GOD-MAN

1. THE investigation of truth would be far easier than it is, if truth lay at the end of a straight line, so that we could advance to it step by step, making sure of each step before we passed on to the next. As a matter of fact, truth is like an arch, in which every part must be carefully articulated to the rest; and until the last brick is fitted into its place, we cannot be said to have anything of the arch at all. We may single out one piece as the keystone; but for practical purposes, every piece is the keystone to the rest. So with our own argument in the preceding chapters. We have not advanced—we could not advance—step by step; we have been laying bricks, for no one of which could we be completely ready, till every other brick had been put into its proper place.

We have seen already that right conduct, which it is the aim of ethics to analyse, springs from right relations between persons, and that a completely ethical society would embody the relations of members of the same family to one another. To restore these relations when broken, is the work of a personal reconciliation;—a reconciliation which cannot be accomplished by the person who has done the wrong, but only by the instrumentality of a third person, capable of occupying the positions of both injurer and injured alike. This process of reconciliation we have found, displayed at

THE GOD-MAN 217

its fullest, in the accounts of the Atonement given in the New Testament. We have seen that there is nothing in these accounts contrary to the notions of ethics; and where they seemed to import ideas alien to ethics, such as ceremonialism or sacrifice, they were in reality only emphasising the ethical ideal of acquiring and manifesting a goodness otherwise despaired of. But we have so far made one great assumption. We are not alone in making it; it is made in the every-day dealings of ordinary people with one another as constantly as it is made in theological treatises. We have assumed that it is possible for one person to place himself in the position occupied by a second, and by so doing, to bring that second person back with him to the position which is his own. Further, we have assumed that one person can at the same time occupy the position of two others, and thereby make those two at one with each other. This seems hopelessly paradoxical. What ground have we for maintaining that it is possible? We may reply that all reconcilement and mediation, all operations of personal influence, imply its possibility. We are always transcending the limits of our own personalities to pass over to other people; and other people are always passing over to us; this is the essence of all personal intercourse, the basis on which all human society is built. We live far more outside our own skin than inside. I can only influence other people by projecting myself into them; and if I ever know the happiness of reconciling two people who have been estranged, it is simply by passing into each of them, and drawing them into myself.

But, natural as this may sound when applied to ordinary human intercourse, it is far otherwise when expressed in the language of theology. Christ, we are told, and Christ alone, was able to accomplish the Atonement, because he was at once God and man. But this statement would seem to pass beyond the powers of reason altogether. How can an individual, living at a definite period of history like the rest of us, be "one with" God? And how can any individual, however exalted, be not only a man, but "man," that is to say, "one with" humanity or the race? This is the eternal wonder which has made some regard speculation in theology as almost impious; and has made others turn from theology as if it were treason to the human intellect. Either way of thinking would be fatal to our argument. All truth, even where it exceeds a man's grasp, must be capable of being reached by him, if not by reason, then by that subtle intuition, which is the precursor of reason and perhaps a higher form of reason, wherein we are unconscious of the step while we are sure of the conclusion. There is no rest in a mystery as such; if there is any rest in thoughts which we cannot understand, it is because they contain certain elements which we can understand—which, as we say, mean something for us. However deep the sea, we ought to be able to sail on it, and reach the haven where we would be. There are mysteries enough in science; we are not yet a step nearer the knowledge of the origin of free-will, of consciousness, or of life; we comprehend neither the cause of natural selection, as we call it, nor the composition of matter; but no scientific thinker would ask us to accept a theory on any of these problems on the ground that it transcended our human comprehension. It may indeed lie beyond us to comprehend how matter as we know it can be made up of electrons; but we can claim to understand the reasons which have lead to the adoption of this view.

THE GOD-MAN

And can theology teach us in any other fashion? Theology is as much a science—a body of ordered, though perhaps far from complete, knowledge—as is biology or physics. Every science begins with faith, and ends with faith; but like every man of science, the theologian must be prepared to give a reason for the faith that is in him. What reason has theology, then, for speaking of Christ as one with God?

II. There are two ways of answering this question; we may take the path of metaphysics, consider the nature of God, and show that the nature which was in Christ was one with this. It was by following this method that the Greek fathers formulated the great creeds of Christendom. But to our own generation, their arguments have failed to carry conviction. We have come to feel the wide gulf which separates the technical language of the creeds of Asia Minor from the simple teaching of Galilee and Jerusalem. Jesus himself never bade us wrestle with the metaphysical subtleties involved in his unity of substance and person with the Father. He cared nothing for definitions, distinctions, or dogmatic assertions of any sort. For this reason, Ritschl and his followers have called us to the other extreme, and advised us to give up trying to define the Godhead of Christ. It is enough, they say, to recognise that Christ has for Christians the value of God; we think of him, that is to say, as God, and we receive through him all that God has to give. Let us be satisfied with this, and rid our minds both of metaphysics, or the consideration of the unity of Christ and God, and mysticism, or the hope of attaining union with God ourselves. We cannot be too thankful to Ritschl for reminding us of the importance of the practical in religion and in theology. With teaching that

220 ETHICS AND ATONEMENT

had no practical moral value, Jesus had no sympathy. To say that there is no metaphysics in the Bible would perhaps lead us too far; but we can say that whatever metaphysics the Bible contains, is grounded in the moral and the spiritual.

There is another course. Assuming the idea of Christ's Godhead, we may ask how it grew up. Twelve Galilean peasants were to bequeath the thought that Jesus was the Son of God to all after ages; how did they acquire it themselves? We naturally turn to the records of their intercourse with Jesus. What do we find? First, that the disciples hardly ever use language which directly ascribes divinity to Christ. Second, that Christ hardly ever lays any direct claim to divinity for himself. Third, that he asserts in himself a unique obedience to God, and he claims a unique knowledge of God, and a unique right to act as God. Fourth, that in the earliest Christian writings, which are—it must not be forgotten—earlier than any of our existing gospels, Christ is accorded a supremacy which, to say the least, is unshared and unsharable by any other human being. If they do not say, Christ is God, they do say, with entire explicitness, Christ is more than man.

The actual process by which Christ came to possess this pre-eminence in their thought was as follows. Their religion, like that of all Jews, was monotheism; for the truth that Jehovah their God was one God, all of them would have been ready to die, as one of them at least, Simon the Zealot, had been ready to fight. To them, Jesus was at first, as he had been to Nicodemus, simply a teacher come from God; their religious system admitted of his being no more. But that he was no ordinary teacher, they speedily discovered. Hitherto,

THE GOD-MAN

the only teaching they had known had been the didactic and artificial expositions of the scribes; now they listened to one who taught with authority. Others besides themselves were compelled to confess that never man spake like this man; they knew that he had the words of eternal life. It was his meat, he told them, his daily sustenance, to do the will of his father; he performed startling works, and claimed to do so by the finger of God. He went further, and made surprising assertions of his first-hand knowledge of God; "no man knoweth the Father but the Son, and he to whomsoever the Son willeth to reveal him"; just as he had previously said, in an equally surprising manner, "no man knoweth the Son save the Father." This was impressive; but how much more so was his claim that he, the man who lived and taught among them, would come "in his glory," and "the holy angels with him," to judge the whole earth? Three times over, at the beginning, the middle, and the end of his public life, had there been, as we are told, "voices from heaven," saying "this is my beloved Son." What it meant to be "Son of God" he never explained to them, and they never asked; but that it meant that he stood to them almost in the place of God became evident to these monotheistic Jews when he told them that to live, they must eat his flesh and drink his blood. Unconsciously the disciples had been prepared for the only thing left to be said, in order to identify him with their "one God";—"I and the Father are one thing" (not εἰς but ἕν).

On the other hand, Jesus never used the title "Son of God," of himself. It is worth while to notice the passages which seem to contradict this statement. In S. Matthew, the title is used in reference to Christ by

222 ETHICS AND ATONEMENT

Satan, the demons, the disciples, the heavenly voice, Caiaphas, the passers-by at Calvary, and the centurion; but when we read the words "for he said, I am the Son of God" used either by the evangelist himself or inserted as a quotation from the bystanders at the crucifixion, we look in vain, as far as this Gospel is concerned, for the occasion of their utterance, unless it be in Christ's quiet "Thou sayest it," in answer to Caiaphas. S. Mark adduces no further instance. S. Luke refers also to the words of Gabriel, but gives us nothing fresh, and quotes the centurion witnessing Christ's death as saying "this was a righteous man."

S. John, in his own statements, is far more explicit than the other evangelists: he gives the confessions of Nathaniel and Martha and Thomas, and he quotes the significant words "Father, glorify thy Son." The Jews accuse Jesus before Pilate of having made himself the Son of God; he himself refers to his having said "I am the Son of God": he tells the Jews that the dead will hear the voice of the Son of God: and he asks the man who had been born blind "Dost thou believe on the Son of God?" adding immediately "I that speak unto thee am he." Here it must be noticed that perhaps stronger evidence exists for the reading "the Son of man." But apart from this it is quite clear that S. John does everything except make Jesus say categorically, "I am the Son of God." More usually, however, Jesus spoke of himself as "the Son," simply; still more often as "the Son of man." He needed to pray, like any other man, though he knew that his Father heard him always; he never sought to make the least secret of this need. If judgment was in his hands, it had been committed to him by the Father; committed to him, that is to say, in virtue of his sonship. He did

THE GOD-MAN

not hesitate to say, "the Father is greater than I"; and he was ready to explain that with regard to the final "day," the passing away of the heavens and the earth, even he, the Son, was ignorant, as ignorant as the angels or as man; only the Father knew;—an explanation which follows the assertion that his words shall never pass away like the transitory universe. To a casual questioner, he used words almost suggesting that there was no special connexion between himself and God; "Why callest thou me good? none is good, save one, that is, God"; and in the crisis of his own inner life, as he subsequently described it to the disciples, he resolutely bent his own will to that supreme will with which he had so often in their hearing identified himself, "not as I will, but as thou wilt."

III. It has been objected, indeed, that Jesus' claim to unity with the Father cannot be traced to his own lips, but results from the ecstatic brooding of his disciples over his magnificence, until they could stop short at nothing less than his godhead. Most of the assertions of this unity, as we have noticed, occur in the fourth Gospel; the fourth Gospel is later than the other three, and it is strongly urged that we cannot rely upon its being an authentic presentation of the character of Jesus as revealed by himself. But the same claims occur in the other Gospels; if they are not as numerous, they are quite as emphatic; the statement that no one knows the Father save the Son is not in the fourth Gospel, but the first. In all three, Jesus claims the power to heal, to forgive sins, and to judge the world. But that suggestion raises an even greater difficulty; if the rapt devotion of the disciples exalted Jesus into unity with Jehovah, how came they to record at the same time words which so strikingly emphasised his manhood and his subservience to that supreme Jehovah with whom they were identifying him? If they had imagined the one, must they not have forgotten the other? The picture of Jesus as we have it in the Gospels, is highly complex. How could one describe an individual at once equal with God and lower than God without glaring inconsistency? To have made such a picture harmonious, to have given it that strangely convincing air of verisimilitude, would have been impossible for a skilled writer of the present day; how much more for ignorant peasants who in course of time could dream themselves into exalting to divinity their friend and comrade?

But the case is still stronger; the divinity of Jesus does not for the first time appear in a memoir written by an unknown adherent, as it is suggested, nearly a century after its subject's death; within twenty-five years of the crucifixion of Jesus, his divinity was being proclaimed in the great centres of commerce and government by one who was no ignorant peasant, but a skilful dialectician, trained in the very schools where the belief in monotheism had become almost a fanaticism. The attempt to explain away words like "I and the Father are one," or "as the Father hath life in himself, so hath he given unto the Son to have life in himself," as the products of a hundred years of systematic rhapsodizing, would seem hardly worth while, when Saul of Tarsus could declare that he learnt, and taught, that Jesus died for our sins, and rose again the third day, and was declared to be the Son of God with power. If Jesus did not himself declare his divinity, the fact that a generation after his death, no one among his followers so much as thought of doubting it, is an even greater marvel.

THE GOD-MAN 225

Natural speculations about that divinity, some of them grotesque enough, soon became rife, in what we call the early heresies; but that there was divinity to be examined and explained, no one ever denied.

As a matter of fact, the memoirs of Jesus make it quite plain that his calm assumption of divine functions puzzled every one who listened to him. They could not even make up their minds as to whether he was the Messiah or not. "How long dost thou hold us in suspense? If thou be the Messiah, tell us plainly." Long before this, many of his disciples had found his sayings hard, and had gone back and walked no more with him. Others again, not altogether unnaturally, felt that the Nazarene carpenter's claim to pronounce forgiveness was sheer blasphemy; "Who can forgive sins but God only?" When Jesus at the last stood as a prisoner before the Sanhedrim, the High Priest could only adjure him to say whether he was the Messiah, the Son of God; and when he used words that seemed to admit it, the cry of "Blasphemy!" was repeated. The disciples on their side never addressed Jesus as God; their intercourse with him was not that of worshippers with their God, but of friends with their teacher; it is difficult to see how it could have been anything else. When they were telling Jesus of the current opinions about himself,—that he was Elijah, Jeremiah, or one of the prophets,—Peter, in answer to a direct challenge from Jesus, added "Thou art the Messiah, the Son of God." After the startling news of the resurrection, Thomas, seeing before him the glorified but tangible body of Jesus, burst out into the exclamation, "My Lord and my God!"

It is plain that Jesus exacted no formal and possibly miscomprehended declaration of his divinity from his disciples. Adherence to his cause was conditional on no formula. Nor was any formula of divinity emphasised in the early sermons in the Acts. To judge from their preaching, the main point for the disciples after Pentecost was that Jesus was risen, the risen Messiah, and that God had exalted him to be Saviour and Prince ; and that in him the most pregnant prophecies of the coming deliverer in the Old Testament found their fulfilment. We discover no trace, while the gospel still lingered within Palestine, of the metaphysical speculations which began to spring up so thickly in the second century. The Jew was no metaphysician, and the very terms "Nature" and "Person," inseparable from all Christological discussion, could have found no equivalent in his language. But if there was no metaphysics in early Christian preaching, there was no approach to what might be called "di-theism." Not even the professed enemies of the infant church could suggest this. There is no trace of any Jewish attack on the new Christian sect, on the score of disloyalty to the unity of God ; though, had there been any possibility of making such a charge, it would not have been overlooked. When the gospel travelled into the pagan world, it was confronted by an almost greater danger. The Gentile mind would not have rejected the suggestion of two divinities, a father and a son, with contumely ; on the contrary, it would have been prepared to welcome the idea as an interesting parallel to the relation of Zeus to Heracles, or Demeter to Persephone. On one occasion, indeed, the highly cultivated people of Athens fancied that Paul was preaching two new gods, Jesus and "Anastasis" (the Resurrection); but whatever mistakes were made by the converts from heathenism—and they were numerous

THE GOD-MAN

—there is no sign of any worship of allied divinities, in the sense in which, to the Roman Catholic mind, the Virgin is allied to the Deity.

Without being aware of it, the early Christian preachers vindicated the consistency of two great principles, hitherto held to be diametrically opposite, the unity of God, and plurality within the Godhead. They were monotheists, and it never occurred to them that they were in danger of being anything else. They were convinced of the Godhead of Christ, and of the unity of Christ with God, "the Father";—a unity based, not on metaphysical dogma, nor on physical descent, but on the experienced identity of purpose, will, power, goodness. The introduction of a new personality into the Godhead—to use our modern terms—implied strange processes of generation, hitherto foreign to their conception of the self-contained and solitary magnificence of the "I Am." We cannot say that they developed their Christology; their Christology developed itself in their own minds. The five loaves which Christ once put into their hands multiplied there till they could feed a crowd of thousands; and their daily intercourse with Christ matured a conviction about him which grew into the form which leaped forth from Peter's lips when he uttered the cry, "Thou art the Son of God."

In the epistles, the reticence in calling Christ God is as remarkable as the insistence on the facts which imply his godhead. Paul speaks of Christ as "God blessed for evermore,"[1] and in the Epistle to the Hebrews we find the words "Thy throne, O God, is for ever and ever" directly applied to the Son;[2] which we can only parallel by the expressions "The word was God"[3] and

[1] Rom. 9^5. [2] Heb. 1^8. [3] John 1^1.

"the church of God, ... which he purchased with his own blood."[1] But when they had once recognized in him the risen Messiah, the fulfilment of ancient prophecy, their recognition of what this implied far outstripped any language directly attributing divinity to him. It would even seem that they were so anxious to show that he discharged the functions of Deity, that they did not trouble about the name. If he was the risen Messiah, he could not have come into existence only when he appeared upon earth; as he himself said, "Before Abraham was, I am"; indeed, could there ever have been a time when he was not? the glory which he had with the Father, he must have had, to use the words of his prayer, "before the world was."

Again, if this were so, he could not be thought of as a part of creation; he must be outside of it, Lord of it; "the first born of every creature," all things not only being created for him but through him and in him. Further, he who forgave sins, saved his people, revealed the will of God, and was to judge the world, how could he be otherwise than the image, the visible representation of God? Or with equal appropriateness he could be called "the Word," the message, the expression of the mind of God. But if God, the unchanging, be from the beginning, His Word must have been from the beginning too, even if it had only been fully expressed in the latter days. And since the Word was no lifeless thing but the living Prince and Saviour, it, or rather he, must have been with God, that is (to give the full force of S. John's pregnant expression) in living relation to God, with perpetual activity ever turning towards God. If he was felt to be all this, how could the Christian consciousness avoid

[1] Ac. 20^{28}.

THE GOD-MAN

adding, "the Word was God"? In no angelic being could there have been found, in equal completeness, all human and all divine qualities. And angels themselves are thus part of that creation over which Christ was placed. True, Christ is never confused with the Father. S. Paul goes so far as to write in one place that, when the Lordship of the Son shall have been consummated, "the Son shall himself be subjected to" the Father.[1] But no one can read the New Testament without seeing that throughout its pages the Son is regarded as throned far above all principalities and powers in the undying glory of an endless union with the Father.

IV. And can we say less? Shall we accuse the New Testament writers of having been misled by their affection for their friend and their reverence for his memory into a wild exaggeration of the origin and attributes of his character, and a blasphemous identification with God of a good man who had had a great and salutary influence on themselves? Is it even conceivable that such a conception should grow up in the minds of men born and brought up in the strictest monotheism the world has ever known? The man in the street, whether in Galilee or anywhere else, does not make theology, especially theology of such a daring and adventurous type. Of blasphemy or even irreverence the most searching critics of the New Testament have not discovered a trace. On the contrary, the holiness of God there attains a majesty unknown elsewhere; and if the disciples were simply exaggerating the honour due to their departed friend, how came it that the man who gave the clearest expression to the unity of Christ with God had never been a friend of the man Jesus at all?

[1] Cor. 15^{28}.

Moreover is it not a travesty to describe Christ as a good man who has had a salutary influence on certain associates of his? His is a record more than man's, or at least more than that of any man known to us. It has become fashionable in certain quarters to compare him with Moses, Buddha, Confucius, Mohammed, and other religious leaders of most of whom we know very little, and of none of whom have we records anything like so complete or so trustworthy as of Christ. We may welcome the beauty and strength, the patience, the humility or the wisdom displayed by some of these "pagan Christs," as they have been called; but they all of them differ from Christ in two very striking characteristics; each of the great religious leaders has claimed some special spiritual isolation, of the ascetic, the prophet or the general; Christ alone lived a life indistinguishable, in its outward aspect, from that of ordinary men; he did not retire into the wilderness or the forest; he did not wear a peculiar kind of dress; he was not found in kings' palaces; the great accusation levelled against him was that he ate with publicans and sinners. They aspired to stand above men; he was among men "as one that serveth"; their humanity was incomplete; his was perfect. Secondly, in spite of all this, he made claims that they never dared to make; he spoke of himself as they never did; they point men to God; he pointed men to himself; they said, "follow God as I follow him"; he said simply, "follow me." And this command was supported, not by assertions that he was super-human, but by the witness of an unchallenged sinlessness. The divinity which he thus tacitly claimed was as consistent as his humanity; his relations to God were as complete and unvarying as

THE GOD-MAN

were his relations to the men and women whom he came to save.

More than this, the claim, so astounding and unique, is verified in the experience of those who allow it. Through Christ, they find done for them what God does not do for them apart from Christ. The blessings of God they find mediated through Christ. To use the Ritschlian phrase once more, Christ to them "has the value of God." This is to say more than ever was said or could be said of any other religious luminary; it is to place Christ by himself above creation, and as lord of creation; it is to admit that Christ does, speaks, and blesses, exactly as God does. Can we stop here? Is not this to admit that Christ actually is God? Or is there some third category in the universe—not a third to God and man, but a third to God and all created and subordinate beings? To make such an assertion would only be to remove the matter further from human comprehension and experience than ever. Of whom beside could it be said that he has for us the value of God? To have the value of God is nothing else than to be God for us; and to be God for us is nothing else than to be, as far as we are concerned, God.

Ritschlianism means either that Christ was divine, or it means nothing. No one would deny that this assertion involves philosophical difficulties; every great truth involves philosophical difficulties; but no one has ever successfully faced the dilemma, "aut deus aut homo non bonus"; if Christ was not God, he could not even have been good; the dilemma might indeed be restated more fully, " aut deus, aut deceptor vel deceptus "; if Christ was not God, he was either deceiving others, or he was himself sadly deceived. Which alternative is preferable ; to accuse him of inventing a dishonourable

232 ETHICS AND ATONEMENT

fiction from which every other religious leader would have shrunk, or to discover in him a childish folly which would place him far below the mental level of them all?

Such, then, is the Biblical presentation of Christ as "one" with God; a oneness that was overheard rather than heard; seldom proclaimed from his lips, but hourly proclaimed by his life. The recognition of this oneness arose from no speculation about the basis of his personality or the essence of which his divinity subsisted; speculation follows the recognition of a truth, and cannot precede it. The recognition of Christ's divinity was the recognition that, for the practical purposes of the spiritual life, Christ stood where God did; the deepest elements of personality, as we understand it, thought, purposes, power, will, he shared with God; he taught, spoke, and loved, as God would do; he gave his followers all that God could give; he gave gifts which were not given without him; he was the "Word," the living message, the visible manifestation, of God; and they were ready to die for the vital truth that "the Word was God."

V. Now comes our second question; how could Christ be man? And here too, as in the previous part of the chapter, it will be best to ask, How can the belief be seen developing in the minds of Christ's earliest followers? It is obvious that the oneness of Christ with the race cannot be the same as the oneness of Christ with God. The unity of God is quite different from the unity of the human race; the latter is made up of countless individuals, differing as widely as the poles in every conceivable particular of thought, of knowledge, of ideals, and of goodness. How could there be any unity in such a heterogeneous agglomeration?

THE GOD-MAN

How could Christ identify himself with that unity? And if he could do so, how could he then be one with God? God and man are surely opposites; to deny this would seem to be a contradiction in terms; and if we are to identify Christ, in any sense, with Man, we must forfeit our identification of him with God.

Now, it is safe to say that such questions, in this form, could never have occurred to those who knew Christ upon earth and were the first preachers of the gospel.[1] Humanity, as a general term, was at that time quite foreign to the Jewish intellect, or indeed to any intellect, save, perhaps that of a few Roman lawyers. Christian thought, also, has for the most part been far more anxious to prove that Jesus was really human, and not simply God masquerading, so to speak, in a human guise, than that he was one with the race as a whole. That he was human, indeed, cannot be doubted, if we are to place the slightest reliance on our records; he grew, suffered, needed sleep and food, like the rest of us; but that is not our point at present; we want to see, not how he was a man, but how he was Man. To our minds, Christ's unity with the race is suggested by his customary use of the title, "the Son of Man," to indicate himself. But it is doubtful whether this title would suggest such a unity to his hearers. To speak of a man as the son of anything (consolation, or wisdom, or peace, or folly), meant, in Hebrew or Aramaic, that he possessed the essential qualities of that thing; but the Jew, with his memories of phrases

---

[1] We can apply to the gospels, and to the whole of the New Testament, Prof. A. B. Davison's words about the Old: "The sphere of the Old Testament is the practical religious sphere, out of which it never wanders into the sphere of ontology. The whole question is the question of the relation of a living, active, moral, personal God to the world and men. It asks as little what the essence of God is as it asks what the essence of man is" ("Theology of the Old Testament," p. 115).

234   ETHICS AND ATONEMENT

in the Psalms, in Ezekiel and Daniel, or in the apocalyptic books of Enoch, would think of the words " Son of Man," as meaning either man as opposed to brutes, or man in his weakness, yet cared for by God. In any case, we see from a significant passage in the fourth gospel, that Christ's use of the term puzzled the Jews ; " Who is this Son of Man ? " nor, we gather, was it any better understood by Christians; only once did the words fall from Christian lips after Christ's death.[1]

At first, Christ was not even "the Christ," the Messiah, save to a very few ; he was simply a "teacher" sent from God ; a man with a strange power of attracting, or repelling, his fellow-men, just as he was felt to have a strange affinity with God. Nor did he, before his death, emphasise anything in his teaching which would have shown him to be different, in his relation to mankind, from other teachers. He said far more about the relation of the Father to mankind than about his own. But a fresh note might have been overheard when he invited men to himself, not only as the giver of rest, but as the source of life, and when he bade them eat his flesh and drink his blood ; when he told them how he was to give his life a ransom for many ; and when, alone with the disciples at the last, he commanded them to find the fulfilment of his joy in them, by abiding in him, as he would abide in them. Such language would be meaningless, unless there were some importation of personality from Christ to his followers; something more than the influence of one person over another ; some fusion of Christ with the Self, the person, of the believer. These words could hardly fail to be ambiguous at the time ; nor would the ambiguity be removed when Christ

[1] John 12^{34} ; Acts 7^{56}.

THE GOD-MAN

spoke in one and the same breath of never leaving them, and of departing from them so as to send another "Comforter," who was to guide them into all truth, and to be in them. They could only gather from this, what they must have been learning before, that the gift which Christ came to bestow was not a law to be set before them, but a life to be lived within them. But as soon as Christ finally left them, there came a great change. All that he had done for them, they now found that they were able to do for themselves. Before, they had looked for help and inspiration from without; now, they found it within.

VI. When reading the story of the early years after the death of Christ, we seem at first sight to have moved away from the standpoint of the gospels. There is striking insistence on Christ as Lord, and as Redeemer; but there is also a constant reliance on the Spirit for every practical need, and a constant reference to the Spirit, which we do not find in the pages of the gospels. We are inclined to ask whether the devotion of the infant church was shared between the Spirit and Christ. When we read the speeches of the Apostles as recorded in the Acts, we have to confess that of any such sharing, if it existed, the Apostles themselves were as unconscious as they were of any division between their reverence for Christ and for God. But when we turn to the Epistles, we find not only that such sharing did not exist, but that it was impossible.

The Epistles are records of Christian experience; and all Christian experience, as we find it in the epistles, is the consciousness of two things; religious satisfaction in the forgiveness of sin, and a new power over sin joined to a new insight into the will of God. The first of these, the forgiveness of sin, is uniformly ascribed to

Christ; the latter is ascribed to the Spirit; but it is also ascribed to Christ, or, more fully, to Christ through the Spirit. It would be superfluous to point out how in the Epistles, the whole activities of the believer spring from the presence of the Spirit within him. He lives by the Spirit; he walks by the Spirit; by the Spirit he puts to death the deeds of the flesh; he minds the things of the Spirit; he is sealed by the Spirit; he has access by the Spirit to the Father; he knows himself to be a child of God by the Spirit given unto him, who is thus the earnest of his future bliss; he brings forth the fruits of the Spirit; and he even knows that Christ abides in him, by his Spirit which he gave him. These statements, which might be multiplied almost indefinitely, are enough to show that the Spirit is considered as being the source of the believer's thought, of his acts, his experience, and his will; in other words, that the Spirit has actually taken the place of the believer's former personality.

What of the relation of Christ to all this? The student of Christ's own words will remember how Christ not only identified God with himself (" I and my Father are one "), but also identified God with the Spirit (" God is Spirit "); and he will connect this with the double premise that Christ would abide in the disciples, and that the Spirit would abide in the disciples. Will he not conclude that the promise is not double but single; that Christ, as one with God, is Spirit, and that the Spirit is simply Christ let loose, so to speak, from the limitations of the body, so as to enter into the lives of individuals? Christ, as he will apprehend, was the Word, the Message, the Logos, of God, spoken and received: the Spirit was the breath; and the breath of God not only conveys the word, but is breathed

THE GOD-MAN 237

into man, is inhaled, received, as it were, into the lungs.

This conclusion will be strengthened by two things that he will notice in the writings of S. Paul; first, that the Spirit is definitely connected with Christ, and even identified with him; "if any man have not the Spirit of Christ, he is none of his"; "this shall turn to my salvation through . . . the supply of the Spirit of Christ Jesus"; "the last Adam (Christ) was made a life-giving Spirit"; and, still more explicitly, "the Lord is the Spirit."[1] Secondly, S. Paul assigns to Christ the same position, as source of the new life and activity in the believer, that he has previously assigned to the Spirit; and he even goes further, and not only asserts that Christ enters into the believer's experiences, but that the believer enters into those of Christ. Christians must have this mind ($\tau o \hat{v} \tau o\ \phi \rho o \nu \epsilon \hat{\iota} \nu$) "which was also in Christ Jesus"; he claims that "we have the mind ($\nu o \hat{v} s$) of Christ." They must be "transformed by the renewing of (their) minds," and it is Christ that is to be formed in them.[2] They are to put away the "old man"; to be renewed in the spirit of their mind, and to "put on the new man," which he expresses elsewhere as putting on Christ.[3] About himself S. Paul says explicitly that he has given up living; Christ has taken the place of his old self in his life; "no longer do I live, but Christ liveth in me";[4] his life in the flesh is a life of faith in the Son of God. Christ is to be in them; and just as they are to live in the Spirit and walk in the Spirit, so they are to be, and as believers or sanctified ones they actually are, "in Christ."

[1] Rom. 8^9; Phil. 1^{19}; 1 Cor. 15^{45}; 2 Cor. 3^{17}.
[2] Phil. 2^5; 1 Cor. 2^{16}; Rom. 12^2; Gal. 4^{19}.
[3] Eph. 4^{22}; Rom. 13^{14}.   [4] Gal. 2^{20}.

238   ETHICS AND ATONEMENT

The use of such language, to indicate the intimacy, the "mystical union," as it has been called, between the believer and Christ or the Spirit of Christ, is striking enough; but, according to S. Paul's view, the believer is actually to find the experiences of Christ repeated throughout his own life. He has "crucified the flesh" with its passions and desires; he has been buried with Christ in baptism; he has been raised with Christ, and as risen with Christ, he and his fellows must seek the things which are above, where Christ sits at the right hand of God; or, to quote a slightly different expression of what is really the same conception, "our old man was crucified with Christ, that the body of sin might be done away . . . but if we died with Christ, we believe that we shall also live with him." "Ye died," he writes elsewhere, "and your life is hid with Christ in God."[1] Christ is thus the true life of every believer, the common life which all share; the bond of union whereby each individual becomes part of one great body; he is the head of the church, the "second man," the "last Adam," a life-giving spirit,[2] alike immanent and transcendent in relation to the great living whole which he has "redeemed with his own blood."

But do not these passages suggest the union of Christ, not with the race, but with the church, with believers? And does not our view of reconciliation make it necessary that the reconciler should be one with all those whom he was to bring back, before they acknowledged him? Here, it is the acknowledgment that makes all the difference. Before such acknowledgment, personal union can at best be only potential. The reconciler can at most enter into the feelings, the shame, the fear,

---

[1] Rom. $6^{6\ 8}$; Col. 3^3.   [2] 1 Cor. 15^{45}.

THE GOD-MAN 239

the separation, of those whom he comes to save. The reality of the union can only be shown by the fact that, after the acknowledgment, they can enter into his feelings, and that what their estrangement had prevented, their reconciliation can effect, producing naturally the fusing of his personality with theirs, the inflowing of his love of the good, his confidence in the right, into them. The union of Christ with the church proves his union, at least implicit, with the race. Here S. John strikes the most definite note, in his continual references to Christ as Life. "I am Resurrection and Life"; "I am the Way, Truth, Life."[1] "In him was Life, and the Life was the light of men; that was the true light that lighteth every man that cometh into the world." Their very need of reconciliation made it impossible for Christ to be the head of all members of the race in an absolute sense; the possibility of reconciliation showed their real though hidden union with him from whom, at their reconciliation, life was to be in its fulness received. That he really did enter into their feelings before the reconciliation, that he became one with them before they could become one with him, the Biblical writers are confident. "We have not an high priest that cannot be touched with the feeling of our infirmities, but one that hath been tempted in all points like as we are." "He took the form of a slave . . . becoming obedient to death."[2] The mysterious words, "Surely he hath borne our griefs and carried our sorrows . . . he was wounded for our transgressions, he was bruised for our iniquities,"[3] though uttered centuries before the death on Calvary, were yet immediately recognised by the

---

[1] The Greek definite article with these abstract nouns can surely be best translated by omission.
[2] Heb. 4^{15}; Phil. $2^{7\,8}$. [3] Is. $53^{3\,4}$.

240 ETHICS AND ATONEMENT

first disciples as the perfect expression of what gave that death its abiding significance.

VII. Such then is the point to which the Bible leads us when we consider the union of Christ with God and with man. On neither side is that union a matter of speculation or theologising; it is based on no grounds that lie outside the limits of our own reason; and it is not even a matter for faith, if faith means that which is opposed to reason; only if faith is the evidence of things not seen but guaranteed to us by our experience, is the union based on faith. It begins in experience, and in experience it ends, so far as it can be said to end at all. Christ is God, not because he is of one metaphysical or supra-sensuous substance with the Father, but because he speaks, acts, and thinks, as God does. In his representing God perfectly lies his divinity. All that we could ever know in God we find in Christ; "he that hath seen me hath seen the Father." The union is personal, and rests on the springs of personality, as far as personality can be known to us,—on emotion, thought, will. On exactly the same basis rests Christ's union with man. The belief in that union, as it was held in the early church, was not based on any medieval theory of realism, by which Christ shared the substance or attributes of the "genus homo"; nor was it based on any abstract conception of the solidarity of the race, any more than the ethics of Christianity flowed from any abstract conception of the "rights of man." On the contrary, the first Christians were compelled to think of a large part of their fellow-men as perishing or being lost; the system of the world was being "brought to nought"; the whole world was "lying in the evil one." Their thought of Christ was of one "who loved me and gave himself for me." But that

THE GOD-MAN 241

love for me could not be confined to me, nor to any special section of humanity. "The arms of love that compass me should all mankind embrace." There can be neither racial nor social distinctions where his approach is recognised. If he is the "new man," the new personality in me, so he must be in everyone who comes to him as I have done. Thus, what he did for me, he did for all; and what I have done in him, all have done, if they would but recognise it. "One died for all; therefore all died; and he died for all, that they which live, should no longer live unto themselves . . . wherefore if *any* man is in Christ, he is a new creature."[1] We are not bound to Christ because we are bound to others; we are bound to others because we are bound to Christ.

Thus the teaching of the parable of the Good Samaritan, that a neighbour is anyone who needs us, broadens out into the principle that no one can love Christ without loving his brother also. At the beginning of our discussion we were wondering how right relations between man and man, when once broken, were to be restored. Ethics alone seemed able to give us no answer. The answer is here. Union with life, with the personal source of life, means union with all living men and women. If I know Christ, I must feel to others as he does. If my attitude to them is wrong, so must be also my attitude to Christ. It is not strange that "eternal punishment" is foretold only for those who have not fed the hungry or clothed the naked; that is to say, for those who have shown by their neglect of men, that they have had no real relations with Christ. "If ye love me, keep my commandments"; "a new commandment

[1] 2 Cor. $5^{15\ 16}$.

give I unto you, that ye love one another." It is because he is the head of the Church,—of redeemed humanity,—that he is the head of humanity as a whole; of humanity, that is to say, as it is implicitly, as it is meant to become explicitly; and because he is the head of humanity, he is the head of the universe; the "first-born of all creation"; all things are to be summed up in him.

To say this is not to eliminate metaphysics from theology. The attempt to do without metaphysics simply results, as has often been pointed out, in bad metaphysics. The apostles were in fact metaphysicians for the reason that makes us all metaphysicians; there are certain questions, "why cannot I always do as I would?" "why am I influenced by something outside me?" "what is it that influences me?" "what am I, and what am I meant to become?" which sooner or later demand an answer from us all. The answers to these questions cannot be obtained from the realm of physics; they are metaphysical; but they may none the less be matters of immediate certainty and experience. They may lead on to subtleties; but in themselves, they are not subtle. Attacks on the metaphysical theology of Christian dogma have in these latter years been frequent; and these attacks have been believed, both by those who delivered them and by those who resisted, to be attacks on Christianity itself. There could be no greater mistake. Metaphysical discussion cannot affect the foundations of Christianity. Theology must come second to religion; she is "the younger child." Every familiar path of the mind leads to the road which passes out of our sight into the unknown. The simplest statement of religious belief, or any other belief, may suggest ineffable

THE GOD-MAN

mysteries. But let us not find fault with theology for making mistakes about what lies along the unknown stretches of the road, until we have become acquainted with the path that traverses our common world. It is as difficult for theologians as for common men to tell what is hidden beyond the bend of the road. We must start, when we consider the meaning of the first teachers of Christianity about him whom we have come to call the "God-man," from the thought of the stainless life and mysterious power and knowledge which made men say of their possessor, "in him dwelleth all the fulness of the Godhead bodily." It was the unquenchable and infectious zeal for service and sacrifice which lived for men and worked in them till they knew him to be "the true light that lighteth every man that cometh into the world," "of whose fulness we have all received." Christ became all that we are, apart from sin: we become all that Christ is, purged from the sin which never could enter into him.

CHAPTER IX

PERSONALITY

I. THE previous chapter has not led us to a complete answer to the question which it propounded. It asked, What reason has theology for speaking of Christ as one with God and with man? It then proceeded to examine the basis of the unity which theology has tried to formulate. That unity, we found, is not metaphysical, but spiritual; it is not speculative, but experimental. Christ was one with God, because, from his first appearance among men, he was felt by those who came most nearly into contact with him, to be speaking and thinking and acting as God; he represented God; he did what God would do; but more than this, he did what God was doing; and he did this, not instead of God, or apart from God; but—if the resources of language are equal to these demands—with God, and in God, and as God.

However few the direct assertions of that unity, our investigation will allow us to stop at nothing short of this. The phrase used most commonly to express this unity is, as we have observed, "the Son of God." But this phrase must not mislead us into supposing that the unity of Christ with God was no more than is implied by a term denoting the ordinary relationship, both physical and spiritual, between earthly sons and fathers. We have already pointed out that the words Son and Father are the best that language can use in hinting at a relation which it is beyond the power of language to express. They may shadow forth the conception that all which Christ, as the Son, possesses, he derives from the Father; and even that in all that he does, he is "about his Father's business," that is, he is representing his Father; but they do not suggest that independent unity of purpose and activity which Christ expressed by the phrase "abiding in the Father," and made still clearer when he said "the Father worketh hitherto, and I work"; nor do they suggest that the ultimate truth about the relation of Christ to the Father is the truth of two personalities in one, of distinction in unity. Yet this is the conclusion to which we are driven.

This is also true of Christ's unity with Man. It was not a new thing, an event in time, that Christ should descend from heaven to become the head of the human race. As Son of God, he was necessarily, and from the beginning, united with mankind. He spoke of himself as the Son of Man; this does not mean that the bond which united him to man was the same as the bond which united him to God; he did not derive anything from mankind; but he showed himself as the type of all that is best in man,—of what man really is, when he is in dependence on God and in communion with God. If he was God made visible to man, he was man set before the face of God. Nor was he the type, simply, of what man was meant to be; he exerted in himself the renewing energy which actually approximated man to that type; as men drew near to him, they became like him; he was "formed in" them. He thus represented man before God; he was, in attitude, purpose and will, what man was to become when reconciled to God, and what man would actually become through him. And this has always been verified in the experience of believers. It is by no paradox, and by no false humility, that the best men have felt themselves the "chief of sinners," and have had no ground of hope save in the "merits of Christ." It is the best men, and not the worst, whose hearts will most readily echo the cry of such words as these—

> "And can it be, that I should gain
> An interest in the Saviour's blood?
> . . . 'Tis mercy all, immense and free,
> For O my God, it found me out."

Far more than the newly repenting sinner, will the mature saint regard his old self as an impure thing, and rejoice that there is a new self within him, which he knows to be Christ; he has found himself in Christ.

But now a further step is needed. Granted that the above is the teaching of the New Testament, is it philosophically justifiable? What reason has theology, in the nature of things, for asserting this unity of Christ with man and with God? If this unity is justified in the experience of the men and women whom we call believers, must it not also be capable of justification in the thought of men in general? Otherwise, we are left with the old division between reason and revelation. Either reason cannot lead us to the highest truth, but can only mislead us by leaving us at a point where we are not meant to stop; or else revelation leaves us with a conception which, as being inconceivable by reason, appears a delusion. In the latter case, the hopes and beliefs of the best men the world has seen are no better than a will-o'-the-wisp; in the former, if we must part company with reason sooner or later, we need hardly trouble with it at all; and we are brought to that very perilous form of agnosticism which says "we cannot

PERSONALITY

know anything definite about these matters; we can only believe." What then has philosophy to say about the possibility of the Christian doctrine? Can we conceive that two personalities, or what appear to be such, can become one, or can be one from the beginning, through identity of purpose, thought and will,—that is to say, through community of spiritual attitude?

II. On the subject of Personality, indeed, philosophy has had much to say, though it has hardly succeeded even yet in saying anything definite. The meaning of Personality, in truth, has been the problem on which philosophy has subsisted from the very commencement. The relation of the One to the Many and to the All was the centre from which all Greek philosophical discussion radiated, the relations of the Limited to the Unlimited and of Form to Matter being only corollaries thereto. Oriental speculation, with its dreams of metempsychosis, emanation and absorption, has been occupied with nothing else, though Personality and even individuality it has long since surrendered. In Modern Europe, in spite of the invasion of what was once thought the domain of pure philosophy by psychology and biology, the question of the Absolute, so hotly debated in Germany a century ago, and since then with hardly less vigour in England, still holds the key of the position to be won; and the question of the Absolute is nothing but the question of Personality; of the nature of our consciousness, and its relation to the Universe and to the origin of the Universe, if any origin it can be said to have.

It is obvious that we cannot attempt an adequate discussion of this vast subject here, although every philosophical investigation must lead to its margin. On the other hand, it is equally impossible, especially for us, to treat it as if it did not exist. As a matter of fact, though the views held on the question at different times are practically innumerable, there are only three types of answer which have any serious claim to be considered at present. What is Personality? The first answer is that which we gather in the main from Transcendentalism. Most people hold that our personality is our feeling of separateness, in thought and action and initiative, from other people. But this feeling, like all our other feelings, is a part of our consciousness in general. Transcendentalism holds that the consciousness of each individual is a fragment of a Universal Consciousness, a Spiritual Principle, which is eternal. There can only be, for all thinking things, one Consciousness, just as there can only be, for all living things, one Life. Even our own thought is freed from the limitations of time and space; it can move backwards or forwards in either as it likes; how much more the Universal Thought? This Universal Thought, this Spiritual Principle, is the only existence that can properly be called real; for all material things exist only for thought; and all forms and modes of thought are but fragments of the Universal Thought. Hence, Personality, it would seem, cannot properly be called real; it cannot be predicated of the Absolute; and as a consciousness of distinctness, it must be swallowed up in the Universal Consciousness, in which all separate existence is swept away.

If this were true, Personality would at once retire to a position of very secondary importance; and, in addition to this, our whole view, not only of religion, but also of ethics, as a consideration of the facts of moral life which leads directly to the need of reconciliation for the divisions caused by wrong-doing, becomes

PERSONALITY

untenable. How can there be either reconciliation or division or even wrong-doing, if we are to agree that "all are but parts of one stupendous whole"? If we are to have no permanent and no independent existence of our own, even right and wrong will become only fleeting shadows. In the next place, if Personality is thus to be pushed aside, we cannot help suspecting that there is something wrong somewhere. We cannot get rid of Personality from our own consciousness; all our consciousness is consciousness of Personality; whatever else we are conscious of, we are always conscious of that; can it be a mere phase of thought, "staining the bright radiance of eternity"? The fault of what we have called the Transcendentalist view is that it has taken mental life in its lowest instead of in its highest terms. This Absolute Consciousness is, for most people, during the greater part of their lives, an abstraction and even an unreality. We cannot usefully consider consciousness without considering the content of consciousness. Consciousness does not, and we may even say cannot, exist apart from emotion, reason, and will: and the Absolute Consciousness, the Spiritual Principle, must be that in which these three elements of mental activity exist absolutely. But these three elements, inseparable from consciousness, are also inseparable from any valid conception of Personality. What is our Personality but the way in which we love and hate, think and desire—our "admiration, hope, and love"? The Spiritual Principle must be the Universal Personality, and instead of saying that our consciousness is an individualized fragment of the Absolute Consciousness, it would seem truer to say that our personalities must be gathered up into the Supreme Personality.

Next, let us consider what we might term "the Common Sense" view of Personality. Personality is that which gives us distinctness from our fellows and makes us remain distinct. I am not you and I never can be you, and to talk about an Absolute Personality in which both you and I might be merged is unmeaning. For the essence of Personality on this view is limitation; and to overstep such limitations in the "merging" of two separate persons is to overstep Personality altogether. To this conclusion the consciousness of the plain man is held to bear witness. He is as sure that he is himself and not someone else, as he is that his will is free and his own. Now, if we had to choose between this view and that of Transcendentalism we could hardly avoid being led to the side of Common Sense. Personality, as something separate and distinct, we all know. The "Absolute Consciousness" can never seem anything but strange and unreal. But if we insist on this distinctness we shall be just as unable as before to regard any one personality as becoming "one with" another; and reconciliation, even if it survives in a negative sense, as the removal of the cause of suspicion and hatred, can have no positive existence as the union or even the approximation of two sundered persons.

But it is not only our argument to which this view runs counter. Previous chapters have shown us that if it is true at all it can only be true in a very restricted sense. Ours are not "hermit spirits," and we must admit that if consciousness proves that Richard is not William, experience shows that Richard and William may react very remarkably on one another, and may come very near to identification with one another in various important respects. The fault of the "common sense" view is that it confuses Individuality with Personality. Something there is which keeps us distinct and prevents us being lost in others, but this is not Personality. The three essentials of our personal life, emotion, thought and will, are the magnetic forces that draw us together.

III. This brings us to the third view, which is as much a contrast to the other two as they are to each other. This view regards Personality as inclusive and not exclusive; and this in a double sense: first, as the total of a man's powers, the sum of his mental and spiritual activities,—as that which, in short, embraces the whole round of his conscious life; and secondly, as that which diffuses rather than isolates itself; draws other personalities to itself, and itself enters into them; its mark is not limitation, but expansion. First, to identify a man's personality with the whole of his conscious life rather than with some one part of it which we may call consciousness, must surely be correct. As we advance further in our knowledge of a man's character, his emotions, his plans, his will, we do not advance past the knowledge of his personality, but towards it. Conscious life is one and indivisible; we may talk about our wishes, our dislikes, and our hopes, as if each were separate, for the sake of distinctness in language; but in every mental act, each so-called "faculty" of the mind takes part in the unity of the whole. When the circle moves, each segment must move with it; and when one limb suffers, the whole body must suffer at the same time. To know and understand any one function of a man's mind or spirit, we must become acquainted with all the rest, for each acts and reacts upon every other; and if we know all, it is hardly worth while to pay special attention to one. To speak about a man's personality is to speak, not about his reason or his affections or his consciousness, but about his complete self, as thinking, willing, feeling, and acting. Should a time come when he should cease to think, feel, and act for himself, his personality would come to an end ; for practical purposes, he would cease to exist.

The second " note " of Personality, its expansiveness, has been to some extent defended in an earlier chapter. It is the nature of the individual to unite with other individuals, for a common purpose, and in a common life. The family, the tribe, the nation, are as "real" as the individual himself. A livelihood is not a life ; the isolated individual can gain the former ; the latter can be attained only by union. The very constituents of Personality, emotions, desires and will, refuse to be confined within the limits of the individual ; they must pass over into other personalities, and influence and be influenced by them, or wither away into feebleness and death. " No man liveth to himself." But this is not the whole truth. As the life of communities, whether large or small, broadens and deepens, the complexity of the interaction and co-operation of the individuals therein proportionately increases. And the reverse is equally true ; man is to man as air is to the lungs ; as individuals are bound more closely together, their personalities grow ; their powers of thinking, feeling, willing, are sharpened into a new intensity. Life and Personality were greater things in Rome and Athens than in Scythia or Persia ; and the integrating forces of modern times have developed Personality to a degree unsuspected by either Socrates or Cicero. " A man were better," says Bacon in his quaint way, " to relate himself to a statua, than to keep his thoughts in smother"; even a pretence of personal intercourse is better than nothing at all for the rousing of a man's personal faculties. Thoreau, shut in to the solitude of his forest lake, talking much of time and eternity, had cut himself off from the fountain head of wisdom by cutting himself off from the companionship of his fellow-men. Emerson, hardly less quaint than Bacon, has remarked, "every soul is a celestial Venus to every other soul"; and elsewhere, " our intellectual and active powers increase with our affection. The scholar sits down to write, and all his years of meditation do not furnish him with one good thought or happy expression; but it is necessary to write a letter to a friend,— and forthwith troops of gentle thoughts invest themselves on every hand with chosen words." The union of two personalities, in every degree of closeness, is not mechanical, but chemical or rather organic; one and one do not make two, but a larger and better third.

IV. Further, it has always been observed that there are natures which have this inspiring power to a pre-eminent extent. A character cast into a large mould of feeling and willing, we call a great personality. And such a character will always prove to be able to awake latent powers in the souls of others, and to attach them to himself. When it can be said of a man, as it was of Brutus, that whatever he wills, he wills strongly, that man, like Brutus, however limited in other directions, will be capable of enchaining the allegiance of those who come under his influence. This sway over the affections of others, sufficiently wonder-compelling when seen on a large scale, can be exercised by bad men and good men alike; but in evil there is something inherently isolating and segregative; and this attracting influence, when exercised by evil minds or for evil ends, must in the nature of things be only temporary; further, it could not exist save for the fact that no man's character is wholly devoid of good, and therefore every man must hold within himself these mystic seeds of power and attraction. Greatness of personality, if it is not to be hampered and hindered at every turn, must always be joined to goodness.

On a closer examination, the influence of great personalities will be found to be threefold. In the first place, every great character is a teacher and revealer,—in the truest sense, an educator; not because he puts hitherto unknown facts in other people's brains, but because he draws out of them new possibilities of love, admiration, and hope. The officer, cheering on his men to the charge; the Hindu ascetic, recalling to men by his mute example the value of the contemplative life; the leader in church or state, moving in the light that beats on every exalted position, and copied, consciously or unconsciously, by his followers in his words and his actions; and the mother, living and moving in the midst of her children; all teach their own life, and, in their degree, reproduce their own life in those who watch them, drawing their own life afresh, as it were, out of the souls of those whom they benefit. Hence, secondly, those who are thus taught by the great character are necessarily raised nearer to his level; while the very fact that they are thus drawn out of themselves, that they obey the call of a higher nature, and surrender themselves to the impulse that sweeps them towards the heights of goodness or bravery or self-denial, must of itself deepen and intensify their own powers. Thirdly, this means a real fusing of the personalities of the strong individual and of those who surround him. He draws them

PERSONALITY

into himself; his aims, his emotions, his very thoughts, replace theirs in their own breasts. But besides this, he will be capable of entering into them; or else, his power of attracting them will be but short-lived. He will understand their fears, their temptations, their ambitions; he will actually feel them; and while his adherents are living in him, he will be living in them. Examples might easily be multiplied; Savonarola, turning half his Florentine fellow-citizens into men as stern and pious as himself; Mohammed, inspiring the pagan hordes of Arabia with his boundless ambition and zeal, and Gordon, inspiring both raw Chinese levies and the destitute street-boys of Gravesend with his passion for discipline and courage; these, like all other great leaders of men, knew the secret of evolving an orderly cosmos out of chaos; and could find their way into the lives of others, in order to impregnate crude or feeble natures with their own spirit of order, enthusiasm, and power.

We have called this a secret; no one who has it can explain it; it cannot be learned, it must be possessed. But if we cannot explain it, we can know what it involves. And whenever it is complete, or approaches completeness, this losing myself to find myself, this drawing others into myself, involves suffering. In the lives of all the greater men, and especially of the greatest, "the heights and pinnacles of human mind," there has been a strain of melancholy. To concentrate upon a high ambition, to toil for an arduous purpose, is to forsake all that is low, and, at the earlier stages at least, all that is natural and easy. To use every part of the personality, thought, emotion and will, in the task of accomplishing the utmost for the highest, means a continuous and painful sacrifice, even to the extent of cutting off the right hand or plucking out the right eye. Even if the main end, the τέλος ἀρχιτεκτονικόν, as Aristotle would call it, is a bad one, the sacrifice of smaller and hampering desires will still be painful; while, if the end is a good one, and is not at the same time held to justify the use of every means—the doing of evil that good may come— a further sacrifice is necessary, the sacrifice not only of lower aims but of lower methods. The story of the Temptation in the Wilderness is meant to be typical of the experience of every great soul. To refuse to turn the stones into bread, or to cast one's self down from the pinnacle of the Temple, is often as painful as to refuse the ends for which those cheap and easy methods were suggested.

And into such a life suffering flows in by yet another channel. The great personality which is to live in others must spend and be spent for them; he must cramp his nature into the narrower limits of theirs, if he is to widen theirs into the breadth of his own. As George Eliot says of one of her finest characters, "her full nature, like that river of which Cyrus broke the strength, spent itself in channels which had no great name on the earth. But the effect of her being on those around her was incalculably diffusive; for the growing good of the world is partly dependent on un-historic acts." And many of these unhistoric acts will consist in the bearing of pain or distress which he who endures it might otherwise have avoided, but which he will feel more intensely than those for whom he thus acts vicariously. No Italian peasant could feel the daily oppression of Austrian tyranny as keenly as Mazzini felt it for him; no leper could feel his own loathsomeness of disease with the same poignancy as did Father

PERSONALITY

Damien and the noble women who laboured with him. So bitterly did Moses groan over the sorrows of his brethren that while they were content to labour he revolted, until his revolt became their own; and when, later on, repeated disobedience brought down on them the righteous anger of Jehovah, so deeply was he moved by the sense of their sin that he was willing to endure any punishment himself that they might escape. The words " Surely he hath borne our griefs . . . and with his stripes we are healed " apply in some degree to every true servant of mankind.

By the purifying and uplifting spectacle of such vicarious suffering more than by anything else are the narrower lives drawn into the wider. There is no appeal, even to the rudest nature, like the appeal of, " I suffer this for you." An army may be roused to enthusiasm by the general who spurs it on to conquest; but the leader to whom his soldiers' hearts are knit is he who shares with them the toils of a long campaign; who sits by their bedside when they are wounded, and who is their comrade, not only in the rapture of victory, but in the bitterness of retreat. It was an old observation that the emotions are purified by pity and terror; but when that pity is roused by sufferings intimately connected with the welfare of the spectator, the will, as well as the emotions, may be touched and strengthened. There are some natures whom this appeal will only touch slowly and with difficulty; suffering and pain always contain within themselves an element of the repulsive; and a deliverer whose visage is marred more than any man's will often be despised by those whose rescue he comes to effect. But all vigorous action of the personality, or of any part of it, exerts a magnetic force; we cannot live

R

earnestly in any direction, loving, hating, aspiring, without communicating that life and earnestness to others; and history can show no more earnest and intense life, and no more persuasive and effectual argument, than that of him who said " I, if I be lifted up from the earth, will draw all men unto me."

V. Our rapid survey of Personality, then, leads us first, to think of it as a man's whole mental and spiritual activity as exerted in the midst of other men, and secondly, to hold that the exertion of this personality is a force, or sets up a force, which necessarily unites him to others and others to him. The more completely he lives, the more he will live in others, and the more they will live in him. What is the bearing of these conclusions on the Biblical view, as expressed in our last chapter, of the relations of Christ to man? There is no *a priori* necessity for the existence of a supreme Personality, who should be to the whole of humanity what every great character is to his immediate circle. We might indeed consider the appearance of such a crown of humanity as distinctly probable. If humanity has been made, as it were, with hands outstretched to grasp other hands, we might well look for some central force, by which the whole circle might be united and so become conscious of its unity. But Theology, or at least Biblical Theology, troubles itself little about the *a priori*. It is more to the point to consider whether there has not lived one who showed himself what we should expect such a Personality, if it existed, to be. Now it is universally admitted that of all the great teachers of mankind, Jesus of Nazareth stands first. No words about God have ever approached his, in far-reaching scope and penetrating power. His words about man were equally remarkable. Not only did he flash upon man glimpses—and far more than glimpses—of what he was and what he might become; but the light of those flashes quickened seeds of the new life, which only the prophetic eye of Jesus could discern—the new life which is likeness to the Father in whose image man had been created. He did not, as some philosophers have desired to do, make men in love with virtue; he made them in love with himself, and in so doing, gave them his spirit, that is, the new personal force which saved the world by making those who received him in the world like himself. He raised them to his own level; and he stooped to theirs. He made them feel that he understood and sympathised with all that was in their minds; every struggling hope, every threatening doubt and anxiety; and he made them able to appreciate and reproduce all that was in his; the ambition to minister rather than to be ministered to, and the hunger for that food which was the doing of his Father's will.

Nor was this effect wrought on his contemporaries alone. S. Paul had not seen him in the flesh; yet the writings of S. Paul breathe a note of personal intimacy as intense as anything that we can find in the letters of S. Peter or of S. John. And this intimacy S. Paul expected to be shared by the wide circle of foreign disciples to whom he wrote. Nor did he expect this in vain. In every subsequent age, the devotion of Christians has not been to a cause, or to the representative leaders of that cause who have from time to time appeared, but to him who summoned them to be one with him as he was one with the Father. The devout though critical Augustine writes in his Confessions, " thou didst expel from me the pleasures of folly, thou who art the true, the highest pleasure, and didst thyself make thy entrance, sweeter than all delight, though not to flesh and blood, more glorious than all light, but more intimate than any secret thing"; the grave author of the "Theologia Germanica" says "Christ is greater than his own life," and "if the inward man have any 'Wherefore' in the actions of the outward man, he saith only that such things must be, and ought to be, as are ordained by the eternal will. And where God himself dwelleth in the man, it is thus; as we plainly see in Christ"; and we understand that what actuates them both, is not religious reverence, but a personal devotion rising into a reverent friendship and intimacy.

Lastly, we find Christ's very type of excellence reproduced in his followers; or perhaps we should say, his absence of type. For to speak about a type of goodness implies the existence of other types; but the peculiarity of Christ was that he transcended types; all the various excellences of mankind meet in him;—the gentleness of the Buddhist, the mingled fervour and resignation of the Mohammedan, the stern devotion to lawful authority which exalted the name of Roman, the versatile delight in harmonious beauty and in logical subtlety which characterised the Greek, the Englishman's practical common-sense and the mysticism of the German, the hatred of priesthood and of soulless ritual which has sharpened the weapons of the Protestant, and the ardour of rapt contemplation which has been the glory of the medieval saint. All goodness runs up into the general goodness exhibited in his character, as all the separated colours of the spectrum find their fulfilment and their union in the white light of the sun; and with men of the most diverse temperaments, from S. Paul to Francis Xavier, from Xavier to Luther, and from Luther to Pascal, as their goodness has approached that of Christ, so it has approached that of each other.

In this way Christ comes before us, from the standpoint of history, as the supreme person, the head of the race. All goodness is found in him; every man of whom goodness can be predicated, becomes so far like him; every man who comes spiritually near him must become like him, not simply by imitating his high example, but by experiencing his transforming spiritual energy; and all national and collective progress is a progress towards the ideal that was laid down once for all by him. It is on this consideration that Christ's claim to be the second man, the last Adam, is based. As the supreme person, he enters into the lives of others; he bears their griefs and carries their sorrows; he understands their sins, feels the weight of them, bears them, and by so doing, "saves his people from their sins"; he draws them into himself, opens the gates of life to them, and is himself the way and the life. We do not claim that this analysis exhausts the relation of Christ to the human race; or that it explains how different personalities can grow up into one, while remaining distinct from that one and from each other—how a man can be "one with Christ," in short, while still being himself, though purified and transformed. This must remain a mystery; a mystery which not even the apostles have enabled us to fathom—perhaps they did not fathom it themselves; but it is not more insoluble than the more familiar but equally perplexing mystery of the union in distinctness of parent and child, of lover and beloved.

VI. If such, then, be the account of the union of Christ with man to which we are led, not only by the

New Testament, but by reason and history, what shall we say of the union of Christ with God? How can we substantiate the claim that God himself was in any sense one with the Jewish teacher whom Pilate condemned to suffer as a revolutionary upon Calvary? The claim cannot be substantiated at all if we are forbidden, as so many would forbid us, to attribute Personality to God. And if Personality means limitation, we cannot of course call God a Person. Nor can persons, if as such they are essentially limited, be ever united to an unlimited being. But our argument has led us to the opposite conclusion. Personality implies inclusiveness; the more completely a man possesses personality, the more surely is limitation precluded.

And further, are we to attribute love, will, thought, to God, or not? Surely we must do so, or God will not be an intelligible being at all; while if we do, we at once give Him what makes Him a person, and, as such, able to communicate Himself, since these qualities of necessity pass outside themselves to others. To say that God is absolutely unlimited, that He is shut out from no living being, and from no person, is to call Him in the highest degree personal. Further, if God is to communicate Himself to a world of personal beings, it must be through a person; for Personality is the highest thing we know; the highest form of creation is life, and Personality is the fullest manifestation of life that is possible; and therefore we can hardly conceive that God should reveal Himself through any impersonal form of being, or in anything lower than a person. And the person which will thus be the medium of communication must be united with God; and yet he must be distinct from Him, or he would not be a person at all.

It may be asked at this point, Why should God reveal Himself? The answer is that if God is personal, He cannot remain out of contact with other persons; He must communicate Himself to them, and draw them to Himself. He may do this in many ways; all men, in all ages, and at all steps in the development of the race, will not be arrested by the same impressions; but sooner or later He will appear as a person in the midst of persons; He must approach them at their own highest level. True, any great quality seen in men, may make us say "that is like God; that helps me to understand God"; but we cannot tell the true nature, either of man or of God, from one great quality or from one great virtue. Men touch one another, not by this or that characteristic, but by the sum, or the resultant, of them all. So with God; if He is to show Himself at all—as He must, unless we are to think of Him as an irrational force or an unknown quantity—He will best show Himself, not as a conquering Messiah, object of mistaken Jewish hopes; nor as a refined and solitary ascetic, nor as a wonder worker, to make people think that the gods are come down in the likeness of men, nor in any special guise of magnificence or wisdom, thus making a part obscure the whole; but He will surely come with the characteristics of true Personality; attracting others, entering into them, making them leave their old selves and enter into life in Him,—and doing this, above all, by suffering, with them, and for them. God can only reveal Himself, in fact, if the conditions we have learnt to look for are fulfilled, by such a supreme personality as we have just been considering. There may indeed be something in God far higher than Personality; there may be some such thing, as yet unsuspected, possible to man; just as there may be a world in which the very axioms of mathematics are quite different from what we know them to be here. In that case, the ultimate revelation of God may be something hitherto undreamed of; but till that purely hypothetical stage is reached, or guessed at, the revelation by a complete person must be the complete revelation for us. There may be "other heights in other lives, God willing"; yet we may be forgiven if we cannot conceive of a greater or more god-like thing, even in other spheres of life, than the self-abnegating love by which the completest personality is crowned.

VII. We are thus led back to the great act whose necessity to the race has been unfolded to us in the previous chapters. The end of ethics and of religion alike, is righteousness. Righteousness consists in the right relation between persons—that is, righteousness is fully reached when persons act to one another as if united to one another by the closest of known human ties, the ties of the family. But these ties are severed; instead of the sympathy and union of the true family, there is suspicion, hatred, injury, between person and person; between man and man, and between man and God; and consequently misery, self-reproach, helplessness and despair. How can the Reconciliation, the Atonement, be made? When the injured can pass over into the injurer, expelling the latter's evil nature, and instilling his own goodness. This can only be accomplished by mediation, and by suffering; and that is simply to say, by a person, taking the word in its highest and completest sense. It is the strength of Personality to make possible this passing over, this drawing of apparent opposites into one; and it is the glory of Personality to attain this by suffering, by laying down life to take it again, and to bestow it on others. Personality, the impulse and the power to share the worst that another can bear, and to impart the best that one can oneself possess, is the true ladder which is let down from heaven to earth, and along which we mortals can emulate the angels by passing back and forth; it is the royal road of spiritual communication, by which what is true of one becomes true of another, and what is done to one becomes done to another; even as the supreme person said, "he that receiveth you receiveth me; and he that receiveth me receiveth him that sent me."

CHAPTER X

ATONEMENT AND THE RACE

1. WE have now found that the end of the path on which we were started by ethics is a doctrine of Atonement. In other words, we have found that the commands of ethics imply a personal relation; that conquest over evil can only be secured by reconciliation; and that reconciliation, in its complete form, is only possible through the suffering of one who is distinct from the wrong-doer and yet has identified himself with him. Here, we might think, we have found a way of uniting morals adequately with religion, each being the necessary completion and supplement of the other. Religion without morality is not worth calling religion at all; religion must go to morality constantly for her codes of rules; while without religion, morality is but a voice crying in the wilderness, with no power to compel passers-by to obey or even to listen. Yet, even supposing that the adherents of "mere morality" and of religion will both go with us so far, there is still the ground for the old disagreement which perplexed us at the beginning of our journey. The moralist will still ask "Has anything which has gone before lessened the worth of a good act in itself, apart from the religious profession or belief of the agent, or the absence thereof?" while the champion of religion will rejoin, "whatever we have said, Christ's words remain, 'I am the door; no man

ATONEMENT AND THE RACE 267

cometh unto the Father but by me.'" It is still true, he will assert, that "without faith, it is impossible to please him." The problem seems as far from solution as ever.

We may however state the problem in slightly different terms. Granted that apart from the truth of the Atonement, any theory of ethics must be incomplete, we may still ask, what is the value of good actions, apart from a conscious relation to Christ in the doer of them—a definite relation, that is, to the Atoning Christ, or, if we may borrow the Biblical phrase, to "Christ's blood"? Christianity asserts that works without faith are dead; all religion asserts the necessity of something more than a good act in itself; if that is so, must the religious man, and especially the Christian, refuse admiration and reverence to truth, honesty, purity, and self-denial, if they are not "mixed with faith"? On the other hand, if this admixture with faith is unnecessary, and if goodness is goodness, through whomsoever it is manifested, do we not at once assert Christ to be unnecessary, and so deny the value of the Atonement altogether?

This question has seldom been faced by theology except in the abstract, although the opponents of theology will always use it as a convenient weapon of attack. How then shall we understand the theological declaration that there is no goodness apart from Christ? It is as easy to lay down dogmatically that without faith in Christ there can be no real good, as to asseverate of men in general that "there is none that doeth good, no, not so much as one"; and that "the heart is deceitful above all things." But as soon as we apply such a generalisation to actual men and women around us, it has to be modified immediately.

268   ETHICS AND ATONEMENT

If this were for a single day accepted as true of the society in which we are living, the ordinary traffic of life would be impossible. The commonest business transactions are based on what we call credit, which is nothing but trust in the ordinary honesty of our fellow-men; and our everyday intercourse, both with friends and strangers, proceeds on the assumption that ingratitude and deceit are the exception and not the rule. Nor could such a sweeping statement be applied for a moment to the saints and heroes of the Old Testament. They had no conscious relation to any atonement, and certainly none to the Atonement of Christ. Sacrifice itself, as it enters into the lives of a David, a Samuel, or a Gideon, appears an element in the accepted form of worship, but contains no suggestion of vicarious satisfaction. Of a Son of God, as the only medium of righteousness, without which their own natural goodness would be but as filthy rags, they knew nothing. The womb of time still contained the secret.

Nor again can this assumption of universal evil apart from Christ be made indiscriminately when we are dealing with the characters of the pagan world before Christ. Socrates, Aristides, Epaminondas, will never be denied admiration, however deep be the heathen darkness which we imagine to have enveloped their spirit. And if Fabricius, Cincinnatus, and Laelius have served as models of patriotism and wisdom to Christian generations succeeding them, we must not surely find fault with their light because it shone out of a darkness which has since passed away. Was family affection a different thing in Cicero from what it is in a modern member of Parliament, because Cicero could not know that family relationship, properly under-

ATONEMENT AND THE RACE

stood, springs from the relationship of Christ to the Father? Does even a member of Parliament always bear in mind this truth? Was Brutus any less loyal to principle than Cavour or Pym, because behind the ideal of the State there could be for him no commonwealth which is in heaven, from whence he could look for a Saviour?

Again, if we look at pagans who lived after Christ, and therefore may be said to have rejected him, neither Aurelius nor even Julian need greatly fear comparison in kingly virtues with Edward the Confessor or even with S. Louis. No one can deny that when we survey the long conflict between good and evil, either in the history of nations or in the lives of individuals, the appearance of Jesus of Nazareth upon earth meant the calling of new ideals of virtue into the field to reinforce the old; but the field on which the combatants have fought, and the strategic points which they have striven to gain, have remained the same. No one can read Cicero's "De Officiis" or Plutarch's Lives, or even the old world stories of Herodotus, without feeling that there is a nobility which is noble in its own right, a virtue which is virtuous in itself; and that just as sin exists which needs no rejection of Christ to make it appear hideous, so there exists righteousness which Christ would not have scrupled to acknowledge. Nor need allegiance to Christ compel us to slight the virtuous maxims of Confucius, the blameless life of Buddha, nor the instances of self-control, patriotism, and conspicuous courage furnished by India or Japan, or by peoples far lower in the scale of civilisation. If the followers of Buddha and Confucius, and of the early teachers of Hinduism come short of the highest ideas of their religions, the same thing must be sorrowfully admitted of the followers of Christ. "There can be no greater mistake than to depreciate the ethnic religions in the supposed interests of an exclusive revelation ... (The higher stages of religion) are inseparably joined with the lower steps that have led up to them; and if we held that the mass of mankind had been deceived in supposing themselves capable of intercourse with the spiritual world, we should have no logical right to make a particular exception."[1]

And we may go still further; in the various religious and philosophic sects, among men who have on various grounds rejected the Atonement, Christ, and even God, by whatever names they have been known, we find lives which would not shame a Christian. The test, "by their fruits ye shall know them," cannot be so applied as to leave Arians, Socinians, Deists, Transcendentalists and Positivists on the one side, and believers in the divinity of Christ on the other. True, it is rare to find the highest type of moral excellence among those who have rejected Christ; but then it is rare to find it on the other side; and where it is found, it would seem to have little to do with the intellectual attitude to any particular dogma either on the one side or the other. The influence of scepticism on character does not appear to be universally retrograde; if we put Spinoza, Kant, Mill, Huxley, or many an honest man never seen inside a church in one class, we might find examples to contrast with them, among men whose orthodoxy has never been disputed, which would make us dread the influence on character exerted by the Christian creed. Among the great mass of inconspicuous men untouched by positive Christian

[1] Illingworth, "Personality, Human and Divine."

ATONEMENT AND THE RACE 271

belief, practical experience proves to us the existence of heroism, self-sacrifice, and quiet beauty of character indistinguishable from that of men and women within the pale of the church.

Further, when we consider the various Christian communions, both Catholic and Protestant, what shall be said of the differing views of those who acquiesce in the orthodox declaration of Christ as God? I may hold the divinity of Christ, I may accept all that is said on the subject in the New Testament, and yet if I came to paraphrase my belief, it might seem, to the man who worships next me each Sunday, hardly worth calling belief at all. Every thinking man knows how easily, in attempting to define the divinity of Christ to himself, he falls into the old errors known as Sabellianism, Nestorianism, or Apollinarianism; and how many Christian people have ever tried to define that divinity at all? How many of those brought up in the straitest sects of Christianity possess the righteousnesss of Christ in such a sense that if their belief in Christ were taken away from them, the foundations of their righteousness would be removed?

Can we deny that the majority of Christians are, as Matthew Arnold called us, only "light half-believers in our casual creeds, who never deeply felt or clearly willed"? What wonder is it if "our insight never has borne fruit in deeds, and our vague resolves never have been fulfilled"? It would seem, then, that if we are to make righteousness inseparable from an explicit consciousness of Christ as the source of righteousness, we must rule out from its possession all but a small minority of those to whom the gospel has been presented. For the rest of the human race, even for those who have inspired our own Christian ideals of conduct, righteousness will be plainly impossible. Either we must admit that the great majority of the race has been inevitably deceived as to the real nature of righteousness,—as to what righteousness is, that is to say, in the sight of God ;—or that goodness, having been a matter of morality before Christ appeared, became something very different afterwards, for which there is not the smallest suggestion in any authoritative Christian writing ;—or else we must conclude that the goodness or badness of an act is independent of the agent's conscious relation to Christ.

II. But this is not the only point of view from which the question needs to be considered. There are many who will accept the dilemma in the last paragraph, and unhesitatingly reject all goodness which has not this conscious relation to Christ as being not really goodness at all. But dare we hold that such acts are worthless? Can we even say that there is any difference between truthfulness and honour in a Christian, and truthfulness and honour in a man to whom the Bible is like any other book? Are the latter, as some of the early Christian fathers boldly asserted, merely "splendida vitia"? Here ethics makes its voice heard once more. Acts cannot be considered apart from motives. An act is good only when it is performed from a good motive. A man may do what is recognised as good from selfishness or pride; but the goodness of such an act will be at best only formal or accidental, not material. And an act will only be bad if done from a bad motive. When, however, the motive cannot be called bad, the act may indeed be bad formally, that is, when it involves unforeseen consequences, as when the axe-head slips from the handle I am holding and injures my friend ; materially bad, it

ATONEMENT AND THE RACE 273

cannot be. At any rate, we can hardly conceive that the Judge of all the earth would condemn an act which was the outcome of an honest wish to do right.

But in the last resort, a bad motive springs from some kind of selfishness; an act done purely for self-gratification, to the neglect of others, can never be positively good; it may do no harm, but at best, it is neutral, while it contains within itself all the elements of badness. On the other hand, an act done, not to gain one's own ends, but for the sake either of its goodness, or for the sake of others, cannot but be good. When Cordelia led an expedition into Britain to protect and avenge her aged father, in glorious forgetfulness of the treatment she had received from him, we look upon the act as one of pure filial goodness; had she thought simply of wresting the control of the kingdom from her sisters, she might have done no harm, and perhaps have greatly benefited the country; but we should not have spoken of her act as good, nor could we have readily distinguished it from a piece of wanton aggression. We applaud Harmodius and Aristogeiton, if they slew the tyrant to liberate their country; if their deed was to avenge a private wrong, we can at most refuse to blame. Mankind will never succeed in discovering a finer example of practical goodness than that of the Good Samaritan; the Priest and the Levite might answer every test of religious conscientiousness; if they fail in the duty of ready sympathy, they fail in everything. To prove the reality of goodness, we must love our neighbour as ourselves.

But this is a moral and not a religious test; it depends not on a man's belief, but on his attitude to his own happiness and that of others. If acts cannot be judged apart from motives, however, neither can they be judged apart from characters. Neither the act nor the motive can be criticised apart from the subject; a man's life is not a succession of isolated thoughts and deeds; it is a continuous manifestation of his character. We do not judge the deed, but the man who has done it. What then is the worth to God of a good character, as distinct from the creed of Christianity or definite belief in Jesus Christ?

III. Here the answer of the theologian has often been, as in the case of actions, "it is of no worth at all; an apparently good character cannot but be made really bad by the conscious rejection of Jesus Christ, or of the Holy Spirit; that is the sin which cannot be forgiven." This is undeniably true, for those to whom Christ has plainly been presented, and who have then rejected him. But here we must repeat our statement that Christ has been presented to men in the most various ways, and to many men he has never been presented at all. To present Christ to men is by no means the simple thing that it is sometimes thought. Christ is presented to men, according to some, in the Roman sacrifice of the Mass, wherein, as it is believed, to see God made and eaten—to use Browning's bold phrase—must do far more for them than to hear certain human words about him. The Calvinist claims that he is presenting Christ to men when he describes the sufferings of Calvary as if borne only for the select portion of the race fore-ordained to salvation. Generations of Christians have gazed upon Michel Angelo's terrifying presentation of Christ as the frowning Judge raising his stern right hand to smite the wicked into perdition. The strict Anglican presents to men a Christ whose covenanted mercies are severely confined within the limits of the Apostolical Succession; and the zealous Protestant street preacher

ATONEMENT AND THE RACE

seeks to convert his hearers by a formula, and with perplexing simplicity beseeches them to "come to Christ." Which of these various modes of presentation is the true one?

We shall be reminded that there can be no value in any man's presentation of Christ, whether more or less complete, without the "aid of the Holy Spirit." This must mean, either that the Spirit's revelation of Christ is totally independent of the words and deeds of the human preacher; or that the Spirit carries forward the work which the human preacher has already begun. In the former case, the comparative truth or falsehood of the human words would seem to be alike irrelevant; in the latter, the efficiency of the work of the Spirit will still be dependent, at least in part, on the preacher's skill and insight. If the former were true, why should not the Spirit act without human aid altogether? What need would there be to ask "how shall they hear without a preacher? or how shall one preach unless he be sent?" We shall perhaps be asked to recall S. Paul's words about the foolishness of preaching; but S. Paul's meaning in that place was not that what was said was unimportant; the stumbling-block of the cross lay neither in the unintelligibility nor the illogicality of the preacher's words, nor in its inconsistency with what might otherwise be known of Christ; but rather in the audacity of believing, with a practical energy hitherto unknown, that the weak things of the world might confound the strong, that suffering is better than ruling, and that to give is nobler and more profitable than to receive. If the latter interpretation be true, the view of the preacher must still make a difference to the acceptance of Christ by the hearer.

Christ, then, must be presented to men for their

acceptance or rejection through human agency; but since this fact of human agency necessarily implies variation and imperfection, we must go on to ask, "if the unpardonable sin consists in rejecting Christ, which is the particular view of Christ which it is sin to reject?" Is it the presentation of Christ as made by the Roman Catholic or the Calvinist or the street preacher? Or will a man be safe so long as he accepts any one of these? Is the Frenchman, whose only idea of religion has been gained from the perfunctory ceremonial of Catholicism, as guilty in rejecting such a parody of Christ's service, as the Englishman, who, with healthy contempt for the jugglery of the mass, will at the same time have nothing to do with the simpler and saner teaching of his own Protestantism? Or has the slum-dweller, compelled to herd with the thief and the prostitute, the same responsibility, if he should "reject" or ignore Christ, as an Ananias or a Hymenaeus?

But, it will be argued, every one has free access to the word of God; human imperfection cannot interfere with the preaching of Christ found in its pages; there we have the "truth as it is in Jesus." On the contrary, this free access to the word of God in the Bible only holds good for a third of Christendom, the Protestant churches; and this free access has meant, through the three hundred years in which the Bible has been open to every reader, the drawing of the most diverse conclusions from its words; the Arminian, the Calvinist, and even the Unitarian have proved their positions from the Bible as confidently as the Dominican and the Jesuit. The Bible does not speak by itself; it is as much in need of human presentation as is the person of Christ. The theologian, with a blind reliance on the

ATONEMENT AND THE RACE

Bible's loyalty to him, presses home his question "how can you differ from a view which is so plainly founded on Scripture?" but the question loses its force when we find it urged in the same words from opposing schools. We are far from asserting that the Bible is rightly open to this multiplicity of interpretations; but we cannot deny that they exist. Which is the interpretation, therefore, of the Scriptural teaching of Christ that we reject at our peril? Are we safe so long as we accept some one of them, Catholic, Calvinist, or Unitarian? If on the other hand we merely acknowledge that Christ has some claim to our allegiance, either as the Son of God (however we understand that much disputed term), or simply as one of the great world-teachers, can we be said to accept him in the sense necessary for salvation?

IV. Even to settle this question would not give us a final solution of our difficulty. What of those who have neither read nor heard of Christ, and so have had no chance of either accepting or rejecting him? If, as we supposed our theologian to tell us, an apparently good character cannot but be made bad by the conscious rejection of Christ, what of the apparently good characters to which such rejection is impossible, because of his never having been offered for their acceptance? Are they restricted to a semblance of goodness which in the eyes of God is no more than a worthless imitation? Are such lives as valueless and reprobate as that of the hardened sinner who has said, not only "evil, be thou my good," but also "Christ, I will have none of thee"? In other ages the Christian conscience did not shrink from this harsh assertion. Even Dante could do no more for the best of the heathen, than to consign them, with the exception of a Rhipeus or a Trajan, to a painless limbo on the confines of the infernal regions: and little children, too young to accept or reject consciously any view of Christ, were for ever shut out of heaven if they did not happen to have been baptised. With one who still clings to this view we cannot profess to argue. But if we refuse to exclude either children in age or children in religious education from the mercies of God, we cannot make the simple acceptance or rejection of Christ the test of the worth of character in the sight of God. "Rejection of Christ" must be altered to "rejection of the purest ideal that the individual can conceive"; and this is nothing else than the choice of the lower instead of the higher.

This test, starting from the individual, is applicable to the individual in every case; to Jew and Greek alike, to all sorts and conditions of men, to antiquity and to the present time. We shall believe that Trajan, for example, has found salvation, not because, unlike other virtuous pagans, he had the good fortune to gain Gregory's intercession,[1] but because, as Dante himself admits, his honest and pure love and exercise of justice had made him worthy of a place among the glorified judges of the earth in Paradise. We shall set David in his company, not because, after a grievous sin, he consciously availed himself of the merits of Christ, but because, after committing himself to the lower, he ascended from it, in real sorrow of heart, to the higher, in reliance on all that could be then known of a merciful God. Our condemnation of Nero does not rest on the fact that he neglected the witness to a dead Nazarene said to be alive by a Jew from Tarsus, but on our instinctive horror at one who set himself to outrage everything that the human mind held sacred.

[1] Dante, "Paradise," xx. 112.

But here finally the test of the dogmatist is seen to be inapplicable. The only universal test which we can use is moral rather than distinctly religious; and even for the man who has lived in the full light of the Christian dispensation, the question, whether he has accepted Christ, is really the same as the question propounded to every man of every dispensation, whether he has submitted himself to the highest authority he knows. To many a Christian, religion in practice is little more than morality :—the keeping of certain rules, obeying the law as enunciated by Christ, doing one's duty to God and man. This lower ideal of religion may be brushed aside with the words, "this might be pagan teaching, now hear mine," and religion may be felt by the maturer Christian to rest upon the indwelling power of a love that saves from wrong-doing; still, to reach this higher plane, the first necessity is submission.

Unless we are to confuse all distinction between the religious and the moral elements of life, the religious, which consists in loving communion with God, must be preceded by the moral, deliberate surrender to an acknowledged authority. When once the moral act of this definite surrender has been performed, whether as the result of an "emotional conversion" or an intellectual "closing with" the authority and the conditions imposed, or a mixture of both, in any case what follows will depend upon the disposition and the environment of the individual. Asoka surrendering himself to the solemn charm of Buddha, the high-spirited young Ali devoting himself to the cause of his adopted father Mohammed, Elias of Cortona joyfully embracing poverty for love of the child-like Francis of Assisi, Luther hurling himself, lion-like, against the barrier of circumstance in his determination to be satisfied with nothing less than the soul's immediate access to Christ, all are alike in making the great decision as it is presented to them, but they differ in the extent of spiritual expansion made possible to them by the influences to which they pledged their obedience. Each of them, like all men before or since, had to face the question, moral rather than distinctly religious, "are you willing to follow the best you know, whatever demands it may make?" The test of goodness, therefore, in character as in act, remains a moral one; what makes act or character bad is that which is a fault, not simply to religion, but to ethics.

V. Now, does not all this appear to force us to a still wider divergence from the Biblical conception of God's purpose to save the world through Christ? How can we reconcile what has just been said with such words as "I am the door; by me if any man enter in he shall be saved"; "in none other is there salvation, for neither is there any other name under heaven that is given among men, wherein we must be saved"; and, still more definitely, the familiar words, "he gave his only begotten son that whosoever believeth in him should not perish but have everlasting life"?[1] If the value of character, in God's eyes, consists simply in goodness; and if God's test for goodness, both in character and act, is a moral one, and therefore applicable to all men alike, whether they have heard of Christ or not, and whether they have lived before or after his appearance in the world, then does it not follow that God must deny the unique worth of that appearance? If what God requires are the merely "natural" virtues of kindliness, justice and humility,

[1] Jn. 10^9; Acts 4^{12}; Jn. 3^{16}.

ATONEMENT AND THE RACE

the Incarnation would seem to lose all claim to be considered the turning point in the history of the race, and would become simply one of many stages in the progressive revelation of God's attitude and will to the world.

But the whole argument of the foregoing chapters points to an exactly opposite conclusion. We cannot, as we have just seen, divide good acts or characters into two distinct classes, those that have a personal relation to Christ and those that have not. But instead of concluding from this, that the personal relation to Christ is necessary for none, we can only conclude that it is necessary for all. Good acts or characters are impossible, if our previous conclusions were right, apart from suffering and atonement. For goodness consists in a personal relation; that relation, once broken, is unattainable without reconciliation; and that reconciliation, consummated, is atonement. Goodness, for the race, is impossible apart from atonement made on behalf of the race, and such atonement must also be atonement made by the race, that is to say, by one who holds a special relation of personal unity both with the race and with God, the source and the law of all goodness. In the person of Jesus Christ we have found this dual relationship with the race and with God. Apart from Christ, therefore, there can be no goodness at all.

What then of the statement that the test of goodness is moral and not religious? This difficulty will be inevitable if we regard Christ as the founder of a religion either as distinct from other religions, or as distinct from systems of morality. But if we take into consideration Christ's own claims and regard him as the universal master, the λόγος or Message of God to all

282   ETHICS AND ATONEMENT

men before and after him,[1] the contradiction will vanish. In the first place, if Christ's life and death avail for any members of the race, they avail for all. Christ did not come to impart goodness to individuals who happened to live after a given point of time, nor to narrow down the confines of goodness previously open to all, so as to exclude those who had no chance of hearing his gospel, or who could only hear it in a way that they could not understand, or in words that would prove a stumbling block to them. Many a Christian to-day, if he heard the teaching that Mill heard so often fifty years ago, would be inclined to sympathize with his protest, "If God will send me to hell for not believing this, to hell I will go." Nor can we fairly blame Bradlaugh for rejecting a presentation of Christianity which loyalty to Christ would compel us to reject as vigorously as he did. And how could we conceive a crowd of men, women and children to have "heard the Gospel" when they listen to a street preacher saying: "My friends, you pay a shilling a pound for butcher meat, but here you get Bleeding Lamb for nothing.[2] We must not make the goodness which Christ came to bring dependent on a man's acceptance or rejection of any "other gospel,"[3] however good the intentions of its preachers.

Unless we are altogether to misunderstand the gospel, Christ is the Son of Man, the Light of the World, the Light that lighteth every man that cometh into the world, the head of the race, the true righteousness of every one who accepts him; his mind is formed in every one of his followers. It is into him that they grow up in all things, it is into his image that they are

[1] *Cf.* Jn. 8^{56}, "Your father Abraham rejoiced to see my day, and he saw it and was glad."
[2] See "Britain's Next Campaign," by Julie Sutter, ch. vi.
[3] Gal. 1^8.

ATONEMENT AND THE RACE

changed from glory to glory. Either this is the rhetoric of men trained to make the most of their doctrine, or it means that as man grows up into goodness, into that goodness which has worth in the eyes of God, into all sincere goodness which does not spring from selfishness, he is growing up into Christ. This is true even of the individual who has no idea, when he thinks a noble thought or performs a good deed, of the great act in whose results he participates. How diverse have been the views held on the relation of the atonement to practical life may be gathered from any history of doctrine.[1] But the widest diversity of views cannot alter the fact that, for every man, goodness means communion with Christ. Nor must we neglect the sublime tolerance of Christ himself, often forgotten by his exponents, "he that is not against us is for us." For every act of goodness the world has ever known, Christ has been the inspiration and the soul. In every age protests have been raised against the narrow view which identifies belief in Christ with intellectual or verbal assent to certain propositions about Christ. "John the Baptist was canonised as having died a martyr, not for refusing to deny Christ, but for refusing to deny the truth. Christ is truth and righteousness, and he who dies for truth and righteousness dies for Christ." These noble words of Anselm the Catholic are echoed by the Quaker Penn : " The humble, meek, merciful, just, pious and devout souls are everywhere of one religion, and when death has taken off the mask, they will know one another, though the divers liveries they wear have made them strangers." Both would

---

[1] For a concise account of these, the reader may consult Lidgett's "Spiritual Principle of the Atonement," Appendix, or Moberly, "Atonement and Personality," Supplementary Chapter.

have welcomed Matthew Arnold's description of the
"small transfigured band" of saints,

> "Christian and Pagan, king and slave,
>   Soldier and anchorite,—
> Distinctions we esteem so much
>   Are nothing in thy sight.
>
> They do not ask who pined unseen,
>   Who was on action hurled,
> Whose one bond is that all have been
>   Unspotted from the world."

VI. It will readily be seen that the foregoing argument, if it is correct, implies the pre-existence of Christ. That belief has often been represented as a later elaboration of dogma after the memory of Christ's human life had grown dim, the product of the minds of S. Paul and others working at a system which was to become a world religion, but unknown to the simple teaching of Galilee. As a matter of fact, the accounts of the Synoptics themselves would be unintelligible without this belief in the pre-existence of Christ. The Son of Man who was to lay down his life and to take it again, who bade the weary put his own mild yoke upon them, who was to come in the glory of his Father, with all the holy angels with him, to judge the world, and who alone knew the Father and was known by Him alone—how shall we say of him that he came into existence only in the latter half of the reign of Augustus? The riddle of such words from such a man would be insoluble if we had not the key furnished by the fourth gospel. There we find that he who spoke with authority as never man spake, who forgave sins as if he were God, whose one demand from men was for confidence in him, and who admitted his friends

ATONEMENT AND THE RACE 285

even into Paradise, claimed to be not only the light of the world, but life itself. "Before Abraham was," he said, "I am." "Glorify thou me," he prays, "with thine own self with the glory which I had with thee before the world was . . . for thou lovedst me before the foundation of the world." The author's own comment, "in the beginning was the word . . . all things were made by him, and without him was not anything made that hath been made,"[1] can add nothing more. This tone is strikingly echoed in the Apocalypse; Christ is "he that is and was, and is to come"; "I am the first and the last, and the Living one"; "the beginning of the creation of God."[2] These writings may well date from near the end of the first century; but S. Paul's letters, which take us back to within a generation of Christ's life on earth, are equally unflinching. "Who, being in the form of God, thought it not a prize to be retained to be equal with God, but emptied himself." Apart from explicit statements like this, the pre-existence of Christ underlies all his theological thought. "(God)chose us in him before the foundation of the world"; "his own purpose and grace which was given us in Christ Jesus before times eternal";[3] where God's original purpose for the salvation of men is made dependent on Christ's presence at his side from the beginning. In the early days of their preaching, the apostles could say, "him, being delivered up by the determinate counsel and foreknowledge of God, ye by the hand of lawless men did crucify and slay"; this can only point to the fully developed belief expressed in the words, "the Lamb that hath been slain from the foundation of the world."[4]

[1] Jn. 17^6 ^{24} 1$^{1\ 2}$.
[2] Rev. 1$^{4\ 17}$ 3^{14}.
[3] Phil. 2^6; Eph. 1^4; 1 Tim. 1^9.
[4] Acts 2^{23}; Rev. 13^8.

VII. But this pre-existence implies something more than chronological priority. It would be an absurdity to suppose that Christ only existed before certain other events in time, such as the birth in Bethlehem, or even the creation of man. The only logical conclusion from Christ's existence with God, "in the bosom of the Father," before the world was, is that there never was a time when Christ was not; that his existence, like God's, is timeless; not simply everlasting, but eternal. Future and past are but parts of one eternal Now; there are no events in time for him; all that takes place for him is complete through all time, as for God.

Now we may think of God in one of three ways; as a being in the universe, in the same sense as we are in it, but with greater, perhaps enormously greater powers of knowledge, foresight, and control, than our own; as a being outside the universe who is a spectator of its history and action, and indeed controls it from outside, either as a watchmaker may be said to control the action of the watch he has made, or as an employer of labour can be said to control the action of his men; or, in the third place, we may think of Him as a being, neither wholly outside the universe, nor wholly inside it, who, instead of being a spectator of its history as that history unrolls itself, sees the whole at one glance, or as we should say, in a single moment; sees, that is, both the middle and the end in the beginning and the beginning in the middle and the end. Of these three views, the third alone is tenable. The first, the "outworn creed" of paganism, surrenders the supremacy of God, and makes him only a member, however important, of the great organism, even as we are. The second, by surrendering God's knowledge of the future, leaves to him only the function of a divine artificer. In

ATONEMENT AND THE RACE   287

the third we have the only view of God which is worth preserving. Either God is ignorant of the future as we are, though to a less degree, or he sees the first together with the last. In the former case, the course of events is independent of him; that is, he is no God at all. In the latter, his existence must be not only everlasting, but timeless.

This consideration, though simple, is far-reaching. It follows that nothing can "happen" for God, as things happen in the world or in history for us, altering our views, our environment, or our purposes and actions. To speak of an event in the life of God would be as absurd as to call the excellence of truthfulness or the equality of the three angles of a triangle to two right angles an event in our own lives. Least of all can the Atonement, whether we regard it as the central act of history or not, be an "event" to God. We concluded previously, on other grounds, that we cannot speak of God's attitude, either to man or to Christ, as changing on account of what either may do. Now we must assert further that the Atonement, Christ's own great act, could produce no change in God; He must have known it from the beginning. He must have seen man in the light of the Atonement, not merely for the last two thousand years, but ever since there was any man to see;—ever since He first thought of man; which can only mean, from all eternity. Christ was the "Lamb slain from before the foundation of the world." In that region which transcends and yet surely permeates all time and all existence, the abode of God, Christ was, is, and will be, continually obeying his Father's will, sacrificing himself, reconciling men to God. What we see projected on the screen of history, God sees in that point of light, that eternal present, which embraces His

Godhead. What Christ did on earth in the first century was only the outworking, made visible to men, of the attitude that is eternal and timeless; as eternal and timeless as is his love to God. Only in our human limitation do we think of that act as producing a change in God's thought of us; the act was known, and, for God, it was also done, from the beginning. There could be no difference in the position of men before God in the year 100 B.C. and the year 100 A.D. The Atonement holds good for the whole of humanity, and not simply for that part of it which came into existence at a time when the world was already growing old.

But we shall be reminded that if the Atonement existed for God from all time, it did not so exist for man; that man could not know what Christ was, or what God really was, until Christ had appeared; and that with this knowledge, man could not be the same, or be judged by the same standards, as he had been while without it. This is undeniable. The Atonement, whatever else it was, was a revelation; and a revelation takes place in time, and alters the world for those to whom it is vouchsafed. But what did it reveal? It did not reveal new virtues, but it laid fresh emphasis on old ones; it did not reveal a new God, but it revealed attributes of God which men had guessed at and talked of, but not clearly understood; it did not reveal a new law, but reaffirmed the essentials of the old one, known to Jew and Gentile alike though constantly disobeyed or forgotten. What it did reveal was a new way of salvation, nothing less than a personality which was the motive power and fulfilment of righteousness in the individual,—God fulfilling his own law in the heart of man. And yet, the more we look at this revelation, the more we see that God, who revealed himself by a son in the last times, had yet revealed himself at sundry times and in divers manners to the fathers. Conviction, repentance, mercy, long-suffering, forgiveness, acceptance, were all known before Christ. No passage in the Bible is more saturated with the longing for salvation and its joyous experience than the fifty-first psalm; and of sin, righteousness, judgment, and salvation, the mind of man is half convicted and dimly conscious, in the psalms of Babylonia, the hymns of ancient India, the choruses of Greek tragedy, and the confused records of the struggles, failures, and glories of ancient history Goodness, where it is not an interested and selfish obedience to an external precept, and therefore no goodness at all, is one and the same wherever it is met. Confidence in right, hatred of wrong-doing, loyalty to principle in the face of danger, sacrifice of self to the commands of the highest authority,—the laws, the state, duty, the gods of the country or the Lord of heaven and earth—these are the marks of goodness inside as outside the pages of the Bible. If God does not approve of these, he can approve of nothing. The difference which has been made by the Atonement, considered as a divine revelation, has been that what before was dim and fluctuating is now clear and unmistakable; the people that walked in darkness have seen a great light.

VIII. But is the Atonement primarily a revelation? Have we not been discussing it all along as if it were something very different? Was Christ's death the repetition, though on a stupendous scale, of the messages of the prophets to previous generations? Surely to regard it merely as a symbolical expression, however remarkable, of God's love of men and hatred of sin, would be to empty it of its essential characteristics. The Atonement is a revelation, and something more.

T

In the first place, the real work of Christ was not done on Calvary; nor was it done simply in the three crowded years of his ministry; it has lasted from the first moment when sin entered into the world. His death outside Jerusalem was that work contracted to a span, brought under conditions which made it visible to us, just as a star, after passing through space, might enter the field of vision of our human eyes. The Atonement itself—the Reconciliation—is thus more than a revelation; it is Christ's essential activity. The Atonement, as we saw it on the cross, is the revelation of the Atonement as Christ performs it, and as God knows it, for all eternity.

But, secondly, such a revelation must itself be a work. To unveil a truth hitherto unknown is to set free a force hitherto unemployed. Every new message of God, when really learnt, becomes a new activity of God within the heart; how much more the message of God's ultimate law and love for man? It is the risen sun which brings to us the consciousness of the sun's beneficent action. Through the hours of darkness, the sun still controls every movement of the earth, and is responsible for all its varied life. But when it appears above the horizon, it calls forth every slumbering faculty for which hitherto all its light and warmth had been non-existent. Precisely in the same way, Christ's work of reconciliation, through the ages of ignorance, had been unsuspected, and so without direct influence on any conscious human endeavour; when it had become known under conditions of time and space, that very revelation became a unique factor in the formation of Christ-like character, in the uplifting of the heart and the purifying of the life.

It was as bearers of good news, heralds of a mystery

ATONEMENT AND THE RACE

long hid, but now made ready for universal proclamation, prophets of the revelation of an accomplished work which was to end the long centuries of baffled groping and futile conflict, that the early apostles "turned the world upside down." In Judea, righteousness had been sought, and sought in vain, by the dead works of the law; the result of enthusiasm for the law, as the law had come to be understood, was made manifest in the horrors of the siege of Jerusalem; but what the law could not do was made triumphantly possible by the knowledge of a personal word of God, who had reconciled sinners once for all upon the cross. In the pagan world, the old ideals of patriotism, reverence, and order, the "pietas" and the "prisca fides," the ideals which were enshrined in the pages of Virgil and inspired the author of the "De Monarchia," had been transformed into the monotonous and hopeless wickedness which needed, for its due description, the pen of a Tacitus, a Juvenal, or a Petronius. The knowledge that sin could be fought, not merely by philosophies or codes of morals, but by a divine force before which it had already yielded at discretion; that the God who had never left himself without witness was now waiting to become the covenant God of man, —this knowledge it was which transformed the world by the renewing of its mind.

It has been pointed out that every great revival of religion in Christendom has sprung from a rediscovery of S. Paul. This means that whenever the fires of religion, almost quenched by worldliness, indifference, or "legalism," have burst forth again, they have been re-kindled by the knowledge of a present salvation;— by the knowledge that the work has been already done, and that through "faith in Christ," every man may be as dead to the world and as victorious over sin, as Christ has been and is. It was in fact the same knowledge as that which, when only half-revealed, and on a far smaller scale, accomplished the revivals of religion in ancient Israel; when the Hebrews, after giving up the struggle with idolatry and oppression, suddenly became convinced, at some prophetic word, that the Lord was with them, that they were, or could be, mighty men of valour, and that, when their sins were repudiated and therefore no longer a bar between themselves and God, victory and purity were assured. Every conversion is a spiritual battle of Marengo; just when the position of sin appears to be unassailable, and books, sermons, deterrents, incentives, and the will itself, have done their best in vain, a new force appears and drives the victorious enemy off the field. "I have sinned; but God loves me still; the burden that was keeping me from him has actually been borne by Christ for me; the strength for which I vainly sought is ready to be wielded in me by him"; when a man can say this, he has learnt the secret of the gospel.

And what has been true of Europe, the land of Augustine, Luther, and Wesley, is equally true of the mission field. The heathen does not perish simply because he is a heathen, and has never heard of Christ; the follower of Mohammed or the worshipper of Vishnu may be a just man, and as such he may be accepted before God, and come from the east or the west to sit down with Abraham and Isaac and Jacob in the kingdom of heaven. But is he for that reason placed beyond the need of the knowledge by which Europe has been regenerated? On the contrary, it is this knowledge alone which can offer protection from the destructive effects of the religions of the pagan world as we observe

ATONEMENT AND THE RACE 293

them at present. Outside Christendom, the influence of religion has come to be what we in Europe know only as the influence of infidelity or atheism. When religion teaches, as one or other of the great religions teach to-day, that there is no hope, no personality, no God, that licentiousness may be enshrined and sanctified within the temple courts, that the scoundrel has as good a chance of God's favour as the saint—that it does not matter, in fact, what he believes or does, so long as the ceremonies he performs are sufficiently in order, and that heaven itself is a place of unlimited opportunity "to revel in a sensual sty," the wonder is that the "virtuous heathen" exists at all.

The evils of the non-Christian world, like the vices of classical paganism, may have been exaggerated; such exaggeration is natural to those who see at once the darkness and the light; but who can be unconscious of the enormous difference in the helps and the hindrances to goodness in the case of a devout English Christian, and a native of Ceylon or of Borneo? It is true that much is given to some and, as it seems to us, appallingly little to others, as, for example, to a Kingswood collier before Wesley began his preaching, or to a Jane Cakebread; nevertheless, true goodness, in act or in character, is possible to all, because, in the sphere of personality, all men may become one with Christ. The Incarnation means this or it means nothing. To some, a Cetawayo or a Thakombau might seem too degraded and brutal to have anything to do with goodness, if goodness means something shared with Christ, as the result of the Incarnation; but are not we ourselves, as imperfect human beings, far nearer to them than to Christ? and if they are "too degraded" for an act which Christ will recognise as done through and by himself, may not we be too degraded also? The possibility for all men, in all ages, of being saved from sin—that in which Christ can have no part—into goodness—that which apart from Christ is impossible—is the essential work of the eternally begotten Son, put into outward visible act upon the cross.

IX. To answer the question with which we started this chapter now becomes comparatively easy. If it is asked how we are to reconcile the conclusions just reached with the emphasis laid by the whole of the New Testament on faith in Christ, our answer is twofold. In the first place, the question as now asked did not occur to the New Testament writers themselves; for them, the pagan world was the world of the first chapter of Romans, of the corruption and vice of Corinth, Ephesus, and Antioch; unbelief and evil corresponded and coincided. The virtues of a Cato or a Trajan never entered their calculations; had they done so, their reply would doubtless have been, "thou art not far from the kingdom of heaven." In the second place, faith—that faith, without which "it is impossible to be well-pleasing unto him"—must be taken in a wide sense; it must include not only the reasoned confidence of the apostle of the Gentiles, or the burning fire of devoted intimacy in the disciple whom Jesus loved; but it must include also the untutored and spontaneous reliance and confidence of the Syro-phœnician woman; or of the paralytic who had only heard of Christ as a healer; or of missionary converts who have never learnt about the doctrines of the Atonement and only know that somehow through Christ they have come into the light. It will include the faith of those who have never heard of Christ at all, but who have faith to act on the principle

ATONEMENT AND THE RACE 295

that good is better, in itself, than evil, purity than impurity, giving than getting, and serving than being served; and many Christians have little more faith than this. Faith cannot be restricted to a man's particular view of the personal and historical Christ, or even to a personal and historical Christ at all; if we ventured to claim this we might unchurch more than Roman and Anglican together would wish. If Rahab had faith, so had Hypatia, so had the mother of the Gracchi.

Completely to reconcile the "objective" and "subjective" elements in the Atonement may prove to be beyond all human powers; certainly the earliest Christian teachers did not attempt to draw a rigid line between what Christ did for us on the cross, and what we have to do in appropriating his blessings. But we see that men are saved by goodness, destroyed by sin; men are capable of salvation, because, as men,—as sharing the humanity of Christ,—they can, by virtue of Christ's reconciliation, reach to the only goodness, which is Christ's. This goodness springs from Christ, and is given through Christ, through union with Christ, whether men are conscious or not of that great person with whom they are united.

Such goodness consists in the personal relation of filial obedience and love to God. To reach it, namely to take up that relation which for us all has been broken, is impossible, as all experience teaches, except through atonement. The only atonement of which we know is Christ's atoning death on Calvary, or rather the reconciliation effected through his death and resurrection. But that event, completed in the fulness of the times, stands for much more than itself. The act upon Calvary, and the whole drama of the perfect life, as events in time, and apart from the eternal purpose of the

Godhead, have introduced no change into the principles of God's dealing with men; but the knowledge of that act indefinitely increases both man's powers and man's responsibilities. For when the Son of Man is lifted up before his eyes, the dim guesses of the past are suddenly transformed into knowledge. He knows what complete goodness is; he knows that it is now attainable for him; and he knows how solemn and urgent is the force of the appeal from the cross. By deliberate acceptance of the message, or rather by frank and full confidence in the messenger,—the Word,—by explicit "faith in Christ," that is to say,—he can reach a far higher degree of goodness than was ever possible before; by rejecting it he incurs a condemnation far severer than could ever follow from the rejection of dimmer ideals and vaguer demands. "To whomsoever much is given, from him shall much be required."

X. "Supposing, then, that there had been no Atonement?" But that is just what we cannot suppose, unless there had been no human race, or else no sin. The only God of whom we can conceive is a God at once of righteousness and of love. If He has created mankind, He must both demand righteousness from them, and yearn for their love. The end of his purpose must be the unbroken confidence between two persons who are after all not two, but one. To the recognition of this ideal we were led by our study of ethics, which showed us that goodness consists in those personal relations which are seen in their completest form in the family, between parent and child. But what if that personal bond has been broken, and instead of joyful obedience, there is only the gulf of suspicion and instinctive hate? In that case, love could only be love by being reconciliation

ATONEMENT AND THE RACE

as well; and righteousness could only be righteous by action that would bring back the righteousness in man which disobedience had expelled. From the first moment that the breach appeared, God must have been reconciling the world unto Himself; and this He could only do in Christ. Unless He was to deny himself, He must ever have been sending forth that personal energy, the mediator and the bond between Himself and man, which is for ever rendering to Him a stainless obedience, even to the point of the agony of death, on behalf of man. The real difficulty does not consist in "believing in the Atonement," but in conceiving of either God or the world without the Atonement. The Atonement, the Reconciliation, is no ingenious plan or device for salvation; it is God's love, God's very being, viewed from the side of human sin. It is no article of the Christian creed to be dispensed with or not at will; it is the expression of God's nature, without which all that we know of God would form one vast contradiction. It is no theological dogma "tacked on" to the principles of morality, introducing a new and artificial goodness to replace the goodness of everyday life; it is the underlying truth of man's relation to goodness and to God, which alone has made practicable the simplest commands of morality.

"No man cometh unto the Father, but by me." These words mean exactly what they say; if any man has ever come unto the Father, or even, in ignorance of the Father, has approximated to the Father in righteousness or love, it is because, however little he may have suspected it, he has been drawn thither by Christ. "Love is of God, and every one that loveth is begotten of God, and knoweth God . . . he that abideth in love abideth in God, and God in him . . . we love, because he first loved us." And this community of love which is community of nature has been secured, as alone it could be secured, by one who shared man's deepest degradation and bore his heaviest burdens, and so was made unto him righteousness and life; "that in the name of Jesus every knee should bow, of things in heaven and things on earth and things under the earth, and that every tongue should confess that Jesus Christ is Lord to the glory of God the Father."

INDEX

The references to words marked with an asterisk are intended simply to supplement the Table of Contents, and to mark the more important passages.

ABSOLUTE, the, 43, 247.
Adoption, 18.
Alcestis, 129.
Ali, 279.
Angelico, Fra, 180.
Anger, 151 ff., 171.
Anselm, 81, 135, 150, 283.
Anthropomorphism, 157 ff.
Antigone, 129.
Apollinarianism, 271.
Aquinas, Thomas, 33, 150.
Arianism, 270.
Aristides, 268.
Aristotle, 2, 21, 29, 32, 65, 72, 83, 151, 256.
Arnold, Matthew, 271, 284.
Arthur, King, 59.
Asoka, 279.
Atheism, 120.
*Atonement, the, 125, 133, 142 ff., 179, 264, 267, 281, 287 ff., 296.
Atonement, Day of, 205, 212.
Augustine, 17, 80, 150, 259.
Aurelius, Marcus, 269.

BACON, Francis, 151, 160, 252.
Barnabas, Epistle of, 2.
Bayard, Chevalier, 81.
Behmen, Jacob, 33.
Benevolence, 75.
Bentham, Jeremy, 27, 41.
Bernard of Clairvaux, 150.
*Blood of Christ, the, 182 ff., 210, 267.
Blood, as the life, 204.
Bradlaugh, Charles, 282.
Bravery, 63, 72, 80.
Browning, Robert, 102, 116, 166, 274.
Brutus, 253, 268.

Buddha and Buddhism, 12, 96, 112, 151, 197, 230, 269.
Bunyan, John, 102.
Butler, Bishop, 28, 41, 45, 85, 152, 164.

CÆSAR, 108.
Calvin, John, 37, 118.
Carton, Sidney, 63.
Casuistry, 78.
Categorical Imperative, 42, 62, 64.
Catholicism, 182, 271, 276.
Cato, 294.
Cavour, Count, 269.
Celsus, 11.
Child, Mrs, 161.
Church, the, 238.
Cicero, 87, 252, 268, 269.
Cincinnatus, 268.
"Cloister and the Hearth," 57.
Clovis, 214.
"Common-sense" morality, 48, 65.
—— philosophy, 250.
Confucius, 96, 230, 269.
Conrad, Joseph, 101.
Conscience, 66, 85.
Contrition, 106, 125.
Conversion, 81.
Cordelia, 273.
Cornelia, 295.
Covenant, the, 15 ff., 196.
Covenanters, the, 37.
Cowper, William, 165, 183.
Crucifixion of Christ, 180, 194, 195.
—— with Christ, 193.

DALE, R. W., 176.
Damien, Father, 257.
Dante, 79, 81, 103, 141, 277, 291.

INDEX

Davidson, A. B., 233.
*Death of Christ, 129, 132, 182, 189, 195, 201.
Decalogue, the, 62.
Deism, 37, 120, 270.
Divinity of Christ, 228 ff.
Driver, S. R., 138.
Duty, 33, 37, 40, 53. *See* Ethics.

EDWARD the Confessor, 269.
Elias of Cortona, 279.
Eliot, George, 57.
Emerson, R. W., 114, 253.
Epaminondas, 268.
Epictetus, 152.
Epicureans, 33.
*Ethics, 26 ff., 49, 83, 85, 98, 184, 196, 241, 272, 296.
—— Greek, 29 f., 33, 43, 49.
Ethnic religions, 149, 197, 199, 203, 209, 270, 293.
Experience, Christian, 231, 235, 240.

FABRICIUS, 268.
*Faith, 19, 127, 147, 280, 294.
Family, the, 25, 57 f., 66, 80, 124, 296.
*Fatherhood of God, 176 ff., 210.
*Forgiveness, 105 ff., 156, 159.
Frazer, J. G., 166.
Freedom, 23.

GAMBETTA, L. M., 4.
Garvie, A. E., 169.
Gilds, mediæval, 58.
Gladstone, W. E., 118, 160.
Gobbo, Lancelot, 46.
Golden Rule, the, 64.
Good Samaritan, Parable of the, 241, 273.
Goodness, 281 ff., 289.
Gordon, "Chinese," 255.
Green, T. H., 2, 27, 72, 141, 173.

HAMMURABI, Code of, 5.
Harmodius and Aristogeiton, 273.
Hartley, D., 41.
Haym, R., 50.
Heathen, the unevangelised, 292.
Hedonism, 34 f.
Hegel, G. F. W., 43, 60.
Hermas, 2.
Herodotus, 269.

Hildebrand, 81.
Hinduism, 254, 269.
Hobbes, T., 28, 39, 45, 151.
Holiness, 202.
Howard, J., 81.
Humanitarianism, 152.
Hutcheson, F., 73.
Hutten, Ulrich von, 81.
Huxley, T., 270.
Hypatia, 295.
Hypnotism, 114.

ILLINGWORTH, J. R., 117, 270.
Incarnation, the, 232 f., 281, 293.
Initiation ceremonies, 149.
Intuitionism, 34.

JACKSON, "Stonewall," 115.
James, S., 2, 6, 20, 37, 97, 190.
Jealousy, human and divine, 159 f.
Jesuits, 60.
*Jesus Christ, 2, 14, 15, 20, 23, 68, 91, 94, 112, 158, 171, 175, 185, 218 ff., 258, 274 ff. *See also* Death, Divinity, Incarnation, Manhood, Pre-existence.
John, S., 2, 14, 17, 20, 175, 190, 222, 228.
Judaism, modern, 198.
Julian, the Emperor, 269.
Justice, 76.
Justin Martyr, 29.

KANT, Immanuel, 42, 53, 72, 270.
Kingdom of Heaven, 21, 29.

LAELIUS, 268.
Law, in Old Testament, 3, 4, 7, 16, 23, 64, 88, 199, 291.
Law, the Moral, 179. *See* Categorical Imperative and Conscience.
Lecky, W. E. H., 35.
Lidgett, J. S., 178, 283.
Lodge, Sir Oliver, 130.
Louis, S., 81, 269.
Lucian, 11.
Lucretius, 149.
Luther, Martin, 37, 118, 150, 261, 279.

MAGNETISM, animal, 113.
Manchester School, the, 65.
Mandeville, Bertrand de, 151.
Manhood of Christ, 232 ff.

INDEX 301

Martineau, J., 45, 84.
Mazzini, G., 4, 81, 256.
*Mediation, 18, 110, 120 ff., 139, 212.
Meredith, G. 162.
Messiah, the, 196, 234.
Metaphysics, 84, 226, 242.
Michael Angelo, 274.
Mill, J. S., 2, 4, 27, 70, 270, 282.
Mirandola, Pico de, 81.
Moberley, R. C., 283.
Mohammed, 12, 96, 118, 198, 230, 255.
Monastic system, the, 58.
Monotheism, 224 f.
Morality. *See* Ethics.
—— Hebrew ideals of, 9.
Moses, 230, 257.

NAPOLEON, 115.
Nelson, Lord, 63, 115.
Nero, 278.
Nestorianism, 271.
Nicholson, General, 115.

OBLIGATION, 87.
Original sin, 86.

PALEY, W., 27, 41.
Palmer, G. H., 67.
Pascal, Blaise, 261.
Paul, S., 1, 6, 7, 14, 20, 23, 37, 64, 67, 96, 118, 153, 175, 191, 237, 260.
Penitence, 124.
Penn, W., 283.
Persius, 74.
*Personality, 38, 61, 232, 247 ff.
Petronius, 291.
Pitt, William, 118.
Plato, 29, 31, 63, 81, 148, 151, 165, 171.
Platonists, Christian, 40.
Pleasure, 33, 43.
Plutarch, 269.
Polycarp, 2.
Pope, W. B., 134.
Positivism, 270.
Pre-existence of Christ, 284 ff.
*Propitiation, 88, 148 ff.
Protestantism, 182, 271, 276.
Psychology, 39, 42, 45, 114.
*Punishment, 102 ff., 134, 148, 164 f.
—— eternal, 241.

Puritans, 37.
Pusey, E. B., 183, 188.
Pym, John, 269.

RACE, the, 238.
Rahab, 295.
*Ransom, 95, 134, 143.
Reade, C., 57.
*Reconciliation, 92, 97, 99, 118, 125, 179, 212, 238, 264, 297.
Reformation, the, 37.
Reid, T., 65.
Religion, 1, 98, 149.
Repentance, 106, 125, 169 ff.
Resurrection of Christ, 191.
Ritschl, A., 154, 168, 231.
"Romola," 57.
Rubens, 180.

SABBATH, the, 4.
Sabellianism, 271.
*Sacrifices, 88 ff., 97, 182, 198, 207, 212, 268.
Satisfaction, 100.
Savonarola, 255.
Schoolmen, the, 36.
Seeley, J. R., 6, 69.
Self-realisation, 55 ff., 60, 72.
Semites, 8, 200.
Seneca, 152.
Sermon on Mount, 1, 9, 62.
Shaftesbury, 3rd Earl of, 41, 45, 65, 73.
Shakespeare, 59, 106.
Sidgwick, H., 27, 71, 77.
Smith, Ad., 73.
Socinianism, 270.
Socrates, 2, 29, 30, 49, 252, 268.
"Son of Man," 233.
Spencer, H., 27, 59, 69, 110, 149.
Spinoza, B., 41.
Spirit, the Holy, 235 ff.
State, the, 57.
Stewart, D., 65.
Stoicism, 24, 33.
Substitution, 135 ff.
Suffering, 91, 98, 111, 141.
Suggestion, 114.

TABOO, 204.
Tacitus, 291.
Temperance, 80.
Temptation in Wilderness, 256.
"Theologia Germanica," 260.

INDEX

Thoreau, H. D., 253.
Tintoretto, 180.
Tolstoi, Count, 6, 13.
Totemism, 204.
Trajan, 278, 294.
Transcendentalism, 248 ff., 270.
Trinity, the, 27, 176.
Truthfulness, 76.

UNITARIANISM, 37, 277.
Unity, between Father and Son, 175, 176, 227.
Utilitarianism, 34, 41, 52, 77.

*VICARIOUSNESS, 133 ff., 257.
Virgil, 291.
Virtue, 32, 83, 294.
Virtues, the, 19, 21, 80, 83.

WESLEY, J., 72, 81, 116.
Westcott, B. F., 194.
Whitman, Walt, 56.
Wilberforce, W., 160.
Wordsworth, W., 50, 61.

XAVIER, Francis, 260.

PRINTED BY
TURNBULL AND SPEARS,
EDINBURGH

A CATALOGUE OF BOOKS PUBLISHED BY METHUEN AND COMPANY: LONDON 36 ESSEX STREET W.C.

CONTENTS

	PAGE		PAGE
General Literature,	2-19	Little Blue Books,	27
Ancient Cities,	19	Little Books on Art,	27
Antiquary's Books,	20	Little Galleries,	28
Beginner's Books,	20	Little Guides,	28
Business Books,	20	Little Library,	28
Byzantine Texts,	21	Miniature Library,	30
Churchman's Bible,	21	Oxford Biographies,	30
Churchman's Library,	21	School Examination Series,	30
Classical Translations,	21	Social Questions of To-day,	31
Commercial Series,	22	Textbooks of Science,	31
Connoisseur's Library,	22	Textbooks of Technology	31
Library of Devotion,	23	Handbooks of Theology,	31
Standard Library,	23	Westminster Commentaries,	32
Half-Crown Library,	24		
Illustrated Pocket Library of Plain and Coloured Books,	24	Fiction,	32-36
		The Shilling Novels,	37
Junior Examination Series,	26	Books for Boys and Girls	38
Junior School-Books,	26	Novels of Alexandre Dumas,	38
Leaders of Religion,	27	Methuen's Sixpenny Books,	39

JULY 1906

A CATALOGUE OF

MESSRS. METHUEN'S
PUBLICATIONS

Colonial Editions are published of all Messrs. METHUEN's Novels issued at a price above 2s. 6d., and similar editions are published of some works of General Literature. These are marked in the Catalogue. Colonial editions are only for circulation in the British Colonies and India.

An asterisk denotes that a book is in the Press.
I.P.L. represents Illustrated Pocket Library.
S.Q.S. represents Social Questions Series.

PART I.—GENERAL LITERATURE

Abbot (Jacob). See Little Blue Books.
Abbott (J. H. M.). Author of 'Tommy Cornstalk.' AN OUTLANDER IN ENGLAND: BEING SOME IMPRESSIONS OF AN AUSTRALIAN ABROAD. *Second Edition.* Cr. 8vo. 6s.
A Colonial Edition is also published.
Acatos (M. J.). See Junior School Books.
Adams (Frank). JACK SPRATT. With 24 Coloured Pictures. *Super Royal* 16mo. 2s.
Adeney (W. F.), M.A. See Bennett and Adeney.
Æschylus. See Classical Translations.
Æsop. See I.P.L.
Ainsworth (W. Harrison). See I.P.L.
Alderson (J. P.). MR. ASQUITH. With Portraits and Illustrations. *Demy 8vo.* 7s. 6d. net.
A Colonial Edition is also published.
Aldis (Janet). MADAME GEOFFRIN, HER SALON, AND HER TIMES. With many Portraits and Illustrations. *Second Edition.* Demy 8vo. 10s. 6d. net.
A Colonial Edition is also published.
Alexander (William), D.D., Archbishop of Armagh. THOUGHTS AND COUNSELS OF MANY YEARS. *Demy* 16mo. 2s. 6d.
Alken (Henry). THE NATIONAL SPORTS OF GREAT BRITAIN. With descriptions in English and French. With 51 Coloured Plates. *Royal Folio. Five Guineas net.* The Plates can be had separately in a Portfolio. £3, 3s. *net.*
See also I.P.L.
Allen (Jessie). See Little Books on Art.
Allen (J. Romilly), F.S.A. See Antiquary's Books.
Almack (E.). See Little Books on Art.
Amherst (Lady). A SKETCH OF EGYPTIAN HISTORY FROM THE EARLIEST TIMES TO THE PRESENT DAY. With many Illustrations. *Demy 8vo.* 7s. 6d. *net.*

Anderson (F. M.). THE STORY OF THE BRITISH EMPIRE FOR CHILDREN. With many Illustrations. *Cr. 8vo.* 2s.
Anderson (J. G.), B.A., Examiner to London University, NOUVELLE GRAMMAIRE FRANÇAISE. *Cr. 8vo.* 2s.
EXERCICES DE GRAMMAIRE FRANÇAISE. *Cr. 8vo.* 1s. 6d.
Andrewes (Bishop). PRECES PRIVATAE. Edited, with Notes, by F. E. BRIGHTMAN, M.A., of Pusey House, Oxford. *Cr. 8vo.* 6s.
Anglo-Australian. AFTER-GLOW MEMORIES. *Cr. 8vo.* 6s.
A Colonial Edition is also published.
Aristophanes. THE FROGS. Translated into English by E. W. HUNTINGFORD, M.A. *Cr. 8vo.* 2s. 6d.
Aristotle. THE NICOMACHEAN ETHICS. Edited, with an Introduction and Notes, by JOHN BURNET, M.A., Professor of Greek at St. Andrews. *Cheaper issue. Demy 8vo.* 10s. 6d. *net.*
Ashton (R.). See Little Blue Books.
Atkins (H. G.). See Oxford Biographies.
Atkinson (C. M.). JEREMY BENTHAM. *Demy 8vo.* 5s. *net.*
Atkinson (T. D.). A SHORT HISTORY OF ENGLISH ARCHITECTURE. With over 200 Illustrations. *Fcap. 8vo.* 3s. 6d. *net.*
A GLOSSARY OF TERMS USED IN ENGLISH ARCHITECTURE. Illustrated. *Fcap. 8vo.* 3s. 6d. *net.*
Auden (T.), M.A., F.S.A. See Ancient Cities.
Aurelius (Marcus). See Standard Library and W. H. D. Rouse.
Austen (Jane). See Little Library and Standard Library.
Aves (Ernest). See Books on Business.
Bacon (Francis). See Little Library and Standard Library.

General Literature 3

Baden-Powell (R. S. S.), Major-General. THE DOWNFALL OF PREMPEH. A Diary of Life in Ashanti, 1895. Illustrated. *Third Edition. Large Cr. 8vo. 6s.*
A Colonial Edition is also published.
THE MATABELE CAMPAIGN, 1896. With nearly 100 Illustrations. *Fourth Edition. Large Cr. 8vo. 6s.*
A Colonial Edition is also published.
*Bagot (Richard). THE LAKE OF COMO. *Cr. 8vo. 3s. 6d. net.*
Bailey (J. C.), M.A. See Cowper.
Baker (W. G.), M.A. See Junior Examination Series.
Baker (Julian L.), F.I.C., F.C.S. See Books on Business.
Balfour (Graham). THE LIFE OF ROBERT LOUIS STEVENSON. *Second Edition. Two Volumes. Demy 8vo. 25s. net.*
A Colonial Edition is also published.
Bally (S. E.). See Commercial Series.
Banks (Elizabeth L.). THE AUTOBIOGRAPHY OF A 'NEWSPAPER GIRL.' *Second Edition. Cr. 8vo. 6s.*
A Colonial Edition is also published.
Barham (R. H.). See Little Library.
Baring (The Hon. Maurice). WITH THE RUSSIANS IN MANCHURIA. *Third Edition. Demy 8vo. 7s. 6d. net.*
A Colonial Edition is also published.
Baring-Gould (S.). THE LIFE OF NAPOLEON BONAPARTE. With over 450 Illustrations in the Text, and 12 Photogravure Plates. *Gilt top. Large quarto. 36s.*
THE TRAGEDY OF THE CÆSARS. With numerous Illustrations from Busts, Gems, Cameos, etc. *Fifth Edition. Royal 8vo. 10s. 6d. net.*
A BOOK OF FAIRY TALES. With numerous Illustrations by A. J. GASKIN. *Second Edition. Cr. 8vo. Buckram. 6s.*
OLD ENGLISH FAIRY TALES. With numerous Illustrations by F. D. BEDFORD. *Second Edition. Cr. 8vo. Buckram. 6s.*
A Colonial Edition is also published.
THE VICAR OF MORWENSTOW. Revised Edition. With a Portrait. *Cr. 8vo. 3s. 6d.*
DARTMOOR: A Descriptive and Historical Sketch. With Plans and numerous Illustrations. *Cr. 8vo. 6s.*
A BOOK OF DEVON. Illustrated. *Second Edition. Cr. 8vo. 6s.*
A BOOK OF CORNWALL. Illustrated. *Second Edition. Cr. 8vo. 6s.*
A BOOK OF NORTH WALES. Illustrated. *Cr. 8vo. 6s.*
A BOOK OF SOUTH WALES. Illustrated. *Cr. 8vo. 6s.*
A BOOK OF BRITTANY. Illustrated. *Cr. 8vo. 6s.*
A BOOK OF THE RIVIERA. Illustrated. *Cr. 8vo. 6s.*
A Colonial Edition is also published.

*THE RHINE. Illustrated. *Cr. 8vo. 6s.*
A BOOK OF GHOSTS. With 8 Illustrations by D. MURRAY SMITH. *Second Edition. Cr. 8vo. 6s.*
A Colonial Edition is also published.
OLD COUNTRY LIFE. With 67 Illustrations. *Fifth Edition. Large Cr. 8vo. 6s.*
A GARLAND OF COUNTRY SONG: English Folk Songs with their Traditional Melodies. Collected and arranged by S. BARING-GOULD and H. F. SHEPPARD. *Demy 4to. 6s.*
SONGS OF THE WEST: Folk Songs of Devon and Cornwall. Collected from the Mouths of the People. By S. BARING-GOULD, M.A., and H· FLEETWOOD SHEPPARD, M.A. New and Revised Edition, under the musical editorship of CECIL J. SHARP, Principal of the Hampstead Conservatoire. *Large Imperial 8vo. 5s. net.*
See also Little Guides and Half-Crown Library.
Barker (Aldred F.). See Textbooks of Technology.
Barnes (W. E.), D.D. See Churchman's Bible.
Barnett (Mrs. P. A.). See Little Library.
Baron (R. R. N.), M.A. FRENCH PROSE COMPOSITION. *Second Edition. Cr. 8vo. 2s. 6d. Key, 3s. net.* See also Junior School Books.
Barron (H. M.), M.A., Wadham College, Oxford. TEXTS FOR SERMONS. With a Preface by Canon SCOTT HOLLAND. *Cr. 8vo. 3s. 6d.*
Bartholomew (J. G.), F.R.S.E. See C. G. Robertson.
Bastable (C. F.), M.A. See S.Q.S.
Batson (Mrs. Stephen). A BOOK OF THE COUNTRY AND THE GARDEN. Illustrated by F. CARRUTHERS GOULD and A. C. GOULD. *Demy 8vo. 10s. 6d.*
A CONCISE HANDBOOK OF GARDEN FLOWERS. *Fcap. 8vo. 3s. 6d.*
Batten (Loring W.), Ph.D., S.T.D. THE HEBREW PROPHET. *Cr. 8vo. 3s. 6d net.*
Beaman (A. Hulme). PONS ASINORUM; OR, A GUIDE TO BRIDGE. *Second Edition. Fcap. 8vo. 2s.*
Beard (W. S.). See Junior Examination Series and Beginner's Books.
Beckford (Peter). THOUGHTS ON HUNTING. Edited by J. OTHO PAGET, and Illustrated by G. H. JALLAND. *Second Edition. Demy 8vo. 6s.*
Beckford (William). See Little Library.
Beeching (H. C.), M.A., Canon of Westminster. See Library of Devotion.
Begbie (Harold). MASTER WORKERS. Illustrated. *Demy 8vo. 7s. 6d. net.*
Behmen (Jacob). DIALOGUES ON THE SUPERSENSUAL LIFE. Edited by BERNARD HOLLAND. *Fcap. 8vo. 3s. 6d.*

4 Messrs. Methuen's Catalogue

Belloc (Hillaire). PARIS. With Maps and Illustrations. *Cr. 8vo.* 6s.
*****MARIE ANTOINETTE.** With many Portraits and Illustrations. *Demy 8vo.* 12s. 6d. net.
A Colonial Edition is also published.
Bellot (H. H. L.), M.A. THE INNER AND MIDDLE TEMPLE. With numerous Illustrations. *Crown 8vo.* 6s. net.
See also L. A. A. Jones.
Bennett (W. H.), M.A. A PRIMER OF THE BIBLE. *Third Edition. Cr. 8vo.* 2s. 6d.
Bennett (W. H.) and Adeney (W. F.). A BIBLICAL INTRODUCTION. *Third Edition. Cr. 8vo.* 7s. 6d.
Benson (Archbishop) GOD'S BOARD: Communion Addresses. *Fcap. 8vo.* 3s. 6d. net.
Benson (A. C.), M.A. See Oxford Biographies.
Benson (R. M.). THE WAY OF HOLINESS: a Devotional Commentary on the 119th Psalm. *Cr. 8vo.* 5s.
Bernard (E. R.), M.A., Canon of Salisbury. THE ENGLISH SUNDAY. *Fcap. 8vo.* 1s. 6d.
Bertouch (Baroness de). THE LIFE OF FATHER IGNATIUS. Illustrated. *Demy 8vo.* 10s. 6d. net.
A Colonial Edition is also published.
Betham-Edwards (M.). HOME LIFE IN FRANCE. Illustrated. *Fourth Edition. Demy 8vo.* 7s. 6d. net.
A Colonial Edition is also published.
Bethune-Baker (J. F.), M.A. See Handbooks of Theology.
Bidez (M.). See Byzantine Texts.
Biggs (C. R. D.), D.D. See Churchman's Bible.
Bindley (T. Herbert), B.D. THE OECUMENICAL DOCUMENTS OF THE FAITH. With Introductions and Notes. *Cr. 8vo.* 6s.
Binns (H. B.). THE LIFE OF WALT WHITMAN. Illustrated. *Demy 8vo.* 10s. 6d. net.
A Colonial Edition is also published.
Binyon (Laurence). THE DEATH OF ADAM, AND OTHER POEMS. *Cr. 8vo.* 3s. 6d. net.
*****WILLIAM BLAKE.** In 2 volumes. *Super Royal Quarto.* £1, 1s. *each.*
Vol. I.—THE BOOK OF JOB.
Birnstingl (Ethel). See Little Books on Art.
Blackmantle (Bernard). See I.P.L.
Blair (Robert). See I.P.L.
Blake (William). See I.P.L. and Little Library.
Blaxland (B.), M.A. See Library of Devotion.
Bloom (T. Harvey), M.A. SHAKESPEARE'S GARDEN. Illustrated. *Fcap. 8vo.* 3s. 6d.; leather, 4s. 6d. net.
See also Antiquary's Books

Blouet (Henri). See Beginner's Books.
Boardman (T. H.), M.A. See Textbooks of Science.
Bodley (J. E. C.), Author of 'France.' THE CORONATION OF EDWARD VII. *Demy 8vo.* 21s. net. By Command of the King.
Body (George), D.D. THE SOUL'S PILGRIMAGE: Devotional Readings from his writings. Selected by J. H. BURN, B.D., F.R.S.E. *Pott 8vo.* 2s. 6d.
Bona (Cardinal). See Library of Devotion.
Boon (F. C.). See Commercial Series.
Borrow (George). See Little Library.
Bos (J. Ritzema). AGRICULTURAL ZOOLOGY. Translated by J. R. AINSWORTH DAVIS, M.A. With 155 Illustrations. *Cr. 8vo. Third Edition.* 3s. 6d.
Botting (C. G.), B.A. EASY GREEK EXERCISES. *Cr. 8vo.* 2s. See also Junior Examination Series.
Boulton (E. S.), M.A. GEOMETRY ON MODERN LINES. *Cr. 8vo.* 2s.
Boulton (William B.). THOMAS GAINSBOROUGH With 40 Illustrations. *Second Ed. Demy 8vo.* 7s. 6d. net.
SIR JOSHUA REYNOLDS, P.R.A. With 49 Illustrations. *Demy 8vo.* 7s. 6d. net.
Bowden (E. M.). THE IMITATION OF BUDDHA: Being Quotations from Buddhist Literature for each Day in the Year. *Fifth Edition. Cr. 16mo.* 2s. 6d.
Boyle (W.). CHRISTMAS AT THE ZOO. With Verses by W. BOYLE and 24 Coloured Pictures by H. B. NEILSON. *Super Royal 16mo.* 2s.
Brabant (F. G.), M.A. See Little Guides.
Bradley (J. W.). See Little Books on Art.
Brailsford (H. N.). MACEDONIA. Illustrated. *Demy 8vo.* 12s. 6d. net.
Brodrick (Mary) and Morton (Anderson). A CONCISE HANDBOOK OF EGYPTIAN ARCHÆOLOGY. Illustrated. *Cr. 8vo.* 3s. 6d.
Brooke (A. S.), M.A. SLINGSBY AND SLINGSBY CASTLE. Illustrated. *Cr. 8vo.* 7s. 6d.
Brooks (E. W.). See Byzantine Texts.
Brown (P. H.), LL.D., Fraser Professor of Ancient (Scottish) History at the University of Edinburgh. SCOTLAND IN THE TIME OF QUEEN MARY. *Demy 8vo.* 7s. 6d. net.
Browne (Sir Thomas). See Standard Library.
Brownell (C. L.). THE HEART OF JAPAN. Illustrated. *Third Edition. Cr. 8vo.* 6s.; also *Demy 8vo.* 6d.
A Colonial Edition is also published.
Browning (Robert). See Little Library.
Buckland (Francis T.). CURIOSITIES OF NATURAL HISTORY. Illustrated by H. B. NEILSON. *Cr. 8vo.* 3s. 6d.

General Literature 5

Buckton (A. M.) THE BURDEN OF ENGELA: a Ballad-Epic. *Second Edition.* *Cr. 8vo.* 3s. 6d. *net.*
EAGER HEART: A Mystery Play. *Fourth Edition. Cr. 8vo.* 1s. *net.*
Budge (E. A. Wallis). THE GODS OF THE EGYPTIANS. With over 100 Coloured Plates and many Illustrations. *Two Volumes. Royal 8vo.* £3, 3s. *net.*
Bull (Paul), Army Chaplain. GOD AND OUR SOLDIERS. *Second Edition. Cr. 8vo.* 6s.
A Colonial Edition is also published.
Bulley (Miss). See S.Q.S.
Bunyan (John). THE PILGRIM'S PROGRESS. Edited, with an Introduction, by C. H. FIRTH, M.A. With 39 Illustrations by R. ANNING BELL. *Cr. 8vo.* 6s.
See also Library of Devotion and Standard Library.
Burch (G. J.), M.A., F.R.S. A MANUAL OF ELECTRICAL SCIENCE. Illustrated. *Cr. 8vo.* 3s.
Burgess (Gelett). GOOPS AND HOW TO BE THEM. Illustrated. *Small 4to.* 6s.
Burke (Edmund). See Standard Library.
Burn (A. E.), D.D., Rector of Handsworth and Prebendary of Lichfield.
See Handbooks of Theology.
Burn (J. H.), B.D. See Library of Devotion.
Burnand (Sir F. C.), RECORDS AND REMINISCENCES. With a Portrait by H. v. HERKOMER. *Cr. 8vo. Fourth and Cheaper Edition.* 6s.
A Colonial Edition is also published.
Burns (Robert), THE POEMS OF. Edited by ANDREW LANG and W. A. CRAIGIE. With Portrait. *Third Edition. Demy 8vo, gilt top.* 6s.
Burnside (W. F.), M.A. OLD TESTAMENT HISTORY FOR USE IN SCHOOLS. *Cr. 8vo.* 3s. 6d.
Burton (Alfred). See I.P.L.
Butler (Joseph). See Standard Library.
Caldecott (Alfred), D.D. See Handbooks of Theology.
Calderwood (D. S.), Headmaster of the Normal School, Edinburgh. TEST CARDS IN EUCLID AND ALGEBRA. In three packets of 40, with Answers. 1s. each. Or in three Books, price 2d., 2d., and 3d.
Cambridge (Ada) [Mrs. Cross]. THIRTY YEARS IN AUSTRALIA. *Demy 8vo.* 7s. 6d.
A Colonial Edition is also published.
Canning (George). See Little Library.
Capey (E. F. H.). See Oxford Biographies.
Careless (John). See I.P.L.
Carlyle (Thomas). THE FRENCH REVOLUTION. Edited by C. R. L. FLETCHER, Fellow of Magdalen College, Oxford. *Three Volumes. Cr. 8vo.* 18s.

THE LIFE AND LETTERS OF OLIVER CROMWELL. With an Introduction by C. H. FIRTH, M.A., and Notes and Appendices by Mrs. S. C. LOMAS. *Three Volumes. Demy 8vo.* 18s. *net.*
Carlyle (R. M. and A. J.), M.A. See Leaders of Religion.
***Carpenter (Margaret).** THE CHILD IN ART. Illustrated. *Cr. 8vo.* 6s.
Chamberlin (Wilbur B.). ORDERED TO CHINA. *Cr. 8vo.* 6s.
A Colonial Edition is also published.
Channer (C. C.) and Roberts (M. E.). LACEMAKING IN THE MIDLANDS, PAST AND PRESENT. With 16 full-page Illustrations. *Cr. 8vo.* 2s. 6d.
Chapman (S. J.). See Books on Business.
Chatterton (Thomas). See Standard Library.
Chesterfield (Lord), THE LETTERS OF, TO HIS SON. Edited, with an Introduction by C. STRACHEY, and Notes by A. CALTHROP. *Two Volumes. Cr. 8vo.* 12s.
***Chesterton (G. K.).** DICKENS. With Portraits and Illustrations. *Demy 8vo.* 7s. 6d. *net.*
A Colonial Edition is also published.
Christian (F. W.). THE CAROLINE ISLANDS. With many Illustrations and Maps. *Demy 8vo.* 12s. 6d. *net.*
Cicero. See Classical Translations.
Clarke (F. A.), M.A. See Leaders of Religion.
Cleather (A. L.) and Crump (B.). RICHARD WAGNER'S MUSIC DRAMAS: Interpretations, embodying Wagner's own explanations. *In Four Volumes. Fcap 8vo.* 2s. 6d. *each.*
VOL. I.—THE RING OF THE NIBELUNG. *Third Edition.*
VOL. II.—PARSIFAL, LOHENGRIN, and THE HOLY GRAIL.
VOL. III.—TRISTAN AND ISOLDE.
Clinch (G.). See Little Guides.
Clough (W. T.). See Junior School Books.
Coast (W. G.), B.A. EXAMINATION PAPERS IN VERGIL. *Cr. 8vo.* 2s.
Cobb (T.). See Little Blue Books.
Cobb (W. F.), M.A. THE BOOK OF PSALMS: with a Commentary. *Demy 8vo.* 10s. 6d. *net.*
Coleridge (S. T.), SELECTIONS FROM. Edited by ARTHUR SYMONS. *Fcap. 8vo.* 2s. 6d.
Collingwood (W. G.). See Half-Crown Library.
Collins (W. E.), M.A. See Churchman's Library.
Colonna. HYPNEROTOMACHIA POLIPHILI UBI HUMANA OMNIA NON NISI SOMNIUM ESSE DOCET ATQUE OBITER PLURIMA SCITU SANE QUAM DIGNA COMMEMORAT. An edition limited to 350 copies on handmade paper. *Folio. Three Guineas net.*
Combe (William). See I.P.L.

Messrs. Methuen's Catalogue

Cook (A. M.), M.A. See E. C. Marchant.
Cooke-Taylor (R. W.). See S.Q.S.
Corelli (Marie). THE PASSING OF THE GREAT QUEEN : *Fcap. 4to. 1s.*
A CHRISTMAS GREETING. *Cr. 4to. 1s.*
Corkran (Alice). See Little Books on Art.
Cotes (Rosemary). DANTE'S GARDEN. With a Frontispiece. *Second Edition. Fcap. 8vo. 2s. 6d.; leather, 3s. 6d. net.*
BIBLE FLOWERS. With a Frontispiece and Plan. *Fcap. 8vo. 2s. 6d. net.*
Cowley (Abraham). See Little Library.
Cowper (William), THE POEMS OF. Edited with an Introduction and Notes by J. C. BAILEY, M.A. Illustrated, including two unpublished designs by WILLIAM BLAKE. *Demy 8vo. 10s. 6d. net.*
Cox (J. Charles), LL.D., F.S.A. See Little Guides, The Antiquary's Books, and Ancient Cities.
Cox (Harold), B.A. See S.Q.S.
Crabbe (George). See Little Library.
Craigie (W. A.). A PRIMER OF BURNS. *Cr. 8vo. 2s. 6d.*
Craik (Mrs.). See Little Library.
Crashaw (Richard). See Little Library.
Crawford (F. G.). See Mary C. Danson.
Cross (J. A.). A LITTLE BOOK OF RELIGION. *Fcap. 8vo. 2s. 6d. net.*
Crouch (W.). BRYAN KING. With a Portrait. *Cr. 8vo. 3s. 6d. net.*
Cruikshank (G.). THE LOVING BALLAD OF LORD BATEMAN. With 11 Plates. *Cr. 16mo. 1s. 6d. net.*
Crump (B.). See A. L. Cleather.
Cunliffe (Sir F. H. E.), Fellow of All Souls' College, Oxford. THE HISTORY OF THE BOER WAR. With many Illustrations, Plans, and Portraits. *In 2 vols. Quarto. 15s. each.*
A Colonial Edition is also published.
Cunynghame (H.), C.B., See Connoisseur's Library.
Cutts (E. L.), D.D. See Leaders of Religion.
Daniell (G. W.), M.A. See Leaders of Religion.
Danson (Mary C.) and Crawford (F. G.). FATHERS IN THE FAITH. *Fcap. 8vo. 1s. 6d.*
Dante. LA COMMEDIA DI DANTE. The Italian Text edited by PAGET TOYNBEE, M.A., D.Litt. *Cr. 8vo. 6s.*
THE PURGATORIO OF DANTE. Translated into Spenserian Prose by C. GORDON WRIGHT. With the Italian text. *Fcap. 8vo. 2s. 6d. net.*
See also Paget Toynbee, Little Library and Standard Library.
Darley (George). See Little Library.
D'Arcy (R. F.), M.A. A NEW TRIGONOMETRY FOR BEGINNERS. *Cr. 8vo. 2s. 6d.*
Davenport (Cyril). See Connoisseur's Library and Little Books on Art.

Davey (Richard). THE PAGEANT OF LONDON With 40 Illustrations in Colour by JOHN FULLEYLOVE, R. I. *In Two Volumes. Demy 8vo. 7s. 6d. net.* Each volume may be purchased separately.
VOL. I.—TO A.D. 1500.
VOL. II.—A.D. 1500 TO 1900.
Davis (H. W. C.), M.A., Fellow and Tutor of Balliol College, Author of 'Charlemagne.' ENGLAND UNDER THE NORMANS AND ANGEVINS : 1066-1272. With Maps and Illustrations. *Demy 8vo. 10s. 6d. net.*
Dawson (A. J.). MOROCCO. Illustrated. *Demy 8vo. 10s. 6d. net.*
Deane (A. C.). See Little Library.
Delbos (Leon). THE METRIC SYSTEM. *Cr. 8vo. 2s.*
Demosthenes. THE OLYNTHIACS AND PHILIPPICS. Translated by OTHO HOLLAND. *Cr. 8vo. 2s. 6d.*
Demosthenes. AGAINST CONON AND CALLICLES. Edited by F. DARWIN SWIFT, M.A. *Fcap. 8vo. 2s.*
Dickens (Charles). See Little Library and I.P.L.
Dickinson (Emily). POEMS. *Cr. 8vo. 4s. 6d. net.*
Dickinson (G. L.), M.A., Fellow of King's College, Cambridge. THE GREEK VIEW OF LIFE. *Fourth Edition. Cr. 8vo. 2s. 6d.*
Dickson (H. N.). F.R.Met. Soc. METEOROLOGY. Illustrated. *Cr. 8vo. 2s. 6d.*
Dilke (Lady). See S.Q.S.
Dillon (Edward). See Connoisseur's Library and Little Books on Art.
Ditchfield (P. H.), M.A., F.S.A. THE STORY OF OUR ENGLISH TOWNS. With an Introduction by AUGUSTUS JESSOPP, D.D. *Second Edition. Cr. 8vo. 6s.*
OLD ENGLISH CUSTOMS : Extant at the Present Time. *Cr. 8vo. 6s.*
See also Half-crown Library.
Dixon (W. M.), M.A. A PRIMER OF TENNYSON. *Second Edition. Cr. 8vo. 2s. 6d.*
ENGLISH POETRY FROM BLAKE TO BROWNING. *Second Edition. Cr. 8vo. 2s. 6d.*
Dole (N. H.). FAMOUS COMPOSERS. With Portraits. *Two Volumes. Demy 8vo. 12s. net.*
Doney (May). SONGS OF THE REAL. *Cr. 8vo. 3s. 6d. net.*
A volume of poems.
Douglas (James). THE MAN IN THE PULPIT. *Cr. 8vo. 2s. 6d. net.*
Dowden (J.), D.D., Lord Bishop of Edinburgh. See Churchman's Library.
Drage (G.). See Books on Business.

General Literature 7

Driver (S. R.), D.D., D.C.L., Canon of Christ Church, Regius Professor of Hebrew in the University of Oxford. SERMONS ON SUBJECTS CONNECTED WITH THE OLD TESTAMENT. *Cr. 8vo.* 6s.
See also Westminster Commentaries.
Dry (Wakeling). See Little Guides.
Dryhurst (A. R.). See Little Books on Art.
Duguid (Charles). See Books on Business.
Dunn (J. T.), D. Sc., and Mundella (V. A.). GENERAL ELEMENTARY SCIENCE. With 114 Illustrations. *Second Edition. Cr. 8vo.* 3s. 6d.
Dunstan (A. E.), B.Sc. See Junior School Books and Textbooks of Science.
Durham (The Earl of). A REPORT ON CANADA. With an Introductory Note. *Demy 8vo.* 4s. 6d. net.
Dutt (W. A.). A POPULAR GUIDE TO NORFOLK. *Medium 8vo.* 6d. net.
THE NORFOLK BROADS. With coloured Illustrations by FRANK SOUTHGATE. *Cr. 8vo.* 6s. See also Little Guides.
Earle (John), Bishop of Salisbury. MICROCOSMOGRAPHIE, OR A PIECE OF THE WORLD DISCOVERED. *Post 16mo.* 2s net.
Edmonds (Major J. E.), R.E. ; D.A.Q.-M.G. See W. Birkbeck Wood.
Edwards (Clement). See S.Q.S.
Edwards (W. Douglas). See Commercial Series.
Egan (Pierce). See I.P.L.
Egerton (H. E.), M.A. A HISTORY OF BRITISH COLONIAL POLICY. New and Cheaper Issue. *Demy 8vo.* 7s. 6d. net.
A Colonial Edition is also published.
Ellaby (C. G.). See The Little Guides.
Ellerton (F. G.). See S. J. Stone.
Ellwood (Thomas), THE HISTORY OF THE LIFE OF. Edited by C. G. CRUMP, M.A. *Cr. 8vo.* 6s.
Epictetus. See W. H. D. Rouse.
Erasmus. A Book called in Latin ENCHIRIDION MILITIS CHRISTIANI, and in English the Manual of the Christian Knight.
From the edition printed by Wynken de Worde, 1533. *Fcap. 8vo* 3s. 6d. net.
Fairbrother (W. H.), M.A. THE PHILOSOPHY OF T. H. GREEN. *Second Edition. Cr. 8vo.* 3s. 6d.
Farrer (Reginald). THE GARDEN OF ASIA. *Second Edition. Cr. 8vo.* 6s.
A Colonial Edition is also published.
Fea (Allan). BEAUTIES OF THE SEVENTEENTH CENTURY. With 100 Illustrations. *Demy 8vo.* 12s. 6d. net.
FELISSA ; OR, THE LIFE AND OPINIONS OF A KITTEN OF SENTIMENT. With 12 Coloured Plates. *Post 16mo.* 2s. 6d. net.
Ferrier (Susan). See Little Library.
Fidler (T. Claxton), M.Inst. C.E. See Books on Business.

Fielding (Henry). See Standard Library.
Finn (S. W.), M.A. See Junior Examination Series.
Firth (C. H.), M.A. CROMWELL'S ARMY: A History of the English Soldier during the Civil Wars, the Commonwealth, and the Protectorate. *Cr. 8vo.* 6s.
Fisher (G. W.), M.A. ANNALS OF SHREWSBURY SCHOOL. Illustrated. *Demy 8vo.* 10s. 6d.
FitzGerald (Edward). THE RUBAIYAT OF OMAR KHAYYÁM. Printed from the Fifth and last Edition. With a Commentary by Mrs. STEPHEN BATSON, and a Biography of Omar by E. D. ROSS. *Cr. 8vo.* 6s. See also Miniature Library.
FitzGerald (H. P.). A CONCISE HANDBOOK OF CLIMBERS, TWINERS, AND WALL SHRUBS. Illustrated. *Fcap. 8vo.* 3s. 6d. net.
Flecker (W. H.), M.A., D.C.L., Headmaster of the Dean Close School, Cheltenham. THE STUDENT'S PRAYER BOOK.
THE TEXT OF MORNING AND EVENING PRAYER AND LITANY. With an Introduction and Notes. *Cr. 8vo.* 2s. 6d.
Flux (A. W.), M.A., William Dow Professor of Political Economy in M'Gill University, Montreal. ECONOMIC PRINCIPLES. *Demy 8vo.* 7s. 6d. net.
Fortescue (Mrs. G.). See Little Books on Art.
Fraser (David). A MODERN CAMPAIGN ; OR, WAR AND WIRELESS TELEGRAPHY IN THE FAR EAST. Illustrated. *Cr. 8vo.* 6s.
A Colonial Edition is also published.
Fraser (J. F.). ROUND THE WORLD ON A WHEEL. With 100 Illustrations. *Fourth Edition Cr. 8vo.*
A Colonial Edition is also published.
French (W.), M.A. See Textbooks of Science.
Freudenreich (Ed. von). DAIRY BACTERIOLOGY. A Short Manual for the Use of Students. Translated by J. R. AINSWORTH DAVIS, M.A. *Second Edition. Revised. Cr. 8vo.* 2s. 6d.
Fulford (H. W.), M.A. See Churchman's Bible.
C. G., and F. C. G. JOHN BULL'S ADVENTURES IN THE FISCAL WONDERLAND. By CHARLES GEAKE. With 46 Illustrations by F. CARRUTHERS GOULD. *Second Edition. Cr. 8vo.* 1s. net.
***Gallaher (D.) and Stead (D. W.).** THE COMPLETE RUGBY FOOTBALLER. With an Account of the Tour of the New Zealanders in England. With Illustrations. *Demy 8vo.* 10s. 6d. net.
Gallichan (W. M.). See Little Guides.
Gambado (Geoffrey, Esq.). See I.P.L.
Gaskell (Mrs.). See Little Library and Standard Library.
Gasquet, the Right Rev. Abbot, O.S.B. See Antiquary's Books.

8 MESSRS. METHUEN'S CATALOGUE

George (H. B.), M.A., Fellow of New College, Oxford. BATTLES OF ENGLISH HISTORY. With numerous Plans. *Fourth Edition.* Revised, with a new Chapter including the South African War. *Cr. 8vo.* 3s. 6d.
A HISTORICAL GEOGRAPHY OF THE BRITISH EMPIRE. *Second Edition.* *Cr. 8vo.* 3s. 6d.
Gibbins (H. de B.), Litt.D., M.A. INDUSTRY IN ENGLAND: HISTORICAL OUTLINES. With 5 Maps. *Fourth Edition.* *Demy 8vo.* 10s. 6d.
A COMPANION GERMAN GRAMMAR. *Cr. 8vo.* 1s. 6d.
THE INDUSTRIAL HISTORY OF ENGLAND. *Eleventh Edition.* Revised. With Maps and Plans. *Cr. 8vo.* 3s.
ENGLISH SOCIAL REFORMERS. *Second Edition.* *Cr. 8vo.* 2s. 6d.
See also Commercial Series and S.Q.S.
Gibbon (Edward). THE DECLINE AND FALL OF THE ROMAN EMPIRE. A New Edition, edited with Notes, Appendices, and Maps, by J. B. BURY, M.A., Litt.D., Regius Professor of Greek at Cambridge. *In Seven Volumes.* *Demy 8vo.* Gilt top, 8s. 6d. each. *Also, Cr. 8vo.* 6s. each.
MEMOIRS OF MY LIFE AND WRITINGS. Edited by G. BIRKBECK HILL, LL.D. *Demy 8vo, Gilt top.* 8s. 6d. *Also Cr. 8vo.* 6s.
See also Standard Library.
Gibson (E. C. S.), D.D., Lord Bishop of Gloucester. See Westminster Commentaries, Handbooks of Theology, and Oxford Biographies.
Gilbert (A. R.). See Little Books on Art.
Gloag (M.). See K. Wyatt.
Godfrey (Elizabeth). A BOOK OF REMEMBRANCE. Edited by *Fcap. 8vo.* 2s. 6d. net.
Godley (A. D.), M.A., Fellow of Magdalen College, Oxford. LYRA FRIVOLA. *Third Edition.* *Fcap. 8vo.* 2s. 6d.
VERSES TO ORDER. *Second Edition.* *Fcap. 8vo.* 2s. 6d.
SECOND STRINGS. *Fcap. 8vo.* 2s. 6d.
Goldsmith (Oliver). THE VICAR OF WAKEFIELD. *Fcap. 32mo.* With 10 Plates in Photogravure by Tony Johannot. *Leather,* 2s. 6d. net. See also I.P.L. and Standard Library.
Goodrich-Freer (A.). IN A SYRIAN SADDLE. *Demy 8vo.* 7s. 6d. net.
A Colonial Edition is also published.
Goudge (H. L.), M.A., Principal of Wells Theological College. See Westminster Commentaries.
Graham (P. Anderson). See S.Q.S.
Granger (F. S.), M.A., Litt.D. PSYCHOLOGY. *Third Edition.* *Cr. 8vo.* 2s. 6d.
THE SOUL OF A CHRISTIAN. *Cr. 8vo.* 6s.

Gray (E. M'Queen). GERMAN PASSAGES FOR UNSEEN TRANSLATION. *Cr. 8vo.* 2s. 6d.
Gray (P. L.), B.Sc. THE PRINCIPLES OF MAGNETISM AND ELECTRICITY: an Elementary Text-Book. With 181 Diagrams. *Cr. 8vo.* 3s. 6d.
Green (G. Buckland), M.A., late Fellow of St. John's College, Oxon. NOTES ON GREEK AND LATIN SYNTAX. *Cr. 8vo.* 3s. 6d.
Green (E. T.), M.A. See Churchman's Library.
Greenidge (A. H. J.), M.A. A HISTORY OF ROME: During the Later Republic and the Early Principate. *In Six Volumes.* *Demy 8vo.* Vol. I. (133-104 B.C.). 10s. 6d. net.
Greenwell (Dora). See Miniature Library.
Gregory (R. A.). THE VAULT OF HEAVEN. A Popular Introduction to Astronomy. Illustrated. *Cr. 8vo.* 2s. 6d.
Gregory (Miss E. C.). See Library of Devotion.
Greville Minor. A MODERN JOURNAL. Edited by J. A. SPENDER. *Cr. 8vo.* 3s. 6d. net.
Grubb (H. C.). See Textbooks of Technology.
Guiney (Louisa I.). HURRELL FROUDE: Memoranda and Comments. Illustrated. *Demy 8vo.* 10s. 6d. net.
Gwynn (M. L.). A BIRTHDAY BOOK. New and cheaper issue. *Royal 8vo.* 5s. net.
Hackett (John), B.D. A HISTORY OF THE ORTHODOX CHURCH OF CYPRUS. With Maps and Illustrations. *Demy 8vo.* 15s. net.
Haddon (A. C.), Sc.D., F.R.S. HEADHUNTERS BLACK, WHITE, AND BROWN. With many Illustrations and a Map. *Demy 8vo.* 15s.
Hadfield (R. A.). See S.Q.S.
Hall (R. N.) and Neal (W. G.). THE ANCIENT RUINS OF RHODESIA. Illustrated. *Second Edition, revised.* *Demy 8vo.* 10s. 6d. net.
A Colonial Edition is also published.
Hall (R. N.). GREAT ZIMBABWE. With numerous Plans and Illustrations. *Second Edition.* *Royal 8vo.* 21s. net.
Hamilton (F. J.), D.D. See Byzantine Texts.
Hammond (J. L.). CHARLES JAMES FOX. *Demy 8vo.* 10s. 6d.
Hannay (D.). A SHORT HISTORY OF THE ROYAL NAVY, Illustrated. *Two Volumes.* *Demy 8vo.* 7s. 6d. each. Vol. I. 1200-1688.
Hannay (James O.), M.A. THE SPIRIT AND ORIGIN OF CHRISTIAN MONASTICISM. *Cr. 8vo.* 6s.
THE WISDOM OF THE DESERT. *Fcap. 8vo.* 3s. 6d. net.
Hare (A. T.), M.A. THE CONSTRUCTION OF LARGE INDUCTION COILS. With numerous Diagrams. *Demy 8vo.* 6s.

General Literature 9

Harrison (Clifford). READING AND READERS. *Fcap. 8vo.* 2s. 6d.
Hawthorne (Nathaniel). See Little Library.
HEALTH, WEALTH AND WISDOM. *Cr. 8vo.* 1s. net.
Heath (Frank R.). See Little Guides.
Heath (Dudley). See Connoisseur's Library.
Hello (Ernest). STUDIES IN SAINT-SHIP. Translated from the French by V. M. CRAWFORD. *Fcap 8vo.* 3s. 6d.
Henderson (B. W.), Fellow of Exeter College, Oxford. THE LIFE AND PRINCIPATE OF THE EMPEROR NERO. Illustrated. *New and cheaper issue. Demy 8vo.* 7s. 6d. net.
AT INTERVALS. *Fcap 8vo.* 2s. 6d. net.
Henderson (T. F.). See Little Library and Oxford Biographies.
Henley (W. E.). See Half-Crown Library.
Henson (H. H.), B.D., Canon of Westminster. APOSTOLIC CHRISTIANITY: As Illustrated by the Epistles of St. Paul to the Corinthians. *Cr. 8vo.* 6s.
LIGHT AND LEAVEN: HISTORICAL AND SOCIAL SERMONS. *Cr. 8vo.* 6s.
DISCIPLINE AND LAW. *Fcap.* 8vo. 2s. 6d.
Herbert (George). See Library of Devotion.
Herbert of Cherbury (Lord). See Miniature Library.
Hewins (W. A. S.), B.A. ENGLISH TRADE AND FINANCE IN THE SEVENTEENTH CENTURY. *Cr. 8vo.* 2s. 6d.
Hewitt (Ethel M.) A GOLDEN DIAL. A Day Book of Prose and Verse. *Fcap. 8vo.* 2s. 6d. net.
Heywood (W.). PALIO AND PONTE: A Book of Tuscan Games. Illustrated. *Royal 8vo.* 21s. net.
Hilbert (T.). See Little Blue Books.
Hill (Clare). See Textbooks of Technology.
Hill (Henry), B.A., Headmaster of the Boy's High School, Worcester, Cape Colony. A SOUTH AFRICAN ARITHMETIC. *Cr. 8vo.* 3s. 6d.
Hillegas (Howard C.). WITH THE BOER FORCES. With 24 Illustrations. *Second Edition. Cr. 8vo.* 6s.
A Colonial Edition is also published.
Hirst (F. W.) See Books on Business.
Hobhouse (Emily). THE BRUNT OF THE WAR. With Map and Illustrations. *Cr. 8vo.* 6s.
A Colonial Edition is also published.
Hobhouse (L. T.), Fellow of C.C.C., Oxford. THE THEORY OF KNOWLEDGE. *Demy 8vo.* 10s. 6d. net.
Hobson (J. A.), M.A. INTERNATIONAL TRADE: A Study of Economic Principles. *Cr. 8vo.* 2s. 6d. net.
PROBLEMS OF POVERTY. *Sixth Edition. Cr. 8vo.* 2s. 6d.
Hodgkin (T.), D.C.L. See Leaders of Religion.

Hodgson (Mrs. W.) HOW TO IDENTIFY OLD CHINESE PORCELAIN. *Second Edition. Post 8vo.* 6s.
Hogg (Thomas Jefferson). SHELLEY AT OXFORD. With an Introduction by R. A. STREATFEILD. *Fcap. 8vo.* 2s. net.
Holden-Stone (G. de). See Books on Business.
Holdich (Sir T. H.), K.C.I.E. THE INDIAN BORDERLAND: being a Personal Record of Twenty Years. Illustrated. *Demy 8vo.* 10s. 6d. net.
A Colonial Edition is also published.
Holdsworth (W. S.), M.A. A HISTORY OF ENGLISH LAW. *In Two Volumes. Vol. I. Demy 8vo.* 10s. 6d. net.
Holland (Canon Scott). See Library of Devotion.
Holt (Emily). THE SECRET OF POPULARITY: How to Achieve Social Success. *Cr. 8vo.* 3s. 6d. net.
A Colonial Edition is also published.
Holyoake (G. J.). THE CO-OPERATIVE MOVEMENT TO-DAY. *Fourth Edition. Cr. 8vo.* 2s. 6d.
Hone (Nathaniel J.). See Antiquary's Books.
Hoppner. See Little Galleries.
Horace. See Classical Translations.
Horsburgh (E. L. S.), M.A. WATERLOO: A Narrative and Criticism. With Plans. *Second Edition. Cr. 8vo.* 5s. See also Oxford Biographies.
Horth (A. C.). See Textbooks of Technology.
Horton (R. F.), D.D. See Leaders of Religion.
Hosie (Alexander). MANCHURIA. With Illustrations and a Map. *Second Edition. Demy 8vo.* 7s. 6d. net.
A Colonial Edition is also published.
How (F. D.). SIX GREAT SCHOOLMASTERS. With Portraits and Illustrations. *Second Edition. Demy 8vo.* 7s. 6d.
Howell (G.). See S. Q. S.
Hudson (Robert). MEMORIALS OF A WARWICKSHIRE PARISH. Illustrated. *Demy 8vo.* 15s. net.
Hughes (C. E.). THE PRAISE OF SHAKESPEARE. An English Anthology. With a Preface by SIDNEY LEE. *Demy 8vo.* 3s. 6d. net.
Hughes (Thomas). TOM BROWN'S SCHOOLDAYS. With an Introduction and Notes by VERNON RENDALL. Leather. *Royal 32mo.* 2s. 6d. net.
Hutchinson (Horace G.) THE NEW FOREST. Illustrated in colour with 50 Pictures by WALTER TYNDALE and 4 by Miss LUCY KEMP WELCH. *Large Demy 8vo.* 21s. net.
Hutton (A. W.), M.A. See Leaders of Religion and Library of Devotion.
Hutton (Edward). THE CITIES OF UMBRIA. With many Illustrations, of which 20 are in Colour, by A. PISA. *Second Edition. Cr. 8vo.* 6s.
A Colonial Edition is also published.

A 2

ENGLISH LOVE POEMS. Edited with an Introduction. *Fcap. 8vo.* 3s. 6d. net.
Hutton (R. H.). See Leaders of Religion.
Hutton (W. H.), M.A. THE LIFE OF SIR THOMAS MORE. With Portraits. *Second Edition. Cr. 8vo.* 5s. See also Leaders of Religion.
Hyett (F. A.). A SHORT HISTORY OF FLORENCE. *Demy 8vo.* 7s. 6d. net.
Ibsen (Henrik). BRAND. A Drama. Translated by WILLIAM WILSON. *Third Edition. Cr. 8vo.* 3s. 6d.
Inge (W. R.), M.A., Fellow and Tutor of Hertford College, Oxford. CHRISTIAN MYSTICISM. The Bampton Lectures for 1899. *Demy 8vo.* 12s. 6d. net. See also Library of Devotion.
Innes (A. D.), M.A. A HISTORY OF THE BRITISH IN INDIA. With Maps and Plans. *Cr. 8vo.* 6s.
ENGLAND UNDER THE TUDORS. With Maps. *Demy 8vo.* 10s. 6d. net.
Jackson (C. E.), B.A. See Textbooks of Science.
Jackson (S.), M.A. See Commercial Series.
Jackson (F. Hamilton). See Little Guides.
Jacob (F.), M.A. See Junior Examination Series.
Jeans (J. Stephen). See S. Q. S. and Business Books.
Jeffreys (D. Gwyn). DOLLY'S THEATRICALS. Described and Illustrated with 24 Coloured Pictures. *Super Royal 16mo.* 2s. 6d.
Jenks (E.), M.A., Reader of Law in the University of Oxford. ENGLISH LOCAL GOVERNMENT. *Cr. 8vo.* 2s. 6d.
Jenner (Mrs. H.). See Little Books on Art.
Jessopp (Augustus), D.D. See Leaders of Religion.
Jevons (F. B.), M.A., Litt.D., Principal of Bishop Hatfield's Hall, Durham. RELIGION IN EVOLUTION. *Cr. 8vo.* 3s. 6d. net.
See also Churchman's Library and Handbooks of Theology.
Johnson (Mrs. Barham). WILLIAM BODHAM DONNE AND HIS FRIENDS. Illustrated. *Demy 8vo.* 10s. 6d. net.
Johnston (Sir H. H.), K.C.B. BRITISH CENTRAL AFRICA. With nearly 200 Illustrations and Six Maps. *Third Edition. Cr. 4to.* 18s. net.
A Colonial Edition is also published.
Jones (R. Crompton), M A. POEMS OF THE INNER LIFE. Selected by. *Eleventh Edition. Fcap. 8vo.* 2s. 6d. net.
Jones (H.). See Commercial Series.
Jones (L. A. Atherley), K.C., M.P., and Bellot (Hugh H. L.). THE MINERS' GUIDE TO THE COAL MINES REGULATION ACTS. *Cr. 8vo.* 2s. 6d. net.
*COMMERCE IN WAR. *Demy 8vo.* 21s. net.
Jonson (Ben). See Standard Library.

Julian (Lady) of Norwich. REVELATIONS OF DIVINE LOVE. Edited by GRACE WARRACK. *Cr. 8vo.* 3s. 6d.
Juvenal. See Classical Translations.
'Kappa.' LET YOUTH BUT KNOW: A Plea for Reason in Education. *Cr. 8vo.* 3s. 6d. net.
Kaufmann (M.). See S. Q. S.
Keating (J. F.), D.D. THE AGAPE AND THE EUCHARIST. *Cr. 8vo.* 3s. 6d.
Keats (John). THE POEMS OF. Edited with Introduction and Notes by E. de Selincourt, M.A. *Demy 8vo.* 7s. 6d. net. See also Little Library, Standard Library, and E. de Selincourt.
Keble (John). THE CHRISTIAN YEAR. With an Introduction and Notes by W. LOCK, D.D., Warden of Keble College. Illustrated by R. ANNING BELL.. *Third Edition. Fcap. 8vo.* 3s. 6d.; *padded morocco*, 5s. See also Library of Devotion.
Kempis (Thomas à). THE IMITATION OF CHRIST. With an Introduction by DEAN FARRAR. Illustrated by C. M. GERE. *Third Edition. Fcap. 8vo.* 3s. 6d.; *padded morocco*, 5s.
Also Translated by C. BIGG, D.D. *Cr. 8vo.* 3s. 6d. See also Library of Devotion and Standard Library.
Kennedy (Bart.). THE GREEN SPHINX. *Cr. 8vo.* 3s. 6d. net.
A Colonial Edition is also published.
Kennedy (James Houghton), D.D., Assistant Lecturer in Divinity in the University of Dublin. ST. PAUL'S SECOND AND THIRD EPISTLES TO THE CORINTHIANS. With Introduction, Dissertations and Notes. *Cr. 8vo.* 6s.
Kestell (J. D.). THROUGH SHOT AND FLAME: Being the Adventures and Experiences of J. D. KESTELL, Chaplain to General Christian de Wet. *Cr. 8vo.* 6s.
A Colonial Edition is also published.
Kimmins (C. W.), M.A. THE CHEMISTRY OF LIFE AND HEALTH. Illustrated. *Cr. 8vo.* 2s. 6d.
Kinglake (A. W.). See Little Library.
Kipling (Rudyard). BARRACK-ROOM BALLADS. 73rd Thousand. *Twenty-first Edition. Cr. 8vo.* 6s.
A Colonial Edition is also published.
THE SEVEN SEAS. 62nd Thousand. *Tenth Edition. Cr. 8vo.* 6s.
A Colonial Edition is also published.
THE FIVE NATIONS. 41st Thousand. *Second Edition. Cr. 8vo.* 6s.
A Colonial Edition is also published.
DEPARTMENTAL DITTIES. *Sixteenth Edition. Cr. 8vo.* 6s.
A Colonial Edition is also published.
Knight (Albert E.). THE COMPLETE CRICKETER. Illustrated. *Demy 8vo.* 7s. 6d. net.
A Colonial Edition is also published.

GENERAL LITERATURE 11

Knowling (R. J.), M.A., Professor of New Testament Exegesis at King's College, London. See Westminster Commentaries.
Lamb (Charles and Mary), THE WORKS OF. Edited by E. V. LUCAS. Illustrated. *In Seven Volumes. Demy 8vo. 7s. 6d. each.*
THE LIFE OF. See E. V. Lucas.
See also Little Library.
Lambert (F. A. H.). See Little Guides.
Lambros (Professor). See Byzantine Texts.
Lane-Poole (Stanley). A HISTORY OF EGYPT IN THE MIDDLE AGES. Fully Illustrated. *Cr. 8vo. 6s.*
Langbridge (F.), M.A. BALLADS OF THE BRAVE: Poems of Chivalry, Enterprise, Courage, and Constancy. *Second Edition. Cr. 8vo. 2s. 6d.*
Law (William). See Library of Devotion and Standard Library.
Leach (Henry). THE DUKE OF DEVONSHIRE. A Biography. With 12 Illustrations. *Demy 8vo. 12s. 6d. net.*
A Colonial Edition is also published.
Le Braz (Anatole). THE LAND OF PARDONS. Translated by FRANCES M. GOSTLING. Illustrated in colour. *Second Edition. Crown 8vo. 6s.*
Lee (Captain L. Melville). A HISTORY OF POLICE IN ENGLAND. *Cr. 8vo. 3s. 6d. net.*
Leigh (Percival). THE COMIC ENGLISH GRAMMAR. Embellished with upwards of 50 characteristic Illustrations by JOHN LEECH. *Post 16mo. 2s. 6d. net.*
Lewes (V. B.), M.A. AIR AND WATER. Illustrated. *Cr. 8vo. 2s. 6d.*
Lewis (Mrs. Gwyn). A CONCISE HANDBOOK OF GARDEN SHRUBS. Illustrated. *Fcap. 8vo. 3s. 6d. net.*
Lisle (Fortunéede). See Little Books on Art.
Littlehales (H.). See Antiquary's Books.
Lock (Walter), D.D., Warden of Keble College. ST. PAUL, THE MASTER-BUILDER. *Second Edition. Cr. 8vo. 3s. 6d.*
THE BIBLE AND CHRISTIAN LIFE. *Cr. 8vo. 6s.*
See also Leaders of Religion and Library of Devotion.
Locker (F.). See Little Library.
Longfellow (H. W.). See Little Library.
Lorimer (George Horace). LETTERS FROM A SELF-MADE MERCHANT TO HIS SON. *Fifteenth Edition. Cr. 8vo. 6s.*
A Colonial Edition is also published.
OLD GORGON GRAHAM. *Second Edition. Cr. 8vo. 6s.*
A Colonial Edition is also published.
Lover (Samuel). See I. P. L.
E. V. L. and C. L.'G. ENGLAND DAY BY DAY: Or, The Englishman's Handbook to Efficiency. Illustrated by GEORGE MORROW. *Fourth Edition. Fcap. 4to. 1s. net.*

Lucas (E. V.). THE LIFE OF CHARLES LAMB. With numerous Portraits and Illustrations. *Third Edition. Two Vols. Demy 8vo. 21s. net.*
A Colonial Edition is also published.
A WANDERER IN HOLLAND. With many Illustrations, of which 20 are in Colour by HERBERT MARSHALL. *Sixth Edition. Cr. 8vo. 6s.*
A Colonial Edition is also published.
THE OPEN ROAD: a Little Book for Wayfarers. *Tenth Edition. Fcap. 8vo. 5s.; India Paper, 7s. 6d.*
THE FRIENDLY TOWN: a Little Book for the Urbane. *Third Edition. Fcap. 8vo. 5s.; India Paper, 7s. 6d.*
Lucian. See Classical Translations.
Lyde (L. W.), M.A. See Commercial Series.
Lydon (Noel S.). See Junior School Books.
Lyttelton (Hon. Mrs. A.). WOMEN AND THEIR WORK. *Cr. 8vo. 2s. 6d.*
M. M. HOW TO DRESS AND WHAT TO WEAR. *Cr. 8vo. 1s. net.*
Macaulay (Lord). CRITICAL AND HISTORICAL ESSAYS. Edited by F. C. MONTAGUE, M.A. *Three Volumes. Cr. 8vo. 18s.*
The only edition of this book completely annotated.
M'Allen (J. E. B.), M.A. See Commercial Series.
MacCulloch (J. A.). See Churchman's Library.
MacCunn (Florence A.). MARY STUART. With over 60 Illustrations, including a Frontispiece in Photogravure. *Demy 8vo. 10s. 6d. net.*
A Colonial Edition is also published. See also Leaders of Religion.
McDermott (E. R.). See Books on Business.
M'Dowall (A. S.). See Oxford Biographies.
Mackay (A. M.). See Churchman's Library.
Magnus (Laurie), M.A. A PRIMER OF WORDSWORTH. *Cr. 8vo. 2s. 6d.*
Mahaffy (J. P.), Litt.D. A HISTORY OF THE EGYPT OF THE PTOLEMIES. Fully Illustrated. *Cr. 8vo. 6s.*
Maitland (F. W.), LL.D., Downing Professor of the Laws of England in the University of Cambridge. CANON LAW IN ENGLAND. *Royal 8vo. 7s. 6d.*
Malden (H. E.), M.A. ENGLISH RECORDS. A Companion to the History of England. *Cr. 8vo. 3s. 6d.*
THE ENGLISH CITIZEN: HIS RIGHTS AND DUTIES. *Fifth Edition. Cr. 8vo. 1s. 6d.*
A SCHOOL HISTORY OF SURREY Illustrated. *Cr. 8vo. 1s. 6d.*
Marchant (E. C.), M.A., Fellow of Peterhouse, Cambridge. A GREEK ANTHOLOGY *Second Edition. Cr. 8vo. 3s. 6d.*
Marchant (C. E.)), M.A., and Cook (A. M.), M.A. PASSAGES FOR UNSEEN TRANSLATION. *Third Edition. Cr. 8vo. 2s. 6d.*

Messrs. Methuen's Catalogue

Marlowe (Christopher). See Standard Library.
Marr (J. E.), F.R.S., F llow of St John's College, Cambridge. THE SCIENTIFIC STUDY OF SCENERY. *Second Edition.* Illustrated. *Cr. 8vo.* 6s.
AGRICULTURAL GEOLOGY. Illustrated. *Cr. 8vo.* 6s.
Marvell (Andrew). See Little Library.
Masefield (John). SEA LIFE IN NELSON'S TIME. Illustrated. *Cr. 8vo.* 3s. 6d. net.
ON THE SPANISH MAIN. With Portraits and Illustrations. *Demy 8vo.* 10s. 6d. net.
A Colonial Edition is also published.
Maskell (A.). See Connoisseur's Library.
Mason (A. J.), D.D. See Leaders of Religion.
Massee (George). THE EVOLUTION OF PLANT LIFE: Lower Forms. Illustrated. *Cr. 8vo.* 2s. 6d.
Massinger (P.). See Standard Library.
Masterman (C. F. G.), M.A. TENNYSON AS A RELIGIOUS TEACHER. *Cr. 8vo.* 6s.
Matheson (Mrs. E. F.). COUNSELS OF LiFE. *Fcap. 8vo.* 2s. 6d. net.
May (Phil). THE PHIL MAY ALBUM. *Second Edition.* 4to. 1s. net.
Mellows (Emma S.). A SHORT STORY OF ENGLISH LITERATURE. *Cr. 8vo.* 3s. 6d.
Methuen (A. M. S.). THE TRAGEDY OF SOUTH AFRICA. *Cr. 8vo.* 2s. net. *Also Cr. 8vo.* 3d. net.
A revised and enlarged edition of the author's 'Peace or War in South Africa.'
ENGLAND'S RUIN: DISCUSSED IN SIXTEEN LETTERS TO THE RIGHT HON. JOSEPH CHAMBERLAIN, M.P. *Seventh Edition. Cr. 8vo.* 3d. net.
Michell (E. B.). THE ART AND PRACTICE OF HAWKING. With 3 Photogravures by G. E. LODGE, and other Illustrations. *Demy 8vo.* 10s. 6d.
Millais (J. G.). THE LIFE AND LETTERS OF SIR JOHN EVERETT MILLAIS, President of the Royal Academy. With many Illustrations, of which 2 are in Photogravure. *New Edition. Demy 8vo.* 7s. 6d. net.
A Colonial Edition is also published.
Millin (G. F.). PICTORIAL GARDENING. Illustrated. *Cr. 8vo.* 3s. 6d. net.
Millis (C. T.), M.I.M.E. See Textbooks of Technology.
Milne (J. G.), M.A. A HISTORY OF ROMAN EGYPT. Fully Illustrated, *Cr. 8vo.* 6s.

Milton (John), THE POEMS OF, BOTH ENGLISH AND LATIN, Compos'd at several times. Printed by his true Copies. The Songs were set in Musick by Mr. HENRY LAWES, Gentleman of the Kings Chappel, and one of His Majesties Private Musick.
Printed and publish'd according to Order. Printed by RUTH RAWORTH for HUMPHREY MOSELEY, and are to be sold at the signe of the Princes Armes in Pauls Churchyard, 1645,
See also Little Library, Standard Library, and R. F. Towndrow.
Minchin (H. C.), M.A. See R. Peel.
Mitchell (P. Chalmers), M.A. OUTLINES OF BIOLOGY. Illustrated. *Second Edition. Cr. 8vo.* 6s.
Mitton (G. E.). JANE AUSTEN AND HER TIMES. With many Portraits and Illustrations. *Second Edition. Demy 8vo.* 10s. 6d. net.
A Colonial Edition is also published.
'**Moil (A.).**' See Books on Business.
Moir (D. M.). See Little Library.
Money (L. G. Chiozza). RICHES AND POVERTY. *Second Edition Demy 8vo.* 5s. net.
Montaigne. See C. F. Pond.
Moore (H. E.). See S. Q. S.
Moran (Clarence G.). See Books on Business.
More (Sir Thomas). See Standard Library.
Morfill (W. R.), Oriel College, Oxford. A HISTORY OF RUSSIA FROM PETER THE GREAT TO ALEXANDER II. With Maps and Plans. *Cr. 8vo.* 3s. 6d.
Morich (R. J.), late of Clifton College. See School Examination Series.
Morris (J.). THE MAKERS OF JAPAN. With many portraits and Illustrations. *Demy 8vo.* 12s. 6d. net.
A Colonial Edition is also published.
Morris (J. E.). See Little Guides.
Morton (Miss Anderson). See Miss Brodrick.
THE MOTOR YEAR-BOOK FOR 1906. With many Illustrations and Diagrams. *Demy 8vo.* 7s. 6d. net.
Moule (H. C. G.), D.D., Lord Bishop of Durham. See Leaders of Religion.
Muir (M. M. Pattison), M.A. THE CHEMISTRY OF FIRE. Illustrated. *Cr. 8vo.* 2s. 6d.
Mundella (V. A.), M.A. See J. T. Dunn.
Munro (R.), LL.D. See Antiquary's Books.
Naval Officer (A). See I. P. L.
Neal (W. G.). See R. N. Hall.
Newman (J. H.) and others. See Library of Devotion.
Nichols (J. B. B.). See Little Library.
Nicklin (T.), M.A. EXAMINATION PAPERS IN THUCYDIDES. *Cr. 8vo.* 2s.
Nimrod. See I. P. L.
Norgate (G. Le G.). SIR WALTER SCOTT. Illustrated. *Demy 8vo.* 7s. 6d. net.

General Literature 13

Norregaard (B. W.). THE GREAT SIEGE: The Investment and Fall of Port Arthur. Illustrated. *Demy 8vo.* 10s. 6d. net.

Northcote (James), R.A. THE CONVERSATIONS OF JAMES NORTHCOTE, R.A., AND JAMES WARD. Edited by ERNEST FLETCHER. With many Portraits. *Demy 8vo.* 10s. 6d.

Norway (A. H.). NAPLES. With 25 Coloured Illustrations by MAURICE GREIFFENHAGEN. A New Edition. *Cr. 8vo.* 6s.

Novalis. THE DISCIPLES AT SAIS AND OTHER FRAGMENTS. Edited by Miss UNA BIRCH. *Fcap. 8vo.* 3s. 6d.

Oldfield (W. J.), Canon of Lincoln. A PRIMER OF RELIGION. *Fcap 8vo.* 2s. 6d.

Oliphant (Mrs.). See Leaders of Religion.

Oman (C. W. C.), M.A., Fellow of All Souls', Oxford. A HISTORY OF THE ART OF WAR. Vol. II.: The Middle Ages, from the Fourth to the Fourteenth Century. Illustrated. *Demy 8vo.* 10s. 6d. net.

Ottley (R. L.), D.D. See Handbooks of Theology and Leaders of Religion.

Overton (J. H.). See Leaders of Religion.

Owen (Douglas). See Books on Business.

Oxford (M. N.), of Guy's Hospital. A HANDBOOK OF NURSING. Third Edition. *Cr. 8vo.* 3s. 6d.

Pakes (W. C. C.). THE SCIENCE OF HYGIENE. Illustrated. *Demy 8vo.* 15s.

Palmer (Frederick). WITH KUROKI IN MANCHURIA. Illustrated. Third Edition. *Demy 8vo.* 7s. 6d. net.
A Colonial Edition is also published.

Parker (Gilbert). A LOVER'S DIARY. *Fcap. 8vo.* 5s.

Parkes (A. K.). SMALL LESSONS ON GREAT TRUTHS. *Fcap. 8vo.* 1s. 6d.

Parkinson (John). PARADISI IN SOLE PARADISUS TERRESTRIS, OR A GARDEN OF ALL SORTS OF PLEASANT FLOWERS. *Folio.* £3, 3s. net.

Parmenter (John). HELIO-TROPES, OR NEW POSIES FOR SUNDIALS, 1625. Edited by PERCIVAL LANDON. *Quarto.* 3s. 6d. net.

Parmentier (Prof. Leon). See Byzantine Texts.

Pascal. See Library of Devotion.

Paston (George). SOCIAL CARICATURES IN THE EIGHTEENTH CENTURY. *Imperial Quarto.* £2, 12s. 6d. net. See also Little Books on Art and I.P.L.

Paterson (W. R.) (Benjamin Swift). LIFE'S QUESTIONINGS. *Cr. 8vo.* 3s. 6d. net.

Patterson (A. H.). NOTES OF AN EAST COAST NATURALIST. Illustrated in Colour by F. SOUTHGATE. Second Edition. *Cr. 8vo.* 6s.

NATURE IN EASTERN NORFOLK. A series of observations on the Birds, Fishes, Mammals, Reptiles, and stalkeyed Crustaceans found in that neighbourhood, with a list of the species. With 12 Illustrations in colour, by FRANK SOUTHGATE. *Second Edition. Cr. 8vo.* 6s.

Peacock (N.). See Little Books on Art.

Pearce (E. H.), M.A. ANNALS OF CHRIST'S HOSPITAL. Illustrated. *Demy 8vo.* 7s. 6d.

Peel (Robert), and **Minchin (H. C.),** M.A. OXFORD. With 100 Illustrations in Colour. *Cr. 8vo.* 6s.

Peel (Sidney), late Fellow of Trinity College, Oxford, and Secretary to the Royal Commission on the Licensing Laws. PRACTICAL LICENSING REFORM. Second Edition. *Cr. 8vo.* 1s. 6d.

Peters (J. P.), D.D. See Churchman's Library.

Petrie (W. M. Flinders), D.C.L., LL.D., Professor of Egyptology at University College. A HISTORY OF EGYPT, FROM THE EARLIEST TIMES TO THE PRESENT DAY. Fully Illustrated. *In six volumes. Cr. 8vo.* 6s. each.

VOL. I. PREHISTORIC TIMES TO XVITH DYNASTY. *Fifth Edition.*
VOL. II. THE XVIITH AND XVIIITH DYNASTIES. *Fourth Edition.*
VOL. III. XIXTH TO XXXTH DYNASTIES.
VOL. IV. THE EGYPT OF THE PTOLEMIES. J. P. MAHAFFY, Litt.D.
VOL. V. ROMAN EGYPT. J. G. MILNE, M.A.
VOL. VI. EGYPT IN THE MIDDLE AGES. STANLEY LANE-POOLE, M.A.

RELIGION AND CONSCIENCE IN ANCIENT EGYPT. Illustrated. *Cr. 8vo.* 2s. 6d.

SYRIA AND EGYPT, FROM THE TELL EL AMARNA TABLETS. *Cr. 8vo.* 2s. 6d.

EGYPTIAN TALES. Illustrated by TRISTRAM ELLIS. *In Two Volumes. Cr. 8vo.* 3s. 6d. each.

EGYPTIAN DECORATIVE ART. With 120 Illustrations. *Cr. 8vo.* 3s. 6d.

Phillips (W. A.). See Oxford Biographies.

Phillpotts (Eden). MY DEVON YEAR. With 38 Illustrations by J. LEY PETHYBRIDGE. *Second and Cheaper Edition. Large Cr. 8vo.* 6s.

UP ALONG AND DOWN ALONG. Illustrated by CLAUDE SHEPPERSON. *Cr. 4to.* 5s. net.
A volume of poems.

Pienaar (Philip). WITH STEYN AND DE WET. Second Edition. *Cr. 8vo.* 3s. 6d.
A Colonial Edition is also published.

Plarr (Victor G.) and Walton (F. W.). A SCHOOL HISTORY OF MIDDLESEX. Illustrated. *Cr. 8vo.* 1s. 6d.

Plato. See Standard Library.

Messrs. Methuen's Catalogue

Plautus. THE CAPTIVI. Edited, with an Introduction, Textual Notes, and a Commentary, by W. M. LINDSAY, Fellow of Jesus College, Oxford. *Demy 8vo.* 10s. 6d. *net.*
Plowden-Wardlaw (J. T.), B.A., King's College, Cambridge. See School Examination Series.
Podmore (Frank). MODERN SPIRITUALISM. *Two Volumes. Demy 8vo.* 21s. *net.*
A History and a Criticism.
Poer (J. Patrick Le). A MODERN LEGIONARY. *Cr. 8vo.* 6s.
A Colonial Edition is also published.
Pollard (Alice). See Little Books on Art.
Pollard (A. W.). OLD PICTURE BOOKS. Illustrated. *Demy 8vo.* 7s. 6d. *net.*
Pollard (Eliza F.). See Little Books on Art.
Pollock (David), M.I.N.A. See Books on Business.
Pond (C. F.). A DAY BOOK OF MONTAIGNE. Edited by. *Fcap. 8vo.* 3s. 6d. *net.*
Potter (M. C.), M.A., F.L.S. A TEXT-BOOK OF AGRICULTURAL BOTANY. Illustrated. *Second Edition. Cr. 8vo.* 4s. 6d.
Power (J. O'Connor). THE MAKING OF AN ORATOR. *Cr. 8vo.* 6s.
Pradeau (G.). A KEY TO THE TIME ALLUSIONS IN THE DIVINE COMEDY. With a Dial. *Small quarto.* 3s. 6d.
Prance (G.). See Half-Crown Library.
Prescott (O. L.). ABOUT MUSIC, AND WHAT IT IS MADE OF. *Cr. 8vo.* 3s. 6d. *net.*
Price (L. L.), M.A., Fellow of Oriel College, Oxon. A HISTORY OF ENGLISH POLITICAL ECONOMY. *Fourth Edition. Cr. 8vo.* 2s. 6d.
Primrose (Deborah). A MODERN BŒOTIA. *Cr. 8vo.* 6s.
Pugin and Rowlandson. THE MICROCOSM OF LONDON, OR LONDON IN MINIATURE. With 104 Illustrations in colour. *In Three Volumes. Small 4to.* £3, 3s. *net.*
'Q' (A. T. Quiller Couch). See Half-Crown Library.
Quevedo Villegas. See Miniature Library.
G. R. and E.S. THE WOODHOUSE CORRESPONDENCE. *Cr. 8vo.* 6s.
A Colonial Edition is also published.
Rackham (R. B.), M.A. See Westminster Commentaries.
Randolph (B. W.), D.D. See Library of Devotion.
Rannie (D. W.), M.A. A STUDENT'S HISTORY OF SCOTLAND. *Cr. 8vo.* 3s. 6d.

Rashdall (Hastings), M.A., Fellow and Tutor of New College, Oxford. DOCTRINE AND DEVELOPMENT. *Cr. 8vo.* 6s.
Rawstorne (Lawrence, Esq.). See I.P.L.
Raymond (Walter). A SCHOOL HISTORY OF SOMERSETSHIRE. Illustrated. *Cr. 8vo.* 1s. 6d.
A Real Paddy. See I.P-L.
Reason (W.), M.A. See S.Q.S.
Redfern (W. B.), Author of 'Ancient Wood and Iron Work in Cambridge,' etc. ROYAL AND HISTORIC GLOVES AND ANCIENT SHOES. Profusely Illustrated in colour and half-tone. *Quarto.* £2, 2s. *net.*
Reynolds. See Little Galleries.
***Rhodes (W. E.).** A SCHOOL HISTORY OF LANCASHIRE. Illustrated. *Cr. 8vo.* 1s. 6d.
Roberts (M. E.). See C. C. Channer.
Robertson (A.), D.D., Lord Bishop of Exeter. REGNUM DEI. The Bampton Lectures of 1901. *Demy 8vo.* 12s. 6d. *net.*
Robertson (C. Grant). M.A., Fellow of All Souls' College, Oxford, Examiner in the Honours School of Modern History, Oxford, 1901-1904. SELECT STATUTES, CASES, AND CONSTITUTIONAL DOCUMENTS, 1660-1832. *Demy 8vo.* 10s. 6d. *net.*
Robertson (C. Grant) and Bartholomew (J. G.), F.R.S.E., F.R.G.S. A HISTORICAL AND MODERN ATLAS OF THE BRITISH EMPIRE. *Demy Quarto.* 4s. 6d. *net.*
Robertson (Sir G. S.), K.C.S.I. See Half-Crown Library.
Robinson (A. W.), M.A. See Churchman's Bible.
Robinson (Cecilia). THE MINISTRY OF DEACONESSES. With an Introduction by the late Archbishop of Canterbury. *Cr. 8vo.* 3s. 6d.
Robinson (F. S.). See Connoisseur's Library.
Rochefoucauld (La). See Little Library.
Rodwell (G.), B.A. NEW TESTAMENT GREEK. A Course for Beginners. With a Preface by WALTER LOCK, D.D., Warden of Keble College. *Fcap. 8vo.* 3s. 6d.
Roe (Fred). ANCIENT COFFERS AND CUPBOARDS: Their History and Description. Illustrated. *Quarto.* £3, 3s. *net.*
OLD OAK FURNITURE. With many Illustrations by the Author, including a frontispiece in colour. *Demy 8vo.* 10s. 6d. *net.*
Rogers (A. G. L.), M.A. See Books on Business.
Roscoe (E. S.). ROBERT HARLEY, EARL OF OXFORD. Illustrated. *Demy 8vo.* 7s. 6d.
This is the only life of Harley in existence.
See also Little Guides.

General Literature 15

Rose (Edward). THE ROSE READER. Illustrated. *Cr. 8vo. 2s. 6d. Also in 4 Parts. Parts I. and II. 6d. each; Part III. 8d.; Part IV.* 10d.

Rouse (W. H. D.). WORDS OF THE ANCIENT WISE: Thoughts from Epictetus and Marcus Aurelius. Edited by. *Fcap. 8vo. 3s. 6d. net.*

Rowntree (Joshua). THE IMPERIAL DRUG TRADE. *Second and Cheaper Edition. Cr. 8vo. 2s. net.*

Rubie (A. E.), D.D. See Junior School Books.

Russell (W. Clark). THE LIFE OF ADMIRAL LORD COLLINGWOOD. With Illustrations by F. BRANGWYN. *Fourth Edition. Cr. 8vo. 6s.*
A Colonial Edition is also published.

St. Anslem. See Library of Devotion.

St. Augustine. See Library of Devotion.

St. Cyres (Viscount). See Oxford Biographies.

St. Francis of Assisi. See Standard Library.

'Saki' (H. Munro). REGINALD. *Second Edition. Fcap. 8vo. 2s. 6d. net.*

Sales (St. Francis de). See Library of Devotion.

Salmon (A. L.). A POPULAR GUIDE TO DEVON. *Medium 8vo. 6d. net.* See also Little Guides.

Sargeant (J.), M.A. ANNALS OF WESTMINSTER SCHOOL. Illustrated. *Demy 8vo. 7s. 6d.*

Sathas (C.). See Byzantine Texts.

Schmitt (John). See Byzantine Texts.

Scott (A. M.). WINSTON SPENCER CHURCHILL. With Portraits and Illustrations. *Cr. 8vo. 3s. 6d.*
A Colonial Edition is also published.

Seeley (H. G.), F.R.S. DRAGONS OF THE AIR. Illustrated. *Cr. 8vo. 6s.*

Sells (V. P.), M.A. THE MECHANICS OF DAILY LIFE. Illustrated. *Cr. 8vo. 2s. 6d.*

Selous (Edmund). TOMMY SMITH'S ANIMALS. Illustrated by G. W. ORD. *Sixth Edition. Fcap. 8vo. 2s. 6d.*

Settle (J. H.). ANECDOTES OF SOLDIERS. *Cr. 8vo. 3s. 6d. net.*
A Colonial Edition is also published.

Shakespeare (William).
THE FOUR FOLIOS, 1623; 1632; 1664; 1685. Each *Four Guineas net*, or a complete set, *Twelve Guineas net.*
Folios 3 and 4 are ready.
Folio 2 is nearly ready.

The Arden Shakespeare.
Demy 8vo. 2s. 6d. net each volume.
General Editor, W. J. CRAIG. An Edition of Shakespeare in single Plays. Edited with a full Introduction, Textual Notes, and a Commentary at the foot of the page.

HAMLET. Edited by EDWARD DOWDEN, Litt.D.
ROMEO AND JULIET. Edited by EDWARD DOWDEN, Litt.D.
KING LEAR. Edited by W. J. CRAIG.
JULIUS CAESAR. Edited by M. MACMILLAN, M.A.
THE TEMPEST. Edited by MORETON LUCE.
OTHELLO. Edited by H. C. HART.
TITUS ANDRONICUS. Edited by H. B. BAILDON.
CYMBELINE. Edited by EDWARD DOWDEN.
THE MERRY WIVES OF WINDSOR. Edited by H. C. HART.
A MIDSUMMER NIGHT'S DREAM. Edited by H. CUNINGHAM.
KING HENRY V. Edited by H. A. EVANS.
ALL'S WELL THAT ENDS WELL. Edited by W. O. BRIGSTOCKE.
THE TAMING OF THE SHREW. Edited by R. WARWICK BOND.
TIMON OF ATHENS. Edited by K. DEIGHTON.
MEASURE FOR MEASURE. Edited by H. C. HART.
TWELFTH NIGHT. Edited by MORETON LUCE.
THE MERCHANT OF VENICE. Edited by C. KNOX POOLER.
TROILUS AND CRESSIDA. Edited by K. DEIGHTON.

The Little Quarto Shakespeare. Edited by W. J. CRAIG. With Introductions and Notes. *Pott 16mo. In 40 Volumes. Leather, price 1s. net each volume. Mahogany Revolving Book Case. 10s. net.*
See also Standard Library.

Sharp (A.). VICTORIAN POETS. *Cr. 8vo. 2s. 6d.*

Sharp (Cecil). See S. Baring-Gould.

Sharp (Mrs. E. A.). See Little Books on Art.

Shedlock (J. S.) THE PIANOFORTE SONATA. *Cr. 8vo. 5s.*

Shelley (Percy B.). ADONAIS; an Elegy on the death of John Keats, Author of 'Endymion,' etc. Pisa. From the types of Didot, 1821. *2s. net.*

Sheppard (H. F.), M.A. See S. Baring-Gould.

Sherwell (Arthur), M.A. See S.Q.S.

Shipley (Mary E.). AN ENGLISH CHURCH HISTORY FOR CHILDREN. With a Preface by the Bishop of Gibraltar. With Maps and Illustrations. Part I. *Cr. 8vo. 2s. 6d. net.*

Sichel (Walter). DISRAELI: A Study in Personality and Ideas. With 3 Portraits. *Demy 8vo. 12s. 6d. net.*
A Colonial Edition is also published.
See also Oxford Biographies.

Sime (J.). See Little Books on Art.

Messrs. Methuen's Catalogue

Simonson (G. A.). FRANCESCO GUARDI. With 41 Plates. *Imperial 4to.* £2, 2s. *net.*

Sketchley (R. E. D.). See Little Books on Art.

Skipton (H. P. K.). See Little Books on Art.

Sladen (Douglas). SICILY: The New Winter Resort. With over 200 Illustrations. *Second Edition. Cr. 8vo.* 5s. *net.*

Small (Evan), M.A. THE EARTH. An Introduction to Physiography. Illustrated. *Cr. 8vo.* 2s. 6d.

Smallwood (M. G.). See Little Books on Art.

Smedley (F. E.). See I.P.L.

Smith (Adam). THE WEALTH OF NATIONS. Edited with an Introduction and numerous Notes by EDWIN CANNAN, M.A. *Two volumes. Demy 8vo.* 21s. *net.*
See also English Library.

Smith (Horace and James). See Little Library.

Smith (H. Bompas), M.A. A NEW JUNIOR ARITHMETIC. *Crown 8vo.* 2s. 6d.

Smith (R. Mudie). THOUGHTS FOR THE DAY. Edited by. *Fcap. 8vo.* 3s. 6d. *net.*

Smith (Nowell C.). See W. Wordsworth.

Smith (John Thomas). A BOOK FOR A RAINY DAY: Or Recollections of the Events of the Years 1766-1833. Edited by WILFRED WHITTEN. Illustrated. *Demy 8vo.* 12s. 6d. *net.*

Snell (F. J.). A BOOK OF EXMOOR. Illustrated. *Cr. 8vo.* 6s.

Snowden (C. E.). A HANDY DIGEST OF BRITISH HISTORY. *Demy 8vo.* 4s. 6d.

Sophocles. See Classical Translations.

Sornet (L. A.). See Junior School Books.

South (Wilton E.), M.A. See Junior School Books.

Southey (R.). ENGLISH SEAMEN. Edited by DAVID HANNAY.
Vol. I. (Howard, Clifford, Hawkins, Drake, Cavendish). *Second Edition. Cr. 8vo.* 6s.
Vol. II. (Richard Hawkins, Grenville, Essex, and Raleigh). *Cr. 8vo.* 6s.
See also Standard Library.

Spence (C. H.), M.A. See School Examination Series.

Spooner (W. A.), M.A. See Leaders of Religion.

Staley (Edgcumbe). THE GUILDS OF FLORENCE. Illustrated. *Second Edition. Royal 8vo.* 16s. *net.*

Stanbridge (J. W.), B.D. See Library of Devotion.

'Stancliffe.' GOLF DO'S AND DONT'S. *Second Edition. Fcap. 8vo.* 1s.

Stead (D. W.). See D. Gallaher.

Stedman (A. M. M.), M.A.
INITIA LATINA: Easy Lessons on Elementary Accidence. *Ninth Edition. Fcap. 8vo.* 1s.
FIRST LATIN LESSONS. *Ninth Edition. Cr. 8vo.* 2s.
FIRST LATIN READER. With Notes adapted to the Shorter Latin Primer and Vocabulary. *Sixth Edition revised.* 18mo. 1s. 6d.
EASY SELECTIONS FROM CÆSAR. The Helvetian War. *Second Edition* 18mo. 1s.
EASY SELECTIONS FROM LIVY. The Kings of Rome. 18mo. *Second Edition.* 1s. 6d.
EASY LATIN PASSAGES FOR UNSEEN TRANSLATION. *Tenth Edition Fcap. 8vo.* 1s. 6d.
EXEMPLA LATINA. First Exercises in Latin Accidence. With Vocabulary. *Third Edition. Cr. 8vo.* 1s.
EASY LATIN EXERCISES ON THE SYNTAX OF THE SHORTER AND REVISED LATIN PRIMER. With Vocabulary. *Tenth and Cheaper Edition, re-written. Cr. 8vo.* 1s. 6d. *Original Edition.* 2s. 6d. KEY, 3s. *net.*
THE LATIN COMPOUND SENTENCE: Rules and Exercises. *Second Edition. Cr. 8vo.* 1s. 6d. With Vocabulary. 2s.
NOTANDA QUAEDAM: Miscellaneous Latin Exercises on Common Rules and Idioms. *Fourth Edition. Fcap. 8vo.* 1s. 6d. With Vocabulary. 2s. Key, 2s. *net.*
LATIN VOCABULARIES FOR REPETITION: Arranged according to Subjects. *Thirteenth Edition. Fcap. 8vo.* 1s. 6d.
A VOCABULARY OF LATIN IDIOMS. 18mo. *Second Edition.* 1s.
STEPS TO GREEK. *Second Edition, revised.* 18mo. 1s.
A SHORTER GREEK PRIMER. *Cr. 8vo.* 1s. 6d.
EASY GREEK PASSAGES FOR UNSEEN TRANSLATION. *Third Edition, revised. Fcap. 8vo.* 1s. 6d.
GREEK VOCABULARIES FOR REPETITION. Arranged according to Subjects. *Fourth Edition. Fcap. 8vo.* 1s. 6d.
GREEK TESTAMENT SELECTIONS. For the use of Schools. With Introduction, Notes, and Vocabulary. *Fourth Edition. Fcap. 8vo.* 2s. 6d.
STEPS TO FRENCH. *Seventh Edition.* 18mo. 8d.
FIRST FRENCH LESSONS. *Seventh Edition, revised. Cr. 8vo.* 1s.
EASY FRENCH PASSAGES FOR UNSEEN TRANSLATION. *Fifth Edition, revised. Fcap. 8vo.* 1s. 6d.

GENERAL LITERATURE 17

EASY FRENCH EXERCISES ON ELEMENTARY SYNTAX. With Vocabulary. *Fourth Edition. Cr. 8vo. 2s. 6d.* KEY. *3s. net.*
FRENCH VOCABULARIES FOR REPETITION: Arranged according to Subjects. *Twelfth Edition. Fcap. 8vo. 1s.* See also School Examination Series.
Steel (R. Elliott), M.A., F.C.S. THE WORLD OF SCIENCE. With 147 Illustrations. *Second Edition. Cr. 8vo. 2s. 6d.* See also School Examination Series.
Stephenson (C.), of the Technical College, Bradford, and **Suddards (F.)** of the Yorkshire College, Leeds. ORNAMENTAL DESIGN FOR WOVEN FABRICS. Illustrated. *Demy 8vo. Third Edition. 7s. 6d.*
Stephenson (J.), M.A. THE CHIEF TRUTHS OF THE CHRISTIAN FAITH. *Cr. 8vo. 3s. 6d.*
Sterne (Laurence). See Little Library.
Sterry (W.). M.A. ANNALS OF ETON COLLEGE. Illustrated. *Demy 8vo. 7s. 6d.*
Steuart (Katherine). BY ALLAN WATER. *Second Edition. Cr. 8vo. 6s.*
Stevenson (R. L.) THE LETTERS OF ROBERT LOUIS STEVENSON TO HIS FAMILY AND FRIENDS. Selected and Edited by SIDNEY COLVIN. *Sixth Edition. Cr. 8vo. 12s.*
LIBRARY EDITION. *Demy 8vo. 2 vols. 25s. net.*
A Colonial Edition is also published.
VAILIMA LETTERS. With an Etched Portrait by WILLIAM STRANG. *Fifth Edition. Cr. 8vo. Buckram. 6s.*
A Colonial Edition is also published.
THE LIFE OF R. L. STEVENSON. See G. Balfour.
Stevenson (M. I.). FROM SARANAC TO THE MARQUESAS. Being Letters written by Mrs. M. I. STEVENSON during 1887-8. *Cr. 8vo. 6s. net.*
A Colonial Edition is also published.
LETTERS FROM SAMOA. Edited and arranged by M. C. BALFOUR. With many Illustrations. *Second Ed. Cr. 8vo. 6s. net.*
Stoddart (Anna M.). See Oxford Biographies.
Stokes (F. G.), B.A. HOURS WITH RABELAIS. From the translation of SIR T. URQUHART and P. A. MOTTEUX. With a Portrait in Photogravure. *Cr. 8vo. 3s. 6d. net.*
Stone (S. J.). POEMS AND HYMNS. With a Memoir by F. G. ELLERTON, M.A. With Portrait. *Cr. 8vo. 6s.*
Storr (Vernon F.), M.A., Lecturer in the Philosophy of Religion in Cambridge University; Examining Chaplain to the Archbishop of Canterbury; formerly Fellow of University College, Oxford. DEVELOPMENT AND DIVINE PURPOSE *Cr. 8vo. 5s. net.*
Straker (F.). See Books on Business.

Streane (A. W.), D.D. See Churchman's Bible.
Stroud (H.), D.Sc., M.A. See Textbooks of Science.
Strutt (Joseph). THE SPORTS AND PASTIMES OF THE PEOPLE OF ENGLAND. Illustrated by many engravings. Revised by J. CHARLES COX, LL.D., F.S.A. *Quarto. 21s. net.*
Stuart (Capt. Donald). THE STRUGGLE FOR PERSIA. With a Map. *Cr. 8vo. 6s.*
Sturch (F.), Staff Instructor to the Surrey County Council. MANUAL TRAINING, DRAWING (WOODWORK). Its Principles and Application, with Solutions to Examination Questions, 1892-1905, Orthographic, Isometric and Oblique Projection. With 50 Plates and 140 Figures. *Foolscap. 5s. net.*
Suckling (Sir John). FRAGMENTA AUREA: a Collection of all the Incomparable Peeces, written by. And published by a friend to perpetuate his memory. Printed by his own copies.
Printed for HUMPHREY MOSELEY, and are to be sold at his shop, at the sign of the Princes Arms in St. Paul's Churchyard, 1646.
Suddards (F.). See C. Stephenson.
Surtees (R. S.). See I.P.L.
Swift (Jonathan). THE JOURNAL TO STELLA. Edited by G. A. AITKEN. *Cr. 8vo. 6s.*
Symes (J. E.), M.A. THE FRENCH REVOLUTION. *Second Edition. Cr. 8vo. 2s. 6d.*
Sympson (E. M.), M.A., M.D. See Ancient Cities.
Syrett (Netta). See Little Blue Books.
Tacitus. AGRICOLA. With Introduction Notes, Map, etc. By R. F. DAVIS, M.A., *Fcap. 8vo. 2s.*
GERMANIA. By the same Editor. *Fcap. 8vo. 2s.* See also Classical Translations.
Tallack (W.). HOWARD LETTERS AND MEMORIES. *Demy 8vo. 10s. 6d. net.*
Tauler (J.). See Library of Devotion.
Taunton (E. L.). A HISTORY OF THE JESUITS IN ENGLAND. Illustrated. *Demy 8vo. 21s. net.*
Taylor (A. E.). THE ELEMENTS OF METAPHYSICS. *Demy 8vo. 10s. 6d. net.*
Taylor (F. G.), M.A. See Commercial Series.
Taylor (I. A.). See Oxford Biographies.
Taylor (T. M.), M.A., Fellow of Gonville and Caius College, Cambridge. A CONSTITUTIONAL AND POLITICAL HISTORY OF ROME. *Cr. 8vo. 7s. 6d.*
Tennyson (Alfred, Lord). THE EARLY POEMS OF. Edited, with Notes and an Introduction, by J. CHURTON COLLINS, M.A. *Cr. 8vo. 6s.*
IN MEMORIAM, MAUD, AND THE PRINCESS. Edited by J. CHURTON COLLINS, M.A. *Cr. 8vo. 6s.* See also Little Library.

A 3

Terry (C. S.). See Oxford Biographies.
Terton (Alice). LIGHTS AND SHADOWS IN A HOSPITAL. *Cr. 8vo.* 3s. 6d.
Thackeray (W. M.). See Little Library.
Theobald (F. V.), M.A. INSECT LIFE. Illustrated. *Second Ed. Revised. Cr. 8vo.* 2s. 6d.
Thompson (A. H.). See Little Guides.
Tileston (Mary W.). DAILY STRENGTH FOR DAILY NEEDS. *Twelfth Edition. Medium 16mo.* 2s. 6d. net. Also an edition in superior binding, 6s.
Tompkins (H. W.), F.R.H.S. See Little Guides.
Towndrow (R. F.). A DAY BOOK OF MILTON. Edited by. *Fcap. 8vo.* 3s. 6d. net.
Townley (Lady Susan). MY CHINESE NOTE-BOOK With 16 Illustrations and 2 Maps. *Third Edition. Demy 8vo.* 10s. 6d. net.
A Colonial Edition is also published.
*****Toynbee (Paget),** M.A., D.Litt. DANTE IN ENGLISH LITERATURE. *Demy 8vo.* 12s. 6d. net.
See also Oxford Biographies.
Trench (Herbert). DEIRDRE WED and Other Poems. *Cr. 8vo.* 5s.
Trevelyan (G. M.), Fellow of Trinity College, Cambridge. ENGLAND UNDER THE STUARTS. With Maps and Plans. *Second Edition. Demy 8vo.* 10s. 6d. net.
Troutbeck (G. E.). See Little Guides.
Tyler (E. A.), B.A., F.C.S. See Junior School Books.
Tyrell-Gill (Frances). See Little Books on Art.
Vardon (Harry). THE COMPLETE GOLFER. Illustrated. *Seventh Edition. Demy 8vo.* 10s. 6d. net.
A Colonial Edition is also published.
Vaughan (Henry). See Little Library.
Voegelin (A.), M.A. See Junior Examination Series.
Waddell (Col. L. A.), LL.D., C.B. LHASA AND ITS MYSTERIES. With a Record of the Expedition of 1903-1904. With 2000 Illustrations and Maps. *Demy 8vo.* 21s. net.
Also Third and Cheaper Edition. With 155 Illustrations and Maps. *Demy 8vo.* 7s. 6d. net.
Wade (G. W.), D.D. OLD TESTAMENT HISTORY. With Maps. *Third Edition. Cr. 8vo.* 6s.
Wagner (Richard). See A. L. Cleather.
Wall (J. C.). DEVILS. Illustrated by the Author and from photographs. *Demy 8vo.* 4s. 6d. net. See also Antiquary's Books.
Walters (H. B.). See Little Books on Art.
Walton (F. W.). See Victor G. Plarr.
Walton (Izaac) and **Cotton (Charles).** See I.P.L., Standard Library, and Little Library.

Warmelo (D. S. Van). ON COMMANDO. With Portrait. *Cr. 8vo.* 3s. 6d.
A Colonial Edition is also published.
Warren-Vernon (Hon. William), M.A. READINGS ON THE INFERNO OF DANTE, chiefly based on the Commentary of BENVENUTO DA IMOLA. With an Introduction by the Rev. Dr. MOORE. In Two Volumes. *Second Edition. Cr. 8vo.* 15s. net.
Waterhouse (Mrs. Alfred). WITH THE SIMPLE-HEARTED: Little Homilies to Women in Country Places. *Second Edition. Small Pott 8vo.* 2s. net. See also Little Library.
Weatherhead (T. C.), M.A. EXAMINATION PAPERS IN HORACE. *Cr. 8vo.* 2s. See also Junior Examination Series.
Webb (W. T.). See Little Blue Books.
Webber (F. C.). See Textbooks of Technology.
Wells (Sidney H.). See Textbooks of Science.
Wells (J.), M.A., Fellow and Tutor of Wadham College. OXFORD AND OXFORD LIFE. *Third Edition. Cr. 8vo.* 3s. 6d.
A SHORT HISTORY OF ROME. *Sixth Edition.* With 3 Maps. *Cr. 8vo.* 3s. 6d.
See also Little Guides.
'Westminster Gazette' Office Boy (Francis Brown). THE DOINGS OF ARTHUR. *Cr. 4to.* 2s. 6d. net.
Wetmore (Helen C.). THE LAST OF THE GREAT SCOUTS ('Buffalo Bill'). Illustrated. *Second Edition. Demy 8vo.* 6s.
A Colonial Edition is also published.
Whibley (C.). See Half-crown Library.
Whibley (L.), M.A., Fellow of Pembroke College, Cambridge. GREEK OLIGARCHIES: THEIR ORGANISATION AND CHARACTER. *Cr. 8vo.* 6s.
Whitaker (G. H.), M.A. See Churchman's Bible.
White (Gilbert). THE NATURAL HISTORY OF SELBORNE. Edited by L. C. MIALL, F.R.S., assisted by W. WARDE FOWLER, M.A. *Cr. 8vo.* 6s. See also Standard Library.
Whitfield (E. E.). See Commercial Series.
Whitehead (A. W.). GASPARD DE COLIGNY. Illustrated. *Demy 8vo.* 12s. 6d. net.
Whiteley (R. Lloyd), F.I.C., Principal of the Municipal Science School, West Bromwich. AN ELEMENTARY TEXT-BOOK OF INORGANIC CHEMISTRY. *Cr. 8vo.* 2s. 6d.
Whitley (Miss). See S.Q.S.
Whitten (W.). See John Thomas Smith.
Whyte (A. G.), B.Sc. See Books on Business.
Wilberforce (Wilfrid). See Little Books on Art.
Wilde (Oscar). DE PROFUNDIS. *Sixth Edition. Cr. 8vo.* 5s. net.
A Colonial Edition is also published.

General Literature 19

Wilkins (W. H.), B.A. See S.Q.S.
Wilkinson (J. Frome). See S.Q.S.
*Williams (A.). PETROL PETER: or Mirth for Motorists. Illustrated in Colour by A. W. MILLS. *Demy 4to.* 3s. 6d. *net.*
Williamson (M. G.). See Ancient Cities.
Williamson (W.). THE BRITISH GARDENER. Illustrated. *Demy 8vo.* 10s. 6d.
Williamson (W.), B.A. See Junior Examination Series, Junior School Books, and Beginner's Books.
Willson (Beckles). LORD STRATHCONA: the Story of his Life. Illustrated. *Demy 8vo.* 7s. 6d.
A Colonial Edition is also published.
Wilmot-Buxton (E. M.). MAKERS OF EUROPE. *Cr. 8vo. Fifth Ed.* 3s. 6d.
A Text-book of European History for Middle Forms.
THE ANCIENT WORLD. With Maps and Illustrations. *Cr. 8vo.* 3s. 6d.
See also Beginner's Books.
Wilson (Bishop.). See Library of Devotion.
Wilson (A. J.). See Books on Business.
Wilson (H. A.). See Books on Business.
Wilton (Richard), M.A. LYRA PASTORALIS: Songs of Nature, Church, and Home. *Pott 8vo.* 2s. 6d.
Winbolt (S. E.), M.A. EXERCISES IN LATIN ACCIDENCE. *Cr. 8vo.* 1s. 6d.
LATIN HEXAMETER VERSE: An Aid to Composition. *Cr. 8vo.* 3s. 6d. KEY, 5s. *net.*
Windle (B. C. A.), D.Sc., F.R.S. See Antiquary's Books, Little Guides and Ancient Cities.
Winterbotham (Canon), M.A., B.Sc., LL.B. See Churchman's Library.
Wood (J. A. E.). See Textbooks of Technology.
Wood (J. Hickory). DAN LENO. Illustrated. *Third Edition. Cr. 8vo.* 6s.
A Colonial Edition is also published.
Wood (W. Birkbeck), M.A., late Scholar of Worcester College, Oxford, and **Edmonds (Major J. E.)**, R.E., D.A.Q.-M.G. A HISTORY OF THE CIVIL WAR IN THE UNITED STATES. With an Introduction by H. SPENSER WILKINSON. With 24 Maps and Plans. *Demy 8vo.* 12s. 6d. *net.*

Wordsworth (Christopher). See Antiquary's Books.
*Wordsworth (W.). THE POEMS OF. With Introduction and Notes by NOWELL C. SMITH, Fellow of New College, Oxford. *In Four Volumes. Demy 8vo.* 5s. *net* each. See also Little Library.
Wordsworth (W.) and Coleridge (S. T.). See Little Library
Wright (Arthur), M.A., Fellow of Queen's College, Cambridge. See Churchman's Library.
Wright (C. Gordon). See Dante.
Wright (J. C.). TO-DAY. *Fcap.* 16mo. 1s. *net.*
Wright (Sophie). GERMAN VOCABULARIES FOR REPETITION. *Fcap. 8vo.* 1s. 6d.
Wrong (George M.), Professor of History in the University of Toronto. THE EARL OF ELGIN. Illustrated. *Demy 8vo.* 7s. 6d. *net.*
A Colonial Edition is also published.
Wyatt (Kate) and Gloag (M.). A BOOK OF ENGLISH GARDENS. With 24 Illustrations in Colour. *Demy 8vo.* 10s. 6s. *net.*
Wylde (A. B.). MODERN ABYSSINIA. With a Map and a Portrait. *Demy 8vo.* 15s. *net.*
A Colonial Edition s also published
Wyndham (George). THE POEMS OF WILLIAM SHAKESPEARE. With an Introduction and Notes. *Demy 8vo. Buckram, gilt top.* 10s. 6d.
Wyon (R.). See Half-crown Library.
Yeats (W. B.). AN ANTHOLOGY OF IRISH VERSE. *Revised and Enlarged Edition. Cr. 8vo.* 3s. 6d.
Young (Filson). THE COMPLETE MOTORIST. With 138 Illustrations. *Sixth Edition. Demy 8vo.* 12s. 6d. *net.*
A Colonial Edition is also published.
Young (T. M.). THE AMERICAN COTTON INDUSTRY: A Study of Work and Workers. *Cr. 8vo. Cloth,* 2s. 6d. ; *paper boards,* 1s. 6d.
Zimmern (Antonia). WHAT DO WE KNOW CONCERNING ELECTRICITY? *Fcap. 8vo.* 1s. 6d. *net.*

Ancient Cities

General Editor, B. C. A. WINDLE, D.Sc., F.R.S.

Cr. 8vo. 4s. 6d. *net.*

CHESTER. By B. C. A. Windle, D.Sc. F.R.S. Illustrated by E. H. New.
SHREWSBURY. By T. Auden, M.A., F.S.A. Illustrated.
CANTERBURY. By J. C. Cox, LL.D., F.S.A. Illustrated.
EDINBURGH. By M. G. Williamson. Illustrated by Herbert Railton.
LINCOLN. By E. Mansel Sympson, M.A., M.D. Illustrated by E. H. New.
BRISTOL. By Alfred Harvey. Illustrated by E. H. New.

Antiquary's Books, The

General Editor, J. CHARLES COX, LL.D., F.S.A.

A series of volumes dealing with various branches of English Antiquities; comprehensive and popular, as well as accurate and scholarly.

Demy 8vo. 7s. 6d. net.

ENGLISH MONASTIC LIFE. By the Right Rev. Abbot Gasquet, O.S B. Illustrated. *Third Edition.*

REMAINS OF THE PREHISTORIC AGE IN ENGLAND. By B. C. A. Windle, D.Sc., F.R.S. With numerous Illustrations and Plans.

OLD SERVICE BOOKS OF THE ENGLISH CHURCH. By Christopher Wordsworth, M.A., and Henry Littlehales. With Coloured and other Illustrations.

CELTIC ART. By J. Romilly Allen, F.S.A. With numerous Illustrations and Plans.

ARCHÆOLOGY AND FALSE ANTIQUITIES. By R. Munro, LL.D. Illustrated.

SHRINES OF BRITISH SAINTS. By J. C. Wall. With numerous Illustrations and Plans.

THE ROYAL FORESTS OF ENGLAND. By J. C. Cox, LL.D., F.S.A. Illustrated.

THE MANOR AND MANORIAL RECORDS. By Nathaniel J. Hone. Illustrated.

SEALS. By J. Harvey Bloom. Illustrated.

Beginner's Books, The

Edited by W. WILLIAMSON, B.A.

EASY FRENCH RHYMES. By Henri Blouet. Illustrated. *Fcap. 8vo.* 1s.

EASY STORIES FROM ENGLISH HISTORY. By E. M. Wilmot-Buxton, Author of 'Makers of Europe.' *Cr. 8vo.* 1s.

EASY EXERCISES IN ARITHMETIC. Arranged by W. S. Beard. *Fcap. 8vo.* Without Answers, 1s. With Answers, 1s. 3d.

EASY DICTATION AND SPELLING. By W. Williamson, B.A. *Fifth Edition. Fcap. 8vo.* 1s.

Business, Books on

Cr. 8vo. 2s. 6d. net.

A series of volumes dealing with all the most important aspects of commercial and financial activity. The volumes are intended to treat separately all the considerable industries and forms of business, and to explain accurately and clearly what they do and how they do it. Some are Illustrated. The first volumes are—

PORTS AND DOCKS. By Douglas Owen.

RAILWAYS. By E. R. McDermott.

THE STOCK EXCHANGE. By Chas. Duguid. *Second Edition.*

THE BUSINESS OF INSURANCE. By A. J. Wilson.

THE ELECTRICAL INDUSTRY: LIGHTING, TRACTION, AND POWER. By A. G. Whyte, B.Sc.

THE SHIPBUILDING INDUSTRY: Its History, Science, Practice, and Finance. By David Pollock, M.I.N.A.

THE MONEY MARKET. By F. Straker.

THE BUSINESS SIDE OF AGRICULTURE. By A. G. L. Rogers, M.A.

LAW IN BUSINESS. By H. A. Wilson.

THE BREWING INDUSTRY. By Julian L. Baker, F.I.C., F.C.S.

THE AUTOMOBILE INDUSTRY. By G. de H. Stone.

MINING AND MINING INVESTMENTS. By 'A. Moil.'

THE BUSINESS OF ADVERTISING. By Clarence G. Moran, Barrister-at-Law. Illustrated.

TRADE UNIONS. By G. Drage.

CIVIL ENGINEERING. By T. Claxton Fidler, M.Inst. C.E. Illustrated.

THE IRON TRADE. By J. Stephen Jeans. Illustrated.

MONOPOLIES, TRUSTS, AND KARTELLS. By F. W. Hirst.

THE COTTON INDUSTRY AND TRADE. By Prof. S. J. Chapman, Dean of the Faculty of Commerce in the University of Manchester. Illustrated.

GENERAL LITERATURE 21

Byzantine Texts
Edited by J. B. BURY, M.A., Litt.D.
A series of texts of Byzantine Historians, edited by English and foreign scholars.

ZACHARIAH OF MITYLENE. Translated by F. J. Hamilton, D.D., and E. W. Brooks. *Demy 8vo.* 12s. 6d. *net.*

EVAGRIUS. Edited by Léon Parmentier and M. Bidez. *Demy 8vo.* 10s. 6d. *net.*

THE HISTORY OF PSELLUS. Edited by C. Sathas. *Demy 8vo.* 15s. *net.*

ECTHESIS CHRONICA. Edited by Professor Lambros. *Demy 8vo.* 7s. 6d. *net.*

THE CHRONICLE OF MOREA. Edited by John Schmitt. *Demy 8vo.* 15s. *net.*

Churchman's Bible, The
General Editor, J. H. BURN, B.D., F.R.S.E.

A series of Expositions on the Books of the Bible, which will be of service to the general reader in the practical and devotional study of the Sacred Text.

Each Book is provided with a full and clear Introductory Section, in which is stated what is known or conjectured respecting the date and occasion of the composition of the Book, and any other particulars that may help to elucidate its meaning as a whole. The Exposition is divided into sections of a convenient length, corresponding as far as possible with the divisions of the Church Lectionary. The Translation of the Authorised Version is printed in full, such corrections as are deemed necessary being placed in footnotes.

THE EPISTLE OF ST. PAUL THE APOSTLE TO THE GALATIANS. Edited by A. W. Robinson, M.A. *Second Edition. Fcap. 8vo.* 1s. 6d. *net.*

ECCLESIASTES. Edited by A. W. Streane, D.D. *Fcap. 8vo.* 1s. 6d. *net.*

THE EPISTLE OF ST. PAUL THE APOSTLE TO THE PHILIPPIANS. Edited by C. R. D. Biggs, D.D. *Second Edition. Fcap 8vo.* 1s. 6d. *net.*

THE EPISTLE OF ST. JAMES. Edited by H. W. Fulford, M.A. *Fcap. 8vo.* 1s. 6d. *net.*

ISAIAH. Edited by W. E. Barnes, D.D. *Two Volumes. Fcap. 8vo.* 2s. *net each.* With Map.

THE EPISTLE OF ST. PAUL THE APOSTLE TO THE EPHESIANS. Edited by G. H. Whitaker, M.A. *Fcap. 8vo.* 1s. 6d. *net.*

Churchman's Library, The
General Editor, J. H. BURN, B.D., F.R.S.E.

THE BEGINNINGS OF ENGLISH CHRISTIANITY. By W. E. Collins, M.A. With Map. *Cr. 8vo.* 3s. 6d.

SOME NEW TESTAMENT PROBLEMS. By Arthur Wright, M.A. *Cr. 8vo.* 6s.

THE KINGDOM OF HEAVEN HERE AND HEREAFTER. By Canon Winterbotham, M.A., B.Sc., LL.B. *Cr. 8vo.* 3s. 6d.

THE WORKMANSHIP OF THE PRAYER BOOK: Its Literary and Liturgical Aspects. By J. Dowden, D.D. *Second Edition. Cr. 8vo.* 3s. 6d.

EVOLUTION. By F. B. Jevons, M.A., Litt.D *Cr. 8vo.* 3s. 6d.

THE OLD TESTAMENT AND THE NEW SCHOLARSHIP. By J. W. Peters, D.D. *Cr. 8vo.* 6s.

THE CHURCHMAN'S INTRODUCTION TO THE OLD TESTAMENT. By A. M. Mackay, B.A. *Cr. 8vo.* 3s. 6d.

THE CHURCH OF CHRIST. By E. T. Green, M.A. *Cr. 8vo.* 6s.

COMPARATIVE THEOLOGY. By J. A. MacCulloch. *Cr. 8vo.* 6s.

Classical Translations
Edited by H. F. FOX, M.A., Fellow and Tutor of Brasenose College, Oxford.
Crown 8vo.

A series of Translations from the Greek and Latin Classics, distinguished by literary excellence as well as by scholarly accuracy.

ÆSCHYLUS—Agamemnon, Choephoroe, Eumenides. Translated by Lewis Campbell, LL.D. 5s.

CICERO—De Oratore I. Translated by E. N. P. Moor, M.A. 3s. 6d.

CICERO—Select Orations (Pro Milone, Pro Mureno, Philippic II., in Catilinam). Translated by H. E. D. Blakiston, M.A. 5s.

CICERO—De Natura Deorum. Translated by F. Brooks, M.A. 3s. 6d.

[*Continued.*

22 MESSRS. METHUEN'S CATALOGUE

CLASSICAL TRANSLATIONS—*continued.*

CICERO—De Officiis. Translated by G. B. Gardiner, M.A. 2s. 6d.
HORACE—The Odes and Epodes. Translated by A. D. Godley, M.A. 2s.
LUCIAN—Six Dialogues (Nigrinus, Icaro-Menippus, The Cock, The Ship, The Parasite, The Lover of Falsehood) Translated by S.

T. Irwin, M.A. 3s. 6d.
SOPHOCLES—Electra and Ajax. Translated by E. D. A. Morshead, M.A. 2s. 6d.
TACITUS—Agricola and Germania. Translated by R. B. Townshend. 2s. 6d.
THE SATIRES OF JUVENAL. Translated by S. G. Owen. 2s. 6d.

Commercial Series

Edited by H. DE B. GIBBINS, Litt.D., M.A.

Crown 8vo.

A series intended to assist students and young men preparing for a commercial career, by supplying useful handbooks of a clear and practical character, dealing with those subjects which are absolutely essential in the business life.

COMMERCIAL EDUCATION IN THEORY AND PRACTICE. By E. E. Whitfield, M.A. 5s.
An introduction to Methuen's Commercial Series treating the question of Commercial Education fully from both the point of view of the teacher and of the parent.
BRITISH COMMERCE AND COLONIES FROM ELIZABETH TO VICTORIA. By H. de B. Gibbins, Litt.D., M.A. *Third Edition.* 2s.
COMMERCIAL EXAMINATION PAPERS. By H. de B. Gibbins, Litt.D., M.A. 1s. 6d.
THE ECONOMICS OF COMMERCE, By H. de B. Gibbins, Litt.D., M.A. *Second Edition.* 1s. 6d.
A GERMAN COMMERCIAL READER. By S. E. Bally. With Vocabulary. 2s.
A COMMERCIAL GEOGRAPHY OF THE BRITISH EMPIRE. By L. W. Lyde, M.A. *Fourth Edition.* 2s.
A COMMERCIAL GEOGRAPHY OF FOREIGN NATIONS. By F. C. Boon, B.A. 2s.

A PRIMER OF BUSINESS. By S. Jackson, M.A. *Third Edition.* 1s. 6d.
COMMERCIAL ARITHMETIC. By F. G. Taylor, M.A. *Fourth Edition.* 1s. 6d.
FRENCH COMMERCIAL CORRESPONDENCE. By S. E. Bally. With Vocabulary. *Third Edition.* 2s.
GERMAN COMMERCIAL CORRESPONDENCE. By S. E. Bally. With Vocabulary. *Second Edition.* 2s. 6d.
A FRENCH COMMERCIAL READER. By S. E. Bally. With Vocabulary. *Second Edition.* 2s.
PRECIS WRITING AND OFFICE CORRESPONDENCE. By E. E. Whitfield, M.A. *Second Edition.* 2s.
A GUIDE TO PROFESSIONS AND BUSINESS. By H. Jones. 1s. 6d.
THE PRINCIPLES OF BOOK-KEEPING BY DOUBLE ENTRY. By J. E. B. M'Allen, M.A. 2s.
COMMERCIAL LAW. By W. Douglas Edwards. *Second Edition.* 2s.

Connoisseur's Library, The

Wide Royal 8vo. 25s. net.

A sumptuous series of 20 books on art, written by experts for collectors, superbly illustrated in photogravure, collotype, and colour. The technical side of the art is duly treated. The first volumes are—

MEZZOTINTS. By Cyril Davenport. With 40 Plates in Photogravure.
PORCELAIN. By Edward Dillon. With 19 Plates in Colour, 20 in Collotype, and 5 in Photogravure.
MINIATURES. By Dudley Heath. With 9 Plates in Colour, 15 in Collotype, and 15 in Photogravure.

IVORIES. By A. Maskell. With 80 Plates in Collotype and Photogravure.
ENGLISH FURNITURE. By F. S. Robinson. With 160 Plates in Collotype and one in Photogravure. *Second Edition.*
EUROPEAN ENAMELS. By H. CUNYNGHAME, C.B. With many Plates in Collotype and a Frontispiece in Photogravure.

General Literature

Devotion, The Library of

With Introductions and (where necessary) Notes.

Small Pott 8vo, cloth, 2s. ; leather, 2s. 6d. net.

These masterpieces of devotional literature are furnished with such Introductions and Notes as may be necessary to explain the standpoint of the author and the obvious difficulties of the text, without unnecessary intrusion between the author and the devout mind.

THE CONFESSIONS OF ST. AUGUSTINE. Edited by C. Bigg, D.D. *Fifth Edition.*
THE CHRISTIAN YEAR. Edited by Walter Lock, D.D. *Third Edition.*
THE IMITATION OF CHRIST. Edited by C. Bigg, D.D. *Fourth Edition.*
A BOOK OF DEVOTIONS. Edited by J. W. Stanbridge. B.D. *Second Edition.*
LYRA INNOCENTIUM. Edited by Walter Lock, D.D.
A SERIOUS CALL TO A DEVOUT AND HOLY LIFE. Edited by C. Bigg, D.D. *Second Edition.*
THE TEMPLE. Edited by E. C. S. Gibson, D.D. *Second Edition.*
A GUIDE TO ETERNITY. Edited by J. W. Stanbridge, B.D.
THE PSALMS OF DAVID. Edited by B. W. Randolph, D.D.
LYRA APOSTOLICA. By Cardinal Newman and others. Edited by Canon Scott Holland and Canon H. C. Beeching, M.A.
THE INNER WAY. By J. Tauler. Edited by A. W. Hutton, M.A.
THE THOUGHTS OF PASCAL. Edited by C. S. Jerram, M.A.

ON THE LOVE OF GOD. By St. Francis de Sales. Edited by W. J. Knox-Little, M.A.
A MANUAL OF CONSOLATION FROM THE SAINTS AND FATHERS. Edited by J. H. Burn, B.D.
THE SONG OF SONGS. Edited by B. Blaxland, M.A.
THE DEVOTIONS OF ST. ANSELM. Edited by C. C. J. Webb, M.A.
GRACE ABOUNDING. By John Bunyan. Edited by S. C. Freer, M.A.
BISHOP WILSON'S SACRA PRIVATA. Edited by A. E. Burn, B.D.
LYRA SACRA : A Book of Sacred Verse. Edited by H. C. Beeching, M.A., Canon of Westminster.
A DAY BOOK FROM THE SAINTS AND FATHERS. Edited by J. H. Burn, B.D.
HEAVENLY WISDOM. A Selection from the English Mystics. Edited by E. C. Gregory.
LIGHT, LIFE, and LOVE. A Selection from the German Mystics. Edited by W. R. Inge, M.A.
AN INTRODUCTION TO THE DEVOUT LIFE. By St. Francis de Sales. Translated and Edited by T. Barns, M.A.

Methuen's Standard Library

In Sixpenny Volumes.

THE STANDARD LIBRARY is a new series of volumes containing the great classics of the world, and particularly the finest works of English literature. All the great masters will be represented, either in complete works or in selections. It is the ambition of the publishers to place the best books of the Anglo-Saxon race within the reach of every reader, so that the series may represent something of the diversity and splendour of our English tongue. The characteristics of THE STANDARD LIBRARY are four :—1. SOUNDNESS OF TEXT. 2. CHEAPNESS. 3. CLEARNESS OF TYPE. 4. SIMPLICITY. The books are well printed on good paper at a price which on the whole is without parallel in the history of publishing. Each volume contains from 100 to 250 pages, and is issued in paper covers, Crown 8vo, at Sixpence net, or in cloth gilt at One Shilling net. In a few cases long books are issued as Double Volumes or as Treble Volumes.

The following books are ready with the exception of those marked with a †, which denotes that the book is nearly ready :—

THE MEDITATIONS OF MARCUS AURELIUS. The translation is by R. Graves.
THE NOVELS OF JANE AUSTEN. In 5 volumes. VOL. I.—Sense and Sensibility.
ESSAYS AND COUNSELS and THE NEW ATLANTIS. By Francis Bacon, Lord Verulam.

RELIGIO MEDICI and URN BURIAL. By Sir Thomas Browne. The text has been collated by A. R. Waller.
THE PILGRIM'S PROGRESS. By John Bunyan.
REFLECTIONS ON THE FRENCH REVOLUTION. By Edmund Burke.
THE ANALOGY OF RELIGION, NATURAL AND REVEALED. By Joseph Butler, D.D.

[Continued.

MESSRS. METHUEN'S CATALOGUE

THE STANDARD LIBRARY—*continued.*

THE POEMS OF THOMAS CHATTERTON. In 2 volumes.
Vol. I.—Miscellaneous Poems.
†Vol. II.—The Rowley Poems.
†VITA NUOVA. By Dante. Translated into English by D G. Rossetti.
TOM JONES. By Henry Fielding. Treble Vol.
CRANFORD. By Mrs. Gaskell.
THE HISTORY OF THE DECLINE AND FALL OF THE ROMAN EMPIRE. By Edward Gibbon. In 7 double volumes.
Vol. v. is nearly ready.
The Text and Notes have been revised by J. B. Bury, Litt.D., but the Appendices of the more expensive edition are not given.
†THE VICAR OF WAKEFIELD. By Oliver Goldsmith.
THE POEMS AND PLAYS OF OLIVER GOLDSMITH.
THE WORKS OF BEN JONSON.
†VOL. I.—The Case is Altered. Every Man in His Humour. Every Man out of His Humour.
The text has been collated by H. C. Hart.
THE POEMS OF JOHN KEATS. Double volume. The Text has been collated by E. de Selincourt.
ON THE IMITATION OF CHRIST. By Thomas à Kempis.
The translation is by C. Bigg, DD., Canon of Christ Church.
A SERIOUS CALL TO A DEVOUT AND HOLY LIFE. By William Law.
THE PLAYS OF CHRISTOPHER MARLOWE.
†Vol. I.—Tamburlane the Great. The Tragical History of Dr. Faustus.
THE PLAYS OF PHILIP MASSINGER.
†Vol. I.—The Duke of Milan.

THE POEMS OF JOHN MILTON. In 2 volumes.
Vol. I.—Paradise Lost.
THE PROSE WORKS OF JOHN MILTON.
VOL. I.—Eikonoklastes and The Tenure of Kings and Magistrates.
SELECT WORKS OF SIR THOMAS MORE.
Vol. I.—Utopia and Poems.
THE REPUBLIC OF PLATO. Translated by Sydenham and Taylor. Double Volume. The translation has been revised by W. H. D. Rouse.
THE LITTLE FLOWERS OF ST. FRANCIS. Translated by W. Heywood.
THE WORKS OF WILLIAM SHAKESPEARE. In 10 volumes.
VOL. I.—The Tempest; The Two Gentlemen of Verona ; The Merry Wives of Windsor ; Measure for Measure ; The Comedy of Errors.
VOL. II.—Much Ado About Nothing ; Love's Labour's Lost ; A Midsummer Night's Dream ; The Merchant of Venice ; As You Like It.
VOL. III.—The Taming of the Shrew ; All's Well that Ends Well; Twelfth Night ; The Winter's Tale.
Vol. IV.—The Life and Death of King John ; The Tragedy of King Richard the Second ; The First Part of King Henry IV. ; The Second Part of King Henry IV.
Vol. V.—The Life of King Henry V. ; The First Part of King Henry VI. ; The Second Part of King Henry VI.
THE LIFE OF NELSON. By Robert Southey.
THE NATURAL HISTORY AND ANTIQUITIES OF SELBORNE. By Gilbert White.

Half-Crown Library

Crown 8vo. 2s. 6d. net.

THE LIFE OF JOHN RUSKIN. By W. G. Collingwood, M.A. With Portraits. *Sixth Edition.*
ENGLISH LYRICS. By W. E. Henley. *Second Edition.*
THE GOLDEN POMP. A Procession of English Lyrics. Arranged by A. T. Quiller Couch. *Second Edition.*
CHITRAL : The Story of a Minor Siege. By Sir G. S. Robertson, K.C.S.I. *Third Edition.* Illustrated.

STRANGE SURVIVALS AND SUPERSTITIONS. By S. Baring-Gould. *Third Edition.*
YORKSHIRE ODDITIES AND STRANGE EVENTS. By S. Baring-Gould. *Fourth Edition.*
ENGLISH VILLAGES. By P. H. Ditchfield, M.A., F.S.A. Illustrated.
A BOOK OF ENGLISH PROSE. By W. E. Henley and C. Whibley.
THE LAND OF THE BLACK MOUNTAIN. Being a Description of Montenegro. By R. Wyon and G. Prance. With 40 Illustrations.

Illustrated Pocket Library of Plain and Coloured Books, The

Fcap 8vo. 3s. 6d. net each volume.

A series, in small form, of some of the famous illustrated books of fiction and general literature. These are faithfully reprinted from the first or best editions without introduction or notes. The Illustrations are chiefly in colour.

COLOURED BOOKS

OLD COLOURED BOOKS. By George Paston. With 16 Coloured Plates. *Fcap. 8vo. 2s. net.*
THE LIFE AND DEATH OF JOHN MYTTON, ESQ. By Nimrod. With 18 Coloured Plates by Henry Alken and T. J. Rawlins. *Third Edition.*

[Continued.

GENERAL LITERATURE 25

ILLUSTRATED POCKET LIBRARY OF PLAIN AND COLOURED BOOKS—*continued.*

THE LIFE OF A SPORTSMAN. By Nimrod. With 35 Coloured Plates by Henry Alken.

HANDLEY CROSS. By R. S. Surtees. With 17 Coloured Plates and 100 Woodcuts in the Text by John Leech. *Second Edition.*

MR. SPONGE'S SPORTING TOUR. By R. S. Surtees. With 13 Coloured Plates and 90 Woodcuts in the Text by John Leech.

JORROCKS' JAUNTS AND JOLLITIES. By R. S. Surtees. With 15 Coloured Plates by H. Alken. *Second Edition.*

This volume is reprinted from the extremely rare and costly edition of 1843, which contains Alken's very fine illustrations instead of the usual ones by Phiz.

ASK MAMMA. By R. S. Surtees. With 13 Coloured Plates and 70 Woodcuts in the Text by John Leech.

THE ANALYSIS OF THE HUNTING FIELD. By R. S. Surtees. With 7 Coloured Plates by Henry Alken, and 43 Illustrations on Wood.

THE TOUR OF DR. SYNTAX IN SEARCH OF THE PICTURESQUE. By William Combe. With 30 Coloured Plates by T. Rowlandson.

THE TOUR OF DOCTOR SYNTAX IN SEARCH OF CONSOLATION. By William Combe. With 24 Coloured Plates by T. Rowlandson.

THE THIRD TOUR OF DOCTOR SYNTAX IN SEARCH OF A WIFE. By William Combe. With 24 Coloured Plates by T. Rowlandson.

THE HISTORY OF JOHNNY QUAE GENUS: the Little Foundling of the late Dr. Syntax. By the Author of 'The Three Tours.' With 24 Coloured Plates by Rowlandson.

THE ENGLISH DANCE OF DEATH, from the Designs of T. Rowlandson, with Metrical Illustrations by the Author of 'Doctor Syntax.' *Two Volumes.*

This book contains 76 Coloured Plates.

THE DANCE OF LIFE: A Poem. By the Author of 'Doctor Syntax.' Illustrated with 26 Coloured Engravings by T. Rowlandson.

LIFE IN LONDON: or, the Day and Night Scenes of Jerry Hawthorn, Esq., and his Elegant Friend, Corinthian Tom. By Pierce Egan. With 36 Coloured Plates by I. R. and G. Cruikshank. With numerous Designs on Wood.

REAL LIFE IN LONDON: or, the Rambles and Adventures of Bob Tallyho, Esq., and his Cousin, The Hon. Tom Dashall. By an Amateur (Pierce Egan). With 31 Coloured Plates by Alken and Rowlandson, etc. *Two Volumes.*

THE LIFE OF AN ACTOR. By Pierce Egan. With 27 Coloured Plates by Theodore Lane, and several Designs on Wood.

THE VICAR OF WAKEFIELD. By Oliver Goldsmith. With 24 Coloured Plates by T. Rowlandson.

THE MILITARY ADVENTURES OF JOHNNY NEWCOME. By an Officer. With 15 Coloured Plates by T. Rowlandson.

THE NATIONAL SPORTS OF GREAT BRITAIN. With Descriptions and 51 Coloured Plates by Henry Alken.

This book is completely different from the large folio edition of 'National Sports' by the same artist, and none of the plates are similar.

THE ADVENTURES OF A POST CAPTAIN. By A Naval Officer. With 24 Coloured Plates by Mr. Williams.

GAMONIA: or, the Art of Preserving Game; and an Improved Method of making Plantations and Covers, explained and illustrated by Lawrence Rawstorne, Esq. With 15 Coloured Plates by T. Rawlins.

AN ACADEMY FOR GROWN HORSEMEN: Containing the completest Instructions for Walking, Trotting, Cantering, Galloping, Stumbling, and Tumbling. Illustrated with 27 Coloured Plates, and adorned with a Portrait of the Author. By Geoffrey Gambado, Esq.

REAL LIFE IN IRELAND, or, the Day and Night Scenes of Brian Boru, Esq., and his Elegant Friend, Sir Shawn O'Dogherty. By a Real Paddy. With 19 Coloured Plates by Heath, Marks, etc.

THE ADVENTURES OF JOHNNY NEWCOME IN THE NAVY. By Alfred Burton. With 16 Coloured Plates by T. Rowlandson.

THE OLD ENGLISH SQUIRE: A Poem. By John Careless, Esq. With 20 Coloured Plates after the style of T. Rowlandson.

*THE ENGLISH SPY. By Bernard Blackmantle. With 72 Coloured Plates by R. Cruikshank, and many Illustrations on wood. *Two Volumes.*

PLAIN BOOKS

THE GRAVE: A Poem. By Robert Blair. Illustrated by 12 Etchings executed by Louis Schiavonetti from the original Inventions of William Blake. With an Engraved Title Page and a Portrait of Blake by T. Phillips, R.A.

The illustrations are reproduced in photogravure.

ILLUSTRATIONS OF THE BOOK OF JOB. Invented and engraved by William Blake. These famous Illustrations—21 in number—are reproduced in photogravure.

ÆSOP'S FABLES. With 380 Woodcuts by Thomas Bewick.

[*Continued.*

MESSRS. METHUEN'S CATALOGUE

ILLUSTRATED POCKET LIBRARY OF PLAIN AND COLOURED BOOKS—*continued*.

WINDSOR CASTLE. By W. Harrison Ainsworth. With 22 Plates and 87 Woodcuts in the Text by George Cruikshank.

THE TOWER OF LONDON. By W. Harrison Ainsworth. With 40 Plates and 58 Woodcuts in the Text by George Cruikshank.

FRANK FAIRLEGH. By F. E. Smedley. With 30 Plates by George Cruikshank.

HANDY ANDY. By Samuel Lover. With 24 Illustrations by the Author.

THE COMPLEAT ANGLER. By Izaak Walton and Charles Cotton. With 14 Plates and 77 Woodcuts in the Text. This volume is reproduced from the beautiful edition of John Major of 1824.

THE PICKWICK PAPERS. By Charles Dickens. With the 43 Illustrations by Seymour and Phiz, the two Buss Plates, and the 32 Contemporary Onwhyn Plates.

Junior Examination Series

Edited by A. M. M. STEDMAN, M.A. *Fcap. 8vo.* 1s.

This series is intended to lead up to the School Examination Series, and is intended for the use of teachers and students, to supply material for the former and practice for the latter. The papers are carefully graduated, cover the whole of the subject usually taught, and are intended to form part of the ordinary class work. They may be used *vivâ voce* or as a written examination.

JUNIOR FRENCH EXAMINATION PAPERS. By F. Jacob, M.A. *Second Edition.*
JUNIOR LATIN EXAMINATION PAPERS. By C. G. Botting, B.A. *Fourth Edition.*
JUNIOR ENGLISH EXAMINATION PAPERS. By W. Williamson, B.A.
JUNIOR ARITHMETIC EXAMINATION PAPERS. By W. S. Beard. *Second Edition.*
JUNIOR ALGEBRA EXAMINATION PAPERS. By S. W. Finn, M.A.
JUNIOR GREEK EXAMINATION PAPERS. By T. C. Weatherhead, M.A.
JUNIOR GENERAL INFORMATION EXAMINATION PAPERS. By W. S. Beard.
A KEY TO THE ABOVE. *Crown 8vo.* 3s. 6d. *net.*
JUNIOR GEOGRAPHY EXAMINATION PAPERS. By W. G. Baker, M.A.
JUNIOR GERMAN EXAMINATION PAPERS. By A. Voegelin, M.A.

Junior School-Books

Edited by O. D. INSKIP, LL.D., and W. WILLIAMSON, B.A.

A series of elementary books for pupils in lower forms, simply written by teachers of experience.

A CLASS-BOOK OF DICTATION PASSAGES. By W. Williamson, B.A. *Eleventh Edition. Cr. 8vo.* 1s. 6d.
THE GOSPEL ACCORDING TO ST. MATTHEW. Edited by E. Wilton South, M.A. With Three Maps. *Cr. 8vo.* 1s. 6d.
THE GOSPEL ACCORDING TO ST. MARK. Edited by A. E. Rubie, D.D. With Three Maps. *Cr. 8vo.* 1s. 6d.
A JUNIOR ENGLISH GRAMMAR. By W. Williamson, B.A. With numerous passages for parsing and analysis, and a chapter on Essay Writing. *Third Edition. Cr. 8vo.* 2s.
A JUNIOR CHEMISTRY. By E. A. Tyler, B.A., F.C.S. With 78 Illustrations. *Second Edition. Cr. 8vo.* 2s. 6d.
THE ACTS OF THE APOSTLES. Edited by A. E. Rubie, D.D. *Cr. 8vo.* 2s.
A JUNIOR FRENCH GRAMMAR. By L. A. Sornet and M. J. Acatos. *Cr. 8vo.* 2s.
ELEMENTARY EXPERIMENTAL SCIENCE. PHYSICS by W. T. Clough, A.R.C.S. CHEMISTRY by A. E. Dunstan, B.Sc. With 2 Plates and 154 Diagrams. *Third Edition. Cr. 8vo.* 2s. 6d.
A JUNIOR GEOMETRY. By Noel S. Lydon. With 276 Diagrams. *Second Edition. Cr. 8vo.* 2s.
A JUNIOR MAGNETISM AND ELECTRICITY. By W. T. Clough. Illustrated. *Cr. 8vo.* 2s. 6d.
ELEMENTARY EXPERIMENTAL CHEMISTRY. By A. E. Dunstan, B.Sc. With 4 Plates and 109 Diagrams. *Cr. 8vo.* 2s.
A JUNIOR FRENCH PROSE COMPOSITION. By R. R. N. Baron, M.A. *Cr. 8vo.* 2s.
THE GOSPEL ACCORDING TO ST. LUKE. With an Introduction and Notes by William Williamson, B.A. With Three Maps. *Cr. 8vo.* 2s.

General Literature

Leaders of Religion

Edited by H. C. BEECHING, M.A., Canon of Westminster. *With Portraits.*
Cr. 8vo. 2s. net.

A series of short biographies of the most prominent leaders of religious life and thought of all ages and countries.

CARDINAL NEWMAN. By R. H. Hutton.
JOHN WESLEY. By J. H. Overton, M.A.
BISHOP WILBERFORCE. By G. W. Daniell, M.A.
CARDINAL MANNING. By A. W. Hutton, M.A.
CHARLES SIMEON. By H. C. G. Moule, D.D.
JOHN KEBLE. By Walter Lock, D.D.
THOMAS CHALMERS. By Mrs. Oliphant.
LANCELOT ANDREWES. By R. L. Ottley, D.D. *Second Edition.*
AUGUSTINE OF CANTERBURY. By E. L. Cutts, D.D.
WILLIAM LAUD. By W. H. Hutton, M.A. *Third Edition.*
JOHN KNOX. By F. MacCunn. *Second Edition.*
JOHN HOWE. By R. F. Horton, D.D.
BISHOP KEN. By F. A. Clarke, M.A.
GEORGE FOX, THE QUAKER. By T. Hodgkin, D.C.L. *Third Edition.*
JOHN DONNE. By Augustus Jessopp, D.D.
THOMAS CRANMER. By A. J. Mason, D.D.
BISHOP LATIMER. By R. M. Carlyle and A. J. Carlyle, M.A.
BISHOP BUTLER. By W. A. Spooner, M.A.

Little Blue Books, The

General Editor, E. V. LUCAS.

Illustrated. Demy 16mo. 2s. 6d.

A series of books for children. The aim of the editor is to get entertaining or exciting stories about normal children, the moral of which is implied rather than expressed.

1. THE CASTAWAYS OF MEADOWBANK. By Thomas Cobb.
2. THE BEECHNUT BOOK. By Jacob Abbott. Edited by E. V. Lucas.
3. THE AIR GUN. By T. Hilbert.
4. A SCHOOL YEAR. By Netta Syrett.
5. THE PEELES AT THE CAPITAL. By Roger Ashton.
6. THE TREASURE OF PRINCEGATE PRIORY. By T. Cobb.
7. MRS. BARBERRY'S GENERAL SHOP. By Roger Ashton.
8. A BOOK OF BAD CHILDREN. By W. T. Webb.
9. THE LOST BALL. By Thomas Cobb.

Little Books on Art

With many Illustrations. Demy 16mo. 2s. 6d. net.

A series of monographs in miniature, containing the complete outline of the subject under treatment and rejecting minute details. These books are produced with the greatest care. Each volume consists of about 200 pages, and contains from 30 to 40 illustrations, including a frontispiece in photogravure.

GREEK ART. H. B. Walters. *Second Edition.*
BOOKPLATES. E. Almack.
REYNOLDS. J. Sime. *Second Edition.*
ROMNEY. George Paston.
WATTS. R. E. D. Sketchley.
LEIGHTON. Alice Corkran.
VELASQUEZ. Wilfrid Wilberforce and A. R. Gilbert.
GREUZE AND BOUCHER. Eliza F. Pollard.
VANDYCK. M. G. Smallwood.
TURNER. Frances Tyrell-Gill.
DÜRER. Jessie Allen.
HOPPNER. H. P. K. Skipton.
HOLBEIN. Mrs. G. Fortescue.
BURNE-JONES. Fortunée de Lisle. *Second Edition.*
REMBRANDT. Mrs. E. A. Sharp
COROT. Alice Pollard and Ethel Birnstingl.
RAPHAEL. A. R. Dryhurst.
MILLET. Netta Peacock.
ILLUMINATED MSS. J. W. Bradley.
CHRIST IN ART. Mrs. Henry Jenner.
JEWELLERY. Cyril Davenport.
CLAUDE. Edward Dillon.
THE ARTS OF JAPAN. Edward Dillon.

MESSRS. METHUEN'S CATALOGUE

Little Galleries, The
Demy 16mo. 2s. 6d. net.

A series of little books containing examples of the best work of the great painters. Each volume contains 20 plates in photogravure, together with a short outline of the life and work of the master to whom the book is devoted.

A LITTLE GALLERY OF REYNOLDS.
A LITTLE GALLERY OF ROMNEY.
A LITTLE GALLERY OF HOPPNER.
A LITTLE GALLERY OF MILLAIS.
A LITTLE GALLERY OF ENGLISH POETS.

Little Guides, The
Small Pott 8vo, cloth, 2s. 6d. net.; leather, 3s. 6d. net.

OXFORD AND ITS COLLEGES. By J. Wells, M.A. Illustrated by E. H. New. *Seventh Edition.*
CAMBRIDGE AND ITS COLLEGES. By A. Hamilton Thompson. Illustrated by E. H. New. *Second Edition.*
THE MALVERN COUNTRY. By B. C. A. Windle, D.Sc., F.R.S. Illustrated by E. H. New.
SHAKESPEARE'S COUNTRY. By B. C. A. Windle, D.Sc., F.R.S. Illustrated by E. H. New. *Second Edition.*
SUSSEX. By F. G. Brabant, M.A. Illustrated by E. H. New. *Second Edition.*
WESTMINSTER ABBEY. By G. E. Troutbeck. Illustrated by F. D. Bedford.
NORFOLK. By W. A. Dutt. Illustrated by B. C. Boulter.
CORNWALL. By A. L. Salmon. Illustrated by B. C. Boulter.
BRITTANY. By S. Baring-Gould. Illustrated by J. Wylie.
HERTFORDSHIRE. By H. W. Tompkins, F.R.H.S. Illustrated by E. H. New.
THE ENGLISH LAKES. By F. G. Brabant, M.A. Illustrated by E. H. New.
KENT. By G. Clinch. Illustrated by F. D. Bedford.

ROME By C. G. Ellaby. Illustrated by B. C. Boulter.
THE ISLE OF WIGHT. By G. Clinch. Illustrated by F. D. Bedford.
SURREY. By F. A. H. Lambert. Illustrated by E. H. New.
BUCKINGHAMSHIRE. By E. S. Roscoe. Illustrated by F. D. Bedford.
SUFFOLK. By W. A. Dutt. Illustrated by J. Wylie.
DERBYSHIRE. By J. C. Cox, LL.D., F.S.A. Illustrated by J. C. Wall.
THE NORTH RIDING OF YORKSHIRE. By J. E. Morris. Illustrated by R. J. S. Bertram.
HAMPSHIRE. By J. C. Cox. Illustrated by M. E. Purser.
SICILY. By F. H. Jackson. With many Illustrations by the Author.
DORSET. By Frank R. Heath. Illustrated.
CHESHIRE. By W. M. Gallichan. Illustrated by Elizabeth Hartley.
NORTHAMPTONSHIRE. By Wakeling Dry. Illustrated.
THE EAST RIDING OF YORKSHIRE. By J. E. Morris. Illustrated.
OXFORDSHIRE. By F. G. Brabant. Illustrated by E. H. New.
ST. PAUL'S CATHEDRAL. By George Clinch. Illustrated by Beatrice Alcock.

Little Library, The
With Introductions, Notes, and Photogravure Frontispieces.
Small Pott 8vo. Each Volume, cloth, 1s. 6d. net; leather, 2s. 6d. net.

A series of small books under the above title, containing some of the famous works in English and other literatures, in the domains of fiction, poetry, and belles lettres. The series also contains volumes of selections in prose and verse. The books are edited with the most scholarly care. Each one contains an introduction which gives (1) a short biography of the author; (2) a critical estimate of the book. Where they are necessary, short notes are added at the foot of the page.
Each volume has a photogravure frontispiece, and the books are produced with great care.

Anon. ENGLISH LYRICS, A LITTLE BOOK OF.
Austen (Jane). PRIDE AND PREJUDICE. Edited by E. V. LUCAS. *Two Volumes.*

NORTHANGER ABBEY. Edited by E. V. LUCAS.
Bacon (Francis). THE ESSAYS OF LORD BACON. Edited by EDWARD WRIGHT.

General Literature 29

Barham (R. H.). THE INGOLDSBY LEGENDS. Edited by J. B. ATLAY. *Two Volumes.*
Barnett (Mrs. P. A.). A LITTLE BOOK OF ENGLISH PROSE.
Beckford (William). THE HISTORY OF THE CALIPH VATHEK. Edited by E. DENISON ROSS.
Blake (William). SELECTIONS FROM WILLIAM BLAKE. Edited by M. PERUGINI.
Borrow (George). LAVENGRO. Edited by F. HINDES GROOME. *Two Volumes.*
THE ROMANY RYE. Edited by JOHN SAMPSON.
Browning (Robert). SELECTIONS FROM THE EARLY POEMS OF ROBERT BROWNING. Edited by W. HALL GRIFFIN, M.A.
Canning (George). SELECTIONS FROM THE ANTI-JACOBIN: with GEORGE CANNING'S additional Poems. Edited by LLOYD SANDERS.
Cowley (Abraham). THE ESSAYS OF ABRAHAM COWLEY. Edited by H. C. MINCHIN.
Crabbe (George). SELECTIONS FROM GEORGE CRABBE. Edited by A. C. DEANE.
Craik (Mrs.). JOHN HALIFAX, GENTLEMAN. Edited by ANNE MATHESON. *Two Volumes.*
Crashaw (Richard). THE ENGLISH POEMS OF RICHARD CRASHAW. Edited by EDWARD HUTTON.
Dante (Alighieri). THE INFERNO OF DANTE. Translated by H. F. CARY. Edited by PAGET TOYNBEE, M.A., D.Litt.
THE PURGATORIO OF DANTE. Translated by H. F. CARY. Edited by PAGET TOYNBEE, M.A., D.Litt.
THE PARADISO OF DANTE. Translated by H. F. CARY. Edited by PAGET TOYNBEE, M.A., D.Litt.
Darley (George). SELECTIONS FROM THE POEMS OF GEORGE DARLEY. Edited by R. A. STREATFEILD.
Deane (A. C.). A LITTLE BOOK OF LIGHT VERSE.
Dickens (Charles). CHRISTMAS BOOKS. *Two Volumes.*
Ferrier (Susan). MARRIAGE. Edited by A. GOODRICH - FREER and LORD IDDESLEIGH. *Two Volumes.*
THE INHERITANCE. *Two Volumes.*
Gaskell (Mrs.). CRANFORD. Edited by E. V. LUCAS. *Second Edition.*
Hawthorne (Nathaniel). THE SCARLET LETTER. Edited by PERCY DEARMER.
Henderson (T. F.). A LITTLE BOOK OF SCOTTISH VERSE.
Keats (John). POEMS. With an Introduction by L. BINYON, and Notes by J. MASEFIELD.
Kinglake (A. W.). EOTHEN. With an Introduction and Notes. *Second Edition.*
Lamb (Charles). ELIA, AND THE LAST ESSAYS OF ELIA. Edited by E. V. LUCAS.
Locker (F.). LONDON LYRICS. Edited by A. D. GODLEY, M.A. A reprint of the First Edition.
Longfellow (H. W.). SELECTIONS FROM LONGFELLOW. Edited by L. M. FAITHFULL.
Marvell (Andrew). THE POEMS OF ANDREW MARVELL. Edited by E. WRIGHT.
Milton (John). THE MINOR POEMS OF JOHN MILTON. Edited by H. C. BEECHING, M.A., Canon of Westminster.
Moir (D. M.). MANSIE WAUCH. Edited by T. F. HENDERSON.
Nichols (J. B. B.). A LITTLE BOOK OF ENGLISH SONNETS.
Rochefoucauld (La). THE MAXIMS OF LA ROCHEFOUCAULD. Translated by Dean STANHOPE. Edited by G. H. POWELL.
Smith (Horace and James). REJECTED ADDRESSES. Edited by A. D. GODLEY, M.A.
Sterne (Laurence). A SENTIMENTAL JOURNEY. Edited by H. W. PAUL.
Tennyson (Alfred, Lord). THE EARLY POEMS OF ALFRED, LORD TENNYSON. Edited by J. CHURTON COLLINS, M.A.
IN MEMORIAM. Edited by H. C. BEECHING, M.A.
THE PRINCESS. Edited by ELIZABETH WORDSWORTH.
MAUD. Edited by ELIZABETH WORDSWORTH.
Thackeray (W. M.). VANITY FAIR. Edited by S. GWYNN. *Three Volumes.*
PENDENNIS. Edited by S. GWYNN. *Three Volumes.*
ESMOND. Edited by S. GWYNN.
CHRISTMAS BOOKS. Edited by S. GWYNN.
Vaughan (Henry). THE POEMS OF HENRY VAUGHAN. Edited by EDWARD HUTTON.
Walton (Izaak). THE COMPLEAT ANGLER. Edited by J. BUCHAN.
Waterhouse (Mrs. Alfred). A LITTLE BOOK OF LIFE AND DEATH. Edited by. *Ninth Edition.*
Wordsworth (W.). SELECTIONS FROM WORDSWORTH. Edited by NOWELL C. SMITH.
Wordsworth (W.) and Coleridge (S. T.). LYRICAL BALLADS. Edited by GEORGE SAMPSON.

Miniature Library

Reprints in miniature of a few interesting books which have qualities of humanity, devotion, or literary genius.

EUPHRANOR: A Dialogue on Youth. By Edward FitzGerald. From the edition published by W. Pickering in 1851. *Demy* 32*mo. Leather*, 2s. *net.*

POLONIUS: or Wise Saws and Modern Instances. By Edward FitzGerald. From the edition published by W. Pickering in 1852. *Demy* 32*mo. Leather*, 2s. *net.*

THE RUBÁIYÁT OF OMAR KHAYYÁM. By Edward FitzGerald. From the 1st edition of 1859, *Third Edition. Leather*, 1s. *net.*

THE LIFE OF EDWARD, LORD HERBERT OF CHERBURY. Written by himself. From the edition printed at Strawberry Hill in the year 1764. *Medium* 32*mo. Leather*, 2s. *net.*

THE VISIONS OF DOM FRANCISCO QUEVEDO VILLEGAS, Knight of the Order of St. James. Made English by R. L. From the edition printed for H. Herringman, 1668. *Leathe* . 2s. *net.*

POEMS. By Dora Greenwell. From the edition of 1848. *Leather*, 2s. *net.*

Oxford Biographies

Fcap. 8*vo. Each volume, cloth,* 2s. 6d. *net* ; *leather,* 3s. 6d. *net.*

These books are written by scholars of repute, who combine knowledge and literary skill with the power of popular presentation. They are illustrated from authentic material.

DANTE ALIGHIERI. By Paget Toynbee, M.A., D.Litt. With 12 Illustrations. *Second Edition.*
SAVONAROLA. By E. L. S. Horsburgh, M.A. With 12 Illustrations. *Second Edition.*
JOHN HOWARD. By E. C. S. Gibson, D.D., Bishop of Gloucester. With 12 Illustrations.
TENNYSON. By A. C. BENSON, M.A. With 9 Illustrations.
WALTER RALEIGH. By I. A. Taylor. With 12 Illustrations.
ERASMUS. By E. F. H. Capey. With 12 Illustrations.
THE YOUNG PRETENDER. By C. S. Terry. With 12 Illustrations.

ROBERT BURNS. By T. F. Henderson. With 12 Illustrations.
CHATHAM. By A. S. M'Dowall. With 12 Illustrations.
ST. FRANCIS OF ASSISI. By Anna M. Stoddart. With 16 Illustrations.
CANNING. By W. Alison Phillips. With 12 Illustrations.
BEACONSFIELD. By Walter Sichel. With 12 Illustrations.
GOETHE. By H. G. Atkins. With 12 Illustrations.
FENELON. By Viscount St. Cyres. With 12 Illustrations.

School Examination Series

Edited by A. M. M. STEDMAN, M.A. *Cr.* 8*vo.* 2s. 6d.

FRENCH EXAMINATION PAPERS. By A. M. M. Stedman, M.A. *Fourteenth Edition.*
A KEY, issued to Tutors and Private Students only to be had on application to the Publishers. *Fifth Edition. Crown* 8*vo.* 6s. *net.*
LATIN EXAMINATION PAPERS. By A. M. M. Stedman, M.A. *Thirteenth Edition.*
KEY (*Fourth Edition*) issued as above. 6s. *net.*
GREEK EXAMINATION PAPERS. By A. M. M. Stedman, M.A. *Eighth Edition.*
KEY (*Third Edition*) issued as above. 6s. *net.*
GERMAN EXAMINATION PAPERS. By R. J. Morich. *Sixth Edition.*

KEY (*Third Edition*) issued as above. 6s. *net.*
HISTORY AND GEOGRAPHY EXAMINATION PAPERS. By C. H. Spence, M.A. *Second Edition.*
PHYSICS EXAMINATION PAPERS. By R. E. Steel, M.A., F.C.S.
GENERAL KNOWLEDGE EXAMINATION PAPERS. By A. M. M. Stedman, M.A. *Fifth Edition.*
KEY (*Third Edition*) issued as above. 7s. *net.*
EXAMINATION PAPERS IN ENGLISH HISTORY. By J. Tait Plowden-Wardlaw, B.A.

GENERAL LITERATURE 31

Science, Textbooks of
Edited by G. F. GOODCHILD, B.A., B.Sc., and G. R. MILLS, M.A.

PRACTICAL MECHANICS. By Sidney H. Wells. *Third Edition. Cr. 8vo.* 3s. 6d.
PRACTICAL PHYSICS. By H. Stroud, D.Sc., M.A. *Cr. 8vo.* 3s. 6d.
PRACTICAL CHEMISTRY. Part I. By W. French, M.A. *Cr. 8vo. Fourth Edition.* 1s. 6d. Part II. By W. French, M.A., and T. H. Boardman, M.A. *Cr. 8vo.* 1s. 6d.
TECHNICAL ARITHMETIC AND GEOMETRY. By C. T. Millis, M.I.M.E. *Cr. 8vo.* 3s. 6d.
EXAMPLES IN PHYSICS. By C. E. Jackson, B.A. *Cr. 8vo.* 2s. 6d.
*ELEMENTARY ORGANIC CHEMISTRY. By A. E. Dunstan, B.Sc. Illustrated. *Cr. 8vo.*

Social Questions of To-day
Edited by H. DE B. GIBBINS, Litt.D., M.A. *Crown 8vo.* 2s. 6d.

A series of volumes upon those topics of social, economic, and industrial interest that are foremost in the public mind.

TRADE UNIONISM—NEW AND OLD. By G. Howell. *Third Edition.*
THE COMMERCE OF NATIONS. By C. F. Bastable, M.A. *Fourth Edition.*
THE ALIEN INVASION. By W. H. Wilkins, B.A.
THE RURAL EXODUS. By P. Anderson Graham.
LAND NATIONALIZATION. By Harold Cox, B.A. *Second Edition.*
A SHORTER WORKING DAY. By H. de B. Gibbins and R. A. Hadfield.
BACK TO THE LAND. An Inquiry into Rural Depopulation. By H. E. Moore.
TRUSTS, POOLS, AND CORNERS. By J. Stephen Jeans.
THE FACTORY SYSTEM. By R. W. Cooke Taylor.
WOMEN'S WORK. By Lady Dilke, Miss Bulley, and Miss Whitley.
SOCIALISM AND MODERN THOUGHT. By M. Kauffmann.
THE PROBLEM OF THE UNEMPLOYED. By J. A. Hobson, M.A.
LIFE IN WEST LONDON By Arthur Sherwell, M.A. *Third Edition.*
RAILWAY NATIONALIZATION. By Clement Edwards.
UNIVERSITY AND SOCIAL SETTLEMENTS. By W. Reason, M.A.

Technology, Textbooks of
Edited by G. F. GOODCHILD, B.A., B.Sc., and G. R. MILLS, M.A.
Fully Illustrated.

HOW TO MAKE A DRESS. By J. A. E. Wood. *Third Edition. Cr. 8vo.* 1s. 6d.
CARPENTRY AND JOINERY. By F. C. Webber. *Fifth Edition. Cr. 8vo.* 3s. 6d.
MILLINERY, THEORETICAL AND PRACTICAL. By Clare Hill. *Third Edition. Cr. 8vo.* 2s.
AN INTRODUCTION TO THE STUDY OF TEXTILE DESIGN. By Aldred F. Barker. *Demy 8vo.* 7s. 6d.
BUILDERS' QUANTITIES. By H. C. Grubb. *Cr. 8vo.* 4s. 6d.
RÉPOUSSÉ METAL WORK. By A. C. Horth. *Cr. 8vo.* 2s. 6d.

Theology, Handbooks of
Edited by R. L. OTTLEY, D.D., Professor of Pastoral Theology at Oxford, and Canon of Christ Church, Oxford.

The series is intended, in part, to furnish the clergy and teachers or students of Theology with trustworthy Textbooks, adequately representing the present position of the questions dealt with; in part, to make accessible to the reading public an accurate and concise statement of facts and principles in all questions bearing on Theology and Religion.

THE XXXIX. ARTICLES OF THE CHURCH OF ENGLAND. Edited by E. C. S. Gibson, D.D. *Fifth and Cheaper Edition in one Volume. Demy 8vo.* 12s. 6d.
AN INTRODUCTION TO THE HISTORY OF RELIGION. By F. B. Jevons, M.A., Litt.D. *Third Edition. Demy 8vo.* 10s. 6d.
THE DOCTRINE OF THE INCARNATION. By R. L. Ottley, D.D. *Second and Cheaper Edition. Demy 8vo.* 12s. 6d.
AN INTRODUCTION TO THE HISTORY OF THE CREEDS. By A. E. Burn, D.D. *Demy 8vo.* 10s. 6d.
THE PHILOSOPHY OF RELIGION IN ENGLAND AND AMERICA. By Alfred Caldecott, D.D. *Demy 8vo.* 10s. 6d.
A HISTORY OF EARLY CHRISTIAN DOCTRINE. By J. F. Bethune Baker, M.A. *Demy 8vo.* 10s. 6d.

Messrs. Methuen's Catalogue

Westminster Commentaries, The

General Editor, WALTER LOCK, D.D., Warden of Keble College, Dean Ireland's Professor of Exegesis in the University of Oxford.

The object of each commentary is primarily exegetical, to interpret the author's meaning to the present generation. The editors will not deal, except very subordinately, with questions of textual criticism or philology; but, taking the English text in the Revised Version as their basis, they will try to combine a hearty acceptance of critical principles with loyalty to the Catholic Faith.

THE BOOK OF GENESIS. Edited with Introduction and Notes by S. R. Driver, D.D. *Fifth Edition. Demy 8vo.* 10s. 6d.
THE BOOK OF JOB. Edited by E. C. S. Gibson, D.D. *Second Edition. Demy 8vo.* 6s.
THE ACTS OF THE APOSTLES. Edited by R. B. Rackham, M.A. *Demy 8vo. Third and Cheaper Edition.* 10s. 6d.

THE FIRST EPISTLE OF PAUL THE APOSTLE TO THE CORINTHIANS. Edited by H. L. Goudge, M.A. *Demy 8vo.* 6s.

THE EPISTLE OF ST. JAMES. Edited with Introduction and Notes by R. J. Knowling, M.A. *Demy 8vo.* 6s.

PART II.—FICTION

Albanesi (E. Maria). SUSANNAH AND ONE OTHER. *Fourth Edition. Cr. 8vo.* 6s.
THE BLUNDER OF AN INNOCENT. *Second Edition. Cr. 8vo.* 6s.
CAPRICIOUS CAROLINE. *Second Edition. Cr. 8vo.* 6s.
LOVE AND LOUISA. *Second Edition. Cr. 8vo.* 6s.
PETER, A PARASITE. *Cr. 8vo.* 6s.
THE BROWN EYES OF MARY. *Third Edition. Cr. 8vo.* 6s.
Anstey (F.). Author of 'Vice Versâ.' A BAYARD FROM BENGAL. Illustrated by BERNARD PARTRIDGE. *Third Edition. Cr. 8vo.* 3s. 6d.
Bacheller (Irving), Author of 'Eben Holden.' DARREL OF THE BLESSED ISLES. *Third Edition. Cr. 8vo.* 6s.
Bagot (Richard). A ROMAN MYSTERY. *Third Edition. Cr. 8vo.* 6s.
THE PASSPORT. *Fourth Ed. Cr. 8vo.* 6s.
Baring-Gould (S.). ARMINELL. *Fifth Edition. Cr. 8vo.* 6s.
URITH. *Fifth Edition. Cr. 8vo.* 6s.
IN THE ROAR OF THE SEA. *Seventh Edition. Cr. 8vo.* 6s.
CHEAP JACK ZITA. *Fourth Edition. Cr. 8vo.* 6s.
MARGERY OF QUETHER. *Third Edition. Cr. 8vo.* 6s.
THE QUEEN OF LOVE. *Fifth Edition. Cr. 8vo.* 6s.
JACQUETTA. *Third Edition. Cr. 8vo.* 6s.
KITTY ALONE. *Fifth Edition. Cr. 8vo.* 6s.
NOÉMI. Illustrated. *Fourth Edition. Cr. 8vo.* 6s.
THE BROOM-SQUIRE. Illustrated. *Fifth Edition. Cr. 8vo.* 6s.

DARTMOOR IDYLLS. *Cr. 8vo.* 6s.
THE PENNYCOMEQUICKS. *Third Edition. Cr. 8vo.* 6s.
GUAVAS THE TINNER. Illustrated. *Second Edition. Cr. 8vo.* 6s.
BLADYS. Illustrated. *Second Edition. Cr. 8vo.* 6s.
PABO THE PRIEST. *Cr. 8vo.* 6s.
WINEFRED. Illustrated. *Second Edition. Cr. 8vo.* 6s.
ROYAL GEORGIE. Illustrated. *Cr. 8vo.* 6s.
MISS QUILLET. Illustrated. *Cr. 8vo.* 6s.
CHRIS OF ALL SORTS. *Cr. 8vo.* 6s.
IN DEWISLAND. *Second Edition. Cr. 8vo.* 6s.
LITTLE TU'PENNY. *A New Edition.* 6d.
See also Strand Novels and Books for Boys and Girls.
Barlow (Jane). THE LAND OF THE SHAMROCK. *Cr. 8vo.* 6s. See also Strand Novels.
Barr (Robert). IN THE MIDST OF ALARMS. *Third Edition. Cr. 8vo.* 6s.
THE MUTABLE MANY. *Third Edition. Cr. 8vo.* 6s.
THE COUNTESS TEKLA. *Third Edition. Cr. 8vo.* 6s.
THE LADY ELECTRA. *Second Edition. Cr. 8vo.* 6s.
THE TEMPESTUOUS PETTICOAT. Illustrated. *Third Edition. Cr. 8vo.* 6s.
See also Strand Novels and S. Crane.
Begbie (Harold). THE ADVENTURES OF SIR JOHN SPARROW. *Cr. 8vo.* 6s.
Belloc (Hilaire). EMMANUEL BURDEN, MERCHANT. With 36 Illustrations by G. K. CHESTERTON. *Second Edition. Cr. 8vo.* 6s.

FICTION 33

Benson (E. F.) DODO. *Fourth Edition.* *Cr. 8vo. 6s.* See also Strand Novels.
Benson (Margaret). SUBJECT TO VANITY. *Cr. 8vo. 3s. 6d.*
Bourne (Harold C.). See V. Langbridge.
Burton (J. Bloundelle). THE YEAR ONE: A Page of the French Revolution. Illustrated. *Cr. 8vo. 6s.*
THE FATE OF VALSEC. *Cr. 8vo. 6s.*
A BRANDED NAME. *Cr. 8vo. 6s.* See also Strand Novels.
Capes (Bernard), Author of 'The Lake of Wine.' THE EXTRAORDINARY CONFESSIONS OF DIANA PLEASE. *Third Edition. Cr. 8vo. 6s.*
A JAY OF ITALY. *Fourth Ed. Cr. 8vo. 6s.*
LOAVES AND FISHES. *Second Edition. Cr. 8vo. 6s.*
Chesney (Weatherby). THE TRAGEDY OF THE GREAT EMERALD. *Cr. 8vo. 6s.*
THE MYSTERY OF A BUNGALOW. *Second Edition. Cr. 8vo. 6s.* See also Strand Novels.
Clifford (Hugh). A FREE LANCE OF TO-DAY. *Cr. 8vo. 6s.*
Clifford (Mrs. W. K.). See Strand Novels and Books for Boys and Girls.
Cobb (Thomas). A CHANGE OF FACE. *Cr. 8vo. 6s.*
Corelli (Marie). A ROMANCE OF TWO WORLDS. *Twenty-Sixth Edition. Cr. 8vo. 6s.*
VENDETTA. *Twenty-Third Edition. Cr. 8vo. 6s.*
THELMA. *Thirty-Fourth Edition. Cr. 8vo. 6s.*
ARDATH: THE STORY OF A DEAD SELF. *Sixteenth Edition. Cr. 8vo. 6s.*
THE SOUL OF LILITH. *Thirteenth Edition. Cr. 8vo. 6s.*
WORMWOOD. *Fourteenth Ed. Cr. 8vo. 6s.*
BARABBAS: A DREAM OF THE WORLD'S TRAGEDY. *Forty-first Edition. Cr. 8vo. 6s.*
THE SORROWS OF SATAN. *Fiftieth Edition. Cr. 8vo. 6s.*
THE MASTER CHRISTIAN. *167th Thousand. Cr. 8vo. 6s.*
TEMPORAL POWER: A STUDY IN SUPREMACY. *150th Thousand. Cr. 8vo. 6s.*
GOD'S GOOD MAN: A SIMPLE LOVE STORY. *137th Thousand. Cr. 8vo. 6s.*
THE MIGHTY ATOM. *A New Edition. Cr. 8vo. 6s.*
BOY. *A New Edition. Cr. 8vo. 6s.*
JANE. *A New Edition. Cr. 8vo. 6s.*
Crockett (S. R.), Author of 'The Raiders,' etc. LOCHINVAR. Illustrated. *Third Edition. Cr. 8vo. 6s.*
THE STANDARD BEARER. *Cr. 8vo. 6s.*
Croker (B. M.). THE OLD CANTONMENT. *Cr. 8vo. 6s.*
JOHANNA. *Second Edition. Cr. 8vo. 6s.*

THE HAPPY VALLEY. *Third Edition. Cr. 8vo. 6s.*
A NINE DAYS' WONDER. *Third Edition. Cr. 8vo. 6s.*
PEGGY OF THE BARTONS. *Sixth Edition. Cr. 8vo. 5s.*
ANGEL. *Fourth Edition. Cr. 8vo. 6s.*
A STATE SECRET. *Third Edition. Cr. 8vo. 3s. 6d.*
Dawson (Francis W.). THE SCAR. *Second Edition. Cr. 8vo. 6s.*
Dawson (A. J.). DANIEL WHYTE. *Cr. 8vo. 3s. 6d.*
Doyle (A. Conan), Author of 'Sherlock Holmes,' 'The White Company,' etc. ROUND THE RED LAMP. *Ninth Edition. Cr. 8vo. 6s.*
Duncan (Sara Jeannette) (Mrs. Everard Cotes). THOSE DELIGHTFUL AMERICANS. Illustrated. *Third Edition. Cr. 8vo. 6s.* See also Strand Novels.
Findlater (J. H.). THE GREEN GRAVES OF BALGOWRIE. *Fifth Edition. Cr. 8vo. 6s.* See also Strand Novels.
Findlater (Mary). A NARROW WAY. *Third Edition. Cr. 8vo.. 6s.*
THE ROSE OF JOY. *Third Edition. Cr. 8vo. 6s.* See also Strand Novels.
Fitzpatrick (K.) THE WEANS AT ROWALLAN. Illustrated. *Second Edition. Cr. 8vo. 6s.*
Fitzstephen (Gerald). MORE KIN THAN KIND. *Cr. 8vo. 6s.*
Fletcher (J. S.). LUCIAN THE DREAMER. *Cr. 8vo. 6s.*
Fraser (Mrs. Hugh), Author of 'The Stolen Emperor.' THE SLAKING OF THE SWORD. *Cr. 8vo. 5s.*
THE SHADOW OF THE LORD. *Cr. 8vo. 6s.*
Fuller-Maitland (Mrs.), Author of 'The Day Book of Bethia Hardacre.' BLANCHE ESMEAD. *Second Edition. Cr. 8vo. 6s.*
Gerard (Dorothea), Author of 'Lady Baby.' THE CONQUEST OF LONDON. *Second Edition. Cr. 8vo. 6s.*
HOLY MATRIMONY. *Second Edition. Cr. 8vo. 6s.*
MADE OF MONEY. *Cr. 8vo. 6s.*
THE BRIDGE OF LIFE. *Cr. 8vo. 6s.*
THE IMPROBABLE IDYL. *Third Edition. Cr. 8vo. 6s.*
Gerard (Emily). THE HERONS' TOWER. *Cr. 8vo. 6s.*
Gissing (George), Author of 'Demos,' 'In the Year of Jubilee,' etc. THE TOWN TRAVELLER. *Second Ed. Cr. 8vo. 6s.*
THE CROWN OF LIFE. *Cr. 8vo. 6s.*
Gleig (Charles). BUNTER'S CRUISE. Illustrated. *Cr. 8vo. 3s. 6d.*
Harraden (Beatrice). IN VARYING MOODS. *Fourteenth Edition. Cr. 8vo. 6s.*

THE SCHOLAR'S DAUGHTER. *Fourth Edition. Cr. 8vo. 6s.*
HILDA STRAFFORD. *Cr. 8vo. 6s.*
Harrod (F.) (Frances Forbes Robertson). THE TAMING OF THE BRUTE. *Cr. 8vo. 6s.*
Herbertson (Agnes G.). PATIENCE DEAN. *Cr. 8vo. 6s.*
Hichens (Robert). THE PROPHET OF BERKELEY SQUARE. *Second Edition. Cr. 8vo. 6s.*
TONGUES OF CONSCIENCE. *Second Edition. Cr. 8vo. 6s.*
FELIX. *Fifth Edition. Cr. 8vo. 6s.*
THE WOMAN WITH THE FAN. *Sixth Edition. Cr. 8vo. 6s.*
BYEWAYS. *Cr. 8vo. 3s. 6d.*
THE GARDEN OF ALLAH. *Thirteenth Edition. Cr. 8vo. 6s.*
THE BLACK SPANIEL. *Cr. 8vo. 6s.*
Hobbes (John Oliver), Author of 'Robert Orange.' THE SERIOUS WOOING. *Cr. 8vo. 6s.*
Hope (Anthony). THE GOD IN THE CAR. *Tenth Edition. Cr. 8vo. 6s.*
A CHANGE OF AIR. *Sixth Edition. Cr. 8vo. 6s.*
A MAN OF MARK. *Fifth Edition. Cr. 8vo. 6s.*
THE CHRONICLES OF COUNT ANTONIO. *Sixth Edition. Cr. 8vo. 6s.*
PHROSO. Illustrated by H. R. MILLAR. *Sixth Edition. Cr. 8vo. 6s.*
SIMON DALE. Illustrated. *Seventh Edition. Cr. 8vo. 6s.*
THE KING'S MIRROR. *Fourth Edition. Cr. 8vo. 6s.*
QUISANTE. *Fourth Edition. Cr. 8vo. 6s.*
THE DOLLY DIALOGUES. *Cr. 8vo. 6s.*
A SERVANT OF THE PUBLIC. Illustrated. *Fourth Edition. Cr. 8vo. 6s.*
Hope (Graham), Author of 'A Cardinal and his Conscience,' etc., etc. THE LADY OF LYTE. *Second Ed. Cr. 8vo. 6s.*
Hough (Emerson). THE MISSISSIPPI BUBBLE. Illustrated. *Cr. 8vo. 6s.*
Housman (Clemence). THE LIFE OF SIR AGLOVALE DE GALIS. *Cr. 8vo. 6s.*
Hyne (C. J. Cutcliffe), Author of 'Captain Kettle.' MR. HORROCKS, PURSER. *Third Edition. Cr. 8vo. 6s.*
Jacobs (W. W.). MANY CARGOES. *Twenty-Eighth Edition. Cr. 8vo. 3s. 6d.*
SEA URCHINS. *Twelfth Edition. Cr. 8vo. 3s. 6d.*
A MASTER OF CRAFT. Illustrated. *Seventh Edition. Cr. 8vo. 3s. 6d.*
LIGHT FREIGHTS. Illustrated. *Fifth Edition. Cr. 8vo. 3s. 6d.*
James (Henry). THE SOFT SIDE. *Second Edition. Cr. 8vo. 6s.*
THE BETTER SORT. *Cr. 8vo. 6s.*
THE AMBASSADORS. *Second Edition. Cr. 8vo. 6s.*

THE GOLDEN BOWL. *Third Edition. Cr. 8vo. 6s.*
Janson (Gustaf). ABRAHAM'S SACRIFICE. *Cr. 8vo. 6s.*
Keays (H. A. Mitchell). HE THAT EATETH BREAD WITH ME. *Cr. 8vo. 6s.*
Langbridge (V.) and Bourne (C. Harold.). THE VALLEY OF INHERITANCE. *Cr. 8vo. 6s.*
Lawless (Hon. Emily). WITH ESSEX IN IRELAND. *Cr. 8vo. 6s.*
See also Strand Novels.
Lawson (Harry), Author of 'When the Billy Boils.' CHILDREN OF THE BUSH. *Cr. 8vo. 6s.*
Le Queux (W.). THE HUNCHBACK OF WESTMINSTER. *Third Edition. Cr. 8vo. 6s.*
THE CLOSED BOOK. *Third Edition. Cr. 8vo. 6s.*
THE VALLEY OF THE SHADOW. Illustrated. *Third Edition. Cr. 8vo. 6s.*
BEHIND THE THRONE. *Third Edition. Cr. 8vo. 6s.*
Levett-Yeats (S.). ORRAIN. *Second Edition. Cr. 8vo. 6s.*
Long (J. Luther), Co-Author of 'The Darling of the Gods.' MADAME BUTTERFLY. *Cr. 8vo. 3s. 6d.*
SIXTY JANE. *Cr. 8vo. 6s.*
Lowis (Cecil). THE MACHINATIONS OF THE MYO-OK. *Cr. 8vo. 6s.*
Lyall (Edna). DERRICK VAUGHAN, NOVELIST. *42nd Thousand. Cr. 8vo. 3s. 6d.*
M'Carthy (Justin H.), Author of 'If I were King.' THE LADY OF LOYALTY HOUSE. Illustrated. *Third Edition. Cr. 8vo. 6s.*
THE DRYAD. *Second Edition. Cr. 8vo. 6s.*
Macdonald (Ronald). THE SEA MAID. *Second Edition. Cr. 8vo. 6s.*
Macnaughtan (S.). THE FORTUNE OF CHRISTINA MACNAB. *Third Edition. Cr. 8vo. 6s.*
Malet (Lucas). COLONEL ENDERBY'S WIFE. *Fourth Edition. Cr. 8vo. 6s.*
A COUNSEL OF PERFECTION. *New Edition. Cr. 8vo. 6s.*
THE WAGES OF SIN. *Fourteenth Edition. Cr. 8vo. 6s.*
THE CARISSIMA. *Fourth Edition. Cr. 8vo. 6s.*
THE GATELESS BARRIER. *Fourth Edition. Cr. 8vo. 6s.*
THE HISTORY OF SIR RICHARD CALMADY. *Seventh Edition. Cr. 8vo. 6s.*
See also Books for Boys and Girls.
Mann (Mrs. M. E.). OLIVIA'S SUMMER. *Second Edition. Cr. 8vo. 6s.*
A LOST ESTATE. *A New Edition. Cr. 8vo. 6s.*
THE PARISH OF HILBY. *A New Edition. Cr. 8vo. 6s.*

FICTION 35

THE PARISH NURSE. *Fourth Edition.* *Cr. 8vo. 6s.*
GRAN'MA'S JANE. *Cr. 8vo. 6s.*
MRS. PETER HOWARD. *Cr. 8vo. 6s.*
A WINTER'S TALE. *A New Edition.* *Cr. 8vo. 6s.*
ONE ANOTHER'S BURDENS. *A New Edition.* *Cr. 8vo. 6s.*
ROSE AT HONEYPOT. *Third Ed. Cr. 8vo. 6s.* See also Books for Boys and Girls.
Marriott (Charles), Author of 'The Column.' GENEVRA. *Second Edition.* *Cr. 8vo. 6s.*
Marsh (Richard). THE TWICKENHAM PEERAGE. *Second Edition. Cr. 8vo. 6s.*
A DUEL. *Cr. 8vo. 6s.*
THE MARQUIS OF PUTNEY. *Second Edition. Cr. 8vo. 6s.*
See also Strand Novels.
Mason (A. E. W.), Author of 'The Four Feathers,' etc. CLEMENTINA. Illustrated. *Second Edition. Cr. 8vo. 6s.*
Mathers (Helen), Author of 'Comin' thro' the Rye.' HONEY. *Fourth Edition.* *Cr. 8vo. 6s.*
GRIFF OF GRIFFITHSCOURT. *Cr. 8vo. 6s.*
THE FERRYMAN. *Second Edition. Cr. 8vo. 6s.*
Maxwell (W. B.), Author of 'The Ragged Messenger.' VIVIEN. *Eighth Edition.* *Cr. 8vo. 6s.*
THE RAGGED MESSENGER. *Third Edition. Cr. 8vo. 6s.*
FABULOUS FANCIES. *Cr. 8vo. 6s.*
Meade (L. T.). DRIFT. *Second Edition.* *Cr. 8vo. 6s.*
RESURGAM. *Cr. 8vo. 6s.*
VICTORY. *Cr. 8vo. 6s.*
See also Books for Girls and Boys.
Meredith (Ellis). HEART OF MY HEART. *Cr. 8vo. 6s.*
'**Miss Molly**' (The Author of). THE GREAT RECONCILER. *Cr. 8vo. 6s.*
Mitford (Bertram). THE SIGN OF THE SPIDER. Illustrated. *Sixth Edition.* *Cr. 8vo. 3s. 6d.*
IN THE WHIRL OF THE RISING. *Third Edition. Cr. 8vo. 6s.*
THE RED DERELICT. *Second Edition. Cr. 8vo. 6s.*
Montresor (F. F.), Author of 'Into the Highways and Hedges.' THE ALIEN. *Third Edition. Cr. 8vo. 6s.*
Morrison (Arthur). TALES OF MEAN STREETS. *Sixth Edition. Cr. 8vo. 6s.*
A CHILD OF THE JAGO. *Fourth Edition.* *Cr. 8vo. 6s.*
TO LONDON TOWN. *Second Edition.* *Cr. 8vo. 6s.*
CUNNING MURRELL. *Cr. 8vo. 6s.*
THE HOLE IN THE WALL. *Fourth Edition. Cr. 8vo. 6s.*
DIVERS VANITIES. *Cr. 8vo. 6s.*

Nesbit (E.). (Mrs. E. Bland). THE RED HOUSE. Illustrated. *Fourth Edition.* *Cr. 8vo. 6s.*
See also Strand Novels.
Norris (W. E.). THE CREDIT OF THE COUNTY. Illustrated. *Second Edition.* *Cr. 8vo. 6s.*
THE EMBARRASSING ORPHAN. *Cr. 8vo. 6s.*
NIGEL'S VOCATION. *Cr. 8vo. 6s.*
BARHAM OF BELTANA. *Second Edition. Cr. 8vo. 6s.*
See also Strand Novels.
Ollivant (Alfred). OWD BOB, THE GREY DOG OF KENMUIR. *Eighth Edition. Cr. 8vo. 6s.*
Oppenheim (E. Phillips). MASTER OF MEN. *Third Edition. Cr. 8vo. 6s.*
Oxenham (John), Author of 'Barbe' of Grand Bayou.' A WEAVER OF WEBS. *Second Edition. Cr. 8vo. 6s.*
THE GATE OF THE DESERT. *Fourth Edition. Cr. 8vo. 6s.*
Pain (Barry). THREE FANTASIES. *Cr. 8vo. 1s.*
LINDLEY KAYS. *Third Edition. Cr. 8vo. 6s.*
Parker (Gilbert). PIERRE AND HIS PEOPLE. *Sixth Edition.*
MRS. FALCHION. *Fifth Edition. Cr. 8vo. 6s.*
THE TRANSLATION OF A SAVAGE. *Second Edition. Cr. 8vo. 6s.*
THE TRAIL OF THE SWORD. Illustrated. *Ninth Edition. Cr. 8vo. 6s.*
WHEN VALMOND CAME TO PONTIAC: The Story of a Lost Napoleon. *Fifth Edition. Cr. 8vo. 6s.*
AN ADVENTURER OF THE NORTH: The Last Adventures of 'Pretty Pierre.' *Third Edition. Cr. 8vo. 6s.*
THE SEATS OF THE MIGHTY. Illustrated. *Fourteenth Edition. Cr. 8vo. 6s.*
THE BATTLE OF THE STRONG: a Romance of Two Kingdoms. Illustrated. *Fifth Edition. Cr. 8vo. 6s.*
THE POMP OF THE LAVILETTES. *Second Edition. Cr. 3vo. 3s. 6d.*
Pemberton (Max). THE FOOTSTEPS OF A THRONE. Illustrated. *Third Edition. Cr. 8vo. 6s.*
I CROWN THEE KING. With Illustrations by Frank Dadd and A. Forrestier. *Cr. 8vo. 6s.*
Phillpotts (Eden). LYING PROPHETS. *Cr. 8vo. 6s.*
CHILDREN OF THE MIST. *Fifth Edition. Cr. 8vo. 6s.*
THE HUMAN BOY. With a Frontispiece. *Fourth Edition. Cr. 8vo. 6s.*
SONS OF THE MORNING. *Second Edition. Cr. 8vo. 6s.*

36 MESSRS. METHUEN'S CATALOGUE

THE RIVER. *Third Edition. Cr. 8vo. 6s.*
THE AMERICAN PRISONER. *Third Edition. Cr. 8vo. 6s.*
THE SECRET WOMAN. *Fourth Edition. Cr. 8vo. 6s.*
KNOCK AT A VENTURE. With a Frontispiece. *Third Edition. Cr. 8vo. 6s.*
THE PORTREEVE. *Fourth Edition. Cr. 8vo. 6s.*
See also Strand Novels.

Pickthall (Marmaduke). SAÏD THE FISHERMAN. *Fifth Edition. Cr. 8vo. 6s.*
BRENDLE. *Second Edition. Cr. 8vo. 6s.*
'Q,' Author of 'Dead Man's Rock.' THE WHITE WOLF. *Second Edition. Cr. 8vo. 6s.*
THE MAYOR OF TROY. *Fourth Edition. Cr. 8vo. 6s.*

Rhys (Grace). THE WOOING OF SHEILA. *Second Edition. Cr. 8vo. 6s.*
THE PRINCE OF LISNOVER. *Cr. 8vo. 6s.*

Rhys (Grace) and Another. THE DIVERTED VILLAGE. Illustrated by DOROTHY GWYN JEFFREYS. *Cr. 8vo. 6s.*

Ridge (W. Pett). LOST PROPERTY. *Second Edition. Cr. 8vo. 6s.*
ERB. *Second Edition. Cr. 8vo. 6s.*
A SON OF THE STATE. *Second Edition. Cr. 8vo. 3s. 6d.*
A BREAKER OF LAWS. *A New Edition. Cr. 8vo. 3s. 6d.*
MRS. GALER'S BUSINESS. Illustrated. *Second Edition. Cr. 8vo. 6s.*
SECRETARY TO BAYNE, M.P. *Cr. 8vo. 3s. 6d.*

Ritchie (Mrs. David G.). THE TRUTHFUL LIAR. *Cr. 8vo. 6s.*

Roberts (C. G. D.). THE HEART OF THE ANCIENT WOOD. *Cr. 8vo. 3s. 6d.*

Russell (W. Clark). MY DANISH SWEETHEART. Illustrated. *Fifth Edition. Cr. 8vo. 6s.*
HIS ISLAND PRINCESS. *Second Edition. Cr. 8vo. 6s.*
ABANDONED. *Cr. 8vo. 6s.*
See also Books for Boys and Girls.

Sergeant (Adeline). ANTHEA'S WAY. *Cr. 8vo. 6s.*
THE PROGRESS OF RACHAEL. *Cr. 8vo. 6s.*
THE MYSTERY OF THE MOAT. *Second Edition. Cr. 8vo. 6s.*
MRS. LYGON'S HUSBAND. *Cr. 8vo. 6s.*
THE COMING OF THE RANDOLPHS. *Cr. 8vo. 6s.*
See also Strand Novels.

Shannon. (W. F.) THE MESS DECK *Cr. 8vo. 3s. 6d.*
See also Strand Novels.

Sonnischsen (Albert). DEEP-SEA VAGABONDS. *Cr. 8vo. 6s.*
Thompson (Vance). SPINNERS OF LIFE. *Cr. 8vo. 6s.*
Urquhart (M.), A TRAGEDY IN COMMONPLACE. *Second Ed. Cr. 8vo. 6s.*
Waineman (Paul). BY A FINNISH LAKE. *Cr. 8vo. 6s.*
THE SONG OF THE FOREST. *Cr. 8vo. 6s.* See also Strand Novels.
Waltz (E. C.). THE ANCIENT LANDMARK: A Kentucky Romance. *Cr. 8vo. 6s.*
Watson (H. B. Marriott). ALARUMS AND EXCURSIONS. *Cr. 8vo. 6s.*
CAPTAIN FORTUNE. *Third Edition. Cr. 8vo. 6s.*
TWISTED EGLANTINE. With 8 Illustrations by FRANK CRAIG. *Third Edition. Cr. 8vo. 6s.*
THE HIGH TOBY. With a Frontispiece. *Third Edition. Cr. 8vo. 6s.*
See also Strand Novels.

Wells (H. G.). THE SEA LADY. *Cr. 8vo. 6s.*

Weyman (Stanley), Author of 'A Gentleman of France.' UNDER THE RED ROBE. With Illustrations by R. C. WOODVILLE. *Twentieth Edition. Cr. 8vo. 6s.*

White (Stewart E.), Author of 'The Blazed Trail.' CONJUROR'S HOUSE. A Romance of the Free Trail. *Second Edition. Cr. 8vo. 6s.*

White (Percy). THE SYSTEM. *Third Edition. Cr. 8vo. 6s.*
THE PATIENT MAN. *Second Edition. Cr. 8vo. 6s.*

Williamson (Mrs. C. N.), Author of 'The Barnstormers.' THE ADVENTURE OF PRINCESS SYLVIA. *Second Edition. Cr. 8vo. 3s. 6d.*
THE WOMAN WHO DARED. *Cr. 8vo. 6s.*
THE SEA COULD TELL. *Second Edition. Cr. 8vo. 6s.*
THE CASTLE OF THE SHADOWS. *Third Edition. Cr. 8vo. 6s.*
PAPA. *Cr. 8vo. 6s.*
LADY BETTY ACROSS THE WATER. *Third Edition. Cr. 8vo. 6s.*

Williamson (C. N. and A. M.). THE LIGHTNING CONDUCTOR: Being the Romance of a Motor Car. Illustrated. *Fourteenth Edition. Cr. 8vo. 6s.*
THE PRINCESS PASSES. Illustrated. *Seventh Edition. Cr. 8vo. 6s.*
MY FRIEND THE CHAUFFEUR. With 16 Illustrations. *Seventh Edition. Cr. 8vo. 6s.*

Wyllarde (Dolf), Author of 'Uriah the Hittite.' THE PATHWAY OF THE PIONEER. *Fourth Edition. Cr. 8vo. 6s.*

FICTION 37

Methuen's Shilling Novels

Cr. 8vo.   Cloth, 1s. net.

ENCOURAGED by the great and steady sale of their Sixpenny Novels, Messrs. Methuen have determined to issue a new series of fiction at a low price under the title of 'THE SHILLING NOVELS.' These books are well printed and well bound in *cloth*, and the excellence of their quality may be gauged from the names of those authors who contribute the early volumes of the series.

Messrs. Methuen would point out that the books are as good and as long as a six shilling novel, that they are bound in cloth and not in paper, and that their price is One Shilling *net*. They feel sure that the public will appreciate such good and cheap literature, and the books can be seen at all good booksellers.

The first volumes are—

Balfour (Andrew).   VENGEANCE IS MINE.
TO ARMS.
Baring-Gould (S.).   MRS. CURGENVEN OF CURGENVEN.
DOMITIA.
THE FROBISHERS.
Barlow (Jane), Author of 'Irish Idylls. FROM THE EAST UNTO THE WEST.
A CREEL OF IRISH STORIES.
THE FOUNDING OF FORTUNES.
Barr (Robert).   THE VICTORS.
Bartram (George).   THIRTEEN EVENINGS.
Benson (E. F.), Author of 'Dodo.' THE CAPSINA.
Bowles (G. Stewart).   A STRETCH OFF THE LAND.
Brooke (Emma).   THE POET'S CHILD.
Bullock (Shan F.).   THE BARRYS.
THE CHARMER.
THE SQUIREEN.
THE RED LEAGUERS.
Burton (J. Bloundelle).   ACROSS THE SALT SEAS.
THE CLASH OF ARMS.
DENOUNCED.
FORTUNE'S MY FOE.
Capes (Bernard).   AT A WINTER'S FIRE.
Chesney (Weatherby).   THE BAPTIST RING.
THE BRANDED PRINCE.
THE FOUNDERED GALLEON.
JOHN TOPP.
Clifford (Mrs. W. K.).   A FLASH OF SUMMER.
Collingwood (Harry).   THE DOCTOR OF THE 'JULIET.'
Cornford (L. Cope).   SONS OF ADVERSITY.
Crane (Stephen).   WOUNDS IN THE RAIN.
Denny (C. E.).   THE ROMANCE OF UPFOLD MANOR.
Dickson (Harris).   THE BLACK WOLF'S BREED.
Dickinson (Evelyn).   THE SIN OF ANGELS.

Duncan (Sara J.).   *THE POOL IN THE DESERT.
A VOYAGE OF CONSOLATION.
Embree (C. F.).   A HEART OF FLAME.
Fenn (G. Manville).   AN ELECTRIC SPARK.
Findlater (Jane H.).   A DAUGHTER OF STRIFE.
Findlater (Mary).   OVER THE HILLS.
Forrest (R. E.).   THE SWORD OF AZRAEL.
Francis (M. E.).   MISS ERIN.
Gallon (Tom).   RICKERBY'S FOLLY.
Gerard (Dorothea).   THINGS THAT HAVE HAPPENED.
Gilchrist (R. Murray).   WILLOWBRAKE.
Glanville (Ernest).   THE DESPATCH RIDER.
THE LOST REGIMENT.
THE KLOOF BRIDE.
THE INCA'S TREASURE.
Gordon (Julien).   MRS. CLYDE.
WORLD'S PEOPLE.
Goss (C. F.).   THE REDEMPTION OF DAVID CORSON.
Gray (E. M'Queen).   MY STEWARDSHIP.
Hales (A. G.).   JAIR THE APOSTATE.
Hamilton (Lord Ernest).   MARY HAMILTON.
Harrison (Mrs. Burton).   A PRINCESS OF THE HILLS. Illustrated.
Hooper (I.).   THE SINGER OF MARLY.
Hough (Emerson).   THE MISSISSIPPI BUBBLE.
'Iota' (Mrs. Caffyn).   ANNE MAULEVERER.
Jepson (Edgar).   KEEPERS OF THE PEOPLE.
Kelly (Florence Finch).   WITH HOOPS OF STEEL.
Lawless (Hon. Emily).   MAELCHO.
Linden (Annie).   A WOMAN OF SENTIMENT.
Lorimer (Norma).   JOSIAH'S WIFE.
Lush (Charles K.).   THE AUTOCRATS.
Macdonell (Anne).   THE STORY OF TERESA.
Macgrath (Harold).   THE PUPPET CROWN.

Messrs. Methuen's Catalogue

Mackie (Pauline Bradford). THE VOICE IN THE DESERT.
Marsh (Richard). THE SEEN AND THE UNSEEN.
GARNERED.
A METAMORPHOSIS.
MARVELS AND MYSTERIES.
BOTH SIDES OF THE VEIL.
Mayall (J. W.). THE CYNIC AND THE SYREN.
Monkhouse (Allan). LOVE IN A LIFE.
Moore (Arthur). THE KNIGHT PUNCTILIOUS.
Nesbit (Mrs. Bland). THE LITERARY SENSE.
Norris (W. E.). AN OCTAVE.
Oliphant (Mrs.). THE LADY'S WALK.
SIR ROBERT'S FORTUNE.
THE TWO MARY'S.
Penny (Mrs. Frank). A MIXED MARRIAGE.
Phillpotts (Eden). THE STRIKING HOURS.
FANCY FREE.
Pryce (Richard). TIME AND THE WOMAN.
Randall (J.). AUNT BETHIA'S BUTTON.
Raymond (Walter). FORTUNE'S DARLING.
Rayner (Olive Pratt). ROSALBA.
Rhys (Grace). THE DIVERTED VILLAGE.

Rickert (Edith). OUT OF THE CYPRESS SWAMP.
Roberton (M. H.). A GALLANT QUAKER.
Saunders (Marshall). ROSE A CHARLITTE.
Sergeant (Adeline). ACCUSED AND ACCUSER.
BARBARA'S MONEY.
THE ENTHUSIAST.
A GREAT LADY.
THE LOVE THAT OVERCAME.
THE MASTER OF BEECHWOOD.
UNDER SUSPICION.
THE YELLOW DIAMOND.
Shannon (W. F.). JIM TWELVES.
Strain (E. H.). ELMSLIE'S DRAG NET.
Stringer (Arthur). THE SILVER POPPY.
Stuart (Esmè). CHRISTALLA.
Sutherland (Duchess of). ONE HOUR AND THE NEXT.
Swan (Annie). LOVE GROWN COLD.
Swift (Benjamin). SORDON.
Tanqueray (Mrs. B. M.). THE ROYAL QUAKER.
Trafford-Taunton (Mrs. E. W.). SILENT DOMINION.
Upward (Allen). ATHELSTANE FORD.
Waineman (Paul). A HEROINE FROM FINLAND.
Watson (H. B. Marriott). THE SKIRTS OF HAPPY CHANCE.
'Zack.' TALES OF DUNSTABLE WEIR.

Books for Boys and Girls

Illustrated. Crown 8vo. 3s. 6d.

THE GETTING WELL OF DOROTHY. By Mrs. W. K. Clifford. *Second Edition.*

THE ICELANDER'S SWORD. By S. Baring-Gould.

ONLY A GUARD-ROOM DOG. By Edith E. Cuthell.

THE DOCTOR OF THE JULIET. By Harry Collingwood.

LITTLE PETER. By Lucas Malet. *Second Edition.*

MASTER ROCKAFELLAR'S VOYAGE. By W. Clark Russell.

THE SECRET OF MADAME DE MONLUC. By the Author of "Mdlle. Mori."

SYD BELTON: Or, the Boy who would not go to Sea. By G. Manville Fenn.

THE RED GRANGE. By Mrs. Molesworth.

A GIRL OF THE PEOPLE. By L. T. Meade. *Second Edition.*

HEPSY GIPSY. By L. T. Meade. 2s. 6d.

THE HONOURABLE MISS. By L. T. Meade. *Second Edition.*

THERE WAS ONCE A PRINCE. By Mrs. M. E. Mann.

WHEN ARNOLD COMES HOME. By Mrs. M. E. Mann.

The Novels of Alexandre Dumas

Price 6d. Double Volumes, 1s.

THE THREE MUSKETEERS. With a long Introduction by Andrew Lang. Double volume.
THE PRINCE OF THIEVES. *Second Edition.*
ROBIN HOOD. A Sequel to the above.
THE CORSICAN BROTHERS.
GEORGES.

CROP-EARED JACQUOT; JANE; Etc.
TWENTY YEARS AFTER. Double volume.
AMAURY.
THE CASTLE OF EPPSTEIN.
THE SNOWBALL, and SULTANETTA.
CECILE; OR, THE WEDDING GOWN.
ACTÉ.

FICTION 39

THE BLACK TULIP.
THE VICOMTE DE BRAGELONNE.
  Part I. Louise de la Vallière. Double Volume.
  Part II. The Man in the Iron Mask. Double Volume.
THE CONVICT'S SON.
THE WOLF-LEADER.
NANON; OR, THE WOMEN' WAR. Double volume.
PAULINE; MURAT; AND PASCAL BRUNO.
THE ADVENTURES OF CAPTAIN PAMPHILE.
FERNANDE.
GABRIEL LAMBERT.
CATHERINE BLUM.
THE CHEVALIER D'HARMENTAL. Double volume.
SYLVANDIRE.
THE FENCING MASTER.
THE REMINISCENCES OF ANTONY.
CONSCIENCE.
PERE LA RUINE.
*HENRI OF NAVARRE. The second part of Queen Margot.
THE GREAT MASSACRE. The first part of Queen Margot.
THE WILD DUCK SHOOTER.

Illustrated Edition.

Demy 8vo. Cloth.

THE THREE MUSKETEERS. Illustrated in Colour by Frank Adams. 2s. 6d.
THE PRINCE OF THIEVES. Illustrated in Colour by Frank Adams. 2s.
ROBIN HOOD THE OUTLAW. Illustrated in Colour by Frank Adams. 2s.
THE CORSICAN BROTHERS. Illustrated in Colour by A. M. M'Lellan. 1s. 6d.
THE WOLF-LEADER. Illustrated in Colour by Frank Adams. 1s. 6d.
GEORGES. Illustrated in Colour by Munro Orr. 2s.
TWENTY YEARS AFTER. Illustrated in Colour by Frank Adams. 3s.
AMAURY. Illustrated in Colour by Gordon Browne. 2s.
THE SNOWBALL, and SULTANETTA. Illustrated in Colour by Frank Adams. 2s.
THE VICOMTE DE BRAGELONNE. Illustrated in Colour by Frank Adams.
  Part I. Louise de la Vallière. 3s.
  Part II. The Man in the Iron Mask. 3s.
CROP-EARED JACQUOT; JANE; Etc. Illustrated in Colour by Gordon Browne. 2s.
THE CASTLE OF EPFSTEIN. Illustrated in Colour by Stewart Orr. 1s. 6d.
ACTÉ. Illustrated in Colour by Gordon Browne. 1s. 6d.
CECILE; OR, THE WEDDING GOWN. Illustrated in Colour by D. Murray Smith. 1s. 6d.
THE ADVENTURES OF CAPTAIN PAMPHILE. Illustrated in Colour by Frank Adams. 1s. 6d.

Methuen's Sixpenny Books

Austen (Jane). PRIDE AND PREJUDICE.
Bagot (Richard). A ROMAN MYSTERY.
Balfour (Andrew). BY STROKE OF SWORD.
Baring-Gould (S.). FURZE BLOOM.
CHEAP JACK ZITA.
KITTY ALONE.
URITH.
THE BROOM SQUIRE.
IN THE ROAR OF THE SEA.
NOÉMI.
A BOOK OF FAIRY TALES. Illustrated.
LITTLE TU'PENNY.
THE FROBISHERS.
Barr (Robert). JENNIE BAXTER, JOURNALIST.
IN THE MIDST OF ALARMS.
THE COUNTESS TEKLA.
THE MUTABLE MANY.
Benson (E. F.). DODO.
Brontë (Charlotte). SHIRLEY.
Brownell (C. L.). THE HEART OF JAPAN.
Burton (J. Bloundelle). ACROSS THE SALT SEAS.
Caffyn (Mrs.)., ('Iota'). ANNE MAULEVERER.
*****Capes (Bernard).** THE LAKE OF WINE.
Clifford (Mrs. W. K.). A FLASH OF SUMMER.
MRS. KEITH'S CRIME.
Connell (F. Norreys). THE NIGGER KNIGHTS.
Corbett (Julian). A BUSINESS IN GREAT WATERS.
Croker (Mrs. B. M.). PEGGY OF THE BARTONS.
A STATE SECRET.
ANGEL.
JOHANNA.
Dante (Alighieri). THE VISION OF DANTE (CARY).
Doyle (A. Conan). ROUND THE RED LAMP.
Duncan (Sara Jeannette). A VOYAGE OF CONSOLATION.
THOSE DELIGHTFUL AMERICANS.

Eliot (George). THE MILL ON THE FLOSS.
Findlater (Jane H.). THE GREEN GRAVES OF BALGOWRIE.
Gallon (Tom). RICKERBY'S FOLLY.
Gaskell (Mrs.). CRANFORD.
MARY BARTON.
NORTH AND SOUTH.
Gerard (Dorothea). HOLY MATRIMONY.
THE CONQUEST OF LONDON.
MADE OF MONEY.
Gissing (George). THE TOWN TRAVELLER.
THE CROWN OF LIFE.
Glanville (Ernest). THE INCA'S TREASURE.
THE KLOOF BRIDE.
Gleig (Charles). BUNTER'S CRUISE.
Grimm (The Brothers). GRIMM'S FAIRY TALES. Illustrated.
Hope (Anthony). A MAN OF MARK.
A CHANGE OF AIR.
THE CHRONICLES OF COUNT ANTONIO.
PHROSO.
THE DOLLY DIALOGUES.
Hornung (E. W.). DEAD MEN TELL NO TALES.
Ingraham (J. H.). THE THRONE OF DAVID.
Le Queux (W.). THE HUNCHBACK OF WESTMINSTER.
Levett-Yeats (S. K.). THE TRAITOR'S WAY.
Linton (E. Lynn). THE TRUE HISTORY OF JOSHUA DAVIDSON.
Lyall (Edna). DERRICK VAUGHAN.
Malet (Lucas). THE CARISSIMA.
A COUNSEL OF PERFECTION.
Mann (Mrs. M. E.). MRS. PETER HOWARD.
A LOST ESTATE.
THE CEDAR STAR.
Marchmont (A. W.). MISER HOADLEY'S SECRET.
A MOMENT'S ERROR.
Marryat (Captain). PETER SIMPLE.
JACOB FAITHFUL.
Marsh (Richard). THE TWICKENHAM PEERAGE.
THE GODDESS.
THE JOSS.
Mason (A. E. W.). CLEMENTINA.
Mathers (Helen). HONEY.
GRIFF OF GRIFFITHSCOURT.
SAM'S SWEETHEART.
Meade (Mrs. L. T.). DRIFT.
Mitford (Bertram). THE SIGN OF THE SPIDER.
Montresor (F. F.). THE ALIEN.
Moore (Arthur). THE GAY DECEIVERS.
Morrison (Arthur). THE HOLE IN THE WALL.
Nesbit (E.). THE RED HOUSE.
Norris (W. E.). HIS GRACE.
GILES INGILBY.
THE CREDIT OF THE COUNTY.
LORD LEONARD.
MATTHEW AUSTIN.
CLARISSA FURIOSA.
Oliphant (Mrs.). THE LADY'S WALK.
SIR ROBERT'S FORTUNE.
THE PRODIGALS.
Oppenheim (E. Phillips). MASTER OF MEN.
Parker (Gilbert). THE POMP OF THE LAVILETTES.
WHEN VALMOND CAME TO PONTIAC.
THE TRAIL OF THE SWORD.
Pemberton (Max). THE FOOTSTEPS OF A THRONE.
I CROWN THEE KING.
Phillpotts (Eden). THE HUMAN BOY.
CHILDREN OF THE MIST.
Ridge (W. Pett). A SON OF THE STATE.
LOST PROPERTY.
GEORGE AND THE GENERAL.
Russell (W. Clark). A MARRIAGE AT SEA.
ABANDONED.
MY DANISH SWEETHEART.
Sergeant (Adeline). THE MASTER OF BEECHWOOD.
BARBARA'S MONEY.
THE YELLOW DIAMOND.
Surtees (R. S.). HANDLEY CROSS. Illustrated.
MR. SPONGE'S SPORTING TOUR. Illustrated.
ASK MAMMA. Illustrated.
Valentine (Major E. S.). VELDT AND LAAGER.
Walford (Mrs. L. B.). MR. SMITH.
THE BABY'S GRANDMOTHER.
Wallace (General Lew). BEN-HUR.
THE FAIR GOD.
Watson (H. B. Marriot). THE ADVENTURERS.
Weekes (A. B.). PRISONERS OF WAR.
Wells (H. G.). THE STOLEN BACILLUS.
White (Percy). A PASSIONATE PILGRIM.

For Product Safety Concerns and Information please contact our EU
representative GPSR@taylorandfrancis.com
Taylor & Francis Verlag GmbH, Kaufingerstraße 24, 80331 München, Germany

www.ingramcontent.com/pod-product-compliance
Lightning Source LLC
Chambersburg PA
CBHW071758300426
44116CB00009B/1122